IN DIALOGUE WITH
THE OTHER VOICE IN
SIXTEENTH-CENTURY ITALY

The Other Voice in Early Modern Europe:
The Toronto Series, 11

The Other Voice in Early Modern Europe: The Toronto Series

SERIES EDITORS Margaret L. King *and* Albert Rabil, Jr.

Recent Publications in the Series

MADRE MARÍA ROSA
Journey of Five Capuchin Nuns
Edited and translated by Sarah E. Owens
2009

GIOVAN BATTISTA ANDREINI
Love in the Mirror: A Bilingual Edition
Edited and translated by Jon R. Snyder
2009

RAYMOND DE SABANAC AND SIMONE
ZANACCHI
Two Women of the Great Schism: The
Revelations *of Constance de Rabastens
by Raymond de Sabanac and* Life of the
Blessed Ursulina of Parma *by Simone
Zanacchi*
Edited and translated by Renate
Blumenfeld-Kosinski and Bruce L. Venarde
2010

OLIVA SABUCO DE NANTES BARRERA
The True Medicine
Edited and translated by Gianna Pomata
2010

LOUISE-GENEVIÈVE GILLOT DE
SAINCTONGE
Dramatizing Dido, Circe, and Griselda
Edited and translated by Janet Levarie Smarr
2010

PERNETTE DU GUILLET
Complete Poems: A Bilingual Edition
Edited by Karen Simroth James
Translated by Marta Rijn Finch
2010

ANTONIA PULCI
*Saints' Lives and Bible Stories for the Stage:
A Bilingual Edition*
Edited by Elissa B. Weaver
Translated by James Wyatt Cook
2010

VALERIA MIANI
Celinda, A Tragedy: A Bilingual Edition
Edited by Valeria Finucci
Translated by Julia Kisacky
Annotated by Valeria Finucci and Julia
Kisacky
2010

*Enchanted Eloquence: Fairy Tales by
Seventeenth-Century French Women
Writers*
Edited and translated by Lewis C. Seifert
and Domna C. Stanton
2010

*Leibniz and the Two Sophies: The
Philosophical Correspondence*
Edited and translated by Lloyd Strickland
2011

In Dialogue with the Other Voice in Sixteenth-Century Italy: Literary and Social Contexts for Women's Writing

~

Edited by

JULIE D. CAMPBELL

&

MARIA GALLI STAMPINO

Iter Inc.
Centre for Reformation and Renaissance Studies
Toronto
2011

Iter: Gateway to the Middle Ages and Renaissance
Tel: 416/978–7074   Fax: 416/978–1668
Email: iter@utoronto.ca   Web: www.itergateway.org

CRRS Publications, Centre for Reformation and Renaissance Studies
Victoria University in the University of Toronto
Toronto, Ontario M5S 1K7 Canada
Tel: 416/585–4465   Fax: 416/585–4430
Email: crrs.publications@utoronto.ca   Web: www.crrs.ca

Iter and the Centre for Reformation and Renaissance Studies gratefully acknowledge the generous support of James E. Rabil, in memory of Scottie W. Rabil, toward the publication of this book.

Library and Archives Canada Cataloguing in Publication

In dialogue with the other voice in sixteenth-century Italy : literary and social contexts for women's writing / edited by Julie D. Campbell & Maria Galli Stampino.
(The other voice in early modern Europe : the Toronto series ; 11)
Co-published by: Centre for Reformation and Renaissance Studies.
Includes bibliographical references and index.
Issued also in electronic format.
ISBN 978-0-7727-2085-6

1. Women and literature—Italy—History—Renaissance, 1450–1600. 2. Feminism and literature—Italy—History—Renaissance, 1450–1600. 3. Women—Italy—History—Renaissance, 1450–1600. 4. Italian literature—Renaissance, 1450–1600—Women authors. 5. Italian literature—Renaissance, 1450–1600—History and criticism. 6. Italian literature—16th century—History and criticism. I. Campbell, Julie D., 1965– II. Stampino, Maria Galli III. Victoria University (Toronto, Ont.). Centre for Reformation and Renaissance Studies IV. Iter Inc V. Series: Other voice in early modern Europe. Toronto series 11

PQ4055.W6I53 2011
858'.499287   C2011–902793–3

Cover illustration: Eros and Psyche, 16th century (oil on canvas) by Niccolo dell' Abate (c.1509–71) Detroit Institute of Arts, USA/ Founders Society Purchase, R.H. Tannahill Foundation Fund/ Bridgeman Art Library. DTR 140365.

Cover design: Maureen Morin, Information Technology Services, University of Toronto Libraries

Typesetting and production: Iter Inc.

To Al Rabil, Jr.

Contents

Acknowledgments   ix

Introduction
    Julie D. Campbell and Maria Galli Stampino   1

Part 1:   Contexts and the Canon

1.   Contexts and Canonical Authors
    Julie D. Campbell and Maria Galli Stampino   17

2.   Christian Feminine Virtue in Silvio Antoniano's *Three Books on the Christian Education of Children*
    Julie D. Campbell   59

3.   Stefano Guazzo's *Civil conversatione* and the *querelle des femmes*
    Julie D. Campbell   73

4.   Alessandro Piccolomini's *Raffaella*: A Parody of Women's Behavior and Men's Dialogues
    Maria Galli Stampino   89

Part 2:   Cases

5.   Torquato Tasso: *Discourse on Feminine and Womanly Virtue*
    Lori J. Ultsch   115

6.   Giuseppe Passi's Attacks on Women in *The Defects of Women*
    Suzanne Magnanini with David Lamari   143

7.   Love as Centaur: Rational Man, Animal Woman in Sperone Speroni's *Dialogue on Love*
    Janet L. Smarr   195

8.   Francesco Andreini: "On Taking a Wife"
Julie D. Campbell   265

9.   Dishonoring Courtesans in Early Modern Italy: The *poesia puttanesca* of Anton Francesco Grazzini, Nicolò Franco, and Maffio Venier
Patrizia Bettella   289

10.   Giulia Bigolina and Pietro Aretino's *Letters*
Christopher Nissen   313

11.   Centrality and Liminality in Bernardino Ochino's "Sermon Preached… on the Feast Day of St. Mary Magdalen"
Maria Galli Stampino   325

Bibliography

Select List of Male-Authored Texts in Translation   349
Primary Sources   357
Secondary Sources   365

Notes on Contributors   376

Index   379

Acknowledgments

It is our pleasure to acknowledge those whose help has made this project possible. First, we express our deepest thanks to Al Rabil, who in 2001 directed the NEH Summer Institute, "A Literature of Their Own? Women Writing—Venice, London, Paris, 1550-1700." This institute brought together a group scholars of literature, history, and languages all united in their interest in the works of early modern women writers. It provided us a foundation for professional friendships and scholarly support that has enriched our careers enormously. We are also grateful to the National Endowment for the Humanities for their support for this project provided through an NEH Collaborative Research Grant submitted by Al Rabil in 2004.

We would also like to thank the Special Collection staffs at the Humanities Research Center at the University of Texas, at the University of Illinois, and the University of Miami. Thanks are also due to the Interlibrary Loan staffs at the latter institution and at Booth Library of Eastern Illinois University.

Additionally, we owe a great debt of thanks to Elissa Weaver, whose close reading of our manuscript was invaluable. Her meticulous corrections and thoughtful suggestions have greatly improved and enriched our volume. We are also deeply grateful to Diana Robin, who read an early draft and gave us helpful feedback regarding direction and sources. This project has been in process for a long time, and we thus must also heartily thank our contributors, who have stayed the course with us.

Julie Campbell would especially like to thank Maria Galli Stampino for stepping into the co-editor position when help was greatly needed. She would also very much like to thank Anne Larsen and Diana Robin for their advice and support during the last few years that this project has been in progress. Their mentoring has meant much. Thanks are also due to Chris Hanlon and Jad Smith, Directors of Graduate Studies in English at Eastern Illinois University in 2007 and 2008, respectively, for their facilitation of help from a graduate student assistant, Andrea Gleeson, to compile the typescript at that stage of our process and help with the bibliography. She is also very grateful to

Janet Smarr, who allowed her to use an early draft of her translation of Sperone Speroni's *Dialogo d'amore* in the course, Renaissance Women Writers in Context, in the spring of 2009. The trajectory of this project has been followed (and tolerated) with great good humor and friendly advice for nearly ten years by Don and Sharon Campbell, Tom Over, Sharon Michalove, Rosemary Buck, Janet Marquardt, Carol Stevens, Paula Sodders, Mity Myhr, Melissa Benson, Kelly Lowe, and numerous others who have listened patiently to progress reports. To all of them, she is, truly, deeply grateful.

Maria Galli Stampino would first like to thank Julie Campbell for asking her, so many moons ago, to work together on this project. She did not know then how rewarding and enriching this experience would be! Many thanks also go to three University of Miami colleagues who have inspired her to persevere: Anne J. Cruz, Laura Giannetti and Perri Lee Roberts. Valeria Finucci, Guido Ruggiero, Suzanne Wofford and Jane Tylus provide shining examples of dedication to scholarship that are stirring if impossible to match. Robert Strain has heard many, many complaints about not having enough time to work and he absorbed them all with grace and patience. Maria is also very thankful that she was spared major computer mishaps, whether accidental or child-provoked (and therefore, thanks to Lawrence and Beatrice for not messing things up in this department).

Introduction

Just think what would have happened if Madonna Laura had gotten around to writing as much about Petrarch as he wrote about her: you'd have seen things turn out quite differently then!
Tullia d'Aragona[1]

When Tullia d'Aragona (ca. 1510–1556) wrote these prescient words in her *Dialogo della infinità di amore* (1547), she forecast a critical literary dilemma regarding the voice of "the beloved," the glorified female figure whom male writers of the period placed on a pedestal: her silence. Aragona herself, writing with the authority of a learned *cortigiana onesta*, embodied another critical literary dilemma: the sexualized link between voice and body for Renaissance women. Moreover, because she wrote in response to Sperone Speroni's *Dialogo di amore* (1542), partly to protest his stereotypical depiction of courtesans as incapable of any love higher than the carnal on the Neoplatonic ladder of love, she also hints at the ever-present double-standard underscored in men's lives and writing from this period regarding men's own sexuality and spirituality.[2] Her work, on its own a witty representative text of the Renaissance dialogue genre, becomes even more accessible to readers familiar with Petrarch's *Canzoniere* when viewed alongside Speroni's dialogue. Read in this broader literary context, Aragona's dialogue provides an intriguing glimpse into the "other side" of numerous issues related to women during this period, many of which are also examined by the diverse voices of other early modern Italian women writers. However, as in Aragona's case, the rich array of references in such women's texts can be best understood when their works are read alongside those of the men whose pronouncements permeate the literary milieus in which such women wrote. Read against these

1. Tullia d'Aragona, *Dialogue on the Infinity of Love*, trans. Rinaldina Russell and Bruce Merry, The Other Voice in Early Modern Europe (Chicago: University of Chicago Press, 1997), 69.

2. Sperone Speroni, *Dialogo di amore*, in *Opere*, ed. Natale dalle Laste and Marco Forcellini (1740; reprint, Rome: Vecchiarelli, 1989), 1:1–45.

1

prevalent lines of thought during this period, women's works reveal from both literary and historical perspectives why they should be an integral part of early modern literary studies: they bring to light the Other Voice that sometimes questions the dominant philosophies, sometimes colludes with them, but indisputably co-creates the literary society of the period.

Thanks to the availability of new editions and translations of their works and to contemporary scholars' interest in their existence, the works of Italian women writers from the sixteenth and early seventeenth centuries are once again reaching a broad audience.[3] Thus, it is important to bring into focus the cultural and intellectual contexts in which these works were written. Numerous questions about such contexts arise: What views were prominent regarding women's education, spirituality, and sexuality? How were women perceived by their male contemporaries? How, like Aragona's imagined Laura, did they respond to what men wrote about them? To which men's writing did they respond? In men's writing, what did they seek to imitate, and what did they reject?

In the first part of this volume, we explore often-cited male-authored texts that illustrate facets of the literary, social, and cultural stimuli that helped to shape the world of these women writers. In the second part, we provide case studies of specific male writers with whom such women writers were indeed "in dialogue" in some capacity. The goals of this volume are to illustrate the complexity and variety of contexts for sixteenth-century Italian women's works and to present a selection of texts that have not always been easily accessible in English that facilitate the reading and understanding of those works.

There is much to learn about early modern women's writing by examining texts that illustrate the ideological forces at work in their cultural moment. Traditionally, canonical Renaissance literature has mainly included works by authors such as Petrarch, Boccaccio, Ario-

---

3. For examples of the numbers of editions and print runs of the works of numerous sixteenth-century Italian women writers, see Diana Robin's *Publishing Women: Salons, the Presses, and the Counter-Reformation in Sixteenth-Century Italy* (Chicago: University of Chicago Press, 2007), 205–18.

sto, and Castiglione,[4] men whose works have appeared in numerous translations and have been presented to readers as seminal representatives of Renaissance thought. No one would argue that the works of such major authors were not critical influences on the literary milieus of sixteenth- and early-seventeenth-century women writers, but relying solely on the works of major canonical writers to approximate the worldview of women writers leaves large gaps in scholars' impressions of the historical moment. These gaps have too often been filled by timeworn assumptions that do little to illuminate the circumstances of women writers and sometimes even distort them.

Jacob Burckhardt's canonical, authoritative voice on Renaissance Italy assures us that to "understand the higher forms of social intercourse at this period, we must keep before our minds the fact that women stood on a footing of perfect equality with men" and that we "must not suffer ourselves to be misled by the sophistical and often malicious talk about the assumed inferiority of the female sex, which we meet with now and then in the dialogues of this time."[5] Of courtesans, he writes, it is clear that they "were treated with no slight respect and consideration. Even when relations with them were broken off, their good opinion was still desired."[6] Such facile pronouncements have been brought into question by much scholarship from the 1970s onward.

Most famously, perhaps, Joan Kelly interrogates Burckhardt's ideas in her 1977 essay, "Did Women Have a Renaissance?"[7] Her answer to that question, in light of his assumptions, is an emphatic "no." However, as more recent scholars have realized, that answer should probably be a qualified "yes," but one quite different from that as-

4. In *The Italian Renaissance Reader* (New York: Meridian / Penguin, 1987), editors Julia Conaway Bondanella and Mark Musa present Francesco Petrarca, Giovanni Boccaccio, Leon Battista Alberti, Giovanni Pico della Mirandola, Leonardo da Vinci, Baldessare Castiglione, Niccolò Machiavelli, Francesco Guicciardini, Benvenuto Cellini, Michelangelo Buonarroti, and Giorgio Vasari as the "major Italian writers and influential thinkers of the Renaissance" in their subtitle.

5. Jacob Burckhardt, *The Civilization of the Italian Renaissance*, trans. S. C. G. Middlemore (New York: Harper and Row, 1958), 2:389.

6. Burckhardt, *The Civilization of the Italian Renaissance*, 2:394.

7. Joan Kelly, "Did Women Have a Renaissance?" in *Women, History, and Theory* (Chicago: University of Chicago Press, 1984), 19–49; see her note on Burckhardt, 47.

serted by Burckhardt. Beginning with the publication of the writings of Isotta Nogarola (1418–1466),[8] and continuing through numerous works by Italian women writers of the sixteenth century, one finds, for example, a strong trend in protofeminist thought that engaged with the dominant philosophies of the times. The letters of Laura Cereta (1469–1499)[9] and Cassandra Fedele (1465–1558)[10] provide examples of strong protofeminist voices during this period, as do Moderata Fonte (1555–1592),[11] Lucrezia Marinella (1571–1653),[12] and Arcangela Tarabotti (1604–1652).[13] Olympia Morata's (1526–1555) classical education and Calvinist convictions may be seen to embody the humanist interests and religious controversies of her time.[14]

Numerous new editions of such women's works in *belles lettres* are currently available. Among those works never quite as "lost" as others are those of the courtesan-writers Tullia d'Aragona and Veronica Franco (1546–1591), whose poetry may be found along with that of several other early modern Italian women writers in recent translations.[15] Franco's works have also been translated,[16] as has Aragona's *Dialogue*

---

8. Isotta Nogarola, *The Complete Writings*, ed. and trans. Margaret L. King and Diana Robin, The Other Voice in Early Modern Europe (Chicago: University of Chicago Press, 2003).

9. Laura Cereta, *Collected Letters of a Renaissance Feminist*, ed. and trans. Diana Robin, The Other Voice in Early Modern Europe (Chicago: University of Chicago Press, 1997).

10. Cassandra Fedele, *Letters and Orations*, ed. and trans. Diana Robin, The Other Voice in Early Modern Europe (Chicago: University of Chicago Press, 2000).

11. Moderata Fonte (Modesta Pozzo), *The Worth of Women: Wherein Is Clearly Revealed Their Nobility and Their Superiority to Men*, ed. and trans. Virginia Cox, The Other Voice in Early Modern Europe (Chicago: University of Chicago Press, 1997).

12. Lucrezia Marinella, *The Nobility and Excellence of Women and the Defects and Vices of Men*, introd. Letizia Panizza, trans. Anne Dunhill, The Other Voice in Early Modern Europe (Chicago: University of Chicago Press, 1999).

13. Arcangela Tarabotti, *Paternal Tyranny*, ed. and trans. Letizia Panizza, The Other Voice in Early Modern Europe (Chicago: University of Chicago Press, 2004).

14. Olympia Morata, *The Complete Writings of an Italian Heretic*, ed. and trans. Holt Parker, The Other Voice in Early Modern Europe (Chicago: University of Chicago Press, 2003).

15. *Women Poets of the Italian Renaissance*, ed. and trans. Laura Anna Stortoni and Mary Prentice Lillie (New York: Italica Press, 1997).

16. Veronica Franco, *Poems and Selected Letters*, ed. and trans. Ann Rosalind Jones and Margaret F. Rosenthal, The Other Voice in Early Modern Europe (Chicago: University of Chicago Press, 1998).

on the Infinity of Love.[17] Some of the poetry of the similarly renowned noblewoman Vittoria Colonna (1492–1547) appears in a translation of *Sonnets for Michelangelo*,[18] and the poetry of Laura Battiferra (1523–1589) has also been recently published in English.[19] The musical *virtuosa* and poet Gaspara Stampa's (1523–1554) poetry has been translated in part, and a complete edition of her poetry appeared in The Other Voice in Early Modern Europe series in 2010.[20] Musical *virtuosa*, actor, and academician Isabella Andreini's (1562–1604) pastoral *La Mirtilla* has been translated,[21] as has a selection of her poetry.[22] Maddalena Campiglia's pastoral *Flori* has been published in translation,[23] and Giulia Bigolina's (ca. 1516–ca. 1569) prose romance and novella are available in two translations.[24] Fonte's chivalric romance is also now available.[25]

17. Tullia d'Aragona, *Dialogue on the Infinity of Love*, ed. and trans. Bruce Merry and Rinaldina Russell, The Other Voice in Early Modern Europe (Chicago: University of Chicago Press, 1997).

18. Vittoria Colonna, *Sonnets for Michelangelo*, ed. and trans. Abigail Brundin, The Other Voice in Early Modern Europe (Chicago: University of Chicago Press, 2005).

19. Laura Battiferra degli Ammannati, *Laura Battiferra and Her Literary Circle*, ed. and trans. Victoria Kirkham, The Other Voice in Early Modern Europe (Chicago: University of Chicago Press, 2006).

20. Gaspara Stampa, *Selected Poems*, ed. and trans. Laura Anna Stortoni and Mary Prentice Lillie (New York: Italica Press, 1994); *Complete Poems*, trans. Jane Tylus, The Other Voice in Early Modern Europe (Chicago: University of Chicago Press, 2010)..

21. Isabella Andreini, *La Mirtilla: A Pastoral*, ed. and trans. Julie D. Campbell, Medieval and Renaissance Texts and Studies 242 (Tempe: Arizona Center for Medieval and Renaissance Studies, 2002).

22. Isabella Andreini, *Selected Poems of Isabella Andreini*, ed. Anne MacNeil, trans. James Wyatt Cook (Lanham, MD: Scarecrow Press, 2005).

23. Maddalena Campiglia, *Flori: A Pastoral Drama*, ed. and introd. Virginia Cox and Lisa Sampson, trans. Virginia Cox, The Other Voice in Early Modern Europe (Chicago: University of Chicago Press, 2004).

24. Giulia Bigolina, *Urania: A Romance*, ed. and trans. Valeria Finucci, The Other Voice in Early Modern Europe (Chicago: University of Chicago Press, 2004); and Giulia Bigolina, *Urania: The Story of a Young Woman's Love & The Novella of Giulia Camposanpiero and Thesibaldo Vitaliani*, ed. and trans. Christopher Nissen, Medieval and Renaissance Texts and Studies 262 (Tempe, AZ: Arizona Center for Medieval and Renaissance Studies, 2004).

25. Moderata Fonte (Modesta Pozzo), *Floridoro: A Chivalric Romance*, ed. and introd. Valeria Finucci, trans. Julie Kisacky, The Other Voice in Early Modern Europe (Chicago: University of Chicago Press, 2006).

This sample of recently edited and translated works by Italian women of the sixteenth century is by no means comprehensive; the works of numerous others have been or are in the process of being "recovered" and translated. The depth and breadth of the genres represented here, however, suggest that more was happening in the intellectual lives of learned Renaissance women than either Burckhardt or Kelly realized.

Numerous scholars have followed in Burckhardt's and Kelly's footsteps, investigating the contexts and characteristics of Italian Renaissance women's lives from a variety of disciplinary perspectives. Their findings have helped to flesh out details critically important to our understanding of the social and cultural milieus in which such writers lived. Christiane Klapisch-Zuber investigates "how a set of gender-based symbols came to be written into a good part of history" as she explores the material culture of society in Renaissance Florence.[26] She presents data suggesting that the chief value of Florentine women lay not in their erudition and eloquence but in their material wealth and physical necessity for childbearing. Marilyn Migiel and Juliana Schiesari deconstruct Burckhardt's views, noting that after the first passage from his work quoted above, "[b]arely masked inequalities emerge shortly thereafter."[27] Their volume contains essays that further interrogate received notions about women of the Renaissance in history, art, and literature. Pamela Joseph Benson examines issues regarding female independence as it has been depicted in the literature of Renaissance Italy and England.[28] More recently, Benson and Victoria Kirkham have explored the seeming contradiction between the fact that in England, France, and Italy "during the Middle Ages and Renaissance ... contrary to Aristotelian and biblical injunction, women did not keep an obedient, humble silence," and the fact that "women's presence in national literary histories ... has been less stable than men's, their niches more shallow or precarious, their memory

---

26. Christiane Klapisch-Zuber, Women, *Family, and Ritual in Renaissance Italy*, trans. Lydia Cochrane (Chicago: University of Chicago Press, 1987), xiv.

27. *Refiguring Woman: Perspectives on Gender and the Italian Renaissance*, ed. Marilyn Migiel and Juliana Schiesari (Ithaca: Cornell University Press, 1991), 6.

28. Pamela Benson, *The Invention of the Renaissance Woman* (University Park, PA: Pennsylvania State University Press, 1992).

more quickly occluded by time."[29] In a similar vein, Janet Smarr explores the dialogues of early modern Italian and French women who "wanted to insert their voices into the larger cultural conversation" even though of "the many hundreds of dialogues from this period ... few even included women speakers."[30] Diana Robin has examined the thriving world of women writers' engagement in the cultural history of this period, illustrating "the significant roles that Italian women played in tandem with men."[31] Sarah Ross has traced the rise of the "household academies and salons" in which numerous Italian women received humanist educations.[32]

Studies that shine light on the vagaries of individual lives within broader historical contexts continue to emerge. Margaret Rosenthal explores the life of one of the most famous courtesans of the sixteenth century, Veronica Franco, examining the myriad ways in which her life and career bore little resemblance to the women Burckhardt describes.[33] Stanley Chojnacki has published a retrospective of his work from the 1970s to the 1990s in which he examines the "varied and unpredictable circumstances of individual experience" that affected the lives of men and women in Venetian patrician society.[34] With detailed attention to family financial and political issues, he gives the lie to Burckhardt's blithe depiction of fathers giving equal treatment to sons and daughters in the upper classes.[35] Letizia Panizza has edited an array of essays that examine women's relationships with church, state, court, stage, and literary society. These scholarly essays allude

29. Pamela Benson and Victoria Kirkham, "Introduction," in *Strong Voices, Weak History*, ed. Benson and Kirkham (Ann Arbor: University of Michigan Press, 2005), 1.

30. Janet Levarie Smarr, *Joining the Conversation: Dialogues by Renaissance Women* (Ann Arbor: University of Michigan Press, 2005), 1.

31. Diana Robin, *Publishing Women: Salons, the Presses, and the Counter-Reformation in Sixteenth-Century Italy* (Chicago: University of Chicago Press, 2007), xix.

32. Sarah Gwyneth Ross, *The Birth of Feminism: Woman as Intellect in Renaissance Italy and England* (Cambridge, MA: Harvard University Press, 2009), 3, 13.

33. Burckhardt, *The Civilization of the Italian Renaissance*, 2:394; Margaret F. Rosenthal, *The Honest Courtesan: Veronica Franco, Citizen and Writer in Sixteenth-Century Venice* (Chicago: University of Chicago Press, 1992).

34. Stanley Chojnacki, *Women and Men in Renaissance Venice* (Baltimore: Johns Hopkins University Press, 2000), 2.

35. Burckhardt, *The Civilization of the Italian Renaissance*, 2:389.

to numerous documents that help to contextualize the world of early modern Italian women writers. Panizza and Sharon Wood also have published an essay collection that provides a beginning outline of an alternative tradition and canon.[36] Most recently, Virginia Cox has completed a long-needed detailed history of the development of Italian women's writing during this period, as she introduces and contextualizes the work of numerous writers from across the social strata.[37]

We take our cue from such new historical approaches as these as we address texts that facilitate readers' exploration of the intertextual resonances to be found in the interstices of the dialogue that exists between early modern Italian male and female authors. In part 1 we explore general contexts. We include a discussion of three influential canonical literary texts by Petrarch, Castiglione, and Tasso, in which we highlight the views of women they profess and the aspects of such texts that women writers both imitated and rejected. We also present three texts less easily available in English that illustrate a variety of views on issues pertaining to women, including religion, education, societal and family expectations (e.g., marriage, child rearing, and sexuality), the *querelle des femmes*, and Neoplatonic love philosophy. These include excerpts from Silvio Antoniano's *Three Books on the Christian Education of Children* (1589), Stefano Guazzo's *Civil Conversation* (1584), and Alessandro Piccolomini's *Raffaella, or Dialogue about Women's Good Manners* (1540).

Part 2 contains a series of case studies created by scholars familiar with the multifaceted nature of the contexts for early modern Italian women's writing. Each case includes an introduction to a writer and text along with a translation. The texts in question relate in a variety of meaningful ways to works by the women writers who were in dialogue with these male writers in some way. Throughout, we see instances of intertextuality regarding issues from the *querelle des femmes*, which writers treat sometimes as a kind of a literary game and other times as a legitimate forum for adulation and complaint. In either case, the impact regarding the subjection of women is the

---

36. *A History of Women's Writing in Italy*, ed. Letizia Panizza and Sharon Wood (Cambridge: Cambridge University Press, 2000).

37. Virginia Cox, *Women's Writing in Italy, 1400–1650* (Baltimore: Johns Hopkins University Press, 2008).

same. Moreover, the texts give a sense of the enormity of "the woman question" as general subject matter for male writers during this period. Their concentration on how women should be, behave, and believe—in other words, how they should be contained, controlled, and valued according to social and religious norms—gives us insight into the intellectual climate within which women writers worked. Before the list of Works Cited, we include a bibliography of related texts readily available in translation.

The second part opens with a case by Lori Ultsch, who presents Torquato Tasso's *Discorso della virtù femminile e donnesca* (1582), a key text in the Italian *querelle des femmes*. Tasso's text was an impetus for the added chapters of the 1601 edition of *The Nobility and Excellence of Women, and the Defects and Vices of Men*, in which Lucrezia Marinella deconstructs patriarchal praise of women and thus provides some of "the first examples of feminist literary criticism."[38] In the same vein, Tasso's discourse also resonates with Moderata Fonte's *The Worth of Women: Wherein Is Clearly Revealed Their Nobility and Superiority to Men* (1600), another example of a critical feminist voice in early modern Italy. In his piece, Tasso demonstrates his mastery of the courtier's duty to pay homage to his patron's family—in this case the House of Gonzaga in Mantova, represented by Duchess Eleonora, to whom he dedicates his work—while he surveys philosophical thought regarding feminine virtue. The resulting text is, as Ultsch puts it, "a morally didactic survey of philosophical thought on virtues that most befit women." She argues, however, that this discourse is actually "a prime period example of how the ostensible praise of virtuous women is in reality an insidious rehearsal of received notions of female inferiority handed down from Aristotle."

Another case that overtly invokes the Italian *querelle des femmes* is that presented by Suzanne Magnanini, who translates excerpts from *I donneschi diffetti* (1599) by Giuseppe Passi. David Lamari provides translations of the Latin passages in these excerpts. Magnanini points out that although Passi's second published work would ironically be "a manual for speaking tactfully so as not to give offense to others, *The Defects of Women* deeply angered many readers and led to the publication of no fewer than three women-authored

---

38. *A History of Women's Writing in Italy*, ed. Panizza and Wood, 73.

texts: Lucrezia Marinella's *The Nobility and Excellence of Women, and the Defects and Vices of Men* (1600), Moderata Fonte's *The Worth of Women: Wherein Is Clearly Revealed Their Nobility and Superiority to Men* (1600), and Bianca Nardi's *A Response by Signora Bianca Nardi to a Letter from Giacomo Violati, Bookseller in Venice, Written on the Occasion of Thanking Him for Having Sent Her* I donneschi diffetti *by Giuseppe Passi* (1614)." Although Passi would later write *La monstruosa fucina delle sordidezze de gl'huomini* (The monstrous smithy of men's foul deeds) (1603), he is especially remembered for his engagement in the *querelle des femmes* and the ire with which women writers responded to his work.

From these treatises, we move on to Sperone Speroni's *Dialogo di amore* (1542), translated by Janet Smarr. As noted above, this dialogue was the impetus for Tullia d'Aragona's *Della infinità di amore*. Speroni's work was inspired in part by his encounters with Aragona at salon gatherings in Venice around 1535.[39] He casts this dialogue in a salon setting and makes Aragona a key figure in the debate about the nature of love. While he gives a passing nod to the idea that his character Tullia should enjoy her Diotima-like status as a *cortigiana honesta*, that status is not reflected in his portrayal of her. On the contrary, his version of her character is that of a stereotypically lustful, jealous, wheedling courtesan who begs to be enlightened by the men in the group. Aragona's dialogue paints quite a different picture of herself; thus, as Smarr demonstrates, the two dialogues should be read together in order to fully understand the context for Aragona's work.

Next we include a dialogue that examines attitudes toward women and marriage. "Sopra del pigliar moglie" (1612) by Francesco Andreini is introduced and translated by Julie D. Campbell. Andreini is the husband of the celebrated actor, poet, and playwright Isabella Andreini. Together they led one of the most popular *commedia dell'arte* troupes, the Gelosi, during the height of this group's fame in the late sixteenth century. This *ragiomento* between Calistene, an old man, and Teofilo, the head of a family, is especially of interest for its subject matter: an old man giving a younger one advice on choosing a wife for his son. In the process, the two discuss the reasons why mar-

---

39. For more on Aragona, Speroni, and salon gatherings, see Julie D. Campbell, *Literary Circles and Gender in Early Modern Europe* (Surrey, UK: Ashgate, 2006), 21–49.

riage is more important than the state of virginity, the origins of marriage (beginning with Adam and Eve), the problems associated with marrying a bad woman, and the blessings associated with marrying a good one. In terms of the *querelle*, Calistene has the role of the misogynist, and Teofilo, who ultimately has the final word, is the defender of women. Yet, as was demonstrated in Ultsch's work above, here too the resulting impression this dialogue leaves is one of women as chattels. It is especially intriguing to consider that this piece is authored by a man married to one of the most autonomously famous women of the period, renowned for her intellectual acumen and traditional feminine virtue, as well as her talents for acting and writing. Their case underscores the ways in which the literary and social traditions of the *querelle* trumped expression of individual experience, a phenomenon common during this period, when imitation (with only minimal innovation) was highly valued.

Patrizia Bettella explores examples of *poesia puttanesca*, the burlesque poetry of academicians and *letterati* who wrote verse about courtesans. She examines the lives and works of Anton Francesco Grazzini, Nicolò Franco, and Maffio Venier, three minor poets whose satirical poetry illustrates the popularity of attacking courtesans in verse. Bettella notes that while literary pieces written in honor of famous courtesans are widely published, the majority of satirical texts about them, particularly the *poesia puttanesca*, remain largely unknown today, in part because of the obscene language and graphic details inherent in such poetry. Given the marginal status of such poets, critics theorize that they sought to elevate their own standing in literary circles by denouncing courtesans—who sometimes were the more famous and accomplished poets.

Next, we include a selection of letters from Pietro Aretino (1492–1556), one of the most controversial literary figures of the age. Although he was especially well-known for his dialogues, translators have paid less attention to Aretino's letters, which illustrate his knowledge of and correspondence with women writers of the period. Here Christopher Nissen introduces and translates three letters from 1549 that Aretino wrote to Giulia Bigolina, author of the romance *Urania* (written ca. 1552). Nissen notes that Aretino's letters refer to something that Bigolina has sent to him, so it would appear that Bigolina initiated their acquaintance, probably in an attempt to advertise her work and thus benefit her fledgling writing career. Nissen examines this epistolary bid for literary fame, commenting on the attitudes toward women writers apparent in Aretino's responses.

We conclude the volume with a sermon, "Predica predicata … il giorno della festa di S. Maria Maddalena" (1539), by Bernardino Ochino, translated by Maria Galli Stampino. Ochino was a charismatic Franciscan monk whose sermons urging reform from within for the Catholic Church attracted the attention of both the great noblewoman Vittoria Colonna and the courtesan Tullia d'Aragona. Both Colonna and Aragona heard Ochino preach in Ferrara in 1537. Stampino points out that Ochino's extant texts are exceedingly rare because of their controversial religious nature. Ochino fled to Geneva and abandoned Catholicism, yet his spiritual influence continued to be felt in northern and central Italy. Regarding connections with women's texts, Stampino notes that linguistic ties have been established between the sermon translated here and some of Colonna's poems. Moreover, his references to the figure of Mary Madgalene seem to be reflected in Lucrezia Marinella's 1602 volume *Life of the Virgin Mary, Empress of the Universe*, recently edited by Susan Haskins for the University of Chicago Press's Other Voice series.

It should come as no surprise that so many of these texts reflect religious or moralistic concerns. The sixteenth century saw many debates on the nature and content of faith and its reflection in the lives of the faithful. Indeed, the culture prevailing in Italy (and in other Catholic countries, such as Spain, France, and portions of the Hapsburg Empire), especially in the second half of the century, reflected the stricter morality and more centrally organized structure of the Catholic Church after the Council of Trent (1545–63). The enclosure of nuns in monasteries was enforced, and weddings transformed from family affairs to a sacrament administered and controlled by the Church.[40] Such attitudes emboldened conservative thinkers to expound their views ever more forcefully—and in turn provoked women to pen their own answers. As Cox has pointed out, however, nonreligious factors were also present in the contexts for women writ-

40. See Gabriella Zarri, *Recinti: Donne, clausura e matrimonio nella prima età moderna* (Bologna: il Mulino, 2000), 100–130 and 203–35.

ers during this century.[41] A pervasive thread of the *querelle des femmes* was frequently combined with religious injunctions to provoke women's responses. Moreover, trends in oratory and literary production in general are reflected in their work.

The many texts now becoming available prove that many women chose to be actively involved in the culture of early modern Italy, rather than remaining passive and silent. To situate their voices, the texts in this volume are necessary, even vital. We hope that these texts will inspire readers to search out others that will help to provide a more complete picture of the cultural and social milieus in which these women wrote. The influences, reactions, echoes, filled interstices, dialogues, and other information that will be revealed will be invaluable for contextualizing the lives and voices of these women writers.

41. Cox, *Women's Writing*, 125–30.

PART 1

CONTEXTS AND THE CANON

1.
Contexts and Canonical Authors

JULIE D. CAMPBELL AND MARIA GALLI STAMPINO

> Chi amò più, e più mutò nella cosa amata, che si
> facesse il Petrarca?
> [Who ever loved more and more changed him-
> self into his beloved than Petrarch?]
> —Grazia to Tullia in Sperone Speroni's *Dialogo
> di amore*[1]

> After all, the poet says,
> "I di miei legger, che nessun cervo… ."
> [My days (flee) swifter than any deer… .]
> —Lucretia to Corinna in Moderata Fonte's *Il
> merito delle donne*[2]

In the works of both male and female authors of sixteenth-century Italy, imitation of and references to canonical writers appear repeatedly; thus, any consideration of literary contexts for the work of women writers should take into account the influence of such canonical texts, as suggested in the introduction. However, when reading such canonical texts as part of the critical literary context for women writers, it is as important to read against them as it is to accept them as literary masterpieces worthy of imitation. Here, we look at ways in which three key canonical texts served as catalysts for women writers.

Francesco Petrarca's *Canzoniere*, Baldassare Castiglione's *Cortegiano*, and Torquato Tasso's *Aminta* are seminal canonical texts for the genres of poetry, dialogue, and drama, respectively, that influenced innumerable writers during the sixteenth century and beyond. Just as the notion of the importance of imitating a master was crucial in the visual arts during the Renaissance, the same was true in the literary arts, and the three works in question especially found imitators

---

1. Translation by Janet Smarr in chapter 7 of this volume.

2. From *Canzoniere*, sonnet 319, in *The Worth of Women*, trans. Virginia Cox, The Other Voice in Early Modern Europe (Chicago: University of Chicago Press, 1997), 159.

among women writers in Italy, as well as across the Continent and in England. These particular examples, however, pointedly illustrate the conflicting nature of such texts for women. On the one hand, they inspire writers of both sexes to imitate them with regard to genre, style, and theme; on the other, they provide highly circumscribed traditional depictions of women that help to cement such views in the cultural consciousness. The resulting paradox for women writers, then, is the need to participate in the trend of imitating such texts while resisting or negotiating the residual stereotypes of women that they support.

In the following sections, we explore the receptions of these works, as well as aspects of them that illustrate notions about women's places in literary and philosophical creation and discussion. Additionally, we examine a selection of women writers' approaches to writing "in dialogue" with these canonical works.

Petrarch

> You may, perhaps, have heard tell of me, though even this is doubtful, since a poor and insignificant name like mine will hardly have traveled far in space or time.
> —Petrarch, "Letter to Posterity"[3]

In numerous dialogues from the sixteenth century, when characters argue from authority, they frequently quote "il Poeta," trusting that their readership is thoroughly familiar with the classical or early Renaissance author whom they reference. In most instances, the "Poeta" they quote is Francesco Petrarca (1304–1374), known in English as Petrarch. Contrary to his own (undoubtedly deliberate) overly modest projection in the epigraph, Petrarch's name has left such an indelible imprint upon literary history that it has become inextricably linked with the development of poetry in the western world. During the sixteenth century, Petrarch's style became the one most often imitated; indeed, poets were exhorted to do so by leading literary figures of the time. In *Prose della volgar lingua* (1525), in which Pietro Bembo seeks

---

3. *Selections from the Canzoniere and Other Works*, ed. and trans. Mark Musa, World's Classics (Oxford: Oxford University Press, 1985), 1.

to classify specific literary models in Italian to serve as examples of preferred style for the development of a national literature, he strongly advocates Petrarch's verse as exemplary.[4] Bembo had edited Petrarch's *Canzoniere* for its 1501 publication by the Aldine Press, so he speaks with authority on this point. Likewise, Baldessare Castiglione, in his *The Book of the Courtier* (1528), frequently refers to Petrarch and Boccaccio as the literary models of the era most worthy of imitation.[5] By midcentury, Petrarch was considered a critical authority to invoke regarding matters of philosophy, poetics, love, and the nature of women. In *La civil conversatione* (1574), Stefano Guazzo's characters Cavaliere and Annibale call repeatedly upon Petrarch's words to underscore their own, especially when discussing women and love.[6] In "Sopra del pigliar moglie," Francesco Andreini's character Teofilo quotes Petrarch to express his fear of evil befalling his son in the form of a bad wife.[7] And, as we have seen in the *Dialogo della infinità di amore*, Aragona was clearly cognizant of this tradition, although she questions men's widely held trust in the validity of Petrarch's views of women, as her references to Petrarch's authority suggest.

4. Pietro Bembo, *Prose della volgar lingua* (1525), ed. Claudio Vela (Bologna: Cooperativa Libraria Universitaria Editrice Bologna, 2001), 12. References to Petrarch permeate this work.

5. Baldessare Castiglione, *The Book of the Courtier*, trans. George Bull (London: Penguin, 1967, rpt. 1976), 73–75, 80–81. In book 3, Cesare Gonzaga says: "Who studies to compose verses, at least in the vernacular, if not to express the emotions aroused by women? Consider how many noble poems we would be deprived of, both Latin and Greek, if our poets had thought little of women. Leaving all the others aside, would it not be a grievous loss if Francesco Petrarch, who wrote about his loves in this language of ours in such an inspired way, had turned his mind only to exercises in Latin, which he would have done if love for madonna Laura had not sometimes distracted him?" (256)

6. For examples, see *La civil conversatione* (Venice: Presso Altobello Salicato, 1584), 157 ("Ultima speme di cortesi amanti," *Canzoniere* 72), 158 ("Amor' alzando il mio debile stile," *Canzoniere* 332), 159v ("Ch'un soverchio orgoglio / Molte virtudi in bella donna asconde," *Canzoniere* 105), and 230 ("Humile in tanta gloria," *Canzoniere* 126). All references to the poems from the *Canzoniere* are from Mark Musa's translation, *Petrarch's Canzoniere* (Bloomington: Indiana University Press, 1996).

7. See "Sopra del pigliar moglie" in *Ragionamenti fantastici* by Francesco Andreini (Venice: Giacom'Antonio Somasco, 1612), 40. Teofilo says, "Come dice il Poeta, 'il mal mi preme, e mi spaventa il peggio'" (*Canzoniere* 244).

It is difficult to overstate the impact of Petrarch's *Canzoniere*, *Rime sparse*, or *Rerum vulgariam fragmenta* (ca. 1330s–1374), as his poetry sequence is variously called. The Aldine Press's small ottavo format edition of the *Canzoniere*, sometimes referred to as the "petrarchino," became what we would call today an object of cult status. Direct or oblique references to it appear frequently during the *cinquecento*. In his letter to Franceso Vettori, ambassador to Rome, dated December 10, 1513, Niccolò Machiavelli writes of passing time by going into his aviary with a book in his pocket to read—"o Dante, o Petrarca, o un di questi poeti minori … ," that is, "either Dante or Petrarch or one of the minor poets."[8] In his *Ragionamento della Nanna e della Antonia* (1534), Pietro Aretino has Nanna describe the suitors who sought her when she was a young *cortigiana*. She notes that they would come dressed to the nines, "col petrarchino in mano," with the little Petrarch in hand.[9] In Agnolo Bronzino's portrait of the poet Laura Battiferra (ca. 1555), she holds a book with two sonnets from the *Canzoniere* for the viewer to see.[10] Similarly, Andrea del Sarto's works include a portrait of a woman holding a "petrarchino" (ca. 1528). Whether as fashion statement or as a mark of cultural and intellectual attainment, the *Canzoniere* permeates *cinquecento* culture.

A monument to Petrarch's idealized beloved, Laura—whom Eric Ormsby notes is "simultaneously the woman by that name, the breeze (*l'aura*), and the laurel, both the plant itself, in its mythological and botanical aspects, and the poet's crown of glory"[11]—the *Canzoniere* has become, as Mark Musa puts it, "one of the most influential books of poetry in Western literature, its metaphors and conceits absorbed into the language of love to such a degree that it would be

8. Machiavelli, "Niccolò Machiavelli a Francesco Vettori," *Lettere a Francesco Vettori e a Francesco Guicciardini (1513–1527)*, ed. Giorgio Inglese (Milan: Biblioteca Universale Rizzoli, 1996), 194. For the translation, see Machiavelli's "Letter to Francesco Vettori," trans. Allan H. Gilbert, in Maynard Mack and others, eds., *Norton Anthology of World Masterpieces*, 7th ed. (New York: W. W. Norton and Company, 1999), 1:1708–9.

9. See Aretino, *Ragionamento della Nanna e dell'Antonia*, IntraText, http://www.intratext.com/IXT/ITA1035/_P4.HTM, or *I ragionamenti* (Milan: dall'Oglio, 1960), 272.

10. A black and white reproduction of this portrait can be seen in Laura Battiferra degli Ammannati, *Laura Battiferra and Her Literary Circle*, ed. Victoria Kirkham, The Other Voice in Early Modern Europe (Chicago: University of Chicago Press, 2006), 2–3.

11. Eric Ormsby, "Petrarch: A Splendid Excess," *The New Criterion*, 23 September 2004, 19.

difficult to calculate the limits of Petrarch's influence."[12] Petrarchism swept across the Continent and England during the sixteenth century, inspiring poetry by both men and women. Petrarch's poetry, however, constitutes a critical locus of conflict for women writers. Laura, the blond, fair, exquisitely beautiful enigma who is virtually silent throughout the 366 poems,[13] is in part Petrarch's imitation of Dante's heavenly guide Beatrice and in part his connection to the beautiful women of whom the medieval troubadours sang. She also partakes of the Neoplatonic love tradition. She is thus a blend of heavenly spiritual beauty and earthly physical beauty, as well as a philosophical construct. As one of the key facets of Petrarch's poetry that came to be imitated, she poses numerous problems for female poets.

Women Poets and Petrarchism

In *Authorizing Petrarch*, William J. Kennedy suggests that a "woman's appropriation of male discourse always entails a Circean transformation that complicates rather than clarifies the reciprocity of lover and beloved, male and female."[14] By "Circean transformation," he seems to mean a transformation involving a metamorphosis of sorts, a complete change of substance; however, in *The Currency of Eros*, Ann Rosalind Jones explores in depth the sites of difference in women's poems, seeing them more as *negotiations* between women writers and the "ideological pressures" of their era than as the more negatively nuanced "complications" of which Kennedy writes.[15] From either perspective, however, there are unavoidable hurdles that women writers must overcome, as Jones points out, beginning with the contradictions women face within writing and the primacy of the male-au-

12. Musa, introduction to *Petrarch's Canzoniere*, xiii. For the vitality of Petrarch's influence even on contemporary popular culture, see Nancy Vickers, "Vital Signs: Petrarch and Popular Culture," *Romantic Review* 79, no. 1 (1988): 184–95, and her "Lyric in the Video Decade," *Discourse* 16, no. 1 (1993): 6–27.

13. After she is dead, Petrarch occasionally gives Laura a few lines from beyond the grave. See *Canzoniere* 250, 279, and 302 for examples.

14. William J. Kennedy, *Authorizing Petrarch* (Ithaca: Cornell University Press, 1994), 167.

15. Ann Rosalind Jones, *The Currency of Eros: Women's Love Lyric in Europe, 1540–1620* (Bloomington: Indiana University Press, 1990), 1.

thored model of lyric love poetry.[16] Because the ideal for women was to live as silently and chastely as the female beloveds depicted in men's Petrarchan poetry, for a woman to write from the position of lover could be construed as tantamount to an advertisement for the dissolution of her chastity. The act of writing was, first, an act of rebellion against the code of silence for women; second, it was an admission of a passionate, intelligent, articulate nature, which was typically considered characteristic of males, not of females, and was thus connected ideologically with the freedoms only men were to enjoy—including that of being the pursuer in matters of love. The word "ideal," however, should be noted carefully. While women experienced social and religious pressures to conform to idealized behaviors, relatively large numbers of educated women wrote anyway, in spite of the aspersions that might be cast upon their virtue.

At first, the switch to woman as poet/lover and to man as object of inspiration/beloved seems to have been a radical overturning of deeply rooted cultural patterns of behavior; but was it really? This notion, which critics have championed throughout the study and critique of Renaissance literature, needs to be reexamined in light of the fact that much poetry was produced by women writers during this period throughout Europe, in Latin as well as the vernacular languages espoused by Petrarchists.[17] Women's poetry was passed around in both manuscript and printed forms, especially in Italy. As Diana Robin points out, "at the end of the sixteenth century the number of women who had published their work in Italy topped two hundred," and by "midcentury many of their poems were appearing in the new poetry anthologies produced by the Giolito press and several other publishing houses associated with Giolito in Venice, the uncontested center of the print industry in sixteenth-century Italy."[18] Moreover, she notes that the "moral strictures placed on the public appearance of women's names which caused many writers in early modern France and England to publish their works anonymously, simply do not apply

16. Ibid.

17. For more on women Latinists from this period, see Jane Stevenson's *Women Latin Poets* (Oxford: Oxford University Press, 2005).

18. Robin, *Publishing Women*, xviii.

in the commercial print world of sixteenth-century Italy."[19] Could it be that the injunction to silence, with its attendant virtues of chastity and obedience—which critics have long suggested curtailed women's writing—should be seen more as a corrective measure than as illustrative of the status quo? Did such injunctions actually illustrate wishful thinking on the parts of men rather than a universally accepted notion that women should be silent? This question is also taken up by Janet Smarr in *Joining the Conversation: Dialogues by Renaissance Women*, discussed further below, but here it is important to note that the amount of poetry produced by women during the sixteenth century, especially in Italy, requires rethinking the suggested universality of such a notion.

It will be helpful to observe a few ways in which women poets approached the traditions of Petrarchism. First, we discuss how stylistic problems arose, chief among them being the lack of a prototype recommended for real female beloveds who wished to speak for themselves. Second, we consider how Petrarch's emphasis on individual authorship and the crafting of his own persona may have specifically affected two of his female imitators.

Regarding the notion of a female lover writing about a male beloved, it is important to recognize that in this reversal, the Renaissance concepts of honor for men and women stay ideologically the same. The result is poetry by women, ideally meant to be silent, chaste, obedient, and saintly, about men, ideally meant to be valorous and honorable, but for whom the stigma of appearing unchaste in no way equaled that for women. Thus, by writing about real men in their lives, as opposed to Laura-like, unattainable male figures, women poets are implicated from the start in transgressive behavior. They are not silent, and their chastity may be brought into question. In recognizing the implications of this reversal, we can understand why women's writing caused anxiety in some social and religious quarters; women writers were, in effect, acting as men. However, women's writing in this vein was clearly welcomed in other quarters, especially the widely proliferating literary circles, as it contributed intertextually to the ongoing debates about the nature of love and the literary developments that depicted it.

19. Ibid.

Because women writers did not have a singular paragon after which to fashion their male beloveds—a Lorenzo to match Petrarch's Laura—they chose to model them either on the real men in their lives or, more rarely, on Christ as the ideal male. Those who wrote in reference to Christ tended to endow their beloved figures with attributes that resembled the divine aspects of the Renaissance female beloved. Vittoria Colonna describes Christ as a "divina flamma" (divine flame) in sonnet 122 and the "lume del mondo" (light of the world) in sonnet 124 of her *Rime sacre e morali,* with variations on these appellations in many other sonnets in which she emphasizes his holiness and his guidance.[20] A Petrarchan conceit that frequently appears in Colonna's poetry is her use of the word "sole" (sun) to represent her beloved. This device evolves from a reference to her dead husband, Ferrante Francesco d'Avalos, Marquis of Pescara, in her *Rime amorose* to Christ and in her *Rime sacre e morali.* For example, in her first sonnet in the *Rime amorose,* she claims that she writes to assuage her grief over the death of her "beautiful sun, / Who leaves on earth such honored remains";[21] and in the *Rime sacre e morali,* see sonnet 22, "I would like that the true sun, to which I always pray, / send within my mind an eternal flash of light… ."[22] In a blending of the sacred and the profane, Gaspara Stampa invokes the incarnation of Christ in Mary's womb as a conceit for her lover, Collaltino di Collalto, Count of Treviso, making his "nido" (nest) in her heart.[23] In sonnet 2 of her *Sonetti spirituali,* Laura Battiferra degli Ammannati invites the "Loving and holy spirit" to "descend over" her mind to help her sing and speak of God, as well as to translate Latin psalms into Tuscan verses.[24] In sonnet 9, she writes, "This fire so ardent and this flame that comes forth from your breast, sweet Lord, so blazes in / mine with kindled ardor

---

20. Vittoria Colonna, "Rime sacre e morali," in *Rime di tre gentildonne del secolo XVI,* ed. Olindo Guerrini (Milan: Sonzogno, 1882), 127–28.

21. "… bel sole, / Che lasciò in terra sì onorata spoglia." Colonna, "Rime amorose," in *Rime di tre gentildonne del secolo XVI,* 19. Trans. by Campbell.

22. "Vorrei che 'l vero sol, cui sempre invoco, / Mandasse un lampo eterno entro la mente… ." Colonna, "Rime sacre e morali," 89. Trans. by Campbell.

23. Gaspara Stampa, sonnet 2, *Selected Poems,* 4–5.

24. "Spirto amoroso e santo, che scendesti / in forma d'infocate lingue ardenti." *Laura Battiferra and Her Literary Circle,* 220–21.

that it ever more and more / ignites and inflames me."[25] One might argue, especially for Colonna and Battiferra degli Ammannati, who write in clearly delineated categories of sacred and secular poetry, that Petrarch's shift to writing about Mary, the "Vergine bella," at the end of his *Canzoniere* provided a model for female poets to shift their focus from earthly to heavenly figures.[26] Even so, they work with reversals of gendered imagery.

Apart from references to Christ as an ideal male beloved, female Petrarchists adapted more general Petrarchan and classical allusions to illustrate their mortal male beloveds. Stampa puns on the name of her beloved, Collaltino di Collalto, by linking the beautiful hills (*colli*) of his estate with the beauty of his person. Collalto indicates a "high hill," and she turns the reference into praise of her lover's stature.[27] She also uses classical references to allude to his character; however, they may be seen as object lessons for what the ideal lover is not, because she invokes the stories of Orpheus and Eurydice in sonnet 31, Echo and Chimera in sonnet 124, and Procne and Philomela in sonnet 173.[28] Following a rhetorical pattern of praise and blame, Stampa both exalts her beloved and laments his hard heart.[29] In sonnet 4, she first explains how all the planets gave him his gifts of style, intelligence, and good looks, while his coldness came from the moon.[30] The praise-and-blame conceit is also reflected in her blazons[31] as she attempts to depict his physical attributes in the style of the male Petrarchists.

---

25. "Questo foco sì ardente e questa fiamma, / ch'esce del petto tuo, dolce Signore, / avvampa così il mio d'acceso ardore / ch' ognor via più m'infoca e più m'infiamma." *Laura Battiferra and Her Literary Circle*, 230–31.

26. *Canzoniere* 366, "Virgin bella, che di sol vestita," 510–11.

27. Jones, *Currency of Eros*, 127.

28. Fiora A. Bassanese, *Gaspara Stampa*, Twayne's World Authors 658 (Boston: Twayne, 1982), 94–96. These references, moreover, served to prove her knowledge of classical authors to her implied readers.

29. Jones, *Currency of Eros*, 125, 134–41.

30. Stampa, *Selected Poems*, 8–9.

31. A blazon or *blason* is a poem of praise. Typically, it details the beloved's beauty point by point.

In writing their blazons, women poets struggled to come up with ways to make their beloveds blond and fair, yet appropriately manly. In sonnet 7, Stampa adds images of warlike valor to the blond/fair conceit to give Collalto a masculine air. She describes him as being the

> image of glory and valor:
> with blond hair and lively coloring,
> tall in stature with a broad chest,
> and finally in every way perfect,
> except a little (oh me, alas!) pitiless in love.[32]

After introducing this blond warrior and lamenting that he is without pity in love, Stampa addresses her readers, explaining that, thanks to him, she, who is steadily faithful, is the image of death and martyrdom. Even so, he remains cruel. Collalto is clearly no saint in her mind, nor a chaste object on which to reflect. Reflection on him leads to heaven via martyrdom, not by ascension of the Neoplatonic ladder of love. In other words, while Laura is Petrarch's path to glory, Collalto is Stampa's path to suffering. Bassanese notes that in Stampa's poetry there is a collusion of God and Collalto, a mixture of the sacred and the profane, as Stampa manipulates Petrarchan and Neoplatonic ideals to match her own situation.[33] In sonnet 174, Stampa again details Collalto's characteristics that lead to her martyrdom, referring to his "unheard-of, astonishing cruelty, / a prompt and fickle readiness for flight, / a carriage revealing too much pride in his gifts," and "laughter at my death as I lie perishing."[34] Ultimately, Stampa depicts a lover,

---

32. "... imagin de la gloria e del valore: / de pelo biondo, e di vivo colore, / di persona alta e spazioso petto, e finalmente in ogni opra perfetto, / fuor ch'un poco (oimè lassa!) empio in amore." Gaspara Stampa and Veronica Franco, *Rime*, ed. Abdelkader Salza, Scrittori d'Italia (Bari, Italy: Laterza, 1913), 8. Trans. by Campbell.

33. Bassanese, *Gaspara Stampa*, 115.

34. "... inaudita e nova crudeltate, / un esser al fuggir pronto e leggiero, / un andar troppo di sue doti altero" and "rider di mia morte quando pèro." Quoted and translated in Jones, *Currency of Eros*, 136–37.

who is, as Bassanese points out, "both idol and sadist, Platonic sun and demonic assassin."[35]

Tullia d'Aragona depicts a lover, possibly Piero Manelli, a young Florentine nobleman that she meets late in her career,[36] as a blond beloved who leads her to death; but her approach in sonnet 45 is not so darkly tortured as Stampa's regarding Collalto. She sighs,

> Where is (o miserable me) that golden hair
> with which Love made a net to catch me ?
> Where is (alas) the beautiful face, from whence ardor
> is born, that leads my life to the end?[37]

In this poem, she also asks, "where is the white hand" that squeezes her heart, and "where do the angelic words sound"[38] that in a moment give her death and life? Here, Aragona seems to echo Petrarch's sonnet 199, "O lovely hand that squeezes my heart tight," and perhaps his sonnet 299, "Where is the brow that with the slightest movement ..."[39] The "net" to catch her recalls the one that Love spreads in Petrarch's sonnet 181, "Love set amid the grass his pretty net / of gold and pearls, spread out beneath a branch."[40] No matter to whom this poem is actually addressed, it, like others of those Jones calls "free-floating" in Aragona's oeuvre, reflects Aragona's adherence to Petrarchan tradition.[41] The friction, however, arises from the gender of the author. Aside from the

---

35. Bassanese, *Gaspara Stampa*, 111.

36. In *The Currency of Eros*, Jones points out that although Enrico Celani attributes the dedication of this poem to Manelli, the texts that Celani labels "Allo stesso," or to the same man as this one is—in this case, Manelli—"are actually curiously free-floating," and she suggests that it is not completely clear that Manelli is the recipient of this poem; 112.

37. "Ov'è (misera me) quell'aureo crine /di cui fe' rete per pigliarmi Amore /Ov'è (lassa) il bel viso, onde l'ardore / nasce, che mena la mia vita al fine?" Aragona, *Le rime di Tullia d'Aragona cortigiana del secolo XVI*, ed. Enrico Celani (Bologna: Forni, 1968), 49. Trans. by Campbell.

38. "ov'è la bianca man ..." and "ove suonan l'angeliche parole ..."

39. "O bella man che mi destringi 'l core" and "Ov'è la fronte che con picciol cenno ..." *Canzoniere*, 418–19.

40. "Amor fra l'erbe una leggiadra rete / d'oro e di perle tese sott' un ramo." *Canzoniere*, 272–73.

41. Jones, *Currency of Eros*, 112.

external implication that she is writing this poem for a male lover, the internal descriptions of the beloved are very Laura-like. Yet in spite of the implied chaste, distant, unattainable love depicted in this poem, Aragona's poetry was the work of a courtesan poet; thus, much of it would be read as indicative of the real physical relationships she has with her poetic interlocutors. As Colonna and Stampa do, Aragona adapts Petrarchan conceits to fit her own situation, which happens to be very similar to that of the male courtier poets. Like them, she writes for fame and attention, hoping to win support and favor. In praising the handsomeness and the divine souls of her lovers and acquaintances, Aragona seeks, on the one hand, an immortal reputation for her talent, and on the other, clients to support her and act as her protectors.

Actress and poet Isabella Andreini takes diverse approaches to imitating Petrarch's stance toward the beloved. Writing in both male and female voices, she sings passionately of both male and female beloveds. She begins madrigal 104 (*Rime*, 1601), "If, Lady, you were able / To see my suffering the way I see you," and madrigal 4 (*Rime*, 1605), "Whenever upon her silver face / I gaze, on hers who is the only Sun / Of night ..."[42] In madrigal 19 (*Rime* 1601), her "lovely sun" is her male beloved who causes her to blush, and in sonnet 47 (*Rime*, 1601), she writes of her beloved Thyrses, who invokes in her "ardor sweet."[43] She prepares her readers for her appropriation of these voices in the first sonnet of her first poetry collection. In sonnet 1 (*Rime* 1601), she reminds them that "in theaters" she has "in varied style" played "a woman, now a man, / As Nature would instruct and Art as well."[44] In this way, Andreini justifies her play with gender in her poetry by recalling her performance of male and female roles on stage.

42. "Donna se voi poteste / Vedo il mio martir, sicome io veggio," and "Qualhor mio l'argento / Di lei, chè de la notte unico Sole, / Di lei ..." ed. *Selected Poems of Isabella Andreini*, 122–23, 168–69.

43. "M'apparve il mio bel Sole / ... Al cui raggio improviso / Di più colori mi si tinse il viso" and "Tirsi dolce mio ben se dal valore / Onde sì illustre, e glorioso vai / Nasce quest'amor mio, nascono i guai, / M'è soàve'l languir, dolce l'ardore." *Selected Poems of Isabella Andreini*, 78–79, 76–77.

44. "E come ne' Teatri hor Donna, ed hora /Huom fei rappresentando in vario stile / Quanto volle insegnar Natura, ed Arte." *Selected Poems of Isabella Andreini*, 30–31.

The epigraph from Petrarch at the beginning of this section allows us to tease out another aspect of this inheritance with which women writers had to contend: Petrarch's resolute emphasis on individual authorship through carefully crafted self-presentation in written and publicly circulating forms. The emergence of subjectivity has been viewed as an integral part of modernity and a mark of the shift from the cultures prevalent in the Middle Ages. Such an emphasis on a single person's agency has largely prevented us from understanding (or even heeding) the networks and groups through which ideas and manuscript texts circulated that shaped most male and female writers of the early modern period in Italy.[45] In some cases, then, the "dialogues" to which we refer in our title occurred in person, in the contexts of "cercoli, cenacoli, or salons."[46] In other cases, dialogues took place on the written page as poetic tributes and responses between male and female poets published in volumes together and as traditional Renaissance dialogues that recall the classical models (as well as contemporary salon exchanges, in some cases). These categories of "dialogue" were not mutually exclusive, as one occasionally became an intertext for the other.

Although we could choose from numerous examples in which the poetry of women writers from this period is presented alongside that of their male interlocutors, two instances are particularly cogent in this context: Tullia d'Aragona's and Laura Battiferra degli Ammannati's poem collections; or, to use Victoria Kirkham's apt phrase, "choral" anthologies.[47] The title of Aragona's collection, originally printed in Venice by Giolito in 1547, indicates its nature: *Rime della Signora Tullia di Aragona et di diversi a lei* makes explicit that the poems it contains were composed by many, not by a single author. As Julia L. Hairston explains, "She penned forty-nine of the poems whereas

---

45. This situation was also prevalent in the rest of western Europe and in the British Isles; see, for example, Arthur F. Marotti, *John Donne, Coterie Poet* (Madison: University of Wisconsin Press, 1986), and chapters 3 through 6 in Campbell, *Literary Circles and Gender in Early Modern Europe.*

46. Robin, *Publishing Women*, 2.

47. See Victoria Kirkham, "Laura Battiferra degli Ammannati's *First Book* of Poetry: A Renaissance Holograph Comes Out of Hiding," *Rinascimento* 36 (1996): 351–91.

eighteen different men wrote sixty-five poems to or about her."[48] The title gives pride of place to the woman who was responsible for the collection as a whole. Similarly, Laura Battiferra's *Il primo libro dell'opere toscane* (Florence: Giunti, 1560) "collects 187 poems. Of these, 146 are by the author and 41 are by her distinguished male correspondents, among them Annibal Caro, Benedetto Varchi, il Lasca, Agnolo Bronzino, and Benvenuto Cellini."[49] In both cases, poems written to or about the two women poets are subsumed under their names, recognizing the aggregative influence they exerted on their coterie and the care with which they assembled their volumes.[50] Indeed, as Hairston notes:

> The choral anthology differs from the lyric anthology, a genre that was to have an even wider diffusion in the sixteenth century, in its attribution to a single author, even though a number of different authors may have contributed to it; the lyric anthology comprises lyric poetry by many different authors which is usually catalogued under the editor's name. Another difference between the choral anthology and the lyric anthology is thematic—the choral anthology revolves around a single theme, usually the identity of its compiler and author, whereas the lyric anthology is less restricted; at most, a lyric anthology may be ordered by the geographical origin or sex of its contributors.[51]

48. Julia Hairston, "Out of the Archive: Four Newly Identified Figures in Tullia d'Aragona's *Rime della Signora Tullia di Aragona et di diversi a lei* (1547)," *MLN* 118 (2003): 257.

49. Kirkham, "Laura Battiferra degli Ammannati's *First Book* of Poetry," 353.

50. In Battiferra's case, to quote Kirkham, "*Il primo libro delle opere toscane* reads like a *Who's Who* of mid-sixteenth-century Italy, from Cosimo de' Medici and his key ally King Philip of Spain, to his most trusted architect and sculptor, the author's own husband Bartolomeo Ammannati"; furthermore, "she anchors her *canzoniere* to Cosimo's conquest of Siena," demonstrating her keen understanding of the politics and practice of patronage and homage. Kirkham, "Introduction," in Laura Battiferra degli Ammannati, *Laura Battiferra and Her Literary Circle*, ed. and trans. Victoria Kirkham, The Other Voice in Early Modern Europe (Chicago: University of Chicago Press, 2006), 40.

51. Hairston, "Out of the Archive," 257.

We cannot be certain that either poet was responsible for showcasing her name in the anthology's title.[52] Still, either these writers or their editors and publishers cast them as the aggregating force behind these volumes. As Diana Robin has argued, the very books in which women's poetry appeared were designed to emphasize their presence and their interaction with their (male) publishers and editors.[53]

Thus, through their anthologies, Aragona and Battiferra asserted their centrality to their literary, philosophical, and intellectual circles in a more permanent manner than through the typical social exchanges, which were necessarily oral, hence fleeting.[54] In this sense, women poets such as Aragona and Battiferra both adapt to and complicate the emphasis on single authors that Petrarch wanted to convey to posterity and that has traditionally relegated women writers to the margins of the canon in early modern Italy and beyond.[55] They constructed so-called rhetorical spaces[56] that allowed for the creation of ideas and texts, and they crafted works that replicated such spaces in a more permanent medium. In such contexts, dialogues flowed from women to men and vice versa, both in person in literary society and in

52. Nor can we know what influence they had on any part of the printing enterprise, as Susan Broomhall has pointed out in her study *Women and the Book Trade in Sixteenth-Century France* (Surrey, UK: Ashgate, 2002), 112. In the case of Italy, Robin argues, publication occurred though "the bonding of elite women writers with men working at the presses as editors, translators, correctors, printers, and consultants." *Publishing Women*, xxi.

53. Robin, *Publishing Women*, 51–56.

54. The importance of such coteries and their organizers can hardly be overestimated. For Anton Francesco Grazzini (nicknamed il Lasca), inclusion in Aragona's *Rime* coincided chronologically with his expulsion from the Accademica Fiorentina, which he had founded under the name of Accademia degli Umidi. Such a place afforded him an indirect way back into one of the main intellectual circles in Florence; on this case, see Bettella's contribution in part 2 of this volume. His poems also appear in Battiferra's *Rime*: see Laura Battiferra degli Ammannati, *Laura Battiferra and Her Literary Circle*, 172–73. Literary circles were important in smaller Italian cities as well, as Virginia Cox and Lisa Sampson have argued in their volume editors' introduction to Maddalena Campiglia, *Flori, a Pastoral Drama* (Chicago: University of Chicago Press, 2004), 1–35, especially 5–7.

55. See, for example, Joan DeJean, *Tender Geographies: Women and the Origins of the Novel in France* (New York: Columbia University Press, 1991), which focuses on the literary salons in seventeenth-century France.

56. For an incisive definition of "rhetorical space" and its importance for early modern women writers, see Broomhall, *Women and the Book Trade*, 71.

print—even from woman writer to woman writer[57]—and in considerable numbers.

As we examine lyric poems (and dialogues manifested in poetry) written by men and women in early modern Italy, it behooves us to resist the easy categories that pervade past interpretations, lest we continue to impose them on far more nuanced circumstances than have previously been considered.

Castiglione

> In heaven's name, leave all this business of matter and form and male and female for once, and speak in a way that you can be understood. We have heard and understood quite well all the evil said about us by signor Ottaviano and signor Gaspar, but now we can't at all understand your way of defending us.
>
> —Emilia Pia to Magnifico Giuliano[58]

The Courtier (*Il libro del cortegiano*), or *The Book of the Courtier*, by Baldessare Castiglione (1478–1529), was published in 1528 by the Aldine Press. During the sixteenth and early seventeenth centuries, it appeared in numerous editions and was translated into French, German, Spanish, and English.[59] Janet Smarr notes that it became "widely acclaimed as a patternbook for both language and behavior, being reprinted more than twenty times in Italy during the sixteenth century with at least half a dozen more editions or translations in France."[60] Much like Petrarch's *Canzoniere*, Castiglione's *Courtier* became what we might today call a bestseller. Concerned with the education of the ideal courtier—and, to a lesser degree, the ideal woman of the court—it was often read as a conduct book. It was also considered a key Renaissance Neoplatonic dialogue, as it clearly pays homage to Plato's *Symposium*; thus, it was much imitated among writers of that very popular genre during the sixteenth century. Moreover, its setting

57. Robin, *Publishing Women*, 71.

58. Castiglione, *The Book of the Courtier*, 221.

59. It was translated into English by Sir Thomas Hoby and published in 1561.

60. Smarr, *Joining the Conversation*, 5.

and characters—the court of Urbino in March of 1507, where, during the evenings, a distinguished group of noble, learned men and women participate in storytelling and debate some of the most popular philosophical and cultural questions of their time—illustrates a burgeoning phenomenon in Italy that would also spread across the Continent and to England: groups of intellectuals forming their own so-called academies and more informal salons, in part in imitation of Plato's academy.[61] Finally, the subject matter of *The Courtier* is deeply vested in matters of gender, including conversations that attempt to circumscribe masculinity and participate in the *querelle des femmes*. These facets of Castiglione's dialogue intrigued and inspired its imitators.

On the surface, Castiglione's representation of the learned and wise Elisabetta Gonzaga, the Duchess of Urbino (1471–1526), and Emilia Pia (d. 1528), her constant companion known for her wit and intellect, as key interlocutors in this debate would make *The Courtier* appear to further the social acceptance of such women as intellectual equals to their male contemporaries. To some extent, it no doubt did, but a few characteristics of Castiglione's treatment of women in his work illustrate the cultural "glass ceiling" for learned women that *The Courtier* helped to promulgate in the sixteenth century.

In the beginning of book 1 of *The Courtier*, Castiglione gives us a glimpse of what he considers ideal social behavior by the sexes as he describes a typical evening at the court of Urbino. He writes:

> [L]et me say that it was the custom for all the gentlemen of the house to go, immediately after supper, to the rooms of the Duchess; and there, along with pleasant recreations and enjoyments of every kind, including constant music and dancing, sometimes intriguing questions were asked, and sometimes ingenious games played... . And occasionally, there would be discussions on various subjects, or there would be a sharp exchange of spontaneous witticisms; and often "emblems" as we call them nowadays, were devised for the occasion.[62]

61. See Campbell, *Literary Circles and Gender*, 7–14.

62. Castiglione, *The Book of the Courtier*, 44.

Regarding the number and the roles of the women present, he also notes that "the group was arranged alternately one man and one woman, as long as there were women, for invariably they were outnumbered by the men. Then the company was governed according to the wishes of the Duchess, who usually left this task to signora Emilia."[63] Castiglione makes clear that the group is a politely decorous, yet gregarious one in which men and women engage in conversation together. He describes the harmonious relations among the men of the court and states: "It was the same with the ladies, whose company we all enjoyed very freely and innocently, since everyone was allowed to talk and sit, make jokes and laugh with whom he pleased, though such was the respect we had for the wishes of the Duchess that the liberty we enjoyed was accompanied by the most careful restraint."[64]

In his depiction of a historical moment, Castiglione illustrates the freedom of discourse between men and women at the court, and his description depicts how the duchess and her ladies took active roles in the group, participating in the discussions and exchanges of witticisms.[65] However, as author of this particular literary dialogue, Castiglione has his male characters act as the major interlocutors, and his female characters, no matter how highly praised for their wit, wisdom, and virtue, act primarily as referees and audience members. They also act as Neoplatonic guides who lift the tone of the discussions to higher levels of spiritual virtue and as judges who direct and briefly comment on the progress of the debates. The very fact that the gentlemen taking part in the conversation meet in the duchess's chamber indicates both her privileged status and her physical restrictions.

Even though "the group was arranged alternately one man and one woman," the men do the major part of the talking. With regard to the court lady in this setting, Smarr notes that "whatever education or eloquence she may possess, she is viewed as an adornment or en-

---

63. Ibid., 45.

64. Ibid., 43.

65. Bull notes that Margherita Gonzaga, Elisabetta's niece, was reputed to be especially "vivacious, gay and according to Bembo, extremely witty." Castiglione, *The Book of the Courtier*, 26.

tertainment in the service of a totally male-centered culture."[66] Elisabetta Gonzaga and Emilia Pia act as the key female interlocutors,[67] but, as Smarr's observation suggests, their traditional literary roles in the dialogue rapidly become apparent. For example, the male speakers begin and end their discussions at "signs" from the duchess or Signora Emilia,[68] recover the original course of their conversation after going off on tangents when one of these ladies so desires it,[69] and refrain from continuing when one of the two ladies notes that it is time to stop, as Signora Emilia does when she says pointedly to Fregoso and Count Ludovico, "It seems to me that this argument of yours has grown too protracted and tedious. So it would be as well to postpone it to another time."[70] Though these women are ostensibly given the power to limit or control conversation in the *Courtier*, they usually refrain from joining in the argument, even when the topic is the nature of women. Their listening silence, therefore, along with that of the other ladies who are present but quiet, creates a distinct space that signifies ideas and opinions deferred.

It is difficult to judge whether Castiglione keeps the women mostly silent in his work out of a sense of preserving their modesty (his work does not include a courtesan or Diotima-like figure, who might be condoned for taking part in a published discussion), or because he privileges the arguments of the male speakers over theirs, or perhaps because the majority of women present actually behaved in the manner he depicts; however, when we consider his own description of the free flow of conversation between women and men at this court, a conflation of the first two notions seems closest to correct.[71] Critics have speculated widely on the strengths and weaknesses that may be represented by the women's relatively silent presence. Regarding the

---

66. Smarr, *Joining the Conversation*, 6.

67. Margherita Gonzaga does interject a comment in book 3 to protest that the deeds of noble women are not given due attention. Castiglione, *The Book of the Courtier*, 227–28.

68. Castiglione, *The Book of the Courtier*, 65.

69. Ibid., 74.

70. Ibid., 84.

71. Smarr does point out that "women were commonly warned not to argue publicly with men"; however, records of learned women taking part in humanistic disputations or defending their own legal rights are readily available. *Joining the Conversation*, 101.

general power structure of gender relations outlined in *The Courtier,*
some have suggested that the male figures, with their several critiques
of effeminacy, are themselves effeminized in relation to the power of
their prince. Gerry Milligan, building on the work of Harry Berger,
suggests instead that these courtiers are gynephobic, and he argues
that rather "than taking the gender debate to be a reductive one of
male anxiety over female rule, Castiglione is potentially arguing that
women are an integral and powerful discursive force in the bolstering
and policing of a pragmatic masculinity."[72] Milligan persuasively argues that "both the women and men of the court maintain a constant
surveillance over masculinity, and they invoke a shaming mechanism
using men's gender anxieties in order to persuade the courtiers to act
according to their own designs. The text ultimately politicizes masculinity and demonstrates the utility of this gender construction in a
larger project of political reform."[73]

While political reform may be very much the substance of this
facet of the *Courtier,* the form of its depiction of women's interactions
in the dialogue strongly recalls the essentialist notion, espoused by
traditional defenders of women in the *querelle des femmes,* that women
are more morally virtuous than men and that it is thus their responsibility to inspire in men greater moral and spiritual virtue. This concept
is exemplified by Castiglione's use of Elisabetta Gonzaga and Emilia
Pia as guides and referees for the male interlocutors' discourses. From
the early discussions of the attributes of the ideal courtier in book 1 to
considerations of persons of higher importance and even divine love
itself in book 4, the ladies' promptings throughout the dialogue may
be seen to do just that. To illustrate this point, in book 4, Castiglione
has the duchess guide the conversation to the higher, more virtuous
end for the ideal courtier that she has in mind, and the discourse
gradually turns to discussion of an ideal prince and ends with Pietro
Bembo's Neoplatonic reverie.

72. In "The Politics of Effeminacy in *Il cortegiano,*" *Italica* 83, no. 3–4 (2006), Milligan surveys the earlier work of Joan Kelly, Wayne Rebhorn, and Constance Jordan on this topic
and takes his own cue from Berger, who dissects the notion of misogyny, 345–48. Milligan
dissects the notion of effeminacy and concludes that *The Courtier* contains a discourse of
effeminacy meant to "bolster ... pragmatic masculinity" (348).

73. Milligan, "The Politics of Effeminacy," 633.

In book 4, when the dance is finished, Castiglione has Elisabetta Gonzaga announce her desire to "continue the arguments of these gentlemen" concerning the education of the courtier, which she "wholly confirm[s] and approve[s]."[74] As is typical of her role throughout the work, she summarizes the conclusions drawn from the previous argument by the men participating in the discussion, and then she directs and focuses the next installment of the debate. In this passage, she summarizes the virtues and skills Count Lodovico and Federico have deemed crucial for the successful courtier, suggesting that those such as "dancing, entertaining, singing and playing games were vain and frivolous" and that the "elegances of dress, devices, mottoes and other such things that belong to the world of women and romance often … serve simply to make men effeminate." The final result of such "skills," she declares, is that "the name of Italy is brought into disgrace," and a "kind of sterile courtiership" is disclosed. Here, Milligan's thesis is borne out in the text, and we may see how the threat of effeminacy is used rhetorically to shape masculinity. However, the influence of women's supposed superior moral virtue is also illustrated as she then suggests, "[I]f the activities of the courtier are directed as they should be to the virtuous end I have in mind, then I for one am quite convinced not only that they are neither harmful nor vain but that they are most advantageous and deserving of infinite praise."[75] With that prompt to guide the interlocutors, the duchess fulfills her role as the virtuous feminine influence, in this case guiding the male speakers to higher planes of thought on the concept of ideal masculine virtue for the courtier.

Regarding the Neoplatonic movement of the dialogue as a whole, the duchess is also instrumental in directing the conversation to Pietro Bembo's discourse on Neoplatonic love itself. When Bembo enters the conversation, the Duchess remarks: "I am glad, Pietro, that you have had to make little effort in our discussion this evening, because now we can have all the more confidence in giving you the task of speaking, and of teaching us about this kind of love which is so felicitous that it brings with it neither blame nor displeasure; for doubtless it would be one of the most useful and important of the

74. Castiglione, *The Book of the Courtier*, 284.

75. Ibid., 284, for all the quotations here.

endowments yet attributed to the courtier. So please, I beg you, tell us all you know about it."[76]

Thus cued, Bembo begins, as he puts it, "a little discourse in order to make it clear what love is and what is the nature of the happiness that lovers experience." He remarks: "I say, therefore, that as defined by the philosophers of the ancient world Love is simply a certain longing to possess beauty; and since this longing can only be for things that are known already, knowledge must always of necessity precede desire, which by its nature wishes for what is good, but of itself is blind and so cannot perceive what is good. So Nature has ruled that every appetitive faculty, or desire, be accompanied by a cognitive faculty or power of understanding."[77]

He goes on to explain how "man who is rational by his very nature" is "placed between the two extremes of brute matter and pure spirit" and can choose "to follow the senses or to aspire to the intellect," noting that by doing either, he "can long for beauty."[78] Then Bembo launches into his argument on beauty and goodness, contending that contemplation of beauty will lead to true goodness, but the attempt to possess beauty by possessing the beautiful body of the beloved produces "a false and deceptive" pleasure that leads only to "anguish, torment, sorrow, exertion, and distress."[79] Thus, he argues that an older man—rather than a younger man whose physical passions are stronger—is better prepared to seek the higher, Neoplatonic love that leads to perfect love.

In the process of elaborating on connections between true beauty and true goodness, Bembo deplores the lack of chastity in some beautiful women and suggests that the deceptive beauty in which some women indulge when they "display in their eyes and looks a certain enticing and suggestive immodesty which is called beauty" is, in truth, "simply meretricious impudence, and unworthy of so honored and sacred a name."[80] However, he argues that beauty from any source can lead to goodness when the courtier understands that one can

76. Ibid., 324.

77. Ibid., 324–25.

78. Ibid., 325.

79. Ibid., 326–27.

80. Ibid., 332–33.

only experience true love through the enjoyment of beauty through the senses of sight and hearing, because these two "have little to do with corporeal things and are servants of reason."[81] He adds that the courtier will eventually find that contemplation not only of a particular "single woman but the universal beauty which adorns all human bodies"[82] will elevate the quality of his love even further, and that the sacred light of such a universal love, of beauty "indistinguishable from the highest good, which by its light calls and draws all things to it," will refine the soul and destroy everything that is mortal in it. Such a love will "quicken … and beautify … the celestial part which previously, because of the senses, was dead and buried." Finally, this love will lead the courtier to heaven, where he will at last know perfect love in the presence of God. Bembo sums up his explanation by exhorting everyone to "ascend by the ladder whose lowest rung bears the image of sensual beauty to the sublime mansion where dwells the celestial, adorable and true beauty which lies hidden in the secret recesses of the Almighty."[83] Then he falls into a passionate, mystic state in which he prays vehemently to God/Divine Love for the salvation of their souls, and he ends his discourse as he recovers from being "transported out of himself" by "the holy frenzy of love."[84] In effect, the virtue of ladies present, especially that of the duchess, has guided him, at least in part, to this spiritual experience. On the other hand, however, it is the ever-practical Emilia Pia who plucks his sleeve and calls him back from his divine vision. Emilia Pia's action here—suggesting a woman interfering with a man's spiritual attainment—seems to foreshadow the discussion that begins at the open ending of this work.

At the end of *The Courtier*, Gaspare Pallavicino—who always speaks the part of the traditional attacker of women in the *querelle des femmes*, as this debate is embedded in *The Courtier*—suggests that women are not capable of attaining the same spiritual heights as men. The *querelle* thread of the discourse has, however, begun earlier in the work. Smarr reminds us that the "image of dialogue as a battle fought with rhetorical weapons is part of a broader strategy to exclude wom-

81. Ibid., 334.

82. Ibid., 339.

83. Ibid., 341.

84. Ibid., 343.

en," and she points out that in *The Courtier*, Emilia Pia helps to illustrate this notion as she says to Gaspare in response to his misogynistic views: "You will not succeed in your plans, for when you saw that Bernardo was tired from talking so long you began to say so much evil about women in the belief that no one would contradict you: but now we shall appoint a fresh champion who will fight with you so that your crime doesn't go unpunished."[85] Ultimately, Castiglione's female interlocutors must rely on male defenders in the skirmishes of the *querelle* that unfold right before them.

Intriguingly, it is with yet another introduction of a *querelle* topic that *The Courtier* concludes. Just as Castiglione seems to be about to draw *The Courtier* to a close on the final, dramatic note of Bembo's Neoplatonic revelation, a new but related topic is introduced. Gaspare suggests that "to travel this road [to enlightenment] would be difficult for men, but impossible for women," and he presents examples of famous men, such as Plato, Socrates, Plotinus, St. Francis, St. Paul, and St. Stephen, but he cannot recall examples of any women who have "ever received this grace."[86] Magnifico Giuliano reminds him, however, that even Socrates "confessed that all the mysteries of love that he knew had been revealed to him by a woman, the famous Diotima," and Giuliano continues, "the angel who pierced St. Francis with the fire of love has also made several women of our own time worthy of the same seal." The duchess, like Emilia Pia earlier, chooses a male champion, stating that she wants Bembo to be the judge of "whether or not women are as capable of divine love as men," but as it is almost dawn, they decide to postpone this discussion until the next evening.[87] Unfortunately, Castiglione chooses to end his book at this point, and the debate is never "recorded," a ploy used routinely in Socratic/Neoplatonic dialogues.

Women Writers and the Dialogue

When women writers take on the dialogue genre, they tend to give female interlocutors far more loquacious and opinionated voices than

---

85. Smarr, *Joining the Conversation*, 11; Castiglione, *The Book of the Courtier*, 200.

86. Ibid., 343.

87. Ibid., 344.

Castiglione does, although his text is clearly a touchstone for them. Dialogues by women that especially reflect the characteristics of those in *The Courtier* are those that Smarr categorizes in her chapter "Dialogue and Social Conversation" in *Joining the Conversation: Dialogues by Renaissance Women*.[88] Secular dialogues by women writers, as she notes, are either educative, seeking to help educate the reader, or oppositional, presenting disputation. Typically, they are concerned with gender issues. Moreover, they are usually framed by social occasions in which one or more characters are visiting in another character's home or garden. Smarr points out that this type of framing "is the female equivalent of humanist friends gathering in a garden for informal reflective talk: it is a realistic situation that can mix relaxed humor with frank and serious discussion."[89] It may also be compared to the gathering of friends in the evenings at the court of Urbino, as well as to the conversations about gender issues that Castiglione constructs in *The Courtier*.

It is important to recall that Castiglione's description of exchanges between men and women at the court of Urbino, which he offers as introductory background material, differs from his illustration of the four nights in question in *The Courtier*. In the opening of book 1 of *The Courtier*, Castiglione recalls the "polite conversations" and "innocent pleasantries" that entertained groups of guests during the evenings in the chamber of Elisabetta Gonzaga after the duke had gone to bed early, due to his physical infirmities. As noted above, Castiglione states that "it was the same with the ladies, whose company we all enjoyed very freely and innocently, since everyone was allowed to talk and sit, make jokes and laugh with whom he pleased."[90] According to this glimpse of court life, men and women participated equally, in equally circumspect ways, in the discourses and games of the evenings; however, in the four evenings depicted in his dialogue, only the duchess and Emilia Pia have voices (and limited ones at that) in the discussions. Female authors of dialogues, it would seem, were willing to appropriate the dialogue framework and social situations that Castiglione offers, but they give female characters much larger parts in the discourse.

88. Smarr, *Joining the Conversation*, 98–129.

89. Ibid., 98–99.

90. Castiglione, *The Book of the Courtier*, 43.

In her *Dialogo della infinità di amore*, Aragona makes use of a namesake character, Tullia, to argue with learned wit the nature of honest love, which she construes as an inseparable combination of impulses of body and soul. Moreover, she takes advantage of the rhetorical space of the dialogue to ameliorate Speroni's portrait of herself as the courtesan interlocutor in his *Dialogo di amore*, in which he associates courtesans with the lowest rungs of the Neoplatonic ladder of love and reserves the highest rung for men's love for other men. Both Aragona and Speroni engage in topics that arise in Castiglione's *Courtier* (especially in books 3 and 4), and both clearly have Plato's *Symposium* in mind, but Aragona is the one who takes a firm interrogational stance regarding notions of Platonic love as male writers of the Renaissance portray it. In her dialogue, when Tullia and Benedetto Varchi speak of Plato and Socrates, Varchi praises the love of men for men, arguing that Plato's and Socrates's love for young men came from their desire to generate beautiful souls rather than beautiful bodies.[91] Tullia responds by disputing the notion that women cannot be loved for the same reason: "I wouldn't like to let that point slip by in such a hurry. Despite my awareness that what you are saying is perfectly true, I should still like to know why a woman cannot be loved with this same type of love. For I am certain that you don't wish to imply that women lack the intellectual soul that men have and that consequently they do not belong to the same species as males, as I have heard a number of men say."[92] Varchi swiftly reassures her that he means no such thing, and Tullia expresses her relief.[93] Smarr's observation that "feminist persuasion" lies at the heart of most dialogues by Renaissance women is exemplified in this exchange.[94]

Aragona keeps the focus in her dialogue on her learning and her ability to hold her own socially among her male interlocutors, ultimately suggesting that women can indeed compete in intellec-

---

91. Aragona, *Dialogue on the Infinity of Love*, 96–97.

92. Ibid., 97.

93. For more on exchanges between the dialogues of Aragona and Speroni, see Smarr, *Joining the Conversation*, 106–17, and Campbell, *Literary Circles and Gender*, 21–49.

94. Smarr, *Joining the Conversation*, 98.

tual realms and social situations.[95] Unlike Castiglione's mostly silent female interlocutors, she both guides and participates in the discussions she orchestrates, in much the same way that women both hosted and participated in salon entertainments during this period. Aragona fashions her character Tullia to appear well-educated, in spite of Tullia's rhetorically correct assertions that she is not (her use of self-effacement here is a standard rhetorical ploy), and above all to be capable of reason, a characteristic that attackers of women in the *querelle* suggested was lacking in women.[96] The protracted emphasis on Tullia's intellect, knowledge, and ability to debate with her male interlocutors underscores Aragona's intentions: first to ameliorate her own reputation, and second to intimate that other women, too, are as capable as she of competing in male-dominated intellectual society.

Virginia Cox points out that the authors of dialogues presented as "documentary accounts of conversations between named contemporary speakers" are "considerably restricted" in their representations of women by the necessity to protect their reputations.[97] Castiglione was clearly mindful of this notion, as his restricted references to the duchess and her ladies suggest. When the female character in question is a courtesan, as in the depiction of Tullia in Speroni's dialogue, the tenor of the situation changes according to what Speroni considered appropriate for depicting a learned courtesan. As we have just seen, Aragona's self-representation through her character Tullia revises the notion further through her deliberate tactics to promote herself as a virtuous and learned *cortegiana onesta*. Another twist on the tradition occurs when the writer in question is a gentlewoman who makes the self-protective gesture of writing under a pseudonym but who creates fictional female characters who speak their minds loudly and clearly on issues of gender. Such is the case in Moderata Fonte's *Il merito delle donne* (ca. 1592; published in 1600).

95. In *Literary Circles and Gender*, Campbell notes that Speroni and Aragona's "exchange illustrates the friction generated during this period over women's, and in this case a courtesan's, abilities to participate in the life of the mind" (22).

96. Campbell, *Literary Circles and Gender*, 32.

97. Cox, "Seen but Not Heard: The Role of Women Speakers in Cinquecento Literary Dialogue," in *Women in Italian Renaissance Culture and Society*, ed. Letizia Panizza (Oxford: European Humanities Research Centre, University of Oxford, 2000), 387.

Fonte, whose real name was Modesta Pozzo, depicts seven female interlocutors who gather at the home of the widow Leonora, who has just inherited "a lovely house with a very lovely garden."[98] Over the course of two days, the women enjoy the beauty of the home, talking together in a "light and airy room" with a balcony that overlooks the Grand Canal and a window that overlooks the garden; they also talk in the garden itself (46). As cited above, Smarr notes that the gracious setting for this dialogue creates a frame that lends it dignity and provides an intimate space in which the women can freely and comfortably speak their minds. Sarah Ross points out that although Fonte follows aspects of Castiglione's *Courtier* and Pietro Bembo's *Gli Asolani*, she shifts the focus "from abstract ideals to social realities."[99] As we will see, Fonte's characters give clear voice to their own beliefs and opinions in ways that create important counterpoints to consider alongside men's topics of debate.

First, Fonte's characters debate the nature of men, turning the *querelle des femmes* on its head as they create a parallel set of attacks on and defenses of the nature of men like those typically formulated regarding the nature of women. Adriana, the elderly widow who is the "queen," or the director of their discussion, orders that Leonora, a young widow with no desire to remarry, speak "as much evil of [men] as she can" (57), assisted by Corinna, a *dimessa* (i.e., a respectable young woman living at home), and Cornelia, a young woman who has been married for a few years. Helena, a new bride still infatuated with her husband, is given leave to speak in defense of men, assisted by Virginia, a young daughter of Adriana on the marriage market, and Lucretia, a woman who has been married for some years. Taking a cue from the *Courtier*, Corinna argues that "if a man has some virtues, it is because he has picked them up from the woman he lives with, whether mother, nurse, sister, or wife"; moreover, she argues, "that men study at all, that they cultivate the virtues, that they groom themselves and become well-bred ... is all due to women" (58–59). In *The Courtier*,

---

98. Fonte, *The Worth of Women*, 46. All page references in parentheses in this section will be to this edition.

99. Ross, *The Birth of Feminism*, 278.

Cesare Gonzaga presents a similar argument in book 3.[100] As Cox has indicated, Fonte makes reference to the *Courtier* several times in this dialogue.[101] She notes that Fonte was "clearly well acquainted with the humanistic tradition of defenses of women, and readers of Castiglione or Agrippa will find much that is familiar here."[102]

Fonte's characters' conversations turn to discussions of astrology, the humors, friendship, and the natural world as they continue to argue about women's superiority to men. During the second day, a thread of conversation similar to one between Tullia and Varchi in Aragona's dialogue arises, regarding men's and women's worthiness to love and be loved,[103] as Fonte's characters discuss who is best capable of loving, women or men. When Virginia asks why men are not as influenced by the stars to love as women seem to be, Corinna responds that women's hearts, "because of the innate goodness of their nature, are perfectly disposed to receive the imprint of true love. But men are both by nature and by will little inclined to love, and so, where love is concerned, they can be influenced only to a limited extent by the stars" (122).

The discussion moves from astrological influences upon human love, and men's "stubborn souls," which impede their ability to be influenced by the stars (122), to friendship and the ways in which "friendship can arise between two people because of the compatibility of their complexions and humors, or because of a similarity of manners" (123). Cornelia asserts that this notion is true but that "it is very uncommon to find this kind of rare, inseparable friendship arising between two men or between a man and a woman, because men's innate malignity stands in the way, even where these points of compatibility exist" (123). As she deplores men's faults that hold them back from such joys, she implies that women have true gifts for friendship. She summarizes: "The upshot is that they are so ridiculously obsessed with their reputations, and with gaining the respect of those around

---

100. Cox makes this point in a footnote, *The Worth of Women*, 59. See Castiglione, *The Book of the Courtier*, 255–57.

101. For examples, see Cox's comments in footnotes, *The Worth of Women*, 88, 90, 94, and 217.

102. Ibid., 13.

103. Aragona, *Dialogue on the Infinity of Love*, 97.

them, that they behave very stiffly and formally in the pretense that courtesy demands it, whereas in fact their behavior is dictated by artifice. Indeed, instead of honoring their friends by behaving this way, they are dishonoring friendship and breaching its sacred laws, which banish all affectation" (124).

Affectation is a characteristic that Castiglione's interlocutors scorn in *The Courtier*. In book 1, Lodovico states that affectation should be "avoided or hidden," a rather contradictory notion, but he emphasizes its negativity by saying that it is "incompatible" with "gracefulness."[104] In book 2, Federico praises the vivacity in certain French courtiers he has met, and he notes that in them it is natural and "carries no suggestion of affectation."[105] Fonte, too, clearly scorns men's affectation, insinuating that it deprives men of cultivating true friendships. Later, her emphasis on the importance of true friendships will be underscored when she has Corinna remark, "True friendship, true affinity, is the cause of all good" (128).

After discussing friendship, the women go on to display their knowledge of the natural world, discussing what they know about various animals. The discussion turns to birds and hunting, and Cornelia observes, "If there's one thing [men] are good at, it's trapping, deceiving, ensnaring: that's their speciality" (140). In due course, fathers, husbands, sons, and lovers are implored to mend their evil ways. Fonte's dialogue concludes with a cautionary narrative poem for women in which she recounts a story about how Cupid was tricked by Juno, along with Pride and Avarice, who teamed up to lull him to sleep, steal his arrows, and blunt them permanently, with the end result being the extinction of "true faith" and "true love" in the world (253–57)—a very different conclusion about love from Castiglione's in *The Courtier* or Aragona's in her *Dialogo*.

In both Fonte's and Aragona's cases, questions about love and issues from the *querelle des femmes* are taken up in ways similar to Castiglione's; however, they are argued from a protofeminist perspective, one that dissects prevalent male-authored laws, philosophies, and power structures from the standpoint of the "other voice." Whether it is the voice of a learned courtesan or those of an array of gentlewomen

104. Castiglione, *The Book of the Courtier*, 87.

105. Ibid., 146.

at various stages in their lives, these female voices strongly state their own views on subjects about which men have long made pronouncements, bringing fresh perspectives to such debates.[106]

Tasso

A lover too respectful is undone.
I counsel him to work at something else,
since he is such a one. Who wants to learn
to love, forget respect: you dare, demand,
solicit, importune, and finally steal;
and if that's not enough, then ravish her.[107]
—Dafne in *Aminta* (2.2.84–89)

Torquato Tasso's pastoral tragicomedy *Aminta* (ca. 1573) is one of the most imitated plays in Renaissance literature. Charles Jernigan and Irene Marchegiani Jones simply call it "a masterpiece and perhaps the most famous pastoral play ever written."[108] Drawing upon classical idylls and eclogues, such as those of Theocritus and Virgil, as well as such Renaissance pastoral works as Angelo Poliziano's *Orfeo* (1471) and Iacopo Sannazaro's *Arcadia* (1504), Tasso crafted his play to suit the tastes of an aristocratic, courtly audience.[109] Most scholars agree that he wrote it for the court of Alfonso II d'Este at Ferrara after joining that court in 1572. Like the "petrarchino" and *Il libro del cortegiano*, *Aminta* was eventually published by the Aldine Press in Venice. However, it was first published in Cremona in 1580, and then in Venice in 1581. Many other editions soon followed.[110] Concerning

---

106. Although their works fall into the category of spiritual dialogues rather than social dialogues, it is also important to note that other Italian women of the sixteenth century also took part in the dialogue genre. In *Joining the Conversation*, Smarr provides close readings and commentary on such works by Olympia Morata (1526–1555) and Chiara Matraini (1515–1604).

107. Tasso, *Aminta, a Pastoral Play*, ed. and trans. Charles Jernigan and Irene Marchegiani Jones (New York: Italica Press, 2000).

108. Ibid., ix.

109. Ibid., x–xi.

110. For the print history of *Aminta*, as well as its production history, see Jernigan and Jones, *Aminta, a Pastoral Play*, xvii–xix, as well as Maria Galli Stampino, *Staging the Pastoral:*

its translation history, Lisa Sampson points out that it "first appeared in Croatian in 1580, then in French, English, Dutch, Spanish, Latin and German."[111] Thanks to the popularity of the play and the Renaissance notion that imitation of a great master is key to good art, Tasso's *Aminta* enjoyed unprecedented adulation and imitation across the Continent and in England.

With regard to the influence of *Aminta* in Italy, Jernigan and Jones posit that by 1700, it had "spawn[ed]" more than two hundred plays. They also note that it is the source for "numerous plays in France, Spain, and England."[112] Although they mention *Aminta's* influence upon such works as Antoine de Montchrestien's *Bergerie* (1601) and William Shakespeare's *A Midsummer Night's Dream*, *As You Like It*, and *Twelfth Night*, among others, they fail to point out the profound effect Tasso's play had on female playwrights. Barbara Torelli's *Partenia* (ca. 1587), Maddalena Campiglia's *Flori* (1588), and Isabella Andreini's *Mirtilla* (1588) are three female-authored Italian pastorals that respond in varying ways to *Aminta*. Lady Mary Wroth's *Love's Victory* (ca. 1620s) in England, and possibly Catherine des Roches' *Bergerie* (1583) in France, also echo Tasso's play. *Aminta's* pastoral tragicomic story—enacted by its winsomely shy but heroic eponymous *innamorato* and its chaste, beautiful *innamorata*, Silvia, accompanied by friends and a foe in the form of a satyr—attracted both male and female imitators from a variety of backgrounds. Women writers, however, especially sought to subvert some of the play's key elements.

In particular, women reconfigure the parts of Silvia and her female friends, revising the agency of female characters. Additionally, they adapt the love story in interesting ways. In *Aminta*, Silvia, a chaste follower of Diana, at first fiercely resists love in spite of the urging of her friend Dafne, who tries to convince her to love Aminta by means of a pep talk regarding the mating habits of sheep, cattle, and turtledoves, among other animals (1.1.122–50). When that does not work, she resorts to the *carpe diem* approach, emphasizing that

Tasso's Aminta and the Emergence of Modern Western Theater (Tempe: Arizona Center for Medieval and Renaissance Studies, 2005), 17–25.

111. Lisa Sampson, *Pastoral Drama in Early Modern Italy. The Making of a New Genre* (London: Modern Humanities Research Association / Maney, 2006), 2.

112. Tasso, *Aminta, a Pastoral Play*, xviii.

Silvia might refrain from love until she found herself "all alone" and "all wrinkled, gray" (1.1.177–78) and thus out of luck regarding men. Dafne, too, is the "friend" who urges Aminta to resort to raping Silvia if she persists in her resistance (see the epigraph for this section): she suggests that if his bold approaches do not work on Silvia, he should simply ignore her protests and "ravish her" (2.2.89). Soon, however, Silvia is forced into the role of a damsel in distress who must submit to rescue by Aminta, although she still refuses to love him until, finally, caught in the grip of guilt over his seeming suicide for love of her, she becomes an ardent beloved whose tears of regret revive him. We are told that "she screamed and beat her lovely breast, / and fell upon his body lying there / and brought them face to face and mouth to mouth" (5.1.103–5). After Aminta is revived by her tears "filled with rare virtues," the two embrace and "so conjoined lay" (5.1.114, 126), enjoying the prospect of their passionate, happy union.[113] Torelli, Campiglia, and Andreini alter these aspects of the play to illustrate their own, sometimes surprising, notions of what constitutes true love, as well as true friendship.

Female Playwrights and the Pastoral

As Lisa Sampson has argued, women writing pastoral plays build on various aspects of Tasso's *Aminta* and anticipate a crucial development of this genre, embodied in Giovan Battista Guarini's *Pastor fido*: its attention to moralizing issues and tone.[114] Reacting at least in part to the atmosphere prevailing in Counter-Reformation Italy, women writers appropriated pastoral dramatic performance as a genre in which they could express their thoughts regarding religious and moral issues being heatedly debated in their society. They found that pastoral drama's focus on private events and affections constituted a useful middle mode between lofty tragedy and lowly comedy in which they could

---

113. It is interesting that Tasso did not depict or describe a wedding between Aminta and Silvia, which is different from Giovanni Battista Guarini's *Pastor fido* (1590). Despite this, it was often staged for wedding festivities, such as those in Parma in 1628. See Stampino, *Staging the Pastoral*, 97–234.

114. Sampson, *Pastoral Drama*, 102.

present their opinions and experiences.[115] Cox points out that during the latter half of the sixteenth century, "a radical departure" from the predominance of lyric verse took place in women's writing, noting that narratives and dramatic forms authored by women began appearing in the wake of Fonte's works.[116] She notes that five years after the publication of Fonte's *Le feste* and *La passione de Christo* (both 1582), "we find the first female experiment with the modish form of pastoral drama, with Torelli's unpublished but much lauded *Partenia*, written in Parma, around 1587, followed swiftly by the first published pastorals by women, Campiglia's *Flori* and Andreini's *Mirtilla*" (both 1588).[117] Here we examine these three pastorals in light of their authors' appropriations and critiques of Tasso's play.

Torelli's *Partenia* bears a strong resemblance to *Aminta*, a circumstance possibly engendered by its early appearance in the line of female-authored pastoral tragicomedies that were written in this period. It was apparently the first imitation of Tasso's play by a female writer. Having remained in manuscript form in the Biblioteca Statale in Cremona until its current edition and translation by Barbara Burgess-Van Aken and Lisa Sampson,[118] Torelli's play borrows heavily from Tasso's in its characterization, action, and, of course, its conclusion. Torelli herself, as Cox points out, "came from a branch of the noble family in Parma that produced the tragedian Pomponio Torelli (1529–1608)," and she was "well connected within the courts and highly praised" for her work.[119] Torelli's elevated circumstances and elite audience may have also influenced her conservative appropriation of *Aminta*.

Somewhat as Tasso's Dafne seeks to convince Silvia that she should acquiesce to love, so Torelli's Talia plays a similar role for Partenia. In response to Partenia's exultation in her "virginitate pretiosa

---

115. Ibid., 104.

116. Cox, *Women's Writing*, 150.

117. Ibid.

118. Burgess-Van Aken also edited and translated *Partenia* for her dissertation project, "Barbara Torelli's *Partenia*: A Bilingual Critical Edition," Case Western Reserve University, May 2007. The edition with Sampson is slated to appear in The University of Toronto's Center for Renaissance and Reformation Studies in the Other Voice Series.

119. Cox, *Women's Writing*, 332, n79.

e cara," Talia comments on Partenia's youth and notes that she has not yet tasted the pleasures that the world has in store (1.3). True to formula, by act 2, scene 5, the satyr Cromi plots to rape her, and in act 3, scene 5, he is planning, in a manner quite similar to that of Tasso's satyr—and Andreini's—to tie her to a tree trunk. Partenia, however, manages to flee the satyr. Torelli's Tirsi is the Aminta-like figure who longs for Partenia and laments greatly when he fears that she will have to marry Leucippo, to whom her father has promised her (4.3). In an exciting soap-operatic turn of events, however, Ergasto, Partenia's father, learns that Leucippo is actually his son, which does ultimately clear the way for Tirsi (5.3). But, in traditional pastoral tragicomic tradition, the way is not smooth for the lovers. In act 5, scene 3, Partenia and Tirsi are feared dead, but by act 5, scene 4 they have reappeared, alive, well, and together at last. Coridone and Talia also end up together, and the play ends with rejoicing over Ergasto's discovery of his long-lost son and the other matches.

The pattern that Tasso establishes in *Aminta*—that of a chaste heroine who resists marital love in favor of worship of the goddess Diana, only to be conquered by the passion and virtue of a good shepherd who risks his life for love of her—is faithfully manifested in Torelli's play. The work does contain an embedded critique of the issue of paternal ownership of daughters and the parental right to arrange marriages in her work, as she concludes her plot with love matches chosen by the characters themselves; but, in general, the action of her play is closely aligned with that in Tasso's. Campiglia and Andreini, however, take significantly more liberties with Tasso's plot. Campiglia, the illegitimate daughter of Carlo Campiglia and Polissena Verlato, members of Vicentine noble families,[120] uses her pastoral as a vehicle to portray chaste love as the ideal; Andreini, a professional actress, uses hers as an opportunity to rewrite Tasso's roles, which she has played herself numerous times, and in the process critiquing numerous aspects of Tasso's take on ideal love.

Campiglia's *Flori*, like Torelli's *Partenia*, reflects the interests and circumstances of the playwright, in this case an upper-class Vicentine female intellectual who chooses to live unconventionally,

---

120. For more on Campiglia's life, see Cox and Sampson, "Volume Editors' Introduction," 2–12.

resides apart from her husband, and gives herself over to the life of the mind. In the introduction to their edition of *Flori*, Virginia Cox and Lisa Sampson describe the thriving cultural scene of Vicenza in the late *cinquecento*, which stemmed in part from the Accademia O-limpica and its connections with Andrea Palladio's Teatro Olimpico.[121] Writing in this elite cultural milieu for a female patron (the dowager Isabella Pallavicino Lupi) and perhaps inspired by the *Partenia* of her contemporary Barbara Torelli, Tasso's *Aminta*, and Battista Guarini's *Il pastor fido*, Campiglia constructs a pastoral fantasy in which female friendship and chaste Neoplatonic love are given precedence over physical love and traditional marriage.

The plot of Campiglia's play focuses on the nymph Flori's great love for and near-madness over the death of her companion Ama-ranta. These two nymphs, along with a third, Licori, are said to have "pledged [their] days to the icy goddess" (Diana) in their girlhoods;[122] thus, the remaining two still seek to avoid the bonds of marriage. Licori, however, falls for Androgeo, a shepherd hopelessly in love with Flori, while Androgeo's brother, Serrano, who hears Licori complain-ing of love's burning sensation in her heart, hopes that she's thinking of him.[123] Naturally, in true pastoral tragicomic form, she is not. In the meantime, Flori alternately cries out to Amaranta and to death, beg-ging for release from her torment. Campiglia's play then follows the fortunes of these would-be lovers in ways that both recall and reject Tasso's prototype.

Flori, lost in her woe, is accosted in act 1, scene 6 by a satyr and a wild man who plan to rape her; but, like Aminta, Androgeo comes swiftly to her rescue. Although Flori is at first grateful for his help, when he pours out his heart to her, she cries that she would pre-fer to be devoured by "those shameless satyrs" or "a thousand fierce beasts"[124] than to love him. Unlike Tasso's Silvia, Flori never recants her rejection of her rescuer's romantic advances. Another rescue sce-nario occurs in act 2, scene 2, in which Serrano fares better than An-drogeo, after taking his turn in the Aminta-like role and saving the

121. Cox and Sampson, "Volume Editors' Introduction," 6.

122. Campiglia, *Flori*, 75.

123. Ibid., 89–91.

124. Ibid., 111.

nymph Urania from a marauding tigress. Urania finds that "Serrano slew [her] heart at the same time that he restored [her] body to life."[125] Yet by act 2, scene 3, Serrano is confessing in a soliloquy his plans to compete with his adoptive brother Androgeo for Flori's love. Serrano's fickleness in love serves as a foil to Androgeo's faithfulness in a manner somewhat similar to Tirsi's rejection of lasting love in the *Aminta*, as opposed to Aminta's slavish devotion. In the end, however, neither man will win Flori.

In "Epithalamium Interruptum: Maddalena Campiglia's New Arcadia," Lori Ultsch suggests that Campiglia should be considered alongside Fonte as a key protofeminist voice advocating secular celibacy for women, noting that this notion "emerges as a dominant motif in Campiglia's repeated engagement with situations that articulate a partial or complete rupture with normative marriage practices and the imposed gender roles within that institution."[126] Ultsch reminds us that Campiglia sent Tasso a copy of her play, so it is clear that she had his *Aminta* in mind as she composed her own work. Ultsch suggests, however, that did she did so "to show herself conversant with the conventions of the genre—in order to claim the authority to diverge from them."[127] A key figure in this play, as well as in her eclogue *Calisa* (1589), is one that Ultsch calls the "recalcitrant nymph."[128] This figure, portrayed by Flori in the play, enacts stubborn, and ultimately triumphant, resistance to the marriage trope that figures prominently at the end of Tasso's play and sets the traditional parameters for a happy ending for the pastoral tragicomedy.

In act 3, scene 5, Flori is finally released from her great torment by the sacrifice that the priest Damone makes on her behalf. Androgeo, too, is cured of his lovesickness for Flori, and the way is cleared for destiny to prevail. The priest has prophesied that Flori will be "smitten by love for a stranger shepherd,"[129] and she promptly falls for Alessi, a shepherd passing through their area, who witnessed the

---

125. Ibid., 115–17.

126. Lori J. Ultsch, "Epithalamium Interruptum: Maddalena Campiglia's New Arcadia," *MLN* 120, no. 1 (2005): 71.

127. Ibid., 72.

128. Ibid., 76

129. Campiglia, *Flori*, 175.

sacrifice. Even so, she continues to embody the "recalcitrant nymph" figure. Having no desire for a traditional marriage, Flori stipulates in act 5 that she wants to love Alessi chastely, without tying the "knot of Hymen" with him, because she is still bound to Delia (Diana).[130] Via the ensuing discussion with the incredulous Licori, who cannot believe a woman could love as Flori claims to without wishing to consummate the relationship, Campiglia develops her theme of Platonic love as she has Flori explain that, rather than be satisfied with Alessi's "external beauty," she wishes to "pursue a worthier object: to penetrate his inner substance with [her] mind, and thence, feathering the wings of [her] fine yearning, to fly on upwards to the highest spheres, where [she] may at last satisfy [her] desires in full."[131] She just wants to use his beauty, she explains, as a guide to lead her to heaven. Fortunately, Alessi's love for Flori is so noble and pure that all he claims to want is "the sweet sunlight of her eyes and the soft harmonies of her sage words."[132] Campiglia's stubborn nymph, evading Tasso's model by taking a cue from Platonic and Neoplatonic predecessors, transgresses the societal norm with her own depiction of an unusual marriage.

After Licori helps this "new and wondrous pair of lovers" to express their "new and wondrous love,"[133] Flori returns the favor, helping Licori and Androgeo make a traditional match, thus providing Campiglia's audience a Tassian model, even though she keeps the main focus on her couple who are intent on creating their alternative lifestyle. In act 5, scene 5, Fronimo tells us that Flori and Alessi "have pledged to love one another eternally, while following together in the footsteps of Diana; they burn in chaste flames and hope in this way to show a shining example to the world, as paragons of continence and fidelity."[134] Campiglia thus rejects the passionate embrace of Silvia and Aminta, choosing instead to depict purely Neoplatonic lovers at her play's end.

Ultsch observes that Campiglia's Flori moves through two key processes during the course of the play. First, she is healed of

130. Ibid., 247.

131. Ibid., 251.

132. Ibid., 261.

133. Ibid., 283.

134. Ibid., 299.

her "strangeness or contrariness," that is, her longing for Amaranta, and brought to "reason or order" by Damone's sacrifice; next she is brought "further into line with social norms and praxes" through her marriage to Alessi.[135] The marriage, however, is to be a spiritual union rather than a physical one, and the resulting relationship will allow Flori to live in "a third state," that of secular celibacy.[136] Ultsch argues that Flori, then, greatly resembles Fonte's character Corinna, a "young *dimessa*, whose freedom allows her the opportunity to pursue 'studi di lettere umane e divine.'"[137] Campiglia, with her iconoclastic "recalcitrant nymph," thus rejects key facets of *Aminta*, even as she deliberately engages it.

In *La Mirtilla*, Andreini creates not just one but three *innamorate* roles, those of Filli, Mirtilla, and Ardelia. Filli, the role that Andreini is thought to have written for herself, is clearly the lead role, but Mirtilla's and Ardelia's parts are also given star turns in which actresses might showcase their acting and musical abilities. Unlike Tasso's play—written to be performed, at least early on, by a mixed cast of nobles and professionals—Andreini's play is clearly written with performances by professional actors in mind, and to that end she gives the traditional pastoral tragicomedy a few twists that audiences no doubt enjoyed. Perhaps the key scene in which Andreini's Filli diverges from Tasso's Silvia by invoking her agency is the so-called "satyr scene" in act 3, in which Filli tricks the satyr into letting her tie him up. Through this ploy, she handily rescues herself from a near-rape and simultaneously shames the satyr to such an extent that he swears off women altogether, choosing instead to worship Bacchus and Ceres.[138] Concerning female friendship, Filli and Mirtilla, who are best friends, find themselves at odds because both are in love with Uranio. However, after participating in a singing contest to see which should win him and being declared equals in beauty and talent, they wisely decide to value their friendship over their infatuation with Uranio, who, in any case, is in love with Ardelia (3.5). Ardelia's character mirrors that of Silvia in a number of ways, with one critical difference. Like Silvia,

135. Ultsch, "Epithilamium Interruptum," 81.

136. Ibid., 85.

137. Ibid.

138. A precedent for this scene may be seen in Agostino Beccari's play *Il sacrificio* (1554).

she is a cold, chaste follower of Diana who at first wants nothing to do with men. Also like Silvia, she experiences the overwhelming heat of passion that makes her recant her vow. In this case, however, she recants her vow of allegiance to Diana when she falls passionately in love with herself, after catching a glimpse of her own reflection in a spring (4.4). Uranio, who longs helplessly for her anyway, ultimately wins her love through his use of the *carpe diem* approach, to which the narcissistic Ardelia, unlike Silvia, is very susceptible (5.5).

At the end of *La Mirtilla*, three pairs of lovers are united: Filli and Igilio, Mirtilla and Tirsi, and Ardelia and Uranio. Although these pairings are celebrated with pastoral joie de vivre, Andreini's approach to the happy endings of her characters' travails in love differs from Tasso's in that she stresses that Filli and Mirtilla must learn to love the "right" men by following the true guidance of Amore instead of being guided by the false "fury" who, according to Amore, roams the earth pretending to be him and leading lovers astray by their passions.[139] Filli and Mirtilla are ultimately guided more by reason than passion as they rescue their lovers from would-be suicides and chide them for their foolishness, even as they promise Igilio and Tirsi their love. Ardelia and Uranio's path to love, on the other hand, seems to parody the highs and lows of Silvia and Aminta's in a manner meant to reveal the potential shallowness of the typically silent, chaste Petrarchan beloved. Ardelia's passion for herself comically overshadows Silvia's desire for chastity, and Uranio's mocking of Ardelia's changeability in love once he has obtained her vow is barely eclipsed by his joy in his successful conquest. He says archly, even as he triumphs in love, "You certainly show just now that you are a woman, / since you have persuaded yourself all of a sudden / to make me wholly yours! Surely / the beautiful feminine sex ... / ... possesses counsel / which is only the wiser for having been little pondered."[140] Ultimately, Andreini creates a pastoral in which she pays homage to Tasso's *Aminta* but also critiques aspects of it, such as Silvia's lack of agency, the superficiality of her friendship with Dafne, and Tasso's depiction of love guided solely by passion.

139. Isabella Andreini, *La Mirtilla*, 6–7.

140. Ibid., 92.

The pastorals of Torelli, Campiglia, and Andreini clearly participate in the vastly popular tradition of imitating Tasso's *Aminta*, yet each woman puts her own stamp on her storylines. Torelli introduces the issue of paternal ownership and disposal of daughters in marriage in her play, creatively envisioning a conclusion to her story that eschews the patriarchal tradition and allows characters who choose each other to form matches. Campiglia turns Platonic tradition upside down by having a female character value her love for a dead female friend over that of heterosexual love. Because her true love, Amaranta, is dead, Flori settles for second best in the form of a Platonic relationship with Alessi. Andreini's professional comic touch may be seen in the development of her female characters as challenging and engaging roles for professional women actors; her protofeminist views emerge as Filli saves herself from the satyr and both Filli and Mirtilla save their male beloveds from untimely deaths. Such playwrights' responses to Tasso's *Aminta* illustrate the profound effects that the play must have had on the women who saw it or read it. Moreover, their plays show us how they, like many of their male contemporaries, joined in the conversation about the popular pastoral genre, the nature of love, and dramatic entertainment that Tasso's play sparked during this period.

As these examples of women's works in dialogue with those by Petrarch, Castiglione, and Tasso show, fascinating frictions existed in the literary production of Renaissance Italy. While the influence of these canonical writers clearly held sway over literary trends during the early modern period, women's responses to them provide important counterpoints to consider when surveying the literature of the era. It is also important to remember as we introduce the works of such sixteenth-century Italian women writers to our students and into our scholarship that they were also writing in response to numerous other voices around them in literary society. In the chapters that follow, we introduce some of those voices.

2.
Christian Feminine Virtue in Silvio Antoniano's
Three Books on the Christian Education of Children

JULIE D. CAMPBELL

Cardinal Silvio Antoniano (1540–1603), a figure well-known in literary, educational, and ecclesiastical circles, moved with ease among high-ranking humanist poets and scholars, as well as cardinals and popes.[1] Although he was lauded for his linguistic abilities, particularly his facility with Latin, Antoniano wrote the work for which he is perhaps most famous—*Tre libri dell'educatione Christiana de i figliuoli* (1584), or *Three Books on the Christian Education*[2] *of Children*—in Italian, a sign of his allegiance to the Counter-Reformation movement. Antoniano was requested to write this treatise by the Archbishop of Milan, Carlo Borromeo (1538–1584), for whom he was a secretary, and he wrote *Dell'educatione* with the goal of creating a text that would be accessible to a relatively broad readership. In keeping with Counter-Reformationist ideals, his treatise is meant to provide readers with a conduct book to instill Catholic Christian virtues in their children. In the process, he has much to say about the role and conduct of women.

In the two *capitoli* from *Dell'educatione* included here— "Dell'adornarsi delle donne in particulare," or "Of the Adornment of Women in Particular," and "Dell'offitio, e cura particulare della madre

---

1. In *Educational Theories and Principles of Cardinal Silvio Antoniano* (Washington, DC: Catholic University of America Press, 1940), 5–15, Sister Mary Lauretana Zanfagna provides an overview of Antoniano's life, emphasizing his precocious linguistic and literary skills, which garnered him attention among some of the most learned scholars and ecclesiastics of his time. Moreover, in *Il popolo fanciullo: Silvio Antoniano e il sistema disciplinare della controriforma* (Milan: Franco Angeli, 1987), 14–15, Vittorio Frajese provides a similar account, emphasizing his association with the sophisticated court of Ercole II d'Este at Ferrara, where he would have encountered such members of literary society as Vincenzo Maggi, Paolo Manuzio, and Benedetto Varchi, among numerous others. Virginia Cox reminds us that Antoniano had been "in his youth an elegant poet who had corresponded with Laura Battiferra." *Women's Writing*, 137.

2. *Educatione* also refers to child rearing or upbringing in general.

di famiglia circa gli adornamenti delle figliuole," or "Of the Duty and Particular Care of the Mother of the Family concerning the Adornments of Daughters"—Antoniano indirectly illustrates the anxieties produced in ecclesiastical circles by perceptions of courtesans' influence on Renaissance family values. He also reveals the church's concerns about how best to control all women's sexuality as he argues that women who favor any but the most modest appearance are a menace to society. This consternation over women's appearance and its relation to their sexuality highlights two important issues for Counter-Reformers. First, aside from the church's general disapproval for sexual promiscuity and the ways in which courtesans encouraged it, Antoniano's concern is suggestive of Counter-Reformers' desire to rid ecclesiastical circles of concubinage, or the practice of priests, cardinals, and even popes taking consorts, some of whom were drawn from the courtesan class. Second, his consternation about women echoes political concern over the governance of families, especially powerful noble families. Stanley Chojnacki reminds us that in early *cinquecento* Venice, the "identities of wives and mothers, officially noted at every stage of a noble's political career, were more than ever the measure of a family's conformity to the standards of patrician culture."[3] The Counter-Reformers, rather like the Venetian Republic before them, sought to promote social order via familial order, and they attempted to do so by instilling a renewed sense of the need for spiritual order in families. Promoting chastity in women was key to their agenda.

Participating in the Counter-Reform tradition of looking *ad fontes*, to the Bible and the early church fathers for spiritual instruction,[4] Antoniano draws upon the words of the apostles Peter and Paul, as well as those of Saint John Chrysostom, to buttress his arguments about women and the potential for evil inherent in their appearance. From the former, he refers to 1 Peter 3:3 and 1 Timothy 2:9 regarding Peter and Paul's charges to women to eschew adornment and tend to the inner beauty of their souls, as well as to submit themselves wholly in obedience to men. Regarding the latter, he draws

---

3. See *Women and Men in Renaissance Venice*, 65.

4. See Dermot Fenlon's discussion in "The Movement 'ad fontes' and the Outbreak of Reformation," in *Heresy and Obedience in Tridentine Italy: Cardinal Pole and the Counter Reformation* (Cambridge: Cambridge University Press, 1972), 1–2.

arguments and imagery from Chrysostom's "Address on Vainglory and the Right Way for Parents to Bring Up Their Children," especially Chrysostom's personification of Vainglory as a harlot who wears "many golden ornaments," "soft raiment," and "many perfumes," whose "exceeding beauty" seems to be that of a young girl of just the right age to "gain possession" of a young man's soul and drive "his mind to a frenzy."[5] The dangerous power that Chrysostom and Antoniano ascribe to embellished female beauty is such that men who experience it are helpless to control their own wills.

Antoniano especially subscribes to this notion in "Dell' adornarsi," in which the entire burden of men's involvement with courtesans is laid at the feet of the women of the household, and men's agency regarding their own choices in female companionship is virtually nonexistent. In "Dell'adornarsi," Antoniano denounces women who "are not content with the looks God has given them" and who make use of cosmetic or sartorial enhancements. He argues that such embellishments show "that beauty is something useless, dangerous, and full of vexation" and seldom "accompanied by the greatest honesty." Moreover, it makes husbands jealous as well as driving them straight into the arms of prostitutes. Antoniano stresses that if a woman "teaches" her husband to appreciate modest dress and chaste behavior, "he will not turn easily to prostitutes," but if she "teaches" him "to let himself be tricked by a sweet laugh" or to be attracted to that which is "soft and lascivious," she will "supply him with arms against [herself]." He will then be helplessly drawn to "the charms and the face of a prostitute." Men, in this instance of Antoniano's rhetoric, are not expected to exercise self-control or good judgment regarding their own sexuality. Women must therefore teach them what and whom to love.

Mothers, moreover, are singularly responsible for their daughters' virtue. In "Dell'offitio," Antoniano stresses that mothers should teach their daughters "to despise bleaches for women's hair" and that "the ugliest thing is an honest gentlewoman adorned like a prostitute." Continuing his excoriation of courtesans, Antoniano warns that "the good mother" should not permit her daughter to be acquainted with

---

5. John Chrysostom, "An Address on Vainglory and the Right Way for Parents to Bring Up Their Children," trans. M. L. W. Laistner, in *Christianity and Pagan Culture in the Later Roman Empire* (Ithaca, NY: Cornell University Press, 1951), 86.

"wicked women, [who are] masters of these and worse devices." He argues that girls who "too much damn themselves through the study of adornment," especially using hair coloring potions and makeup, will "distemper" their heads and ruin their skin. Moreover, he claims that they will contract various illnesses and age prematurely. His description of decay and disease wrought by use of cosmetics is reminiscent of that said to be brought about by courtesans' lifestyles in general, as illustrated by Maffio Venier's scurrilous "tailed sonnet" to Veronica Franco in chapter 9 of this volume. Summarizing his embellished gentlewoman/prostitute analogy, Antoniano posits that a beautiful, charmingly dressed woman in a public place is but "bait for the devil, a rugged rock of ruin, and a stone of scandal for thousands of unfortunate men." Antoniano concludes that no Christian woman should ever wish to appear beautiful, since beauty carries with it "so great an offense to God."

The Venetian writer Moderata Fonte responds to such dire rhetoric regarding women's adornment in her dialogue *The Worth of Women* (written around 1592; published 1600). During the conversation of the Second Day, her character Cornelia asserts the superior fashion sense of Venetian women, noting that women "from outside Venice … often look mannish rather than feminine."[6] Her companion Helena concurs, noting that "more than anything … the Venetian fashion for women to wear their hair blond seems to confer an air of femininity and refinement, even nobility."[7] Cornelia notes that men would mock them if they heard women conversing thus, but Corinna scoffs, "Oh, let them say what they want! … It's not such an insult, anyway, for the refinement and neatness of our appearance is a sign of the nobility of our soul," and she reminds her friends of Lucius Sulla's warning to the Roman senators regarding "that ill-girt youth," Julius Caesar.[8] Near the end of their critique of women's fashion, Corinna again rebuts such rhetoric as Antoniano's, this time attacking men's conflation of a woman's refined appearance with a suspect reputation. "It's not unfitting for us women to express our natural inner refinement outwardly, in feminine dress and adornments," she says, noting:

6. Fonte, *The Worth of Women*, 234.

7. Ibid.

8. Ibid.

Of course, men say that all this finery we wear betrays a corrupt heart underneath, and often endangers our virtue. But they're quite wrong.... Just think how frequent it is to see women of low estate importuned by men and coming to grief, in spite of the fact that they dress plainly and, one might say, without any form of adornment. It is far rarer to see gentlewomen suffering the same fate, in spite of all their finery, for they aren't dressing up for any vicious reason, but simply, as I've said, out of a spirit of gaiety and to follow the custom of the city.[9]

From their complaints about men's criticism of women's engagement with fashion and adornment, the conversation turns to another, even more insidious belief held by men: that women should remain illiterate "on the pretext that learning is the downfall of many women."[10] The women quickly reject this notion as well. On matters both sartorial and educational, Fonte's interlocutors counter the notions set forth by such thinkers as Antoniano, and their forthright denials of many of his assertions, buttressed by examples from "real life" observations, serve to highlight the hysterical edge to his admonishments.

Another polemicist who defends women's use of cosmetics and adornments is Lucrezia Marinella, the daughter of a physician who wrote two medical books on women's health, one of which was titled *Gli ornamenti delle donne*, or *Women's Ornaments* (Venice 1562). In *The Nobility and Excellence of Women*, Marinella examines Greek and Roman sources to buttress her assertion that "women are honored everywhere with the use of ornaments that greatly surpass men's. ... It is a marvellous sight in our city to see the wife of shoemaker or butcher or even a porter all dressed up with gold chains round her neck, with pearls and valuable rings on her fingers."[11]

9. Ibid., 236.

10. Ibid.

11. Lucrezia Marinella, *The Nobility and Excellence of Women and the Defects and Vices of Men*, ed. and trans. Anne Dunhill, The Other Voice in Early Modern Europe (Chicago: University of Chicago Press, 1999), 131.

Regarding artificial beauty enhancement, in *The Defects and Vices of Men*, she writes:

> Why should it be a sin if a woman born with considerable beauty washes her delicate face with lemon juice and the water of beanflowers and privets in order to remove her freckles and keep her skin soft and clean? ... And if writers and poets, both ancient and modern, say that her golden hair enhances her beauty, why should she not color it blonde and make ringlets and curls in it so as to embellish it still further?
>
> ... The Church Fathers do not entirely condemn women for adorning and polishing themselves; they merely condemn this when it becomes excessive and bad in other respects.[12]

She then quotes Augustine in a letter to Possidus regarding the fitness of women "to adorn themselves and for learned fathers to permit them to conserve their beauty, or to make themselves more beautiful than they are as long as they do not fall into error."[13] Of course, Antoniano's text touches on more than issues of ornamentation; he is also concerned with men's susceptibility to women's charms.

When we consider Antoniano's rhetoric as a context for women's voices in society, the paradox is immediately obvious. Women, according to Peter, Paul, and Chrysostom as quoted by Antoniano, are to have no voice in public and very little in private. Their deeds are to speak for them, not their words. Moreover, women's appearances should be such that men, with their innate lack of self-control, find them either negligible or beyond suspicion. His caution that a woman not teach her husband to be "tricked by a sweet laugh, nor to be ensnared by a soft and lascivious gait" and his concern that a woman not make herself "a stone of scandal for thousands of unfortunate men"[14] illustrate a paradoxical notion: men are incapable of controlling themselves, so women must educate their daughters in the ways of modesty

12. Ibid., 167.

13. Ibid., 167–68.

14. See Antoniano, translated below.

and piety to help men avoid sin and damnation, because female nature is considered changeable, whereas male nature is apparently not. Women, then, must carry the responsibility for keeping both sexes out of trouble, and they are to do it more by deeds than by words.

The correlation between voice, appearance, and a woman's promiscuity provides grounds for what Ann Rosalind Jones terms the "injunction to silence and invisibility" for women.[15] This "injunction" serves as the premise of much misogynistic rhetoric designed to keep women sequestered, verbally and physically. While polemicists such as Fonte and Marinella engage directly with this misogynistic rhetoric, others choose more subtle approaches to combat the injunction to silence and invisibility.

For an aspiring poet or *virtuosa*—an actress or a musician—the injunction to silence and the suppression of female beauty would be major career obstacles. Negotiating a place in literary and artistic society during a period informed by such Counter-Reformation views required that women seek support and approval for their endeavors in a variety of ways. Two of the most common strategies for accomplishing this were to incorporate Counter-Reformation values into the content of their writing and to seek the support of a famous male scholar or writer. The former served as a testament to the writer's "correct" moral perspectives, and the latter provided a male defender of her work whose stamp of approval legitimated her efforts. Even though, according to Counter-Reformation thought, she was not supposed to make use of her voice, doing so in a manner that men found pleasing and acceptable—or, at the very least, inoffensive—provided her a loophole through which she could continue to seek an audience.

Two writers whose career choices exemplify these approaches are Giulia Bigolina and Isabella Andreini. In Bigolina's romance *Urania: The Story of a Young Woman's Love*, the eponymous character is described as being so virtuous that "she would have chosen to die a thousand times rather than see her lovely soul give way to a single vice." Moreover, Bigolina makes clear that Urania is not nearly so beautiful as her rival for her lover Fabio's affections, but emphasizes

15. Ann Rosalind Jones, "Surprising Fame," in *Feminism and Renaissance Studies*, ed. Lorna Hutson (Oxford: Oxford University Press, 1999), 320–21.

that Urania's greater *virtue* makes her the finer beloved for Fabio.[16] In addition to ensuring that the content of her composition reflected appropriate views regarding women and virtue, Bigolina also sought support for her work through her correspondence with Pietro Aretino, as is illustrated in part 2 of this volume. Aretino would, from a Counter-Reformation perspective, seem an odd choice for Bigolina, given his own moral perspectives; however, his status, fame, and, most importantly, his use of his *Lettere* to comment on the artistic endeavors of those whom he knew suggest that she was being resourceful. Through Aretino's advertisement of her work, Bigolina hoped to gain a broader audience.

Andreini, like Bigolina, employs both of these techniques. Her play *La Mirtilla* has been called "long on Counter-Reformation moral attitudes"[17] for its resolutely moral stance on love and the sanctity of marriage, and her correspondence with Erycius Puteanus, a Belgian academician and humanist scholar living in Milan,[18] serves as an example of how she "advertised" her gifts to someone who could help her expand her circle of patrons and admirers. In *La Mirtilla*, Andreini has Coridone, a shepherd, explain that women and men were made for marriage, noting that "so sweet and dear / is this heaven-given companionship, / and so sweet is marital passion, / that is sustains them together."[19] At the end of her play, "fierce desires" are denounced in favor of "love's highest delights," which are to be found only in marriage.[20] Andreini's own moral virtues, which seem to genuinely reflect those illustrated in *Mirtilla*, are praised at length by Puteanus. In a letter dated November 9, 1601, he emphasizes that Andreini's virtues are so great that her own sex may be overlooked, and she may be considered a man. In another, dated December 14, 1601, he praises her *Mirtilla* and her *Rime*, begging her to bring forth more of her writing

---

16. Bigolina, *Urania: The Story of a Young Woman's Love*, 85–89. See also Bigolina, *Urania: A Romance*, 85–87.

17. Louise George Clubb, *Italian Drama in Shakespeare's Time* (New Haven, CT: Yale University Press, 1989), 271.

18. For a transcription and translation of their correspondence, see Anne MacNeil's *Music and Women of the Commedia dell'Arte* (Oxford: Oxford University Press, 2003), 305–23.

19. Andreini, *La Mirtilla*, 72.

20. Ibid., 99, 102.

so that "fertile with children as you are, you may also become fertile with books." In a poem included in this letter, he pronounces her "the mother of chaste love."[21] A subsequent letter from Andreini to Puteanus suggests that his approval of her work has indeed paid off. On March 6, 1602, she writes to thank him for communicating her letters to his friends in his "regions" and notes that because of his connections she is welcomed in many places.[22]

Antoniano's rhetoric regarding Christian feminine virtue reflects the Counter-Reformation values with which Italian women writers contended, no matter where their personal values fell on the continuum of moral ideology governing women's behavior. The emphasis on silence and invisibility created cultural taboos that women writers had to negotiate with resourcefulness and rhetorical skill. While such writers as Fonte and Marinella took on the establishment in their polemics, others, such as Bigolina and Andreini, found ways to seek the approval of those who espoused such values and to garner renown for their work. In spite of Counter-Reformationists' best efforts, women writers seldom wholly embraced the movement's tenets; even the most pious ones may be considered to have ultimately broken the rules by asserting their voices in writing.

21. See Puteanus's letters and poem in MacNeil, *Music and Women of the Commedia dell'Arte*, 306 and 311–12.

22. See Andreini's letter, ibid., 318.

Three Books on the Christian Education of Children

SILVIO ANTONIANO

From Book 2: "Of the Adornment of Women in Particular" (Cap. XCIIII)

It is my intention (since elsewhere I warned our head of the house-hold[23] of it) that the reminders given for sons must also be propor-tionately understood by daughters, as much as is suited to the state and condition of their sex, because the things said above are no less useful to their education than to that of the sons. But because the present discussion is on the vain and superfluous ornaments (com-monly abused by women) it has therefore occurred to me to touch on something in particular on this occasion. Now, I do not want to begin to dispute whether the ornamenting and embellishing of themselves that women commonly do is a grave or light sin and how much it is or is not worthy of being excused; that judgment I leave to the scales and the definition of sacred Theologians and wise and learned confes-sors. I will only say that the ancient fathers, in whom shone conjointly the highest doctrine with saintliness of life, reproved women of this abuse all in the same manner. Among them Saint John Chrysostom, bishop of so great and principal a city as Constantinople and a man greatly practiced in the government of souls, inveighs in many places in his divine sermons against this license of ornaments and embel-lishments, which in our times and especially for a few years [now] in many cities in Italy has grown so much that it requires not only good private education, but [also] public redress. That Saint reproaches women who paint their faces with various colors and are not happy with the looks God has given them—as if they were better artificers, and knew how to and could correct the work of God! He shows that beauty is something useless, dangerous, and full of vexation, because where it is found easily, if it is not often accompanied by the greatest honesty, it occasions people to believe the worst and to speak ill of it. And the husband himself lives in jealousy, full of bitterness, know-

---

23. In the Italian this phrase reads "father of the family." I owe many thanks to Maria Galli Stampino for her careful reading of and help with my translations throughout this volume.

ing there are many tempters of [his wife's] chastity, especially when a woman with too much adornment gives her husband just grounds for suspicion. For this reason, that blessed Saint does not accept the excuse that many women put forth, saying that they adorn themselves for the pleasure of their own husbands. We need not talk about those women who adorn themselves to please strangers, since these women clearly are the devil's nets, and even if they don't ensnare anyone, their corrupt intentions condemn them in the sight of God! But speaking of the former, the Saint laughs at such a badly composed argument, because, he says, when such women return home they take off their ornaments, jewelry, perfumes, and other vanities. Considering this same judgment from another point of view, we may say that when women go to parties, to performances, and to those places where a large crowd gathers, and where very often their own husbands are not [present], then they adorn themselves more artificially and with great care. But beyond the fact that this excuse is insufficient and for the most part false, Chrysostom shows that the poor little women greatly fool themselves and, unaware, procure their own loss, precisely teaching their husband not to love them, while in the meantime trying with their adorning and coloring to be loved more! So that you better understand the truth of this paradox, I want to recite in our language[24] the formal words of the Saint, [who] says speaking thusly to women:

> I beg you, let us not teach husbands to consider or pay attention only to the face, because when your husband begins to take pleasure in your care for adorning yourself, very soon he will be taken in by the charms and the face of a prostitute, as one who is accustomed to loving the face. But if on the contrary you teach him to love in his wife good manners and a comeliness full of modesty and gravity, he will not turn easily to prostitutes, because in them these qualities are not found, but completely the contrary. Do not teach your husband to let himself be tricked by a sweet laugh, nor be ensnared by a soft and lascivious gait, other-

24. He writes Chrysostom's words in Italian as opposed to the original Latin in which they were written.

wise you will supply him with arms against yourself!
[Instead] instruct him to delight in chastity and what
goes with it.

Now, as I started to say above, the books of ancient saintly Doctors
[of the Church] are full of complaints and rebukes regarding the immoderate ornaments of women, but it is not necessary to repeat them
here; the doctrine of the two glorious Apostles and teachers of the
world must suffice, Peter and Paul, the first of whom exhorts women
to try to please their husbands, not with braids and charming hairstyles, with gold and gems, and with beautifully ornate dresses, but
with holy conversation.[25] And the other, writing to Timothy, says thus
appropriately: let women be dressed in modest attire, adorning themselves with modesty and sobriety, not with curls, gold and pearls, or
precious dresses, but as becomes women who promote piety and religion through their good deeds.[26]

"Of the Duty and Particular Care of the Mother of the Family Concerning the Adornments of Daughters" (Cap. XCV)

Therefore, in conclusion, we say that a good mother of the family, to
whom this care especially pertains, must bring up daughters to be neat
and clean, yes, but not vain and fickle, and thus by her own example
teach them to despise bleaches for women's hair, and fake white skin
or blushing lies, not only while they are in their paternal home, where
no appearance of embellishment may excuse them, but also when they
are married, teaching them that the ugliest thing is an honest gentlewoman adorned like a prostitute, while the true beauties and ornaments of a wise and worthy wife are chastity, modesty, demureness,
silence, and restraint, love of her husband and her children, knowing
how to manage the home and how to spend prudently, and other similar virtues pleasing to God and men. Therefore, a good mother should
take care that her daughter not see in her shades of perdition, nor
permit some of the worst women [who are] experts in these and worse
devices to stop by the house, but she should watch very carefully over

25. See 1 Peter 3:3.

26. See 1 Timothy 2:9.

the chastity of her daughter, conserving principally in her the beauty of her soul so that she can please her celestial groom, not to mention that [in this way] she will preserve her physical beauty which shines out of her virginal soul. It goes without saying that those who devote themselves too much to the study of adornment lose their heads, often ruin their complexion, and contract various infirmities, growing old faster. Even if the only trouble were that a woman very charmingly adorned in a public place is bait of the devil, a rugged rock of ruin, and a stone of scandal for thousands of unfortunate men, certainly there should never be a Christian woman [who] desires to appear beautiful, [since beauty carries with it] so great an offense to God and damnation of their souls, redeemed with the priceless blood of Jesus Christ.

3.
Stefano Guazzo's Civil conversatione *and the* querelle des femmes

JULIE D. CAMPBELL

La civil conversatione (1574), by Stefano Guazzo, is considered one of the most influential courtesy books of the sixteenth century. It was translated into French, English, and Latin during that period, but it has not been newly translated into English since the work of George Pettie and Bartholomew Young (1581, 1586).[1] It is written as a dialogue between the cavalier Guglielmo Guazzo, Stefano's brother, who is suffering from melancholia, and Annibale Magnocavalli, the learned physician who comes to visit him, hoping to effect a cure via learned, civilized conversation.[2] During the course of his interlocutors' dialogue, Guazzo presents views on the necessary behaviors, beliefs, and abilities of the socially astute, upwardly mobile gentleman. Most critics suggest that Guazzo's *Civil conversation* is both a mark of how influential Castiglione's *Courtier* was earlier in the century as well as a shrewdly modernized discourse meant for a very different audience from Castiglione's, but one aspect of both dialogues is largely the same: their views on women.

In addition to being a popular courtesy book, *La civil conversatione* is, as Edward Sullivan puts it, "a picture, minute in every detail, of Italian life and morals, both public and domestic, during the second half of the sixteenth century."[3] It is, of course, a very subjective picture of those details of Italian culture during this period, and it is inevitably

---

1. Pettie's edition containing the first three books of *La civil conversatione* was published in 1581. It was reprinted in 1586, with the addition of Bartholomew Young's translation of the fourth book. In 1738, an inferior paraphrase of Pettie's work by an anonymous translator appeared, but it could hardly be considered a new translation of Guazzo's discourse. See John Leon Lievsay, "Notes on *The Art of Conversation* (1738)," *Italica* 17, no. 2 (1940): 58–63.

2. Magnocavalli was associated with the Academy of the *illustrati*, of which Stefano Guazzo was a founder. See Edward Sullivan's introduction to the Tudor Translations edition of Pettie's and Young's translations (New York: AMS Press, 1967), 1:viii–ix.

3. Ibid., xxvi.

contrasted with one painted earlier in the century by Castiglione in his *Courtier* (1528). Guazzo purposely leaves aside the discourse of courtly, aristocratic manners and mores with which Castiglione would shape the ideal *cortegiano*, however, focusing instead on a somewhat lower class of the populace represented by one who would be the ideal *gentiluomo*. Daniel Javitch suggests that the "advent of the Counter-Reformation" and "other social and political changes in Italy" were responsible for a shift toward a stronger sense of virtue, rather than birth, being the defining characteristic of nobility.[4] Thus, there existed a potential for upward mobility in gentle society, and Guazzo sought to capitalize upon it. Kirsty Cochrane notes that in comparison to Castiglione, Guazzo offers "a more accessible, pragmatic, and above all more contemporary model" for his readers.[5]

Book 2, from which an excerpt is translated here, illustrates the pragmatic nature of *La civil conversatione*. For the majority of book 2, Guglielmo and Annibale discuss how to speak to men of differing ages and ranks in society. Such knowledge would be considered not only practical but crucial for the gentleman eager to climb the social ladder. However, when that important information is transmitted and the rather arduous conversation is at a close, as a diversion they turn their attention to a conversation about women and women's conversation. Annibale finds the prospect of such a discussion delightful and refreshing; Guglielmo finds it morally suspect and an appalling waste of his time. The scene is thus set for a verbal romp through the clichés of *querelle* attitudes about women, which, according to Guazzo, clearly cannot in good conscience be left out of what is considered a most civil conversation—one meant to instruct the modern gentleman on proper thought, behavior, and values.

Even though it was published forty-eight years after *The Courtier* and was written from Guazzo's contemporary perspective, *La civil conversatione* still partakes of the *querelle des femmes* issues familiar to Castiglione's readers, a fact that underscores the pervasive nature

4. Daniel Javitch, "Rival Arts of Conduct in Elizabethan England: Guazzo's *Civile conversatione* and Castiglione's *Courtier*," *Yearbook of Italian Studies*, 1 (1971): 179.

5. Kirsty Cochrane, "A Civil Conversation of 1582: Gabriel Harvey's Reading of Guazzo," *A.U.M.L.A.: Journal of the Australasian Universities Modern Language Association* 78 (1992): 7.

of *querelle* thought in popular culture. In book 3 of *The Courtier*, Magnifico Giuliano goes to great lengths to outline the ways in which the ideal courtly woman must learn "a certain difficult mean, composed as it were between contrasting qualities," including the display of chastity, prudence, and a completely benign nature, while also exhibiting a "quick and vivacious spirit," wittiness, and discretion.[6] These qualities are to enable her to gain men's respect, and, at the same time, to act as "a shield against the insolence and beastliness of arrogant men."[7] In general, he describes the fine line between honest and dishonest behavior that women must negotiate. The premise that women's honesty is an either/or concept, or at least is perceived as such, is a foregone conclusion that buttresses his and other characters' comments as they then tell stories that support the good/evil dichotomy in the nature of women. Similar reasoning informs the *Civil Conversation*. Within the body of their discussion, women's merits and attributes are freely debated, with the traditional polarities observed: one is either a "ribello delle donne," a rebel against women, as Annibale accuses Guglielmo of being, or a jovial and earnest defender of them, as is Annibale himself. Women are either honest or dishonest, linked with disease and damnation or considered a civilizing influence upon the unruly manners and mores of men. The very notions embodied in this text—that a civil conversation would not be complete without such a discussion and that a well-educated gentleman (both in the sense of *letterato* and *educato*) should be able to dissect the nature of women and their influences upon men in this timeworn fashion—illustrate the ideological morass of sixteenth-century literary and philosophical views of women with which women had to contend.

In the text translated here, Guglielmo and Annibale take on the traditional roles of attacker and defender of women, respectively, and by the end of the passage in question, Annibale is lecturing Guglielmo on the differences between the honest love inspired by the Heavenly Venus and the lascivious love inspired by the Earthly Venus.[8] Counter-Reformation rhetoric echoes in his summation that

6. Castiglione, *The Book of the Courtier*, 212.

7. Ibid., 213.

8. Regarding the tradition of the earthly and heavenly Venuses, in *The Symposium* Plato writes of the two Aphrodites or Venuses. The "Common Aphrodite" he associates with car-

the love inspired by the latter ruins men's wealth, faith, health, and souls, while the love of the former "renders men affable, discreet, prompt, industrious, patient, [and] magnanimous," as well as making them fit company for inclusion in civilized society. To exemplify his meaning, in the fourth book, Guazzo presents a dialogue between six lords and four ladies, ostensibly an account of a dinner party attended by his wife, Francesca. It is meant to serve as an object lesson in civilized social behavior, and the women present are clearly to act as a refining influence upon the men. From this perspective, Guazzo's text resonates with that of Antoniano, who, in "Dell'adornarsi delle donne in particulare" ("On the Adorning of Women in Particular") and "Dell'offitio, e cura particulare della madre di famiglia circa gli adornamenti delle figliuole" ("On the Duties and Particular Responsibilities of the Mother of the Family concerning the Adornment of Daughters"), holds wives responsible for keeping men out of the arms of prostitutes and in good spiritual order.

Guazzo's emphasis on women's civilizing influence upon men, like that noted in Antoniano's chapters, presents women writers with a particularly entrenched stereotype, one that is familiar from the rhetoric of traditional defenders of women in the *querelle des femmes* and that is buttressed by Counter-Reformation ideology. As noted earlier, writers such as Andreini and Bigolina create their own versions of this facet of Counter-Reformation ideology regarding women's behavior and the influence they have over the behavior of men. Both writers, too, make use of the notion, discussed in Guazzo and handed down from Plato in his *Symposium*, that humans can participate in both earthly, carnal love and heavenly, chaste love.

Embracing the dictate that women are responsible for refining men's rash behavior, Andreini's virtuous heroines Mirtilla and Filli rescue their previously scorned lovers Tirsi and Igilio from suicide attempts, but their actions are motivated by more than simple passion.

---

nal love, and the "Heavenly" one he associates with higher, celestial love. Of the latter, he states that she "has had no share of the female, but only of the male." *Great Dialogues of Plato*, trans. W. H. D. Rouse, ed. Eric H. Warmington and Philip G. Rouse (New York: New American Library, 1956), 79. There is, moreover, a visual tradition of this theme: see Titian's *Amor sacro e amor profano* (*Sacred and Profane Love*) at the Galleria Borghese in Rome, http://www.galleriaborghese.it/borghese/it/amor.htm.

Mirtilla, conscious of her own reputation, explains that she goes to "save [Tirsi] from a cruel death and myself from infamy!" (5.1.2711). When she halts him in his attempt, she lectures him on the cowardice of suicide, exhorting him to understand that "time, love, faith, and steadiness never foil other people's hope" (5.3.3007–09). Moreover, like Guazzo—who refers to the chaste, proper love of the heavenly Venus and the lascivious, misleading love of the earthly one—Andreini includes in her play Amore, who represents chaste, proper love, and his nemesis, the fury who takes on his shape and goes about inciting improper passions and misleading mortals in love (prologue, lines 60–70). When Filli saves Igilio, she explains that for a time, someone else (Uranio) "unworthily held me," but now, Amore has led her to Igilio, her proper love (5.3. 2783–2787). True to pastoral tragicomic tradition, as well as notions of men's inability to control their own passions and behave in a civilized manner of their own accord, Andreini's male characters depend upon the chaste love of honest women to set them on the path to sane, happy lives.

Similar lessons in propriety and love are offered by Bigolina. As Nissen puts it, the "central task" of her *Urania* is to "define and depict" the ideal woman, one whose values are closely aligned with Counter-Reformation dictates for good women. Bigolina, writing before Guazzo, also makes use of the trope of the two kinds of Venus, and she does so in a graphic, didactic way. The name of her heroine, Urania, who eschews posing for a portrait and attempts to flee vanity at all costs, is associated with the virginal muse of astronomy; but her name is also a surname for Venus and is connected with the celestial or heavenly version of Venus (Οὐρανία).[9] By contrast, Bigolina also includes an episode of a woman led astray and degraded by the "Carnal Venus." In this scenario, the widowed duchess of Calabria, in love with the prince of Salerno, is convinced to sit for a painting in which she poses "seminude as Venus in an unscrupulous artist's version of the Judgment of Paris."[10] Nissen points out that Bigolina makes use of the same antithetical treatment of female characters in her *Novella of Giulia Camposanpiero and Thesibaldo*

---

9. Nissen, "Introduction," in *Urania: The Story of a Young Woman's Love*, 37. See also Lemprière, *Lemprière's Classical Dictionary* (London: Bracken Books, 1994), 704, on associations between Urania and Venus.

10. Ibid., 37; Bigolina, *Urania, The Story of a Young Woman's Love*, 195–99.

Vitaliani, wherein one finds "the virtuous and wise Giulia juxtaposed with the immoral and misguided Odolarica."[11] Regarding both pieces of Bigolina's writing, Nissen notes that Bigolina clearly prefers "not to put virtue and lack of virtue in direct conflict with each other, but rather to let each exist, emblematically and exemplarily, in its own separate realm and sphere of action."[12]

While these aspects of Andreini's and Bigolina's works conform to Counter-Reformation notions echoed in Guazzo's *Civil Conversation,* they also can be said to represent a bargaining chip, a "safe" approach to subject matter meant to absolve such women from having the temerity to write. That is not to say that Andreini and Bigolina did not believe in the moralistic, didactic messages they convey to their readers; they may have. However, both writers also fully exploit for their audience's enjoyment the titillating aspects of the influence that the "fury" who misrepresents Amore or the "Earthly Venus" has upon their characters. Andreini's character Ardelia, who falls madly in love with herself (4.4.2503–2604), and Bigolina's Odolarica, who causes the death of her secret lover Orsino through too much copulation,[13] certainly provide such entertainment. Thus, the line between didactic exhortation regarding appropriate behavior for women and deliberate engagement of erotic titillation regarding women's sinful nature can be quite fine, even in writing by women. This is also true in Antoniano's chapters, in which he returns repeatedly to his preoccupation with prostitutes, and in Guazzo's work, in Guglielmo's supposed misunderstanding of Annibale's intentions for subject matter regarding the conversation of women. Guazzo has Guglielmo say, "Pardon me … I thought you meant those women with whom one plays at arms," meaning that he thought Annibale wanted to discuss the conversation of loose women or prostitutes. From this perspective, the motives of those who engage in the *querelle* for didactic purposes should be considered from a variety of angles. Sometimes, as Guglielmo seems to understand, vice makes for more interesting conversation than virtue.

In any case, the fact remains that Guazzo felt compelled to include in his "modern" courtesy discourse this *querelle des femmes*

11. Ibid., 38.

12. Ibid.

13. Bigolina, *Urania: The Story of a Young Woman's Love,* 315.

interlude, which adds nothing new to the genre and seems to be as much of a nod to literary convention as it is an object lesson for the learned gentleman. Some women writers took issue with such facile, stale rhetoric. In her introduction to Moderata Fonte's *The Worth of Women* (written around 1592; published 1600), Virginia Cox suggests that Fonte's work "recharges what had, by this time, deteriorated into a somewhat sterile and formulaic academic exercise by bringing it back into contact with the realities of women's lives."[14] Fonte's interlocutors, as noted in chapter 2, interrogate the traditional *querelle* views of women and critique men's behavior and nature. Indeed, their conversation is deliberately undertaken to be a *querelle des hommes*, as Adriana indicates when she assigns the subject for their conversation, giving Leonora, Corinna, and Cornelia the task of "speaking as much evil" about men as they can, and Helena, Virginia, and Lucretia the job of defending them.[15] Especially during the first day of their conversation, the commonplaces of both Counter-Reformation arguments and *querelle des femmes* arguments guide their discussion.

Corinna argues that men are useless without the influence of women; in fact, she posits that men without women are "no good for anything."[16] Pursuing her argument that women are in general superior to men, she takes every opportunity to show that admonishments and dictates directed toward women stem from the poverty of virtues in men. When Virginia asks why, if men are so imperfect, they are always considered women's superiors, Corinna coolly explains that this "preeminence is something they have unjustly arrogated to themselves" and that the notion of women's subjection to men should be "understood in the same sense as when we say that we are subject to natural disasters, diseases, and all the other accidents of this life."[17] The flow of debate among Fonte's characters proceeds along these lines, with the arguments of the attackers of men frequently winning out, from the perspective of logic, over those of the defenders of men,

---

14. Cox, "Moderata Fonte and *The Worth of Women*," in *The Worth of Women: Wherein Is Clearly Revealed Their Nobility and Their Superiority to Men*, by Moderata Fonte, ed. and trans. Virginia Cox (Chicago: University of Chicago Press, 1997), 1.

15. Fonte, *The Worth of Women*, 57.

16. Ibid., 58.

17. Ibid., 59.

whose arguments tend to be clichés about women's inferiority and men's superiority.

As was also noted in chapter 2, Lucrezia Marinella lends her voice to the reinvigoration of the *querelle* in her treatise, *The Nobility and Excellence of Women and the Defects and Vices of Men* (1600). She writes most directly in response to Giuseppe Passi's *Dei donneschi difetti* (1599), but her reasoning also resonates with assertions in Guazzo's work, and in the last sections of the first part of her treatise, she also rebuts misogynist discourses by Ercole Tasso, Sperone Speroni, Torquato Tasso, and Giovanni Boccaccio. While the majority of her text is indeed a defense of women, as her title suggests, she includes a final section devoted to a catalogue of vicious and murderous acts committed by men throughout history. Letizia Panizza observes that Marinella's treatise is the only one of its kind written by a woman and that it presents "a stunning range of authorities, examples, and arguments, which in sheer quantity no other woman had hitherto amassed."[18] Marinella segues easily from quoting early modern writers such as those mentioned, as well as Ariosto, Petrarch, and a host of more minor literary figures, to classical authors such as Aristotle, Plato, Plutarch, Cicero, and Ovid. In the process, she soundly rebuts the "specious" rhetoric, inspired by hate or "proud disdain," that fuels the *querelle*.[19]

Fonte's and Marinella's works, with their scathing oppositional rhetoric directed toward both traditional attackers and defenders of women in the *querelle*, appear at the end of the sixteenth century. The timing suggests that by this point, educated women readers and writers were tired of the notion that the *querelle* was simply a literary game, one that all well-educated men should know how to play, and perhaps one that could also be exploited to engage and hold an audience's interest. In their works, they employ straightforward polemics to interrogate the shopworn clichés adopted by Guazzo and numerous other writers of the period, endeavoring to show their readers what women think about such notions. The result, of course, was certainly not an end to the querelle, but an updated approach to it, thanks to the interjection of such women's voices.

18. Panizza, "Introduction to the Translation," in *The Nobility and Excellence of Women*, 2.

19. Marinella, *The Nobility and Excellence of Women*, 39.

The Civil Conversation

STEFANO GUAZZO

From Book 2: The Conversation of Women and the Celestial and Earthly Venuses

Interlocutors: Cavalier Guglielmo Guazzo and Annibale Magnocavalli

Guglielmo: If I remember correctly the division that you have made between the kinds of conversation, we have nothing left to discuss but the conversation of women.

Annibale: It was quite appropriate that this discourse be reserved for last, as it will lighten our mood and restore us from the fatigue of our long journey today.[20]

Guglielmo: I fear that debating [the issues] of this conversation will not restore us; rather, we will feel even greater exhaustion, or else it is quite necessary to say that your taste is very different from mine, since I have always esteemed the conversation of women not only vain and useless, but also dangerous and harmful. And if you hear any spirit [within you] contrary to this opinion of mine, exorcise it and drive it away by virtue of these three maxims, of which the first is that if the world could be maintained without women, our conversation would not be far from God. The second is that there is nothing in the world worse than a woman, no matter how good [she is]. The third is that the iniquity of a man is better than the goodness of a woman.

20. Up to this point during the course of this day's discourse, the interlocutors have covered such topics as general manners of polite conversation in public and the specific manners to be considered in conversations between young and old men, nobles and commoners, princes and private citizens, the educated and uneducated, citizens and foreigners, and religious and secular persons. See the summary of topics in *La civil conversatione* (Venice: Altobello Salicato, 1584), 66.

Annibale: These three sayings are rather fit to preserve than to destroy my spirit! I perceive that you look only at the bark. But if you push the acuteness of your intellect into the sap, you will find that [these maxims] are not pronounced in blame of women, but they signal the incontinence and the fragility of men, who sin sooner in conversing with women of good reputation than with wicked men. Indeed, when conversing with usurers, thieves, adulterers, backbiters, and other men of evil ways, he will not allow himself to try their wickedness as easily as when conversing with women, however honest; he will feel himself moved by lascivious and disorderly appetites, verified by that saying: you cannot be more learned than David, nor stronger than Samson, nor wiser than Solomon, all of whom sinned because of women. Behold here the true juice[21] of the sayings that you cited, those that, I repeat, are apt sooner to preserve than to destroy my spirit. For if it is the truth that virtue consists of cruel and difficult things, I believe I do a virtuous act [in] accustoming my feelings to be at peace and not disturbed at all in the presence of and in conversation with women, among whom by now I have gotten into the habit of experiencing my natural serenity.[22]

Guglielmo: Your philosophy has perhaps so deadened you that you can promise yourself the steadfastness of that philosopher who was once mistaken by a woman for a statue.[23] But I will remind you that this virtue is given

---

21. Common metaphor for "meaning."

22. In other words, it is as natural for him to converse with women as men.

23. The reference seems to be to Xenocrates, a philosopher known for his discipline and integrity. A common story about Xenocrates tells that the courtesan Lais pledged a large sum of money in a bet that she could seduce the philosopher. In the end, she failed; however, she protested that she should not have to pay her pledge because she had set out to seduce a man, "not a lifeless stone" (*Lemprière's Classical Dictionary*, 724). I am grateful to E. J. Moncada for providing this reference. Amedeo Quondam's modern edition of Guazzo's

to few, and one finds not only common men but even hermits [whose] breviaries drop from their hands and calendars from their belts in the presence of women.[24]

Annibale: If I do not subscribe to the discipline of that philosopher, neither do I have the frivolity of those who become enamored, as the proverb says, at every marketplace[25] and who are so foolish[26] they lose control of themselves at the sight of women. Such is their madness that whatever laughter, nod, or other gesture a woman happens to make, they take it as done for their benefit, and, full of a thousand vain hopes, they promise themselves a thousand pleasures and chase after such a woman, who in her own mind is many miles away from them.

Guglielmo: And this is also a fault of women, who, as they say, are like death since they follow those who flee them and flee those who call them.

Annibale: Honest women flee those who pursue them, as do dishonest women, although they allow themselves to be overtaken. But there was never a woman so unchaste that she did not think it a shame to follow others, and who did not first want to be desired; thus the fault is not, as you say, with the woman but with the man.

Guglielmo: I could easily tell you the reason for this, but I keep it under wraps for a worthy reason!

---

text offers many classical and medieval sources: Guazzo, *La civil conversazione*, ed. Amedeo Quondam (Modena: Franco Cosimo Panini, 1993), 2:299n755.

24. That is to say, they lose track of their daily and yearly duties as listed in their prayer books and church calendars.

25. Markets took place every day in different cities or neighborhoods of larger cities; falling in love at every marketplace thus means falling in love too easily.

26. The Italian phrase is "dolci di sale"—lacking salt, meaning silly or stupid.

Annibale: Oh, you are such a rebel against women!

Guglielmo: A rebel I am not, because I never swore my loyalty to them. How is it that men can love women, if they take their name from the danger that [always] comes with them?[27]

Annibale: Yes, Bembo said so of old women, but the young ones he calls a benefit, because they are of use.[28]

Guglielmo: Perhaps the young ones are more harmful than the old.

Annibale: Now I know the tack you want to take in this conversation! I reply that old women are more harmful, for according to a popular saying, the young goat eats salt, and the old one eats salt and the sack.

Guglielmo: Choose freely from whichever tack you think, because in the end [it's] more or less the same.[29] Recall the man who was caught between a young woman and an old one: the young woman plucked off his white hair, to make him look young, and the old woman plucked off his black hair so that he would look old, whereby the poor fellow, thanks to both, ended up bald! Thus, in the end, you will finally accept that we are put in this world by women to be ruined by women. For that reason, a poor fellow who was dying from the French

27. The word "danno" or danger is misogynistically treated as part of the etymology of "donna" or woman. See Cox in Fonte's *Worth of Women*, 93. Indeed, the expression "chi dice donna, dice danno!" still exists in Italian today.

28. See Pietro Bembo, *Gli Asolani*, ed. Giorgio Dilemmi (Firenze, Italy: Presso l'Accademia della Crusca, 1991), 2:iv. See also Bembo, *Gli Asolani*, trans. Rudolf B. Gottfried (Freeport, NY: Books for Libraries Press, 1954; repr., 1971), 79. The pun in the original is based on a false etymology (similar to the one invoked above of *donna* deriving from *danno*) whereby *giovane* (young) comes from *giovare* (be of use).

29. Literally, one costs six, the other seven.

disease[30] said: "A woman has done me, and a woman has undone me." And it is certain that they undo [us] in two ways, if we believe the gentle poet who says,

> Lesbia sucks dry one's purse and heart,
> Crazy is he who buys love at so great a cost.[31]

Annibale: This is not the conversation we must discuss, and it seems to me a very strange thing that you, as a knight [whose duties are clear] would show yourself to be such an enemy of women!

Guglielmo: Pardon me, but I followed another tack because as soon as you proposed debating the conversation with women, I thought you meant those women with whom one plays at arms.[32] I believe that for men, and for women who make a profession of it, it is also useful to know the modes of conversing among themselves. [Yet] in order to live long in peace and love, you know very well how much I owe to honorable women, that it is my own proper duty not only to honor them, but also to support and defend their reputation no less with my sword than my word. And when I am not constrained to do so for duty, I would do it out of affection, since I am always most envious of their good will.[33]

Annibale: We cannot save our honor and discuss that conversation you had in mind [for] it seems to me we should

---

30. The "French disease" is syphilis.

31. The Italian phrase in the second line reads, "chi compra con due sangui amore," literally, who buys love with two bloods. The lines are reminiscent of those of Horace or Catullus, but the poet could not be identified; Quondam's note comes to the same conclusion: Guazzo, *La civil conversazione*, 2:300n768.

32. The Italian phrase is "con le quali si giuoca alle braccia." Pettie translates it loosely as, "with those whom men trie their manhood withall in amorous incounters" (1:234).

33. This sentence could also be translated "protective of their grace" or "protective of their good graces."

destroy it rather than to construct it, because it is unworthy of any civil conversation! But so as not to leave you in doubt, I would like you to think with me now that to nothing is the nature of man more inclined than to the love of women. So that we do not choose in error, it is appropriate that we know there is one Venus in Heaven and another on earth. The latter is the mother of lasciviousness and the former of honest love. The [earthly] one is none other than a blind passion of the mind, a misleader of the intellect, something that dulls, indeed erases, memory, a dissipater of worldly abilities, a destroyer of bodily strengths, an enemy of youth, and the death of old age, the mother of vices, a dweller in idle breasts, a thing without reason, order, and any stability, a vice of unhealthy minds, and one who drowns human liberty. In brief, her beginning is fear, her middle, sin, her end, grief and sorrow.[34]

Guglielmo: It is quite clear that you are familiar with our Boccaccio since you are so mindful of his lofty sayings, to which one may add that of the Poet,

[Love] … blocks the path of honor
for anyone who trusts too much in him.[35]

Annibale: Indeed, there is nothing that removes man further from the presence of God and that makes him fall into most foul error. The invincible Hercules might well say so, since he was conquered by a blind passion that led him among the womanish delights to take on women's attire in order to obtain the love of a Queen,

---

34. The lines are from Boccaccio's *Il corbaccio*, ed. Giulia Natali (Milan: Mursia, 1992), 49. See also *The Corbaccio*, trans. Anthony K. Cassell, rev. ed. (Binghamton, NY: Medieval and Renaissance Texts and Studies, 1993), 23.

35. The poet is Petrarca. See canzone 264, *Rime*, trans. Mark Musa. Again, I owe thanks to E. J. Moncada for help with this reference.

by whose commandment he resigned himself to taking spindles and wool into those rough hands of his,
which previously had subdued monsters. He could
not demolish this monster of love, which resembled
the chimera: like the latter, it has the head of a lion,
the stomach of a goat, [and] the tail of a dragon, thus
it comes first with the ferociousness of the lion, then
with the lust of the goat, and in the end with the venom of the dragon, bringing ruin and death.

Guglielmo: I also believe that the metamorphoses via which
Medusa with her beauty turned men into stones and
beasts meant nothing more than that is the fate of intemperate people.

Annibale: We will say in conclusion, that when this love has
formed its roots in the heart, one loses in an instant
one's wealth, faith, reputation, virtue, body, and soul;
whence all those who follow this crazy and bestial
love are drawn into conversations with wicked, unchaste women. They are hardly worthy of the presence and entertainment of honest and virtuous
women! Then there is heavenly love, the one desirous of the beauties of the soul. I could not say of how
many good and pleasing effects it is the cause, since
it renders men affable, discrete, willing, industrious, patient, magnanimous, and, as a valorous writer
has already said, it strips men of their rudeness and
brings them into familiar company via feasts, festi-
vals, and theatrical performances.[36] Such love is both
the captain and the president who gives meekness,
banishes fierceness, brings benevolence, and drives
away hate. It is favorable, beneficent, pleasing, desir-

36. Guazzo refers to Agathon's speech in Plato's *Symposium*, in which he argues that Love
"empties us of estrangement, and fills us with friendliness, ordaining all such meetings as
this one, of people one with another, in feasts, in dances, in sacrifices becoming men's guide."
Great Dialogues of Plato, 93.

ous of goodness, and a scorner of evil. In toil, in fear, in desire, in well-governed speech, and finally of human life, it is the most perfect ornament.

4.
Alessandro Piccolomini's Raffaella: *A Parody of Women's Behavior and Men's Dialogues*

MARIA GALLI STAMPINO

Alessandro Piccolomini (1508–1579) was born to a prominent noble family in Siena, which was then an independent republic (and remained so until 1555). He became a member of the Accademia degli intronati (Academy of the Bewildered Men), with the name of "Stordito" (the Stunned One), and he rose to eminence within it, becoming its leader.[1] In 1538 he left Siena for Padua, then an important hub for Aristotelian thinking, including philosophy as well as rhetoric and literature; there he studied and taught alongside Vincenzo Maggi, Federico Delfino, and Marcantonio Genoa. He also helped found and led the local Accademia degli infiammati (Academy of the Inflamed Men), which included such famed writers as the Tuscan Benedetto Varchi and the Paduans Sperone Speroni and Bernardino Tomitano.[2]

Like other Sienese academies, the Intronati promoted and hosted so-called *veglie*, evenings of discussion and entertainment that at times included plays that were either read or performed.[3] In his earlier years, prior to his Paduan education, Piccolomini's printed production includes the dialogue *Raffaella* (1539) and the comedy *L'amor costante* (*Steadfast Love*, written in 1531 and performed in 1536). Women were an important part of *veglie*, and the Intronati had a pro-woman program based on the education and subsequent inclusion of

---

1. The most complete biographical study of Piccolomini is still Florindo Cerreta, *Alessandro Piccolomini: Letterato e filosofo senese del cinquecento* (Siena: Accademia senese degli Intronati, 1960). For his activities within the Intronati, see 10–18.

2. See Andrea Baldi, *Tradizione e parodia in Alessandro Piccolomini* (Lucca: Maria Pacini Fazzi, 2001), 206, 212–14.

3. Many studies center on the Intronati: see Baldi, *Tradizione e parodia*, 7n1. On their dramatic texts and productions in particular, see Daniele Seragnoli, *Il teatro a Siena nel Cinquecento: progetto e modello drammaturgico nell'Accademia degli Intronati* (Rome: Bulzoni, 1980).

ladies in their get-togethers.[4] As Andrea Baldi has asserted, women were idolized in most writings by members of the Intronati, and Piccolomini in particular was an "outstanding representative of such collective tendencies, pay[ing] close attention to [the Accademia's] proposals" vis-à-vis women.[5] This interest followed Piccolomini when he left Siena; as Virginia Cox reminds us, the publication of "a lecture [he] delivered in February 1541 … before the Paduan Accademia degli Infiammati on a sonnet by Laodomia Forteguerri" gave the latter the distinction of becoming "only the third secular Italian female poet to appear in print, after [Vittoria] Colonna and [Veronica] Gambara" and "the first to gain the honor of an academic commentary on her work."[6]

Yet *Raffaella* seems at variance with such an attitude: its tone is that of parody, even of mocking, and its content is inconsistent with the idolization, education, and inclusion of women that were crucial to the Intronati's beliefs and activities. Even its subtitle, "Dialogue about Women's Good Manners," is filled with irony when considered alongside its content. Yet, in keeping with Intronati custom, it is dedicated to "those women who will read it" (quelle donne che leggeranno). In it Piccolomini introduces the key concept of the dialogue: love affairs are not to be eschewed but rather to be conducted in secrecy and with the utmost attention to outward appearances, so that nobody might suspect women of any misconduct.[7]

This is the message that Lady Raffaella, the dialogue's namesake and the older and more experienced of the two interlocutors, conveys to Margarita, a young Sienese bride. By the end of the dialogue, Raffaella's motivations become clear: she is acting as a go-between for a "messer Aspasio," a nobleman smitten with Margarita who

---

4. To quote Baldi, "Ladies were starting points and terminuses *qua* main addressees of literary production" of Sienese academies ("le gentidonne risultano punto d'innesco e termine di approdo, in qualità di principali destinatarie della produzione letteraria"): Baldi, *Tradizione e parodia*, 12. All translations by Stampino.

5. "Rappresentante di spicco delle tendenze collettive … riserva un'attenzione assidua a queste proposte"; Baldi, *Tradizione e parodia*, 47.

6. Cox, *Women's Writing*, 106.

7. Alessandro Piccolomini, *La Raffaella ovvero dialogo della bella creanza delle donne*, ed. Giancarlo Alfano (Rome: Salerno, 2001), 30–31.

would like to bring his sexual desires to fruition. As the excerpt below indicates, Raffaella carefully uses her rhetorical wiles to ensnare the naive Margarita in deceptive reasoning and gain her acceptance of her transgressive advice.[8]

This extended passage captures some important examples of Raffaella's strategy. First, she couches her remarks within the discourse of religious practices, faith, and sin. In this manner, she confirms Margarita's belief that Raffaella is pious, forcing her to ask (indeed, to beg) for advice. Second, she underscores her close emotional relationship with Margarita's beloved deceased mother, in order to build on her reputation as a God-fearing, devout churchgoer, and to deepen Margarita's trust in her. Third, Raffaella uses her own experience, regrets, and consequent sinful thoughts as the reasons behind her desire to show Margarita a different way of behaving and loving. The latter falls only too readily into Raffaella's trap: "What do you think we young women should be aware of, above all?"[9] When Raffaella lists pastimes commonly avoided by young women mindful of their reputation, and Margarita is shocked by her companion's suggestion that she should partake in them to the point of reveling in them, the older lady resorts to another trick: she indicates that she is offended and threatens to leave.

Raffaella's suggestions are grounded in a general consideration, openly and variously stated: were it possible to lead a sinless life, her advice to Margarita would not be needed; but her experience, even including what one hears in church, shows that it is impossible to do so. Hence, a few minor sins are preferable to graver ones: "going often

8. Or, as Baldi asserts, the dialogue "presents the recruitment of a follower and, consequently, its general program cannot elude the necessity of a direct translation into practice" of the rules ("presenta il reclutamento di un'adepta, e, di conseguenza, il programma generale non può trascurare la necessità di un diretto travaso nella prassi)." Baldi, *Tradizione e parodia*, 89. Marie Françoise Piéjus reminds us that Raffaella is the female version of Raphael, the angel that God sent to the young Tobit to escort him on a perilous journey that ended with his marriage to Sara in the Book of Tobit; Marie Françoise Piéjus, "Venus bifrons: le double idéal féminin dans *La Raffaella* d'Alessandro Piccolomini," in *Images de la femme dans la littérature Italienne de la Renaissance: Préjugés misogynes et aspirations nouvelles*, ed. José Guidi, Marie Françoise Piéjus, and Adelin-Charles Fiorato (Paris: Université de la Sorbonne nouvelle, 1980), 126–27.

9. "Di che cosa giudicate che noi giovani doveriamo essere avertite principalmente?"

to celebrations, banquets, get-togethers; dressing prettily; adorning oneself with jewels, aromatic waters, and perfumes; following fashion" are but a few of them. Such suggestions are geared to attract a listener who is not only young and inexperienced but also lacking male companionship. To Raffaella's feigned and exaggerated surprise, Margarita avows that her husband leaves her home alone for long periods of time. This is to the advantage of Raffaella's plan: not only will their conversation remain uninterrupted, but Margarita's behavior is (and will be) less closely controlled, and her sexual curiosity and desires are (and will be) more easily aroused.

Given the emphasis on appearances throughout the dialogue, it is hardly surprising that Raffaella casts her light on clothing first. She advocates using the highest-quality cloth for Margarita's dresses, and plenty of it; she advises adorn her clothes with "ribbons, cuts, embroideries, and other similar things" and to change them often. Such suggestions fly in the face of centuries of treatises instructing women on appropriate behavior, which were based on the belief that women cannot control their wishes, desires, urges, and behavior.[10] By voicing these suggestions, Raffaella ventriloquizes misogynistic beliefs: neither character can be trusted, as Margarita is an example of women's gullibility and naiveté, and her older companion demonstrates her gender's wily and untrustworthy nature.

In 1539 it was still possible for a man of letters to pen and publish a dialogue like *Raffaella*, one that expounds misogynistic values and does not spare criticism, albeit indirect, of such key institutions as the Church and marriage. Though in his 1540 treatise *De la institutione di tutta la vita de l'homo nato nobile in città* Piccolomini dubbed his dialogue a subversion of the prevailing mores, meant only to provoke laughter and born of a carefree mind,[11] and though the rest of Piccolomini's literary production is far more serious in tone, *Raffaella* still circulated in print.[12] Twenty years later, in 1561, circumstances

---

10. See Campbell's introduction to Silvio Antoniano's *Tre libri dell'educatione Christiana de i figliuoli* in this volume for examples from biblical and church father sources.

11. Baldi, *Tradizione e parodia*, 107.

12. It was indeed a very successful piece; as Piéjus points out, it saw nine editions between 1539 and 1574, as well as three separate French editions beginning in 1573. Piéjus, "Venus bifrons," 81.

had drastically changed, as we can see in a letter written by another member of the Intronati, Girolamo Bargagli: Piccolomini "would never take the time to have [his dialogue] reprinted, like one who is busy with far weightier things wouldn't turn his attention to things that he calls 'tales.'"[13] Bargagli recasts this minor work as something meant for a limited circle of readers, in contrast to the scope of Piccolomini's original dedication; this was a safer alternative in a culture that, as Antoniano's treatise attests, does not condone errant behavior, even if presented in jest.[14]

If, on a cultural level, *Raffaella* draws a "contrast between love as a passion to be enjoyed and loveless arranged marriages," as Laura Giannetti cogently argues,[15] the rhetorical target of Piccolomini's parody is not women, young or old, but the model of all Italian dialogues: Baldessare Castiglione's *The Book of the Courtier*. Baldi calls it "the original matrix for 'Raffaella,' but in opposition,"[16] beginning with the characters and extending to the tone and development of the conversation. While the perfect lady outlined in book 3 of *The Courtier* is of noble birth, educated, meant to shine a light of poise on her husband's court, and in control of her environment and of her emotions, the women speaking in Piccolomini's dialogue are the product of a different milieu and atmosphere. Raffaella is of noble birth but emphasizes her dwindling wealth; Margarita is "a disappointed wife, neglected by her husband, yet submissive and devoted to a humiliating observation

---

13. "A farlo ristampare, non pigliarebbe mai questo assunto, come quello che, intento a cose molto maggiori, non rivolterebbe l'occhio … a queste che egli chiama fole." Giancarlo Alfano, "Introduzione," in Alessandro Piccolomini, *La Raffaella*, 20.

14. Indeed, in the same letter of 1561, Bargagli continues: "If it [Piccolomini's *Raffaella*] is reprinted, though, send two [copies], because here too [in Siena] we miss it and wish for it." ("Facendosi ristampare, mandatecene due, che qua anco ce nè carestia e desiderio.") Alfano, "Introduction," 21. Note that Castiglione's *Book of the Courtier* itself was placed on the Index of Forbidden Books in 1590, and only an expurgated edition was available (and reprinted four times between 1584 and 1606): Panizza, "Introduction to the Translation," in *The Nobility and Excellence of Women and the Defects and Vices of Men*, by Lucrezia Marinella, ed. and trans. by Anne Dunhill (Chicago: University of Chicago Press, 1999), 19n43.

15. Laura Giannetti, *Lelia's Kiss: Imagining Gender, Sex, and Marriage in Italian Renaissance Comedy* (Toronto: University of Toronto Press, 2009), 194.

16. "la matrice prima, *e contrario*, della 'Raffaella'": Baldi, *Tradizione e parodia*, 87.

of domestic habits."[17] Margarita's life is limited to the pastimes of the merchant stratum living in the city, rather than the celebrations, lavish festivities, and even occasions for individual betterment that the court affords the noble women depicted in Castiglione's dialogue.

The *Courtier's* key principle of *sprezzatura*, "a certain nonchalance which conceals all artistry and makes whatever one says or does seem uncontrived and effortless,"[18] is stretched in the *Raffaella* into a total separation between outside appearance or behavior and interior beliefs, thus presenting to Piccolomini's readers "a forgiving relativism [that is] well disposed towards stealthy breaches" of the prevailing mores.[19] At the same time, Piccolomini's dialogue "unveils the presumptuousness of the elusive, chimera-like ideal of the lord [i.e., of the seigniorial stratum], by unmasking the haughtiness of those who legislate manners."[20]

Raffaella's parodying intent vis-à-vis Castiglione's dialogue helps to explain why Piccolomini renounces the Intronati's pro-woman stance, which falls on the side of the protofeminist message of book 3 of *The Courtier*. In 1545 Piccolomini had *Oration in Praise of Women* printed (*Oratione in lode delle donne*) and addressed it to the Intronati. Despite its title, as Baldi has pointed out, its content is philosophical in nature; in it, the author limits himself to pointing out how women deserve men's devotion and gallantry, but he does not offer a concrete plan to change women's roles and positions within culture and society.[21] Yet such a political position would be too much to ask of a man (or, for that matter, of a woman) writing in the 1540s and throughout the early modern period; the context within which Piccolomini wrote was rhetorical, rather than practical.[22] In this sense, then, what is remarkable is the fact that the *Oration* relies heavily on

17. "moglie delusa e trascurata dallo sposo, ma remissive e dédita a un'avvilente osservanza dei rituali domestici": Baldi, *Tradizione e parodia*, 94.

18. Castiglione, *The Book of the Courtier*, ed. and trans. George Bull, 67.

19. "un relativismo condiscendente, benevolo verso una tacita infrazione": Baldi, *Tradizione e parodia*, 157.

20. "svela la presunzione del chimerico ideale signorile, smascherando il sussiego dei legislatori del costume:" Baldi, *Tradizione e parodia*, 122.

21. Baldi, *Tradizione e parodia*, 56–59.

22. As pointed out by Virginia Cox, "Moderata Fonte and *The Worth of Women*," 15–16.

the tone and espouses the views of *The Courtier*;[23] hence, it directly contradicts the misogynous views found in *Raffaella*. Rather than casting Piccolomini's dialogue as the divertissement of a young man or as a facet of his self-fashioning,[24] we should frame it as one part of an exercise of rhetorical argument *in utramque partem*, i.e., on both sides of an issue. Thus Raffaella presents the misogynist side of the diatribe, while the Oration takes a pro-woman stance.

Piccolomini's works indicate that both misogynist and pro-woman ideas circulated in the cultural milieus of the 1530s and 1540s in Italy, though these ideas did not equally inform those milieus. Moderata Fonte's *The Worth of Women* (written around 1592, published in 1600) outlines husbands' and lovers' shortcomings and vices, thus indirectly rebutting Raffaella's suggestion that a lover would give Margarita what her husband would not or did not.[25] Similarly, in *The Nobility and Excellence of Women and the Defects and Vices of Men* (1600), Lucrezia Marinella targets husbands' faults and weaknesses as she argues against Ercole Tasso's 1595 treatise *Dello ammogliarsi* (*On Taking a Wife*).[26] *Raffaella* shows the insidious and pervasive nature of misogynist ideas that were so commonplace, they could be attributed to a woman character and turned into mocking weapons against a literary and rhetorical touchstone. In the end, it is less important to ascertain whether Piccolomini espoused such ideas than to note that his dialogue attests to the ease with which they were invoked in Italy in the 1530s and 1540s.

---

23. This point is made, using plentiful citations, in Baldi, *Tradizione e parodia*, 67–87. In one way Piccolomini's dialogue differs from *The Courtier*, in that, as Piéjus points out, women are the addressees, protagonists, and objects of this work; "Venus bifrons," 85.

24. This is Alfano's interpretation of Piccolomini's retraction of *Raffaella* in the dedication of his 1540 treatise *De la institutione di tutta la vita de l'homo nato nobile in città libera*; Alfano, "Introduction," 7. Note that the dedicatee is Laudomia Forteguerri's newly baptized son, not the Sienese poet herself; Baldi, *Tradizione e parodia*, 208.

25. Fonte, *The Worth of Women*, 68–80.

26. Marinella, *The Nobility and Excellence of Women*, 135–36.

Raffaella, or Dialogue about Women's Good Manners

ALESSANDRO PICCOLOMINI

Interlocutors: Lady Raffaella and Margarita

Lady R.:   May God bestow a good day on you, Margarita; your hands are never idle, and I always find you working or embroidering.

Margarita: Welcome, Lady Raffaella; it's high time you came and spent some time with me! What's new?

Lady R.:   Sins and toil, as is always the case with old women; what else could it be?

Margarita: Sit with me awhile! How are you doing?

Lady R.:   I'm older and poorer than ever; my head gets closer to the grave with every passing hour.

Margarita.:   Don't say that. Young and old alike die when God wills it.

Lady R.:   I really wouldn't mind dying, in fact I'd rather die today than tomorrow; after all, what do I have left to do in this world? All things considered, I would bear even poverty patiently, though it is very hard to be poor for those who were born noble, like me; what pains me is to see myself full of sins, and every day I sin more.

Margarita: What should other old women say? You think you have so many sins, but I hold you to be a saint! What sins might you have, since I always see you with a rosary in your hands and you spend all day in various churches?

Lady R.:   I cannot deny that what consolation I have left comes from masses and prayers to Saint Francis; I don't miss a single one if I can help it. And yet, what's that vis-à-vis the many sins committed all day long?

Margarita: You are wrong, Lady Raffaella, to think that you bother me when you come to my house! Indeed, it is always a great pleasure for me to talk to you. You know how much faith my mother placed in your words and advice, and how much consolation she would draw from them. I do the same as she.

Lady R.:   Alas, what consolation can someone give who is too long in this world?

Margarita: That's enough! It is as I said, and you know that we've always been kind to you.

Lady R.:   That is true, more than I deserve.

Margarita: So, why don't you come by any longer?

Lady R.:   To tell you how things are, I keep myself from coming here as much as I can. It's not that I don't enjoy seeing you, but every time I come something occurs to me that I then have to discuss with our Lord God.

Margarita: Why is that?

Lady R.:   Margarita, I am ashamed just to think about it, let alone say it to someone else, so let's drop it.

Margarita: So you're ashamed to tell me what's on your mind, even though you know that I consider you as a mother!

Lady R.:   How can I know that it won't get to other people's ears?

Margarita:	You show that you have little faith in me, if you suspect that I would divulge to others what you don't want me to.
Lady R.:	Promise me, then, that you'll keep your mouth closed.
Margarita:	Have faith in me, and please, tell me—I truly cannot imagine what this might be.
Lady R.:	Since you've given me your word, then, I will unveil my sin to you: I have never revealed it to anyone except my confessor. Every time I see you, Margarita, I observe your beauty and youth, and I immediately remember those years when I was young myself. At the same time I remember, too, that I didn't manage to enjoy myself as I could have. So the devil instills in me some kind of regret or sorrow, such that for many days I am desperate, I cannot go to mass or to prayers, I cannot do anything positive; the devil wants me to break my neck! In order to avoid this sin, as I said, I keep from coming to see you, because my soul is heavy with worry.
Margarita:	How surprising! I would have never thought it! But the same or even something more must occur to you when you meet with other women who are more beautiful than me.
Lady R.:	I never noticed that any woman could wreak as much havoc as you, either because there is no beauty on a par with yours today in Siena, or for some other reason. In any case, that's the way it is.
Margarita:	Every day you seem more devout to me, Lady Raffaella, since your conscience is burdened by something so small.

Lady R.:   Do you think it's little to remember the mistakes one didn't make and regret it? I don't know why the earth does not swallow me up.

Margarita: It would be far worse to remember that one did make mistakes.

Lady R.:   Daughter, don't say that! I think that I have more experience in this world than you, so I know what's big and what's insignificant in matters of conscience.[27]

Margarita: I will believe you, then, since I know that, as my mother told me many times, you know what you're talking about.

Lady R.:   How much faith the beloved soul of your mother placed in me! God knows how strong my love for her was. One could say that I brought her up myself.

Margarita: Who knows better than I that she couldn't live without you?

Lady R.:   We were related: her sister was my nephew's sister-in-law.

Margarita: She used to tell me that.

Lady R.:   Now, Margarita, you know the reason why I avoided your home for a while.

Margarita: I would have thought it was anything but this!

---

27. The original utilizes images that recall more explicitly the gospels by Matthew and Luke. Jesus urges his followers to avoid passing judgment on others, and rhetorically asks: "Why beholdest thou the mote that is in thy brother's eye, but considerest not the beam that is in thine own eye?" (Matthew 7:3 in the King James version; Luke 6:41 utilizes the same vocabulary).

Lady R.:   On the other hand, my soul is racked when I don't come because it doesn't seem to me that I am doing my duty, as the mass commands in a couple of places.

Margarita: Why?

Lady R.:   What do you mean, why? Don't you know that, in the mass for the Virgin Mary, the lord says to help your neighbor? Since I am old and I know good from evil, I should warn young women and give them advice about many mistakes, above all those like you with whom I am a little familiar. Due to their lack of experience with the world, such young women could easily make those mistakes. So thanks to their companions they should learn to recognize those dangers that I and thousands of other old women learned to recognize by ourselves, since we had no one to advise and warn us. This is real charity.

Margarita: Since we started on this topic, tell me a little: what do you think we young women should be aware of, above all?

Lady R.:   You should be aware of many things, among them what I mentioned before: if one doesn't enjoy herself chastely when she's young, she becomes so desperate in her old age that she goes to hell readily. As you can see, I am afraid I'm going there myself.

Margarita: What kind of enjoyments should we have?

Lady R.:   The ones that young women usually have, such as going often to parties, dinners, get-togethers; dressing prettily, adorning oneself with jewels, aromatic waters, and perfumes; following fashion; trying to be considered beautiful and wise at the same time; to be loved by someone; to listen to serenades; to go to see people wearing masks and liveries performed out of love … Such are the honest pleasures for young and noble women such as yourself.

Margarita: I am astonished—I have always heard that these things are sins rather than anything else.

Lady R.:   Daughter—I can call you that, given the time and affection I have given you—I confess to you that it would be a very holy and great feat if we could keep ourselves in relation to the world sinless from birth until death and without stain, if that were possible. The examples of all the people who have existed show us that we were created sinners and thus it is impossible for us to live without any error. So we have to believe that it is more tolerable and worthy of forgiveness, as far as God is concerned, to have made some small mistake when young than to refrain oneself as I did and then later despair because it's too late, which more than any other sin will send us to hell. Just as bodily illnesses are much less dangerous to young people (as we notice when it comes to rubella and smallpox), the more a body is subject to them then, the stronger and freer it gets from illnesses later on. Similarly, a certain madness that is born with each person is far less dangerous to the soul, and it makes one's life freer and more resolute, if it expresses itself in youth rather than if it is pent up and emerges at the time when one tries to be wise and temperate.

Margarita: So you believe that it is useful to live happily and to enjoy oneself a little when one is my age?

Lady R.:   It is very useful, even necessary! If we had time I think I'd be able to show you in detail how you should live and how far you should go in having fun. I know for sure that you would then say that I understand the world.

Margarita: What do you mean, if we had time? What do we have to do? I absolutely want you to reason with me a little about this; we couldn't have a better occasion, since we're alone, and I don't think you want to leave, since it's not vespers or compline.[28]

Ladu R.: Forgive me, but today I cannot stay; I want to go get some money from your aunt.

Margarita: What difference does it make if you get it today or tomorrow?

Lady R.: Alas, Margarita, though you see me dressed like this, you ought to know that I am under much hardship at home; I show it as little as I can because it shames me, but I can swear to you (since I can tell you anything) that I often don't have a single bread crumb at home.

Margarita: Don't think about leaving, you won't lack bread or anything as long as I have any: one must certainly be compassionate towards those who are born nobly and don't have enough to live by.

Lady R.: I thank you, but forgive me for leaving this time; I will come back another day, when I have more time.

Margarita: What are you doing? You shouldn't get up, I truly don't want you to leave, and I'd be very unhappy with you.

Lady R.: What do you care if it's now or some other time?

---

28. That is, you do not have to go to church to say the prayers prescribed for evening or night devotions.

Margarita:	I care! Since you've lit my fire on this topic, I don't want today to go by without having heard your opinion on every detail.
Lady R.:	Margarita, I won't fail you! Yet, to tell you the truth, though I know that every kind woman (such as yourself) should like what I'm about to tell you, nevertheless one never knows people's souls, and people have different ideas ... So who knows? It could be that the opposite would occur and that you would complain about me, which would pain me greatly.
Margarita:	No, no, there's no danger of that! I have known you for a long time and I know that your words always honor God and are useful to any listener.
Lady R.:	As far as God is concerned, I have already said that it would be better if one could avoid all earthly pleasure, indeed that one could always fast and scourge oneself. In order to avoid greater sins then one must agree to a little error, that is, to enjoy oneself a little when young, because this sin is washed away by holy water. This should be your answer, so that I won't have to reiterate it with everything I will tell you, because you will think that it smacks of sin. I will presuppose a little sin in all that I will explain to you, but as it's necessary, I will take into consideration one's honor in the world; I will make sure that these pleasures are enjoyed so clearly and with such intelligence that they will not make people talk.
Margarita:	I am totally sure of this—I was about to say that I have more faith in you than in the Gospel!
Lady R.:	You should. I'd rather lose this piece of jewelry, though it's the only thing of value I still have, than tell you

something that wouldn't be useful to you and bring you honor.

Margarita: Begin, then!

Lady R.: Yes, as long as you promise me that you'll listen quietly to all that I have to say. I don't believe it possible, but even if I don't please you, don't prevent me from continuing to the end of my observations, and then you'll be free to act according to them or not, as you will.

Margarita: So while you speak, if some doubt were to arise in me, you wouldn't want me to freely ask you what I need to know?

Lady R.: This you may do, as long as you lovingly listen to all I'll want to say.

Margarita: This I promise you!

Lady R.: Give me your hand.

Margarita: Here it is—now speak!

Lady R.: I seem to foresee that your husband or someone else will get here in the middle of our conversation, disrupting our plans.

Margarita: Now is not the time when anybody would come here; and as far as my husband is concerned, there's no danger [of him coming]: two months ago he went to the Ambra Valley[29] to be paid for some grains, and he hasn't been back since.

---

29. Alfano explains that this is an older name for the Ombrone River, which has its springs in the Chianti and reaches the Tyrrhenian Sea in the Maremma area of Tuscany; *La Raffaella*, 122n11.

Lady R.: What do you mean, "two months"? He leaves you alone for such long periods at a time when you're in the prime of your youth?

Margarita: My God, he's thick-headed! I can guarantee you that in the two years since I married him, he hasn't been with me four whole months, piecing together all the times we've been together.

Lady R.: Oh my, what are you telling me? What betrayal is this? Seeing that you are always at home, humble and subject, throwing away your great beauty as you foolishly do, I was convinced that at least you were enjoying yourself all the time with your husband! Though of course caresses and pleasures with a husband are only a little less dull and useless than the idle pastimes of nuns. Oh, what have you told me? What will he do in the future, if he treats you like this when you've just arrived in his home, still a bride, practically? Right now I feel the deepest compassion for you that one can ever believe: I see crystal clear, as if in a mirror, that as you get to the age when you understand a bit, you will regret this and you will despair and be angry, so much so that this despair will send you to live in the devil's mouth. Poor girl, how can you live like this?

Margarita: I confess to you that I do find it difficult, but I have always followed the advice that my mother gave me shortly before dying.

Lady R.: Oh, God, how many mistakes occur because one has little familiarity with things! Had she lived another twenty-five or thirty years, she would have realized her mistake and your great harm. Tell me, how loving is your husband toward you in the little time he spends in Siena?

Margarita: Everything I do is well done, and he never scolds me for anything. He is like this because his nature forces him to act this way, that is, because of his ineptitude, not because he loves me very much!

Lady R.: I believe you. If he loved you, he wouldn't stay away from you for so long, indeed he would never leave you, especially because he's very rich, and he doesn't need to roam the Ambra Valley.

Margarita: It is true he's rich, and I could take advantage of everything should I decide to do so, but as I said, I have forced myself not to care, against my very will.

Lady R.: You're such a simpleton because of this! Your behavior would be crazy if Lady Lorena or your sister-in-law or a thousand ugly women acted that way—but you, by God, you who are hailed as the highest beauty existing in Siena today!

Margarita: Now let's go back to our conversation, Lady Raffaella; I am sure that God himself sent you to me today.

Lady R.: You can be quite sure that God inspired me to come here, so that such beauty and grace as yours would not get old while you stay at home busying yourself sewing and tailoring. First, daughter, you have to pay attention that you pursue those pleasures that we will decide are fit for you with such intelligence and art that your husband would rather allow them than feel the least suspicious of you. You'll do this easily, if you're careful to avoid beginning the life that we'll talk about passionately, all of a sudden—especially given that you've lived away from such things, humbly alongside the cats by the fire. Such an abrupt change would lead anyone to suspect. In addition, it is necessary for you to be careful if you chanced [to be] where people talk about fun and parties in the presence of your husband or others. You should not show your eagerness and your deep desire for them; in fact, you should keep everything inside and talk about them as you'd talk about things that aren't important to you. Similarly, [when] coming home from a party and banquet, be careful not to be as if anxious, with your soul agitated, because the walls themselves would notice that your mind is capricious, let alone other people. If you follow this advice and other [ideas] that you will figure out for yourself, you will be able to partake of those enjoyments and at the same time have peace at home with your husband. If one can have that, it's something that one should prize highly.

Margarita: This won't take me much effort, because, as I told you, my husband has the best disposition that you ever saw. If I were to decide to make him believe that fireflies are lamps, he would believe it. Nor do I have anyone else at home that I should be careful about, such as mothers- and fathers-in-law, brothers- and sisters-in-law, nephews and nieces, and others that are ill-disposed.

Lady R.: You are quite lucky. I know many women in this land whose husbands are so angry, annoyed, and upset that they keep criticizing and insulting them, turning their homes into the devil's. On the contrary, those stupid men could be in paradise if they treated their wives right! In the end, the crazier and more upset they are, the more their anger and madness falls back on themselves, because despite them their wives still do what they want, and with greater harm to them. Still, if (as I told you) a young woman could do what she wanted, spare the quiet of her home, and get along with her husband at the same time, this would be very useful, especially as far as her necessary expenses are concerned.

Margarita: As far as my husband is concerned, things couldn't be better for me. Still, tell me, please, what these expenses that you mentioned are.

Lady R.: First, it is highly enjoyable and fitting for young men and women to dress richly, fashionably, and following good judgment. This is especially true for women: they are soft and delicate, and they alone were created by God to better shoulder the miseries of this world. I have heard a young member of the Intronati nicknamed the Stunned One,[30] who has shown much affection toward women, assert many times that dressing neatly seems to become their whiteness and delicacy more than men's roughness and that indefinable thickness they have.

Margarita: Lady Raffaella, I would like for you to be a little more specific in relation to clothes.

Lady R.: I would like a young woman to change her dress every few days. She should never pass on a flattering dress style, and if she had good enough taste to find new and pretty styles, then it would be very fitting for her to choose some; but if she had not, then she should follow the lead of other women known to have the best taste.

Margarita: What characteristics should a style have in order to be called good?

Lady R.: It has to be rich and well-made.

Margarita: What does it mean that it has to be rich?

---

30. This is clearly a reference to Alessandro Piccolomini himself, who was a member and an official of Siena's Accademia degli intronati (Academy of the Bewildered Men) with the name of "Stordito," i.e., the Stunned One; see the introduction to this piece.

Lady R.: Margarita, do you want me to discuss our topics today with reference to you and you alone, or to many other women, according to their many qualities?

Margarita: What do you think is best?

Lady R.: My first goal for today is to show you things for you individually. Nevertheless I think it necessary to consider many different women at the same time, for reasons you will figure out yourself.

Margarita: Let's do it that way.

Lady R.: I say, then, that the richness of clothes very much consists in checking diligently that everyday cloth, heavy cloth, light woolen cloth, and other refined cloths be of the finest quality, the best that one can find. Wearing rough cloth, as for example Lady Lorenza does (who made a skirt of cloth a little less rough than what monks use), is called "poor style."

Margarita: What do you mean, "a little less rough"? It is monk-like, very monk-like!

Lady R.: Even worse! Beyond that, clothes have to be opulent and made with plenty of cloth, but not to the point that a person be made uncomfortable by them. Such fullness matters a lot, as we never see anything worse than some of our noblewomen going around Siena wearing some skimpy dresses made with less than sixteen *braccia* of cloth, with short cloaks that cover their butts by no more than a hand. They put one side around their necks and they hold a part of it in one hand to half-cover their faces, looking like they are wearing a mask in the street; with the other hand they lift the backside of their dress so that it won't get worn out by dragging on the ground. They go in the street with such haste, with such noise made by their slippers, that it seems as if the devil is between their legs. Do they lift their dress like that to show a dainty foot with a little of their thin leg? On the contrary, they show wide feet that are unkempt, and slippers that have lost all varnish because they are very old! I will tell you about these when we get to this detail.

Margarita: It seems to me that you perfectly described my cousin, though she told me she goes around like that not out of stupidity, but out of gallantry.

Lady R.: They all say so; they transform their lack of money into refinement, showing that they do so on purpose and as if they did it after giving careful thought to something that they do out of utter lack of money, poverty, or ineptitude. I also want to add that these full dresses that I've been telling you about should have many ribbons, cuts large and small, embroideries, and other similar things; other times they should all be plain, because such variety of clothing shows great wealth and is to be commended.

Margarita: I would think it to be a sign of an inconstant brain and of lacking steadfastness, which is not a small blemish.

Lady R.: This would be true if a young woman showed such instability in other actions; but if her other actions show her to be wise and prudent, the variety in clothing that I am talking about would be to her great advantage.

Margarita: You've made me think of Bianchetta's strangest behavior—it is the oddest I've ever seen! Among other fantastic things, this extravagant woman gets dressed six times a day to go to a get-together, and six times she changes her mind and strips herself and doesn't go.

Lady R.:   I heard about this! Now, Margarita, what above all shows richness in one's clothing is always having new dresses and never wearing the same one again, I don't want to say for many weeks, but for many months.

Margarita: Lady Raffaella, such things seem fit for ladies and princesses rather than for an individual gentlewoman as I am! I can call myself very rich compared to most other women in Siena, but I cannot afford as great an expense as you indicate; so, what would other women do, who are far poorer than me?

Lady R.:   Wearing the finest brocades and embroidering their dresses with pearls, diamonds, rubies, and other similar things would be fit for a princess or a great lady. Instead, because I understand this, I have spoken of nothing more expensive than good cloth.

Margarita: That's true, but the embroideries, ribbons, and cuts that you mention cost a lot of money!

Lady R.:   Well, I mean according to what one can do, in all I say; those who cannot do everything should do as much as they can and make an effort to do a bit more.

Margarita: Continue, then.

[Lady Raffaella subsequently addresses the topics of skin care, public behavior, keeping house (including how to keep one's husband happy), and choosing a lover. Margarita is both eager to learn and shocked at the suggestion that she take a lover and enjoy him, but she is rather easily convinced. The dialogue ends with Raffaella leaving Margarita's home on her way to tell the latter's would-be lover, Aspasio, that she will follow Raffaella's advice and yield to his wishes.]

PART 2

CASES

5.

Torquato Tasso: Discourse on Feminine and Womanly Virtue

LORI J. ULTSCH

The Discourse on Feminine and Womanly Virtue (1582)[1] by Torquato Tasso (1544–1595) contains an authoritative voice in the Italian
querelle des femmes that helped give rise to the chapters added to the
1601 edition of Lucrezia Marinella's *The Nobility and Excellence of
Women*.[2] In the esteemed company of other misogynistic texts written by Giovanni Boccaccio, Ercole Tasso, and Sperone Speroni, Tasso's
treatise becomes in Marinella's brief exegesis a reviled object of feminist deconstruction and refutation. Marinella specifically takes issue
with three points that Tasso, following Aristotle, argues in the *Discourse*: women are similar to the left hand in their weakness, idleness,
and imperfection; the intellectual or speculative virtues are denied to
women by nature; and the virtue of strength is essentially different in
men and women. Marinella also rejects the premise of Tasso's entire
argument, i.e., that the very distinction between feminine and womanly (or ladylike) virtue is a novel idea. She summarily dismisses this
distinction with the impatience for preposterous ideas that often characterizes her tone in *The Nobility*: "As for Tasso's new distinction between females and ladies—I say new because Boccaccio, Petrarch, and
others have given the name lady to every one of our sex—I will spare
myself the effort of demolishing and reviling it."[3] Her astute observation underscores the gulf that separates biological sex and socially
constructed gender in sixteenth-century discussions of "the woman
question."

Marinella's mordant dismissal notwithstanding, Tasso, writing
during imprisonment in the hospital of Sant'Anna[4] (1579–1586) and

---

1. *Discorso della virtù feminile e donnesca* (Venice: Giunti, 1582).

2. See Marinella, *The Nobility and Excellence of Women*, 119–45.

3. Ibid., 141.

4. Beginning in the late 1570s, Tasso's irrational behavior indicated mental instability, a form
of paranoia that induced the poet to believe himself persecuted by members of the Este

115

effectively exiled from court society, demonstrates in his *Discourse* a mastery of the courtier's exercise par excellence of weaving together citations from numerous authorities in order to pay homage to his patron's family. Duchess Eleonora of the House of Gonzaga in Mantua becomes the female dedicatee of Tasso's morally didactic survey of philosophical thought on the virtues that most befit women. The elegant *Discourse*, however, is a prime period example of how the ostensible praise of virtuous women is in reality an insidious rehearsal of received notions of female inferiority handed down from Aristotle.[5] The argumentation of the *Discourse*, girded by an authoritative

---

court and household. Tasso's actions would ultimately result in his being committed to the hospital of Sant'Anna for seven years. In 1577 Duke Alfonso relegated Tasso to the convent of San Francesco after the poet stabbed a household servant he suspected of spying on him. After leaving the convent and first seeking refuge with his sister in Sorrento and then patronage in various courts in Mantua, Padua, Urbino, and Turin, Tasso returned to Ferrara. Following a perceived slight upon Alfonso's part during the duke's marriage festivities with Margherita d'Austria in 1579, Tasso publicly and vehemently insulted his patron; the duke then pronounced Tasso insane and issued the order to commit him to the hospital of Sant'Anna. Tasso would remain there with his books, notes, and occasional visitors until 1586, when Vincenzo Gonzaga intervened on his behalf to secure his release.

5. Maintaining that the male is natural perfection, Aristotle further postulates that the "the female is, as it were, a mutilated male, and the menstrual fluids are semen, only not pure; for there is only one thing they have not in them, the principle of soul" [*On the Generation of Animals*, in *The Complete Works* (Princeton, NJ: Princeton University Press, 1984), 1:1144]. The binary oppositions that Aristotle delineates between male and female (hot versus cold, dry versus moist, strong versus weak, rational versus irrational, right versus left, etc.) argue the essential superiority of man over woman physiologically and morally. The generation of a female fetus in the womb is cast as a failure of the male, the superior sex that can "concoct form and discharge a semen carrying with it the principle of form" (*On the Generation of Animals*, 1:1184). Generation of a female is the result of the male (or first) principle not prevailing during conception: "When the first principle does not bear sway and cannot concoct the nourishment through lack of heat nor bring it into its proper form, but is defeated in this respect, then must the material change into its opposite" (*On the Generation of Animals*, 1:1185). Aristotle also maintains that "in all genera in which the distinction of male and female is found, nature makes a similar differentiation in the characteristics of the two sexes.... The female is softer in disposition, is more mischievous, less simple, more impulsive, and more attentive to the nurture of the young; the male, on the other hand, is more spirited, more savage, more simple and less cunning. The traces of these characteristics are more or less visible everywhere, but they are especially visible where character is the more developed, and most of all in man. The fact is, the nature of man is the most rounded off and complete, and consequently in man the qualities above referred to are found most clearly.

polyphony of classical and Italian citations (the words of "excellent men" such as Aristotle, Thucydides, Xenophon, Dante, and Petrarch), demonstrates to the reader how the Aristotelian notion of an essential deficiency in the female soul results in the "natural" and "reasonable" law of subjection of women to men (within both the marriage bond and society at large) and its corollary of a necessary differentiation of roles, functions, and duties along gender lines. A typical man of his times, Tasso is oblivious to the irony hidden in the premises of the "courtly compliment" he pays the duchess: he invites Eleonora to gaze, in the virtual mirror of his *Discourse,* upon her spiritual beauty and virtuous nature—in a text where the very point of departure is the proven imperfection of the female soul!

Tasso rejects Plato's argument in the *Republic* that men and women are endowed with the same virtues and faculties and are therefore equally capable of contributing to the formation of an ideal society.[6] Tasso reasons in Aristotelian dualities and encodes gender difference in his every utterance: man is right, finite, rational, strong, hot, dry; woman is left, infinite, irrational, submissive, cold, moist.[7] Women

---

Hence woman is more compassionate than man, more easily moved to tears, at the same time is more jealous, more querulous, more apt to scold and to strike. She is, furthermore, more prone to despondency and less hopeful than the man, more void of shame, more false of speech, more deceptive, and of more retentive memory. She is also more wakeful, more shrinking, more difficult to rouse to action, and requires a smaller quantity of nutriment" (*The History of Animals,* in *The Complete Works,* 1:948–49).

6. Socrates explains, "If it seems that the male and female sex have different qualities making them good at different arts or forms of work, then we will say they are to do different things. But if they seem different only in this: that the female produces and the male begets, we will say that no argument has been made out, and we will go on giving our guardians and these women the same work to do," [Plato, *Republic,* ed. and trans. I. A. Richards (Cambridge: Cambridge University, 1966), 89].

7. "There are three degrees of composition; and of these the first in order, as all will allow, is composition out of what some call the elements, such as earth, air, water, fire. Perhaps, however, it would be more accurate to say composition out of the elementary forces.... For wet and dry, hot and cold, form the material of all composite bodies; and all other differences are secondary to these" (*On the Parts of Animals,* in *The Complete Works,* 1:1005). For example, when discussing the opposition between right and left, Aristotle observes that "the right is naturally better than the left, being separate from it, and so in man the right is more especially the right, more dexterous that is, than in other animals" (*On the Progression of Animals,* in *The Complete Works,* 1:1099).

do not exhibit any of the virtues of a contemplative mind because they are born without the powers of speculation that reside in the rational part of the soul; hence, they are naturally defective in comparison with men. Accordingly, virtuous women in Tasso's gendered hierarchy of virtues are weak and submissive. They require guidance from prudent men who expect them to be chaste, silent, obedient, and thrifty. A virtuous woman's activities should be confined to the home, because her virtues should benefit only the sphere of existence and influence that directly impinges upon household management (specifically the preservation of what the man acquires) and child rearing. Ultimately, if we take these rules of conduct to their logical conclusion, the truly virtuous woman is the woman who is completely silenced and erased from society. Her virtuous reputation or fame is contained within the walls of her home, and only through an act of condemnable immodesty could word of it spread. To counter this specific point, Marinella boldly protests: "I ... say that the fame of women's achievements in the sciences and in virtuous actions should resound, not only in their own cities but in diverse and varying provinces."[8]

After laying the theoretical groundwork for a gendered moral code predicated upon the physical and intellectual superiority of the male of the human species, Tasso then abandons the potentially pejorative *femina* midway through the *Discourse* to philosophize instead solely upon the virtue of the *donna*. In this second movement of the *Discourse* Tasso backtracks, as it were, to subdivide women into two class-based groups and construct an elitist hierarchy that dictates appropriate virtues for each. Using Dante as his authority and critical divide, he makes a substantive distinction between feminine (*feminile*) and womanly (*donnesca*) virtue. The etymological distinction between *femina* (L. *femina, -ae*) and *donna* (L. *domina, -ae,* f. of *dominus, -i*) underscores how class difference affects women's biological destiny and sphere of influence. The *femina* (related to *foetus*)[9] is relegated to the home and the duties of wife and mother, while the *donna* (as in Castiglione's *donna di corte*) exercises her virtues in the vastly different social context of the court.

---

8. Marinella, *The Nobility and Excellence of Women,* 140–41.

9. For a discussion of these etymologies and their classical sources, see Marinella's chapter titled "On the Nobility of the Names Given to the Female Sex," ibid., 45–51.

As we have seen, Marinella did not agree that Tasso's distinction between feminine and womanly (or "ladylike," understood as the feminine manifestation of "lordly") virtue was a novelty, because canonical representations of praiseworthy women in Italian literary tradition had always emphasized a transliteration of the biological category of woman into the concept of "lady," with all the social graces implied therein. Tasso's distinction is useful, however, in that it illustrates how the rhetorical *topos* of praising exceptional women (the *donna*) in effect reinforces the notion of the weakness and unexceptionality of women as a biological category (the *femina*). The common woman or *femina* is excluded from greatness and from traditionally masculine virtues such as strength and wisdom. The traditionally feminine virtues of patience, obedience, thriftiness, chastity, and silence still obtain for her, while those "womanly" virtues that approach the heroic and virile are possible only for the ruling class, where women in positions of authority are called upon to act in a more dominant (*donnesca*) fashion.

According to this class distinction, then, there are women who, by acting in a masculinized, *almost* heroic manner, distinguish themselves as exceptions to traditional expectations regarding femininity. These women belong to a category that transcends femininity, and they are therefore celebrated for their virile virtues. Like men, they can be prudent, strong, wise, and even amorous (within reason). Tasso, we note, defends Dido, although he does admit that Cleopatra would have been a greater woman had she not been so lusty (just as Marc Anthony, who appears later in the treatise, would have been a greater man for the same reason). Thus, in their status as quasi-heroic exceptions to feminine virtue, the pantheon of great women hailed in Tasso's final pages reinforces yet further the Aristotelian paradigm of female inferiority. Challenging the assumptions of the misogynistic tradition that we find embedded in Tasso's *Discourse*, Marinella counters that in *The Nobility and Excellence of Women* she has "produced a thousand examples of strong women, and not just of queens."[10]

Among the many early modern texts that articulate the *querelle des femmes* are discourses on marriage and family, discourses on household management, and manuals for public and private conduct.

10. Ibid., 139.

Tasso's text is a fusion of these genres that approaches the debate by marrying the subject matter with an encomiastic gift addressed specifically to the duke's wife and, by extension, to the House of Gonzaga. A male member of the family will in fact secure Tasso's release from Sant'Anna, but beyond the immediate scope of cultivating allies and securing a potential means of liberation, the courtier's exercise consciously engages with two distinct humanist traditions. In the Ignatian contemplation of the self, in which he invites the duchess to gaze upon a "virtual mirror" of her soul and see reflected there the virtues most befitting a woman of her rank, the *Discourse* dialogues with the humanist models of the *institutio* and the *exemplum*, speaking to the formation of the individual—in this case, the female individual—in private and public life.

Tasso's references to specific discursive instances of *institutio* and *exemplum* (i.e., Xenophon's *Ciropaedia* and Plutarch's *De claris mulieribus*) underscore the fact that the *Discourse* locates itself within a body of classical and humanist literature on the definition and management of female virtue, or, as Tasso states, alongside "the words of excellent men on the subject." In the first part of the *Discourse*, the neo-Aristotelian explicitly takes issue with what he interprets as the counter-discourse on the topic, represented by Plutarch's lives of illustrious women and Plato's treatise on the utopian society. Tasso argues, counter to the positions expressed in *De claris mulieribus* and *The Republic*, that a woman's fame should indeed remain within the walls of her home and that women, essentially different from and inferior to men, are not capable of performing the same actions or possessing the same virtues as men. Here Tasso's construction of the virtuous mother of a household reiterates Aristotelian thought on the gender-differentiated roles of conservation and acquisition: in the context of household management, the wife should preserve in the home that which the husband acquires from without. Tasso's moral conservatism restates the female injunction to silence and closely resonates with received notions of the specifically female virtues of modesty, thriftiness, obedience, and chastity that obtain for the mother of a private household.

Although Tasso limits the scope of his courtly exercise with the affirmation that his work does not seek to exhaustively delineate the perfect model of a queen, it is precisely a class-based distinction that frees Tasso from the shackles, as it were, of praising the "feminine virtue" of common women and provides the transition into the second part of the *Discourse*, where the author considers "womanly virtue" or the exceptional virtue represented by classical exempla and by a secular set of exempla formed by women writers[11] and women from ruling families. In this part of the *Discourse* Tasso engages obliquely with an entire tradition of texts in the sixteenth-century Italian *querelle des femmes*, typified by early texts such as Flavio Galeazzo Capra's *Della eccellenza e dignità delle donne* (1525)[12] and Baldessare Castiglione's *Il libro del cortegiano* (1528). In fact, the virtues that Tasso identifies as womanly rather than feminine resonate closely with those outlined in book 3 of *The Book of the Courtier*, where the perlocutionary force of the debate performs a Pygmalion-like *institutio* of the ideal court lady. In a social climate fueled by an intense preoccupation with the definition and codification of myriad forms of acceptable interaction or *conversazione*,[13] the court lady—like the courtier and Tasso's exempla of womanly virtue in the second half of the *Discourse*—possesses grace, learning, and *sprezzatura* along with traditionally male-gendered virtues of magnanimity, prudence, and fortitude.[14] It is of course this discrimi-

11. The only early modern woman writer that Tasso specifies is Vittoria Colonna.

12. Capra's work during the period will quickly be eclipsed by Castiglione's but is in itself an interesting work that, in short chapters, provides various classical, Christian, and secular exempla arguing women's moral excellence as a privileged gift from nature that they cultivate and refine through their actions. Capra takes as his starting point for refutation the negative views on women expressed by Boccaccio in *Filocolo* and *Il corbaccio*. In *L'anthropologia* (1533) Capra will further contribute to the debate with one chapter in praise of men and another critical of both sexes.

13. For an indication of period interest in the various forms of conversation, see, for example, Stefano Guazzo's *La civil conversazione* (1574), wherein the third book investigates "the domestic conversation between husband and wife" and addresses a variety of topics pertinent to the *querelle*, such as the question of whether marriage is advisable, the virtues and vices of women, the just subordination of wife to husband, the rearing of children, and love between husband and wife.

14. "When she is talking or laughing, playing or jesting, no matter what, she will always be most graceful, and she will converse in a suitable manner with whomever she happens to meet, making use of agreeable witticisms and jokes. And although continence, magnanimity, temperance, fortitude of spirit, prudence, and the other virtues may not appear to be

natory rhetoric of exemplarity with which Marinella will take issue in her response to the *Discourse*, when she notes that Tasso ascribes to the common woman—i.e., the representative of feminine virtue— only one of the four cardinal virtues: temperance.[15] To reserve the cardinal virtues of prudence,[16] fortitude,[17] and justice to only heroic exemplars of womanly virtue, Marinella objects, is a faulty argument solely in service of Tasso's contention that "women are weak and imperfect in comparison to men, similar, in fact, to the left hand."[18] The exempla that Marinella provides in the chapter of *The Nobility*

relevant in her social encounters with others, I want her to be adorned with these as well, not so much for the sake of good company, though they play a part in this too, as to make her truly virtuous, and so that her virtues, shining through everything she does, may make her worthy of honour." Castiglione, *The Book of the Courtier*, 216.

15. Given Tasso's exemplification of the orthodox exegencies of the Counter-Reformation and his redefinition of epic discourse, it is surprising that the author does not enter into a discussion of the theological virtues in the *Discourse*. While other texts, such as the *Discorsi del poema eroico*, the *Apologia in difesa della Gerusalemme liberata*, and the ultimate revision of the *Liberata* into the *Conquistata* speak volumes about the problematic activity of writing as a post-Tridentine classical humanist, here Tasso simply closes with the remark that he will in another place broach the subject of the specific Christian virtues that most befit a woman. With this closing allusion to a further contemplation and future writing on the topics of faith, hope, and charity, Tasso distances his *Discourse* from its immediate post-Tridentine context. This unexplained disengagement can perhaps be read as coming full circle to once again emphasize that the limited scope of his current project is a humanistic survey of classical philosophers' pronouncements on feminine virtue.

16. "I also deny that a woman's prudence is obedient to that of her husband, because Aristotle considers a person to be prudent who is able to advise and recommend what is best in future matters. Who will deny that there have been many very prudent women in both military and peacetime administration? Let them read my section on prudent women. And who will deny that women demonstrate great prudence in managing their households? Nobody, in my opinion. Moreover, this management belongs solely to woman, and not to her husband, as we read in [Aristotle's] *Economics*." Marinella, *The Nobility and Excellence of Women*, 140.

17. "When he adds, incited by Aristotle's authority, that women have no need of fortitude, I say that we do not accept Aristotle's opinions as true, having produced a thousand examples of strong women, and not just of queens, in our book. Nor are these examples merely of obedient fortitude—something that belongs to servants—but of lordly fortitude, because in fortitude, as defined by Aristotle, there is a constancy of spirit in the face of things that are frightening, provided they lead to an honest and praiseworthy end." Ibid., 139–40.

18. Ibid., 139.

and Excellence of Women titled "Of Women's Noble Actions and Virtues, Which Greatly Surpass Men's" constitute a counter-discourse that posits a genealogy of learned, temperate, strong, and prudent women.

Discourse on Feminine and Womanly Virtue[19]

SIGNOR TORQUATO TASSO

Dedicated to the Most Serene Signora, the Duchess of Mantua

My Most Serene Lady,[20] often beautiful women gaze with delight upon a statue or a painting in which some semblance to them is expressed, and young women in particular take great pleasure in contemplating themselves before a mirror and seeing their very likeness therein reflected. But Your Highness—although of great personal beauty and not yet so aged that you could not be pleasing to another or derive great pleasure from your own appearance—you nevertheless do not desire a self-portrait or mirror as much as you desire to see yourself reborn and rejuvenated in your most beautiful children, among whom the Prince[21] is such [a fine young man] that rightly one can cite in his regard the Horatian verse:

> Loved by all the boys, now
> Loved by all the girls, soon[22]

---

19. The recent critical edition of the *Discorso* edited by Maria Luisa Doglio (Palermo: Sellerio, 1997) has proven invaluable to me in its identification of the many noblewomen that Tasso lists at the end of his work.

20. In 1561 Eleanor of Austria (1534–1594) married Guglielmo Gonzaga, third Duke of Mantua, who had succeeded his brother Francesco III in 1540. The House of Gonzaga was one of the most powerful Renaissance families in Europe and ruled Mantua from 1328 to 1707. Its members distinguished themselves in politics and patronage, and they further strengthened their political position through strategic marriage alliances with other ruling families of Europe. In 1586 the Gonzagas will intervene on Tasso's behalf for his release from the hospital of Sant'Anna; after some time in Mantua, Tasso will begin traveling throughout the courts of Italy again and spend the last years of his life in Naples and Rome.

21. Vincenzo Gonzaga (1562–1612) will become the fourth Duke of Mantua in 1587. Tasso's dialogue *Il messaggiero* (1582) is dedicated to Vincenzo. The poet will also write an encomiastic poem in *ottave*, *La genealogia della serenissima Casa Gonzaga*.

22. *Quo nunc calet omnis iuventus, mox virgines tepebunt.* The reference is to the beauty of Lycidas in ode I.4.19–20, where the original reads "quo calet iuventus / nunc omnis et mox virgines tepebunt." This translation is taken from *The Essential Horace: Odes, Epodes, Satires, and Epistles*, trans. Burton Raffel (San Francisco: North Point Press, 1983), 7.

or, rather, the Virgilian one:

Worth, that shows more winsome in a fair form.[23]

And the duchess of Ferrara[24] is so [splendid] that, even though she
has arrived in a family that has both produced and married with some
of the most beautiful ladies, she nevertheless equals in beauty not
only the four ladies[25] that presently shine in this family but also the
fame and memory of all predecessors, with whose virtue she so well
conforms that Alfonso cannot envy in any of his ancestors a happier
choice in a wife.

Since, however, Your Most Serene Highness is not solely that
outer form that converses, acts, and turns to God, the sole object of
your every act and thought, you may desire to see and perhaps are
[even] eager to contemplate in the mirror of your very soul other portraits more truly your own than even your children. And just as the
eye cannot turn its power of sight upon itself to see itself, likewise
only with difficulty does the soul understand itself and with unease
can the eyes of the intellect turn inwards upon themselves. I believe
that when Your Highness searches for a portrait or mirror of your
soul and, when rapt in the zeal of contemplation, you see the Angels
and speak with them, you are accustomed to seeing [in them] some
likeness of yourself. However, you do not see there *every* likeness of
your soul expressed, because the soul, due to the union it has with the
body, comprises many more forces through which it joins to the body.
In addition, our human nature cannot bear that the eyes of our mind
be fixed at great length upon the Sun of eternal truth, whereby it is
sometimes necessary to turn them to other things and, almost like a
crystal, restore their power of sight.

---

23. *Gratior, et pulchro veniens in corpore virtus.* The reference is to Euryalus, victor in the
games, from book 5 of *The Aeneid*, trans. H. Rushton Fairclough (Cambridge, MA: Harvard
University Press, 1978), 469.

24. Margherita di Gonzaga married Alfonso d'Este in 1579. The family or "casa" subsequently referred to is the powerful House of the Estensi.

25. The four ladies are Francesco's daughter, Marfisa d'Este, and the three sisters of Duke
Alfonso: Anna, Lucrezia and Eleonora d'Este.

I have thought, then, that if I offer to Your Highness a brief discourse on human feminine virtue or on the various opinions that excellent men[26] have had on the topic, I will offer you a virtual mirror or portrait in which you would be able to gaze upon some part of your inner beauty. I specify *some part* because my intention is not to form the complete idea of a Queen in the manner that Xenophon[27] did for a King, but rather to philosophize on the opinions of others, briefly however, as Neoptolemus[28] was wont to do, and proffer my judgment in the midst of them. Whatever this labor of mine may be, it merits my affection, requires your courtesy, and aims to please you.

It was the well-known opinion of Thucydides,[29] Most Serene Lady, that the woman who deserved the highest praise was she whose praise and fame were contained within the walls of a private home. This judgment, cited by Plutarch[30] in the brief work he wrote about illustrious women, is in that same work refuted; and both these extremely famous authors can rest their authority upon the authority of an even more esteemed author, because Aristotle[31] concurs with Thucydides while Plato[32] concurs with Plutarch. Plato maintains that

26. Tasso will argue his gendered view of virtue with citations from "excellent men" such as Aristotle (384–322 BCE) and Thucydides (460–ca. 400 BCE). He also pointedly argues against the view espoused by Plato (427–347 BCE.) in *The Republic* that women and men can contribute equally and in the same manner to the formation of a sound society.

27. Xenophon was an Athenian soldier and historian (ca. 430–350 BCE), student of Socrates, and author of the *Cyropaedia*, an eight-volume didactic account of the life of Cyrus the Great of Persia.

28. Neoptolemus was a grammarian and follower of Aristotle who lived in the third century BCE.

29. Thucydides was an Athenian historian of the Peloponnesian war.

30. The treatise to which Tasso refers is *Mulierum virtutes* by Plutarch of Chaeronia (45–125 CE), a philosopher of ethics and moral education, active in the Academy during the period known as Middle Platonism.

31. Greek philosopher (384–322 BCE), student of Plato and tutor of Alexander the Great. Tasso's references to this author draw upon a variety of sources; chief among them, however, is one of Aristotle's most well-known works on practical philosophy, the *Politics*. The *Politics* treats the state as a naturally arising entity in which citizens contribute in different ways to promote both collective and individual *eudaimonia* or happiness.

32. Greek philosopher (427–347 BCE), student of Socrates, and author of *The Republic*, a dialogue in which the philosopher portrays an ideal political community organized according to the principle of justice. In Plato's ideal republic, positions of authority are open to

a woman's virtue and a man's virtue are one and the same, and that if there is some difference between them, it is a difference introduced by custom and not by nature. In his civil works he argues that women should participate in the Republic and even fulfill military offices no less than men. [Plato] maintains that just as nature produces both hands capable of all operations, and it is custom that then imposes between them a difference between right and left, because of this it seems, the one that is continuously used becomes more practiced in its operations and is called "the right." The other that is not incited to action becomes incapable of operation; thus in a similar manner, nature produces man and woman equally fit for all civil and military offices,[33] but since man exercises himself [in these offices] and woman lives in idleness, it comes to pass that the former is almost like the right in his actions and the latter almost like the left. Plato takes this example perhaps from the teachings of the Pythagoreans,[34] who divide evil and good into two orders, putting that which is right, male, and finite in the order of good and that which is left, female, and infinite in the order of evil. Plato concludes, nevertheless, that just as the perfect body in which the left operates no less well than the right is fit for all actions, the perfect Republic can avail itself of its women no less than its men.

This was Plato's opinion. Aristotle, however, judged most differently, because he argues that the right and the left are differences constructed not only by custom, but also by nature, not only among men,[35] but also in the world at large: the right is that part from which

women because biological sex does not determine intellectual or moral capacities. One of the first topics of discussion in book 5 of *The Republic* is whether differences between men and women are essential or accidental.

33. The term *uffici* appears often throughout the *Discourse*, and I have consistently translated it as "offices" in the sense of sex-differentiated roles and/or functions.

34. The Pythagoreans were followers of Pythagoras (570?–495? BCE), a polymath and the founder of a sect in southern Italy, who ordered the world according to harmonious mathematical relations. Divisions in the Pythagorean school and its cultlike secretiveness make core doctrines difficult to identify, but systematic dualism of associated polarities, such as those reported by Tasso here, became an organizational mode that was commonly associated with their thinking.

35. Here I translate Tasso's word choice of *uomini* as "men" in order to emphasize that he does not employ the more inclusive term *umanità* ("humanity").

all movement proceeds, whereby as if it were against nature itself, one takes it as a bad omen when movement proceeds from the left:

> My left foot
> as a young man I placed into his kingdom[36]

says Petrarch. The left, however, is fit for endurance and suffering, and for this reason weighty loads are usually borne on the left shoulder. And all this difference results from bodily temperature: because nature produced man and woman with very different temperatures and complexions,[37] one can conclude that they are not equally fit for the same offices. Instead, the more robust man is disposed toward some, while the more delicate woman is disposed toward others; for this reason in the beginning of the *Politics*[38] Aristotle concludes against Plato that a man's virtue and a woman's[39] are not the same. Accordingly, a man's virtue will be strength and generosity, while a woman's will be

36. "Il manco piede / Giovinetto posi io nel costui regno." See Petrarca, *Rime*, canzone 360, "Quel antiquo mio dolce empio signore," ll.9–10.

37. The term "complexion" in this context does not mean the hue of one's skin but rather the combination of the hot, cold, moist, and dry qualities believed to determine the quality of the body, according to the sixteenth-century persistence of Aristotelian thought on physiology.

38. "For the slave has no deliberative faculty at all; the woman has, but it is without authority, and the child has, but it is immature. So it must necessarily be supposed to be with the excellences of character also; all should partake of them, but only in such manner and degree as is required by each for the fulfillment of his function. Hence the ruler ought to have excellence of character in perfection, for his function, taken absolutely, demands a master artificer, and reason is such an artificer; the subjects on the other hand, require only that measure of excellence which is proper to each of them. Clearly, then, excellence of character belongs to all of them; but the temperance of a man and of a woman, or the courage and justice of a man and of a woman, are not, as Socrates maintained, the same; the courage of a man is shown in commanding, of a woman in obeying." *Politics*, in *The Complete Works*, 2:1999.

39. The opposition constructed in the original Italian is between *uomo* and *femina*, not *uomo* and *donna*.

chastity. And as Gorgias[40] said, just as silence is a woman's virtue, eloquence is a man's,[41] whence Petrarch gracefully said:

In silence words skillful and wise.[42]

Thriftiness is also a feminine virtue. One could ask, however, how it comes to pass that Aristotle in his moral works—where he speaks most exquisitely of virtues—makes no distinction between masculine and feminine virtues, while in his political works—where considering virtue is less appropriate—he makes the distinction. To this [question] one can respond that in the moral works Aristotle considers virtues universally, i.e., not restricted or applied to any one individual. For this [reason], there was no need to make a distinction between civil and feminine virtue. Moreover, the object of the moral works is the happiness of mankind, while the object of the political works is the happiness of cities. A notion of civil virtue (here I mean virtue inasmuch as it is useful to the city) must, however, precede any treatment of civil happiness. Because it often comes to pass that the city has less need of virtue in one citizen and more in another, in servants (who are part of the city) no virtue or very little virtue—only as much as is necessary to obey and execute others' orders—is required. But in women, who are [also] part of the city, some virtue is still required, although not precisely the same as that which is required in men. Thus Aristotle can justly rebuke the Lacedaemonian citizenry[43]

40. Gorgias (ca. 483–ca. 376 BCE) was a celebrated rhetorician from Leontini in Sicily and a prominent figure in the sophistic movement in Athens. His surviving works, such as the *Defense of Helen*, attest to an elegant rhetorical style.

41. This reference to Gorgias is also from Aristotle: "All classes must be deemed to have their special attributes; as the poet says of women, 'Silence is a woman's glory,' but this is not equally the glory of man." *Politics*, in *The Complete Works*, 2:2000.

42. "In silenzio parole accorte, e saggie." See Petrarca, *Rime*, canzone 105, "Mai non vo' più cantar com'io soleva," l.61.

43. Lacedaemon was the area of ancient Greece comprising the city of Sparta and its surroundings. Aristotle characterizes the powerful status of Lacedaemonian (or Spartan) women as contrary to the ideal of a well-ordered state: "This license of the Lacedaemonian women existed from the earliest times, and was only what might be expected. For, during the wars of the Lacedaemonians, first against the Argives, and afterwards against the Arcadians and Messenians, the men were long away from home, and, on the return of peace, they

as an example of a citizenry that, bereft of feminine shame and chastity, was bereft of half of its civil virtue. Most appropriately, therefore, not only nature, but also custom and legislators introduced a distinction between [male and female] virtues. And since the city requires much differentiation in its offices, different offices could not be best executed by the same virtue.

What has been said with regard to the governance of cities [also pertains to] the governance of the family or of the household, however we would like to call it. Because the household comprises acquisition and conservation, a distinction between its offices has been rightly instituted: the office of acquiring is assigned to the man and the office of conserving is assigned to the woman. Man engages in battle to acquire; he plies himself in both agriculture and trade; he exerts himself in the city, and thereby he needs many virtues for such undertakings; the woman, however, conserves that which has been acquired and therefore she needs other virtues that are different from the man's.[44] Thus, her virtue is employed within the household, just as the man's virtue is displayed outside it. But if feminine virtue is

---

gave themselves into the legislator's hand, already prepared by the discipline of a soldier's life (in which there are many elements of excellence), to receive his enactments. But, when Lycurgus, as tradition says, wanted to bring the women under his laws, they resisted, and he gave up the attempt. These then are the causes of what then happened, and this defect in the constitution is clearly to be attributed to them. We are not, however, considering what is or is not to be excused, but what is right or wrong, and the disorder of women, as I have already said, not only gives an air of indecorum to the constitution considered in itself, but tends in a measure to foster avarice." *Politics*, in *The Complete Works*, 2:2014.

44. Men and women "are distinguished in that the powers which they possess are not applicable to purposes in all cases identical, but in some respects their functions are opposed to one another though they all tend to the same end. For nature has made the one sex stronger, the other weaker, that the latter through fear may be the more cautious, while the former by its courage is better able to ward off attacks; and that the one may acquire possessions outside the house, the other preserve those within. In the performance of work, she made one sex able to lead a sedentary life and not strong enough to endure exposure, the other less adapted for quiet pursuits but well constituted for outdoor activities; and in relation to offspring she has made both share in the procreation of children, but each render its peculiar service towards them, the woman by nurturing, the man by educating them." *Politics*, in *The Complete Works*, 2:2131.

contained within the household, it seems that feminine fame[45] must [likewise] be contained within the household. If [word of a] woman's fame spreads, it can spread only because of a flaw in the woman herself or because of some virtue that is not appropriate for her [sex].

Rightly so, therefore, it seems that Thucydides pronounced that famous judgment that was unjustly contested[46] by Plutarch: a fame for chastity, which befits a woman more than any other, cannot spread greatly if the virtue of chastity from which that fame principally derives loves seclusion and private, solitary spaces and flees from theaters, parties, and public performances. And if this fame spreads, it cannot do so intact and clean either to posterity or to nations afar. But whence does it arise that the licentious woman is ill-reputed and the licentious man is not? Perhaps for the same reason that timidity, which is censured in a man, is not shameful in a woman: because man, just as woman, is honored and dishonored according to the vices and virtues which befit him and not according to the others—or at least not as much as one should absolutely attribute the label of honored or dishonored to the individuals. Therefore, since strength is a virtue that befits a man, for strength he is honored, and the ancients erected statues to commemorate strength more than any other virtue. In a like manner, by comparison, man is dishonored for cowardliness. Similarly, woman is honored for chastity and dishonored for licentiousness because the latter is the vice of women and the former the virtue of women.

[In a brief excised passage Tasso discusses Aristotle's opinion that intemperance is a vice worse than timidity. He concedes that this may be true in an ethical context, but he stipulates that in a political context, where men are called upon to expose themselves to danger and exhibit strength, timidity is more deserving of censure.]

45. The term "fame" here should be understood throughout as a chaste reputation, the only fame befitting a wife or mother in a private household.

46. The term *difesa* in the original implies the action of a defense against or contestation of the judgment, because Tasso makes it clear that Plutarch's views follow those of Plato and contrast with those of Thucydides and Aristotle. Tasso makes the same point earlier in the *Discourse* when he specifies that Thucydides's contention that a woman's fame should remain within her own home was refuted by Plutarch. In that passage Tasso employs the term *rifiutata*.

We arrive therefore at this conclusion: man should be dishonored by cowardliness and woman by licentiousness because the
former is the vice of men and the latter the vice of women. I do not
deny, however, that strength is also a feminine virtue. Rather than absolute strength, however, hers is the strength of one who obeys, as
Aristotle states.[47] Nevertheless, many of those deeds that are strong
deeds among women would not be strong deeds among men. And by
the same token, many deeds among women that would be esteemed
temperate deeds cannot in the least be attributed to temperance[48]
among men.

But which order of virtue is more appropriate for man? And
which for woman? One can instruct more universally, which Aristotle
does not do, that virtues are either categorized as affective or intellectual.[49] Among the virtues categorized as affective, however, one order
is housed in the concupiscent force, which is the force that has good
as its object. Temperance, of which chastity is a part, is in this order.
The other order is housed in the irascible force, which has good as
its object even though it is difficult [to attain]. Of these two orders,
the one that moderates the emotions of concupiscence befits women,
while the other that customarily tempers anger and the emotions that
accompany anger seems more appropriate for men. It seems, however,
that woman should partake very little of those other virtues that are
categorized as intellectual, because the qualities of a speculative intellect do not befit her. In addition, woman barely partakes of prudence
and the other qualities that are part of the practical intellect because
prudence, which is precisely the virtue that commands all others and
is their touchstone, in a woman is subject to the prudence of a man
and should exist only in a quantity sufficient to obey virile prudence.

47. See note 38 above.

48. The negative *intemperanza*, reported in the original, is illogical.

49. Here Tasso seems to offer a subtle distinction regarding Aristotle's tripartite division
of the soul and the respective virtues appropriate to the rational, passionate, and appetitive
parts. Tasso's two categories of intellectual and affective would thus correspond to the first
two parts, and his further distinction between the concupiscent and irascible forces would
be a subdivision of the appetitive part; *On Virtues and Vices*, in *The Complete Works*, 2:1982.
Tasso suggests that these orders of the soul predispose men to be more prone to the appetitive vice of anger and women more susceptible to the appetitive vice of lust.

... Here also [i.e., among the virtues of the intellect] there are other virtues of which woman is bereft, and in this order some list justice and clemency (which is part of justice that in turn contains equity). We shall say therefore that the virtues that more than any others least befit a woman are those that are categorized in the intellectual part that knows; and among the other three[50] orders less befitting are the two that are categorized as intellectual and irascible appetites; and more befitting her is the order that is housed in the concupiscent appetite. But since even the virtues of this order are many, most appropriate for her is the virtue of temperance, of which chastity is a part.

And this distinction of appropriate, more appropriate, and most appropriate should not seem new or at all unknown since it is accepted as one of the first principles of logic. If I recollect well, one calls most appropriate that which always befits all animals of a species and only them; accordingly, chastity does[51] seem most appropriate for a woman since it in no way befits a man. And at this point I hope that philosophizing about women's civic virtue has done me some good. If in the course of my philosophizing I have more closely followed Peripatetic rather than Platonic opinion, I have followed as a master not so much authority as reason. And if one can still err with the guidance of reason, errancy of such a manner is better than following a straight path guided by authority.

But to whom am I writing of feminine virtue? Certainly not to a citizen or a private gentlewoman, nor to an industrious mother of a family, but to a woman born of imperial and heroic blood, who with her own virtues equals the virile virtues of all her glorious ancestors! Therefore, no longer feminine virtue but womanly virtue shall be here considered.[52] Nor shall the noun *femina* but rather the attribute

50. Tasso identifies only two orders, the intellectual and the affective; his reference to three orders in addition to the intellectual can perhaps be explained by his subdivision of the affective order into concupiscent and irascible elements.

51. Because Tasso has just stated in the previous sentence that temperance and modesty are the "most appropriate" virtues for a woman, the negative *non* that appears in the original text must be a printing error. I have therefore translated the statement affirmatively.

52. It is at this significant point in the text that Tasso makes his class-based distinction between the *femina* (common woman) and the *donna* (lady) and the virtues appropriate to each, i.e, *virtù feminile e donnesca* (which I translate, respectively, as feminine and womanly virtue). A translation of "donnesco" as womanly is more faithful to the author's intentions

donnesco—which is equivalent to "refined"—be used. Accordingly, in Dante one reads:

With womanly courtesy she said: come with us.[53]

That is, (she spoke) in a refined and imperial manner.

Now, considering not feminine but womanly virtue, I affirm that just as among men those who exceed the human condition are esteemed heroes, likewise among women many are born of heroic spirit and virtue. And among the many born of royal blood, although they cannot precisely be called heroic women, they do nevertheless resemble them greatly. And these women are not part of the city, because heroes are in no manner [part of the city]. One can debate whether kings are or are not [part of the city]; and even when they are, royal virtue is completely distinct from civic virtue. The virtue, therefore, of such women is not civic virtue, nor should it be considered according to the distinctions and opportunities among civic offices. And even less [should it be considered] according to the necessities of household management, because household management is not the purview of heroic and royal women; and if it does fall within their purview, it is of a different sort than civic and private governance.

It is known that Aristotle posits four modes of economy or household management, however we would like to call them: one is

---

than the term "ladylike," because the latter still carries connotations of "proper" feminine behavior, whereas the former suggests, as Tasso would have it, the unsuitability of a proscriptive code of feminine-gendered virtues for the exceptional *donna*. This elitist distinction between the *femina* and the *donna* in turn juxtaposes the rigid code of feminine virtues (virtues that obtain for the common woman only) against the exception of the refined (*signorile*) womanly virtues that obtain only for women of noble lineage.

53. "Donnescamente, disse, vien con nui." See Dante Alighieri, *Purgatory*, ed. and trans. Mark Musa (New York: Penguin, 1985), 135. The adverb *donnescamente* that describes Matelda's manner of speaking to Statius and Dante the pilgrim is rendered differently in different translations of *Purgatory*; however, Mandelbaum's "with womanly courtesy" and Musa's "with queenly modesty" both capture the adverb's connotations of a display of womanly behavior within the context of court society, hence my previous context-dependent translation of *signorile* as "refined." For the sake of clarity and consistence in my translation, I always translate *signorile* as "refined" and *donnesco/a* as "womanly." See Dante Alighieri, *The Divine Comedy*, ed. and trans. Allen Mandelbaum (Berkeley: University of California Press, 1982), 2:296.

Royal, the other Satrapic, the third civic, and the last private.[54] And if royal household management at all applies to the royal woman, it does not mean that the virtue of a royal woman and [that of] a mother of a private household are the same, because the virtue of a mother of a private family should be thriftiness, while the virtue of a royal woman should be gracefulness and delicacy. The former will have utility as her goal, the latter decorum. Nor will it suffice for the royal woman that the ornamentation of her home be magnificent; it is necessary rather that it be magnificent with delicacy and gracefulness and particularly so in the fabrics worked in silk and gold and in the ornamentation of her room and person. And so much so in the magnificence of such things did the queens of Persia exceed all expectations that entire provinces, as Plato says in *Alcibiades*, were designated for and named after expenses such as belts, slippers and other clothing for the body. Royal governance, although a great and noble [office], can be and usually is rejected by the heroic woman because she, transcending and surpassing not only the condition of other woman but even human virtue [itself], takes her sole delight in acting prudently and strongly. Her virtue is not imperfect, but perfect, not half, but whole. Therefore she can rightly be called right or left.

Nor do feminine modesty and chastity any longer suit her, no more than they would suit a gentleman, because these virtues befit those whom other greater virtues cannot befit. Nor can she be called disgraceful even if she commits a deed that is unchaste, because she does not sin against a virtue that is hers. And only a man or woman who sins against his or her own virtue is disgraceful. I will not deny, nevertheless, that Semiramis and Cleopatra[55] would have merited

54. "Now there are four kinds of economy, that of the king, that of the provincial governor [the satrap], that of the city, and that of the individual." *Politics*, in *The Complete Works*, 2:2134.

55. Semiramis and Cleopatra were frequently cited in the Italian *querelle des femmes* as examples of depraved female licentiousness. See Giovanni Boccaccio, *Famous Women*, ed. and trans. Virginia Brown, I Tatti Renaissance Library (Cambridge, MA: Harvard University Press, 2001), where Boccaccio describes the valor and courage of the Assyrian queen Semiramis in battle and how she ensured the continuing allegiance of the army of her late husband by masquerading as a man and pretending to be her own son. She ruled with such skill and intelligence that "it was almost as if she wanted to show that spirit, not sex, was needed to govern," 19. Boccaccio closes, however, with a vehement condemnation of her reputed

more praise had they not been unchaste. But also Caesar, Trojan, and Alexander[56] would have been more deserving of praise had they been more temperate. And if because of the virtue of temperance Zenobia or Artemisia[57] merits preference over Semiramis or Cleopatra, for the same reason one prefers Scipio to Camillus,[58] Caesar, and Alexander.

---

depravity: "Her accomplishments would be extraordinary and praiseworthy and deserving of perpetual memory for a vigorous male, to say nothing of a woman. But with one unspeakable act of seduction Semiramis stained them all. Like others of her sex, this unhappy female was constantly burning with carnal desire, and it is believed that she gave herself to many men. Among her lovers—and this is something more beastly than human—was her own son Ninyas, a very hansome young man. As though he had changed sex with his mother, Ninyas languished idly in bed while she exerted herself in battle against her enemies. What a heinous crime this was!" (*Famous Women*, 21–23). Cleopatra VII, Ptolemaic queen, lover of both Caesar and Marc Anthony, fares even worse in Boccaccio's portrayal: she "had no true marks of glory except her ancestry and her attractive appearance; on the other hand, she acquired a universal reputation for her greed, cruelty, and lust" (ibid., 361). To avoid capture at the hands of Octavian when Egypt fell to Rome, Cleopatra committed suicide by exposing herself to the bite of a poisonous asp.

56. The references are to Julius Caesar (100–44 BCE), the great Roman general, statesman, orator and writer, and Alexander the Great (356–323 BCE), famous Macedonian ruler and conqueror.

57. Zenobia—accomplished princess and Queen of Palmyra, temperate in her habits of dress, ardent in battle, preferring to ride horseback over the litter, and renowned for her beauty, erudition, and talents in jurisprudence, finance, and government—eventually was defeated by the Romans but was spared by Aurelian, who granted her large possessions near the Tiber river. Boccaccio praises not only her virile strength, which did not exclude wrestling with bears or capturing and killing lions, but also her extreme chastity: "She guarded her virtue so jealously that not only did she shun relations with other men but also … she never gave herself to her husband Odaenathus, while he was alive, except for the purpose of procreation. Zenobia was so careful about this that, after sleeping with her husband once, she would abstain long enough before the next time to see whether she had conceived" (*Famous Women*, 433). Artemisia, queen of Caria in Asia Minor (fl. middle of fourth century BCE), was a model of chaste widowhood who erected an ornate mausoleum in her husband's honor at Halicarnassus and drank a potion that contained his ashes in order to always have her husband with her. Her grief, however, did not prevent her from being an admirable and vigorous ruler who conquered the island of Rhodes and Greek cities on the mainland. Boccaccio's references to the alliance between Artemisia and Xerxes, king of the Persians, confuse the queen of Caria with an earlier Artemisia who fought at the Battle of Salamis (ibid., 241).

58. Scipio the Younger (ca. 185–129 BCE), Roman general celebrated as a model of all that was best in the Roman character, renowned as brave and brilliant in battle and as a cul-

So much are the rights of man and woman equal in this matter that neither one nor the other merits greater praise or censure for chastity or licentiousness.

And if the woman does not seek out amorous embraces, moved by an unbridled lust for intemperance, she should reasonably not be rebuked. Accordingly, the Queen of the Amazons deserved praise rather than censure, as Giustino[59] recounts, when she came of her own will and gave herself to Alexander in order to beget a child. And perhaps the Queen of Sheba was motivated by the same reason to seek out Solomon,[60] because it is believed that the kings of Ethiopia are descendants of Solomon and her. In addition, those who seek out embraces moved by love and not moved by an intemperate lust can be compared to these [heroic women]. Nor can they be in any manner judged disgraceful and dishonored, because disgrace and dishonor proceed from a vice, and where there is no vice, there can be no disgrace or dishonor. [True] vice, however, is a confirmed habit; therefore, if intemperance is depraved, [the person] can be dishonored. Reasonably, however, the incontinent person should not be reputed depraved or dishonored. The intemperate person lets himself be conquered without a struggle and once conquered does not regret his defeat or the scorn [resulting from it]; nor does he suffer remorse or shame. The incontinent person, however, struggles against his emotions, and after a long battle is overcome—and overcome by whom? By love, which is the most powerful of all emotions. Who can think Queen Dido dishonorable even though she did give herself over to

---

tivated, honorable, virtuous man; Camillus (d. 365 BCE), Roman general and statesman, called the "second founder of Rome" for his reconstruction of the city after the Gauls had sacked and occupied the city in 389.

59. Tasso's reference is to Justinus's *Trogi Pompei Historiarum Philippicarum Epitoma*, where it is reported that Minithya, queen of the Amazons, spent thirteen days with Alexander the Great, hoping to conceive his child; see Guido A. Guarino's editorial note in his edition of Boccaccio's *Concerning Famous Women*, ed. and trans. Guarino (New Brunswick, NJ: Rutgers University Press, 1963), 65.

60. Legend has it that Queen Makeda (Queen of Sheba or Queen of Saba) travelled from Abyssinia to Jerusalem to test the knowledge of King Solomon. She stayed with him for some time and after returning to her home gave birth to Emperor Menelik I. Rulers of Ethiopia during the Solomonic dynasty (1270–1630 CE) would claim their imperial rights through this bloodline.

Aeneas's love? First she abhors love and [then], rather than violate the laws of widowly chastity, she ardently desires that lightning strike her or the earth swallow her. Then, after a long struggle, in which the powers of love were increased by the persuasions of her sister—who with great effect said, "Wilt thou wrestle also with a love that pleases?"[61]— she was little by little overcome. Love is [such] an extremely powerful emotion that it leaves us unsure whether it is a divine furor or rather an emotion of carnal concupiscence. And even if it does seem that Aristotle identifies no love other than benevolent love and concupiscent love, nevertheless there is no doubt that there exists a third [type], perhaps a mixture of the two to which is added an unidentifiable celestial and truly divine [element].

But since this is not the time to deal with the subtleties of the nature of love, returning to womanly virtue, I declare that womanly virtue in heroic women is heroic virtue that rivals masculine heroic virtue. For women endowed with this virtue, no longer is chastity appropriate, but rather strength and prudence. Nor does one find any difference in acts and offices between them and heroic men—except perhaps only those offices that pertain to the generation and perpetuation of the species which, however, are somewhat neglected or abandoned by heroic women.

This, Most Serene Lady, is the opinion of others and mine on feminine and womanly virtue. And to confirm for you what I have said previously about heroic virtue with some modern examples that equal the ancient ones, I recall in you the memory of the glorious Queen Maria,[62] sister of Charles V and your father Ferdinando, who executed the offices of a valorous captain in wartime and of a prudent king in the governance of state. Nor at all unlike or inferior to

---

61. "Tunc etiam placido pugnabis Amore?" In the *Aeneid*, as Dido bemoans her recognition of "the traces of the olden flame" that dishonor the memory of her dead husband Sichaeus, her sister Anna reacts: "O dearer to thy sister than the light, wilt thou, lonely and sad, pine away all thy youth long, and know not sweet children or love's rewards? Thinkest thou that dust or buried shades give heed to that?" Trans. Fairclough, Loeb Classical Library 399 (Cambridge, MA: Harvard University Press, 1986), 425. Tasso has misquoted from 4.l.38: "Placitone etiam pugnabis amori?"

62. From 1531 to 1555 Maria of Hapsburg (1505–1558) ruled the Netherlands. For the sake of consistency I have left all names in Tasso's Italianized version, except for those commonly recognized in English, such as Charles V.

her is Margherita of Austria, Duchess of Parma,[63] who combines prudence and strength with so many other heroic virtues that the memory of Cleopatra, Semiramis, Zenobia and any other glorious ancient woman seems base in comparison. Nor should the present Queen of England[64] be passed over in silence because although—much to our misfortune—she has separated from the Church, the heroic virtues of her soul and the excellence of her marvelous intellect nevertheless render every genteel and valorous soul most affectionate toward her. But how could I omit Caterina de' Medici,[65] who deserves to be placed in the royal house of France not only in recognition of the greatness and fortune of her ancestors but also in recognition of her own merit? He who desires in heroic women not only the virtue of action but also that of contemplation should remember Renata of Ferrara[66] and Margherita of Savoy,[67] both of whose great marvels my father used to recount to me. Anna, Lucrezia, and Leonora,[68] born of Renata, are so knowledgeable about state matters and appreciation of letters that no one who hears them speak can take leave without being full of extreme wonder. And on the occasions when I read to them some composition of mine, I judged to have as my audience not Sappho,[69]

63. Margherita of Parma (1522–1586), an illegitimate daughter of emperor Charles V, married Ottavio Farnese in 1542 and served as the regent of the Netherlands for Philip II of Spain (1559–1567).

64. Queen Elizabeth I, daughter of Henry VIII, reigned from 1558 to 1603. Elizabeth had a humanistic education and was an expert in both modern and ancient languages as well as being an eloquent orator.

65. Caterina de' Medici (1519–1589), last member of the branch of the Medici founded by Cosimo the Elder, married Henry II of France and became regent after the death of her husband.

66. Renata or Renée of France, daughter of Louis XII, was the wife of Ercole II d'Este.

67. Margherita di Valois Angoulême, wife of Emanuele Filiberto of Savoy, and mother of Carlo Emanuele I, died in 1574.

68. Anna d'Este (1531–1607), Lucrezia d'Este (1535–1598), and Eleonora d'Este (1537–1581) were sisters of Duke Alfonso II, into whose house Eleanor's daughter had married.

69. Sappho of Lesbos (ca. 630 BCE) was perhaps antiquity's greatest love poet. Greeks named her "the tenth muse" and called her "the Poetess," as Homer was called "the Poet."

Corinne,[70] Diotima[71] or Aspasia[72]—these comparisons are too base!—but the mother of the Gracchi[73] herself or another similar [great woman]. And in order not to deprive those who were excellent in the memory of our fathers and ancestors of the praise due them, who can not but mention Lucrezia Borgia,[74] Isabella d'Este Gonzaga,[75] or Anna and Giovanna of Aragon,[76] of whom the last arrived at such an old age that I was able to meet her? And who should not with immortal praise celebrate the excellent intellect, adroit eloquence, and divine poetry of Vittoria Colonna?[77] But why do I go searching for foreigners

70. Corinna was a Greek lyric poet of Boeotia who flourished between the sixth and fifth centuries BCE. She was reputed to have defeated Pindar five times at the public games.

71. Diotima was the Mantinean priestess who taught Socrates about the nature of Love; see Plato, *Symposium*, in *The Collected Dialogues*, trans. Michael Joyce, ed. Edith Hamilton and Huntington Cairns (New York: Bollingen Foundation / Pantheon Books, 1961), 553–63.

72. Aspasia (fifth century BCE) was a courtesan and mistress of Pericles who was renowned for her wisdom, beauty, and wit. Her home became a center of Athenian literary and philosophical life.

73. Cornelia, daughter of Scipius Africanus, wife of Tiberius Graccus, and mother of the Gracchi, was celebrated for her eloquence.

74. Lucrezia Borgia (1480–1519) was the daughter of Pope Alexander VI and pawn or agent (depending upon one's perspective) in the political machinations of both her father and brother Cesare. In 1501 her last marriage was arranged with Duke Alfonso I of Este. Some of the most prominent intellects of the day (such as Pietro Bembo) gathered around her in the court at Ferrara. During Alfonso's frequent absences from Ferrara she often served as regent.

75. In 1490 Isabella d'Este (1474–1539), daughter of Eleanor of Aragon, married Francesco II Gonzaga (1466–1519), the fourth Marquess of Mantua. Known throughout Europe in her day for her learning and her patronage of the arts, Isabella was called "the first lady of the world." Under her auspices the court of Mantua became one of the most cultured in Europe, attracting important artists such as Raphael and Mantegna and advisors such as Baldassare Castiglione. She remains one of the greatest personalities of the Renaissance.

76. Anna of Aragon was the second wife of Vespasiano Gonzaga, Duke of Sabbioneta; Giovanna of Aragon married Ascanio Colonna, brother of the famous poet Vittoria, in 1521.

77. Vittoria Colonna (1490–1547) was one of the most highly regarded women poets of her day. Beautiful, intelligent, and cultivated, she was married to Ferrante, Marquess of Pescara, who died in battle in 1525 after a ten-year tour of duty that had absented him from Pescara. As a widow Colonna became famed for her ascetic lifestyle, good works, and spiritual love sonnets dedicated to the memory of her husband. She was a confidante of Michelangelo and the center of a group of prominent men of letters (Bembo, Sannazaro, Tasso's father Bernardo, and Castiglione). Many contemporaries write with great admiration for her as a person, for her sonnets, and for other poetic compositions on sacred and moral themes.

or examples from afar and not take it upon myself to speak of you and your sister Barbara?[78] In addition to all the fully rich and ornate virtues of the soul and heroic intellect that can be admired, both of you also have—I will speak of Barbara as if she were alive, as she is alive in my memory—Christian virtue in such perfection that the glory of the other examples is in comparison with yours like a weak light against the sun. But although one honors the Christian, sovereign, and perfect virtue of you alone and of the most prudent and chaste Princess Vittoria Farnese[79] and of a very few others, this exquisiteness of Christian virtue is not required in all women, because each person[80] has a different vocation for it and each must adapt to her nation. And it is already much if, in this world full of imperfection, each person partakes of Christian virtue as much as the salvation of her soul requires; without its help, nevertheless, moral virtues are imperfect, nor do they bring any prize beyond a brief and transitory honor.

I will reserve, however, to a better time and a greater convenience the investigation of which and how many are the Christian virtues and in what part of the soul they are lodged. Thus for now I will close with the good grace of Your Highness, expressing to you my most humble reverence, et cetera.

Most devoted and humble servant
of Your Most Serene Highness
Torquato Tasso

---

78. Barbara of Austria, married to Alfonso II of Este, Duke of Ferrara and Tasso's patron, died in 1572.

79. In 1547 Vittoria Farnese married Guidobaldo Maria della Rovere, Duke of Urbino.

80. Tasso changes the gender of *ciascuna* to *ciascun(o)* midsentence, therefore including men in his closing statements on the importance of Christian virtues.

6.
Giuseppe Passi's Attacks on Women in The Defects of Women

SUZANNE MAGNANINI WITH DAVID LAMARI[1]

Born in Ravenna in 1569, Giuseppe Passi honed his skills as a writer in his native city as a member of the Accademia degli Informi (Academy of the Shapeless Men). He made his literary debut with the publication of his misogynistic treatise *The Defects of Women* (*I donneschi difetti*).[2] Ironically, his second published work would be a manual for speaking tactfully so as not to give offense to others;[3] however, *The Defects of Women* deeply angered many readers and led to the publication of no fewer than three woman-authored texts: Lucrezia Marinella's *The Nobility and Excellence of Women, and the Defects and Vices of Men* (1600),[4] Moderata Fonte's *The Worth of Women: Wherein is Clearly Revealed Their Nobility and Superiority to Men* (1600),[5] and Bianca Nardi's *A Response by Signora Bianca Nardi to a Letter from Giacomo Violati, Bookseller in Venice, Written in the Occasion of Thanking Him for Having Sent Her* The Defects of Women *by Giuseppe Passi* (1614). In her direct response to his treatise, Lucrezia Marinella systematically dismantled Passi's argument by providing examples of female virtue to counter each of his discussions of female vice. She then proceeded to decry the defects of men. Moderata Fonte completed *The Worth of Women* in 1592, just before dying of complications from the birth of her fourth child. *The Worth of Women* was published eight years later by her children and her uncle, Niccolò Doglioni, during the contro-

---

1. Suzanne Magnanini selected the passages translated here, translated all of the Italian text and citations, provided the notes for these passages, and wrote the introduction. David Lamari translated all of the Latin and Greek citations and provided the references to and notes on texts in the footnotes.

2. *I donneschi difetti* was printed in 1599 in both Milan and Venice and reprinted in 1601, 1605, and 1618.

3. Published in 1600, Passi's manual on tactful speaking was titled *Discorso del ben parlar per non offendere persona alcuna.*

4. Marinella, *The Nobility and Excellence of Women.*

5. Fonte, *The Worth of Women.*

versy stirred by Passi's attack on women and Marinella's well-argued defense. In Fonte's dialogue, six women meeting in a Venetian garden play a game under the direction of the eldest woman among them. One group is charged with speaking all the good they can of men, while the other must counter with all the defects of the male sex. As the title of the dialogue suggests, the group who speaks ill of men triumphs and, in the process, reveals the merits of the female sex while denouncing the often barbarous behavior of fathers, husbands, and sons. More than a decade later, Bianca Nardi penned a refutation of Passi's arguments in a letter to Giacomo Violato, which he quickly published.[6] Even some fifty years after the initial publication of Passi's treatise, the Venetian nun Arcangela Tarabotti felt it necessary to confront and denounce his misogynistic ideas in her attack on forced monachization, titled *Paternal Tyranny* (1654).[7]

So great was the outcry against the radically anti-woman sentiments expressed in *The Defects of Women* that Passi would dedicate the ten subsequent years of his literary career to redefining his views on women.[8] When he published *The Defects of Women*, he had already envisioned writing a four-volume study of the female sex examining virginity, marriage, widowhood, and monachization.[9] Although he never seems to have written the other three volumes, Passi published *On Marriage (Dello stato maritale)* in 1602. In the letter to his readers, he reveals his motives for commencing the series with the sec-

6. For an insightful discussion of the relationship between the texts of Passi, Marinella, Fonte, and Nardi, see Stephen Kolsky's essay "Moderata Fonte, Lucrezia Marinella, Giuseppe Passi: An Early Seventeenth-Century Feminist Controversy," *Modern Language Review* 94, no. 1 (2001): 973–89.

7. A professed nun in the Benedictine convent of Sant'Anna in Venice, Arcangela Tarabotti (1604–1652) became one of the most outspoken opponents of the practice of forced monachization. She corresponded with major literary figures of her day and wrote and published a number of works during her lifetime. Although the original title of Tarabotti's treatise was *Paternal Tyranny (La tirannia paterna)*, it would be published with the less aggressive title *Innocence Betrayed (La semplicità ingannata)* in 1654 under the pseudonym Galerena Baratotti. Tarabotti, *Paternal Tyranny*. For more on Tarabotti see the volume edited by Elissa Weaver, *Arcangela Tarabotti: A Literary Nun in Baroque Venice* (Ravenna: Longo, 2006).

8. Kolsky, "Moderata Fonte," 984.

9. He mentions this new project, *Porto delle perfettioni donnesche*, at the end of discourse 16 in *The Defects of Women*.

ond volume: "Here is *On Marriage* for now, which I made first (even though it should have been second) in order to enlighten those fools who reading little of my *Defects*, and perhaps without understanding it, pass strange judgments on my work, as if I want to wholly dissuade men from marrying."[10] When Passi published his criticism of the defects of men one year later in *The Monstrous Smithy of Men's Foul Deeds* (*La monstruosa fucina delle sordidezze de gl'huomini*), a work he had already conceived when he wrote *The Defects of Women*, he could claim that he had denounced the vices of both genders.[11] Yet, as Letizia Panizza notes, Passi attributes fewer vices to men than to women (eighteen compared to thirty-five).[12] Passi's interest in the *querelle des femmes* diminished somewhat when he joined the Order of the Camaldolesi monks in Venice around 1609. At that point, he says, he abandoned "writing about jocose and amusing things" and turned his attention to what he deemed to be more serious subjects, such as natural magic and demonology.[13] The public's interest in *The Defects of Women* does not seem to have waned, however, for a new edition was printed in 1618, two years before Passi's death. In a period rife with misogynistic discourse, why did Passi's treatise engender such rage and encourage the publication of woman-authored texts?

As he describes it in the dedicatory letter to Col. Mario Rasponi, the aim of *The Defects of Women* is to teach young men to "avoid women's deceptions." At one point in the letter to his readers, Passi claims that he intends to denounce only those women who commit or have committed "innumerable evils," but he also recalls the Latin maxim *nulla mulier bona* (no woman is good). As he defines woman

10. Giuseppe Passi, *Dello stato maritale* (Venice: Giacomo Antonio Somascho, 1602).

11. Passi mentions this work in discourse 16 of *I donneschi difetti*.

12. See Panizza's "Introduction to the Translation" in Marinella, *The Nobility and Excellence of Women*, 15–16n37.

13. Pietro (Giuseppe) Passi, *Della magic'arte overo della magia naturale* (Venice: Giacomo Violati All'Insegna della Nave, 1614). Passi changed his first name to Pietro after joining the Order of the Camaldolesi monks. Natural magic, an early form of natural history, involved manipulating the forces of nature in order to produce marvelous outcomes. Books on natural magic included both alchemical formulas and more mundane instructions for breeding small dogs, grafting fruit trees, and dyeing hair. In his prologue to *Della magic'arte*, Passi explains that he wishes to distinguish between those marvels that can be explained according to natural laws and those that are the work of demons.

in the first discourse of the treatise, he invokes both the Aristotelian dictum that women are mistakes of nature and the classical and patristic traditions that defined women as a "necessary evil." Passi was certainly not the first nor the last to assume this particular stance in the early modern debate on the status of women, and if he had limited himself to rehashing such tired arguments, his treatise would have provoked little response. In the thirty-four chapters that follow, however, he launches a vicious, unrelenting attack that depicts women as prone to the vices of pride, avarice, treachery, lust, anger, gluttony, envy, vainglory, ambitiousness, ungratefulness, adultery, waywardness, jealousy, inconstancy, hypocrisy, vanity, cowardice, sloth, and impertinence. According to Passi, women have disgraced themselves as prostitutes, panderers, enchantresses, witches, thieves, tricksters, and liars. Women are obsessed with their physical beauty and personal adornment; furthermore, they are inconstant in the face of adversity, and their advice should never be trusted. Passi justifies each of these charges with a plethora of citations drawn from a vast array of sources that include the great authors of antiquity (e.g., Aristotle and Ovid), the Fathers of the Church (e.g., Augustine, Jerome, and Cyprian), canonical Italian authors (e.g., Dante, Petrarch, Boccaccio, and Ariosto), the writings of medieval and early modern jurists, and on occasion even his own personal experience. Together these thirty-five chapters form an encyclopedia of female evil devoid of virtually any mention of good women.

So numerous and varied are the examples of female perfidy that we might assume Passi to be an extraordinary humanist who painstakingly constructed *The Defects of Women* over the course of many years of study. The extensive table found in the opening pages of the book, which lists the more than three hundred authors cited in the treatise, is clearly meant to confirm this impression. The chapters packed with erudite references, however, mark this treatise as a sort of *selva*, a type of compendium of learned citations and anecdotes.[14] Through the practice of *riscrittura* or rewriting, authors

14. Paolo Cherchi has defined this genre, for which the Spanish author Pedro Mexía's *Silva de varia lecciónes* served as a model, as follows: "a sort of reader on various subjects, compiled from a diverse collection of books whose authors do not matter as much as the materials they present. The collected 'lecciónes' were often of an erudite type and contained

in the popular *selva* genre assembled their texts by consulting—and often plagiarizing from—a few intermediary encyclopedic texts rather than the original, cited sources. During the second half of the sixteenth century, myriad texts were written in this manner.[15] Passi, too, utilized this technique when writing *The Defects of Women* and *The Monstrous Smithy*.[16] Our preliminary research into the sources for *The Defects of Women* has revealed that Passi copied portions of discourse 16 from two encyclopedic texts by Tommaso Garzoni, who in turn had depended upon Latin compendia. While Garzoni's oeuvre includes a catalogue of famous women titled *The Lives of Illustrious Women from the Holy Scriptures* (*La vita delle donne illustri della sacra scrittura*) (1586), Passi draws instead from Garzoni's less favorable depictions of women: a discussion of female vanity in *The Theater of Various and Different Minds* (*Il teatro de' vari e diversi cervelli*) (1586) and a chapter on prostitutes in *The Universal Square of All of the Professions of the World* (*La piazza universale di tutte le professioni del mondo*) (1585). Passi utilized his sources in various ways to construct his own treatise; on occasion he copied passages verbatim from Garzoni's text. Compare the following two passages, one from Garzoni's *The Universal Square of All of the Professions of the World* and the other from Passi's discourse 16, concerning the numerous substances women employ to beautify themselves:[17]

---

plenty of quotations and classical authors' names, thus giving the *selva* that veneer of great learning which made more believable the presentation of events and facts which were quite removed from the ordinary cultural context." Paolo Cherchi, "Juan Luis Vives: A Source for Pedro Mexìa's *Silva de varia lecciónes*," in *Sondaggi sulla riscrittura del cinquecento* (Ravenna: Longo, 1998), 149.

15. For an analysis of examples of this sort of encyclopedic rewriting, see the two volumes edited by Paolo Cherchi: *Ricerche sulle selve rinascimentali* (Ravenna: Longo, 1999) and *Sondaggi sulla riscrittura del cinquecento*, cited above.

16. Alessandro Rebonato has shown that Passi copied significant portions of *The Monstrous Smithy* from three works by Tommaso Garzoni: *La piazza universale*, *Il teatro dei cervelli vari e diversi*, and *L'ospedale dei pazzi incurabili*. See his "Di alcuni imitatori di Tommaso Garzoni," *Studi secenteschi* 45 (2004): 195–215.

17. Tommaso Garzoni, *La piazza universale di tutte le professioni del mondo, nuovamente ristampata et posta in luce, da Thomaso Garzoni da Bagnacavallo* (Venice: L'herede di Gio. Battista Somasco, 1592), 599. Giuseppe Passi, *I donneschi difetti* (Venice: Giacomo Antonio Somascho, 1599), 130.

Vuotando le spiciarie di bacca, di solimado, di lume scaiola, di lume zuccarina di fior di Christallo, di borra raffinato, et che si rendon lustre con molle di pane, con aceto lambicato, con acqua di fava, con acqua di sterco di bue, come vacche che sono: et che rinfrescono il viso, mollifican le carne con l'acque d'amadole di Persico, e il sugo di Limoni; e si conservano, con rose, con vino, con lume di rocca; e induriscono le corna dinanzi da bestie come son veramente, con draganti e semenze di codogni, e mettono penuria nel lume di feccia, et nella calcina viva per far liscia perfetta da farsi la bionda.

—Garzoni

Votando le speziarie di biacca, di solimato, di lume scaiola, di lume zuccarina, di fior di cristallo, e per rendersi lustre con molica di pane, con aceto lambiccato, con acqua di fava, con acqua di sterco di bue, e per mollificare la carne con acqua d'amandole di persico, il sugo de' limoni, e si conservano con rose, con vino, con lume di rocca. Induriscono le corna dinanzi con draganti, semenza di cotogno, e mettono penuria nel lume di feccia, nella calcina viva, nel zolfaro per far liscia, perfetta da farsi la bionda.

—Passi

Passi also mined Garzoni's works for citations from and references to both classical and contemporary authors. This is the case at the end of discourse 16, where Passi bolsters his argument about the importance of women modestly covering their heads with a citation from Petrarch and a reference to Homer's *Odyssey*. A comparison of the following passages reveals that Passi simply paraphrased a passage from Garzoni's *The Theater of Various and Different Minds*:[18]

18. Tommaso Garzoni, *Opere di Tomaso Garzoni da Bagnacavallo cioè il theatro de' varii et diversi cervelli mondani, la sinagoga de gli ignoranti, l'hospitale de' pazzi incurabili*, (Venice: Seravalle ad Istanza di Roberto Meglietti, 1605), 37. Passi, *I donneschi difetti*, 141.

Li veli sono il decoro delle teste loro, andando coperte con gravità contra il costume delle vane. Così volendo il divino Petrarca commendare l'honestà della sua Laura disse:	L'andar le donne col capo coperto fù costume lodato da gli antichi Poeti, e da i moderni; come da Omero Penelope, che si copriva, non il capo, ma il viso ancora; così da Museo Hero e dal Petrarca Laura;
Lasciar il velo, o per Sole, o per ombra don non vi vid'io.	Lasciar il velo ò per Sole; ò per ombra Donna non vi vid'io:
Homero nell'Odissea, parlando della casta e pudica Penelope, scrive quei versi, che nella nostra lingua così direbbono;	Diss'egli ma ne ragionaremo meglio, e più copiosamente nel Porto delle perfettioni Donnesche; e per ora basti di questo. —Passi
Quando a gli amanti suoi venne la Donna Illustre; il piede in su la soglia pose Del ben fondato suo palazzo, havendo D'un grosso drappo il bel viso coperto. —Garzoni	

Further study will surely reveal other instances of such literary borrowings in *The Defects of Women.*

It is worth noting that the very compositional techniques that Passi used to create his anti-woman *selva* permitted anyone who was literate and had access to compendia and *selve* (such as Garzoni's texts) to articulate a convincing rebuttal to his misogynistic assertions. Indeed, during the sixteenth century, as the polymath Lodovico Dolce observed, vernacular compendia permitted women to "speak confidently with learned men about the serious things contained in philosophy books."[19] With such texts at their disposal, intelligent

19. Lodovico Dolce, *Dialogo de i colori* (Venice: Gio. Battista et Marchio Sessa, 1565), 5v.

women such as Lucrezia Marinella and Moderata Fonte defended their sex against Passi's demeaning attacks by creating their own collections of citations and anecdotes that depicted women in a positive light. In addition, these writers sometimes would reinterpret the same citations and anecdotes men used to defame women. Like their male counterparts, Marinella and Fonte also used the many citations and anecdotes in their texts to project an image of themselves as learned authors well-schooled in both the classical and contemporary literary traditions. For example, in her dialogue *The Worth of Women*, Fonte depicts her female interlocutors conversing knowledgeably on a vast array of topics, from zoology to the art of memory to Venetian politics. A number of these witty exchanges appear to be crafted from anecdotes borrowed from Spanish author Pedro Mexía's *Silva de varia lecciónes* (*The Forest, or Collection of Histories*) (1540), which was widely available in Italian translation at the end of the sixteenth century.[20]

Like many *selve*, *The Defects of Women* privileges the rare, the curious, and the marvelous. For example, Passi's denunciation of female adornment in discourse 16 lists a fantastic array of unusual substances that women use to beautify themselves, including crocodile dung, coral powder, and Persian almond water, to name but a few.[21] Discourse 4, dedicated to the denunciation of the vice of lust, becomes a lurid catalogue of prodigious female sexuality, replete with examples of unbridled desire: Messalina sleeps with 25 partners in one night without ever being sated, women bed their fathers and brothers through deception, and women copulate with elephants, horses, and dogs. Indeed, at certain moments, Passi seems more interested in surprising his readers by enumerating the exotic ingredients in

20. On Mexía's *selva*, see note 14 above. For further discussion of Moderata Fonte and the *selva* genre, see Suzanne Magnanini, "*Una selva luminosa*: The Second Day of Moderata Fonte's *Il merito delle donne*," *Modern Philology* 101, no. 2 (2003): 278–96.

21. Although he does not instruct his readers in how to make or use these concoctions, Passi's listing of the ingredients of cosmetics recalls the "books of secrets" that were popular at the time. Books in this genre provided actual recipes for both medicines and beauty treatments. See, by way of example, *Gli ornamenti delle donne* (Venice: Francesco de' Franceschi, 1562), written by Lucrizia Marinella's father, the physician Giovanni Marinello. For a discussion of Marinello's treatise, see Maria Luisa Altieri Biagi's introduction to *Medicina per le donne del Cinquecento* (Turin: UTET, 1992), 7–42.

cosmetics or in titillating them with tales of the erotic misdeeds of women than in condemning sinful behavior. One consequence of this preference for the extraordinary example is that Passi unfairly builds his case against all women based upon the outrageous actions of a few. It is precisely this sort of illogical projection that makes his treatise so offensive.

Passi's tendency to provide multiple, detailed citations regarding individual women or female behaviors bespeaks his delight in recounting women's sins. For example, in discourse 4, he tells of not one but two libidinous hermaphrodites, and he lingers over Pasiphae's coupling with the bull, returning to the scene three separate times through citations from Virgil, Propertius, and Ovid. Writing in post-Tridentine Italy, Passi was careful to justify his use of such erotic depictions by pagan authors by ensuring that each discourse included moral lessons drawn from the writings of the Church Fathers and the Bible. In *The Defects of Women*, pagan texts furnish valuable historical examples, but Christian texts serve as the moral compass to guide his readers. In the letter to his readers, Passi justifies his overwhelmingly negative depiction of women, arguing that, like one "moved by charitable zeal," he aims to warn men of the threat that women pose to their spiritual, economic, and moral well-being. As is clear from the published responses to Passi's treatise, not all of his readers accepted this justification for his misogynistic discourse.

A number of criteria guided the selection of the three chapters from the *The Defects of Women* translated here. In keeping with the dialogic spirit of this anthology, the discourses selected from Passi's treatise correspond to chapters from Anne Dunhill's translation of Lucrezia Marinella's *The Nobility and Excellence of Women*, so that readers with no knowledge of Italian can compare their arguments.[22] Each of the three selected discourses also addresses key points taken up by many male and female authors participating in the *querelle des femmes*: how to define woman, female chastity and sexuality, and personal adornment. Furthermore, taken together the three chapters serve to illustrate Passi's rhetorical strategies and literary style.

---

22. Marinella responds to Passi's discourse 1 in part 1, chapter 1 of *The Nobility and Excellence of Women*; to discourse 4 in her part 1, chapter 5, section 2; and to discourse 16 in her part 2, chapter 22.

The Defects of Women[23]

GIUSEPPE PASSI

To the Benevolent and Gentle Readers, from the Author

There is no doubt, gentle readers, that the saying "truthfulness produces hatred" that people utter every day is true.[24] Because if someone, moved by charitable zeal, wants to reprove another for some notable error in order to turn him away from his sin or some perilous entanglement, immediately upon hearing the honest reproof the wretch—no matter that the other had always been a true and faithful friend—becomes indignant, and once indignant he gets upset, and once upset he grows cruel, and once cruel, lo and behold, a friend has turned into a deadly enemy. With foolish words and a thousand rebukes he drives his friend away rather than embrace and give him endless thanks. This happens in thousands upon thousands of cases, but more often because of vain and lascivious women, about whom I intend to speak with you now, than for other reasons. Therefore, were we to wish to examine thoroughly and to discuss the countless incidents that have befallen men on account of women, we would be able sooner to count the stars one by one, or the sea's innumerable grains of sand, and since one cannot do these two things, similarly it would be impossible to relate the countless evils of wicked women. If vain men do not want to take the advice of wiser men, it is for no other reason than a desire to live free and unbridled with unbridled and unchaste women. Then, for love of those women they drive their own houses to ruin, make their own children and disheartened family suffer, and so many times by following this path they dig early graves for their

23. All of the translations—Passi's text, the citations from Latin and Italian texts, and the occasional Greek words—are our own. As explained above in the introduction, Passi most likely drew the majority of his citations from a few compendia or *selve*. In the footnotes, we have endeavored to identify each of the authors, texts, and passages Passi cites rather than the intermediary sources. We supply the standard numeration for these cited texts. Where Passi's citation differs substantially from the current accepted reading, we have noted the variation.

24. Terence, *Andria*, line 68.

grieved fathers and very mournful mothers. Nor do they look out for their honor, which is worth much more than gold. What is worse, they give themselves over to death, like the most brute beasts. Now I do not want to say anything else about men, because I have chosen to speak about Women, particularly those who are in all things the cause of men's ruin. Although I will not be able to tell of each of their iniquities as I would like, because of the infinite number that I said they possess, at least I will say some small bit about their most notable defects, and I will also say something about their most minor sins, in order not to do the harm to them that they merit, even though I know that notable moral saying: "No woman is good." Nonetheless, I am not so arrogant, nor such a harsh and cruel enemy of the female sex, that I think of ignoring the authority of so many excellent and renowned authors who have sung to the Heavens the virtues and glorious deeds of famous and esteemed women whose names live and will live as long as the sun shines on the world.[25] I have been led to this only by my contempt for those who, loving little their own honor and even less that of their flesh and blood, are and have been the cause of innumerable evils. Therefore, Gentlemen Readers, let it please you to bestow your favor upon this weak offspring that is brought to you by one who aims only to be useful to you. Kindly do not let earthly beauty so cloud your reason that you do not regard those words of the Sage: "Charm is deceitful, and beauty is vain."[26] I beg you again that if you find something in this work that offends your ears, correct it kindly, rather than tear me apart, which would do you no honor. Live happily.

---

25. Here Passi has in mind the popular genre of humanist catalogues of famous women such as Giovanni Boccaccio's *Concerning Famous Women* (1362) and his contemporary Tommaso Garzoni's *Lives of Illustrious Women* (1588). See Margaret L. King and Albert Rabil, Jr.'s "The Other Voice in Early Modern Europe Introduction to the Series," in Moderata Fonte, *The Worth of Women*, xvii (and in all other volumes in this series published by the University of Chicago Press).

26. Proverbs 31:30.

The Defects of Women

Discourse I: What is Woman?

Since we have chosen to deal with the many defects and bad behavior of Women, as well as with their blind desires and dishonest acts, we must proceed methodically, as duty requires. As the Philosopher says, "If the beginning is misunderstood, everything is misunderstood,"[27] and Demosthenes used to say that the things we deal with methodically from the beginning always develop better and better. To begin in an orderly fashion we will say that in Latin we find two words that have the same meaning: one is *mulier* and the other *foemina*, and both are equivalent to the Italian words *Donna* and *femina*. The name *Donna* is a special name, properly given to a woman who was a virgin, and after having lost her virginity, becomes a *donna*. I believe that the Poet had this in mind when he said:

The beautiful young girl who now is a woman.[28]

By this he means that in the past she was a virgin, and a short time after, having lost her virginity, she became a *donna*. Varro said it well: "The term 'mulier' rightly applies to one who is not a virgin."[29] For this reason, we read the following words in the *Digesta*: "But if I should think I am buying a virgin when she were in fact not, the sale is void."[30] Having been reproached by many for having in his old age taken as a wife the young virgin girl Popilia, Cicero replied to them: "Cras erit

---

27. Though Passi is referring to Aristotle, the quote is a paraphrase of Thomas Aquinas, *Sententia metaphysicae*, 3.15.9.

28. Petrarch, *Canzoniere*, 127.22.

29. The quote is not found in the works of the ancient Roman philologist Varro, though Robert Estienne's *Dictionarium* of 1531 likewise attributes it to Varro. *Mulier* was, however, commonly an antonym for *virgo*; for example, Cicero uses the phrase "neither *mulier* nor virgin" (*In verres*, I.107).

30. A misquotation of *Digesta* 18.1.11, which says the opposite: the sale would in fact be valid if the matter were concerning virginity; it would only be held void if the mistake were concerning the sex of the slave being sold.

mulier," which means "Tomorrow she will be a *donna*."[31] We read that one morning upon encountering a young woman who was still a virgin, the philosopher Diogenes said to her, "Chiere cure!" which means "God save you, maiden!" Meeting her later that same day and knowing from her eyes that she was no longer a virgin, he said to her "Chiere gyne!" which means "God save you, *donna*!" And this word *donna* has a thousand other meanings, as Signor Girolamo Ruscelli shows in his interpretation of the Illustrious Marquis della Terza's sonnet to the Illustrious Maria d'Aragon, Marquise of Vasto, which begins:

Regal woman, in whose lively splendor.[32]

Now regarding the word *foemina*, it is a word that means nothing other than vile and ignoble female. For this reason, we commonly read that well-known authors wishing to use the word *femina* have always used it accompanied by a wretched and dishonorable word, such as wicked, bad, accursed, roguish, vain, and vile *femina*. Petrarch said:

Vile little female, in her fist she takes him and binds him.[33]

And Boccaccio:

More than any other female [she is] a sad, wicked, bad, accursed, disloyal, malicious, and treacherous female, a universal shame and a disgrace for all women.[34]

31. Quintilian, *Institutio oratoria*, 6.3.75.

32. Here Passi cites from Ruscelli's *Lettura de Girolamo Ruscelli, sopra vn sonetto dell'illustriss. Signor Marchese della Terza alla diuina Signora Marchesa del Vasto* (Venice: Giovan Griffio, 1552). This text is much more than a literary analysis of della Terza's poetry, for it includes Ruscelli's treatise on female perfection as well as a list of famous Italian noblewomen.

33. Petrarch, *Trionfo d'amore*, 3.

34. This citation is pastiche of phrases from two different novellas in the *Decameron*. The first part, "More than any other female she is sad" (Più ch'altra femina dolorosa), can be found in the tragic tale of Lisabetta (4.5.16). The final part, "malicious and treacherous female, a universal shame and a disgrace for all women" (perfida, et rea femina, universale vergogna, e vituperio di tutte le donne), is found in the comic tale at 5.10.44, which tells of Pietro di Vincolo's wife, who hides her lover in a chicken coop. Most likely Passi copied this

And in another place:

More than any other female, full of malice.[35]

Now it is clear that this word *femina* is always accompanied by some wretched word, but let us look at the origins of the etymology of both words, *mulier* and *foemina*.

We say, along with Isidore of Seville, Varro, Firmianus Lactantius in the great book *Officio rei*, and Saint Augustine in sermon 243, *On Time*, that: "The word *mulier* is derived from *mollitie*, with one letter changed and another removed (that is, it was originally *mulier*)."[36] Gratian also writes this in causa 32, question 7.[37] In the eighth book of the *Iliad*, Homer uses this epithet θηλύτεραι for women, which means "soft."[38] It is the same in his *Hymn to Venus*, in which he calls virgins ἀπαλόχροοß, which means "soft-skinned."[39] Saint John Chrysostom refers to women in the same way in the twenty-third homily on Matthew, as does Alberic in his dictionary in the entry for *mulier*. In Ariosto's poem, Rinaldo was well-informed of this fact, and for this reason he did not want to test the faithfulness of his wife, but says:

My wife is a woman, and every woman is weak.[40]

Hence, Aristotle in his book on the animals said that in each species of animal the females are weaker than the males, except in the species

---

citation from an intermediary source. See the introduction for an explanation of his use of sources.

35. Boccaccio, *The Corbaccio*, 4.244.

36. The final word should of course not be *mulier*, but *mollier*. The passage is not found in Augustine, but in Lactantius, *De opificio Dei* 12, 57C, and Isidorus, *De proprietate sermonum* 21.94. The proposed etymology is, as one would expect, false; Alcuin (*Commentaria in apocalypsin* 5.12) rightly rejected it.

37. A monk who taught canon law at the University of Bologna during the middle of the twelfth century, Gratian authored the *Decretum gratiani*, a compendium of canon laws that became the foundational text for Church law.

38. *Odyssey*, 8.324; *Iliad*, 8.520.

39. *Hymnus in venerem*,14; Hesiod, *Works and Days*, 519. The correct spelling is απαλονχροοß.

40. Ariosto, *Orlando furioso*, 43.6.5.

of bears and leopards, and this womanly weakness is affirmed also by Galen in his comment 17 on the fifth part of Hippocrates's *Aphorisms*.[41] For this reason, we commonly say of an accursed and ungodly female that she is a bear or a leopard. Gratian attributes this weakness to the mind, as does the gloss to the first chapter of *de calend. Despon*.[42] Alberic also said that "the word *mulier* is derived from the feebleness of the female mind."[43] But Firmianus Lactantius in the first book of *Divine Institutions* and Galen in the commentaries on *De Pulsibus* attribute it to the body.

Let us turn to the etymology of the word *foemina*, about which one Author says that "the word is derived from *femur*, because women are especially keen for sex, the seat of which is located in the *femora* (thighs)."[44] Hence Juvenal said in the sixth satire:

> The expert masseur pressed his fingers to her muff
> and forced his mistress's upper thigh to cry out.[45]

But it is important to note that this difference exists between *femina* and *femur*: *foemur* means the exterior or posterior part of things, *foemina* the interior or anterior part, as Lorenzo Valla says in the fourth book of his *Eleganze*.[46] Isidore of Seville says that "the word female is derived from the feebleness characteristic of females, for

---

41. Galen (ca. 130–200 CE) was a Greek philosopher, anatomist, and physician. His writings on the body and herbal medicines became the fundamental medical texts in medieval and early modern European universities. Passi cites many of Galen's writings throughout *I donneschi diffetti*.

42. The phrase "*de. calend. Despons.*" is most likely a typographical error or incorrect abbreviation for "*de clandestina desponsatione*," the portion of the canon laws, or decretals, dedicated to clandestine marriage. Passi seems to be referring here to Cardinal Enrico de Susa's (1210–1271) gloss oon these laws, "*Mulier est a molliciae animi*" (in *Hen. de Segusio Cardinalis hostiensis in quartum decretaliu librum commentaria*, 1572, 5.4, t. 3). Our thanks to Maria Teresa Guerra Medici for her help in identifying this reference.

43. Not extant in the corpus of Alberic of Monte Cassino or Alberic of Ostia.

44. Unable to be attributed.

45. Juvenal, *Satires*, 6.423.

46. Lorenzo Valla, *De Elegantia Linguae Latinae* (1444), 4.57. During the Renaissance, this work was a standard textbook for students of Latin.

some hold that female comes from fetus, which is certainly possible."[47] In this way, one can sing with that Poet:

> Such that one is forced to hold one's nose
> Because one cannot suffer the immense stench.[48]

Perhaps Aphrodisius had this in mind when creating the seven properties of Woman, for he placed "a stench in bed" seventh. The others are "saints in the church, angels in procession, demons in the house, owls in the window, magpies on the gate, goats in the garden," and the seventh is the one mentioned above, "a stench in bed."[49] I will omit a discussion of this point, so as not to upset the stomachs of those who now find themselves in good health. The most learned Rabbi David Kimchi says that in Hebrew the etymology of the word *femina* comes from a root which means an inclination toward evil.[50] For this reason I believe that when speaking of spiritual intelligence Saint Jerome said that in scriptures *femina* means every sin and iniquity. Isidore of Seville in his book of etymologies says that *Femina* is a word that derives from the Greek *phos*,[51] which means "fire"; and for this reason some say that wherever a woman enters, she starts a fire. So we read that when the lyric poet Philoxenus was asked why Sophocles introduces wise women in his writings while Philoxenus depicted women as wicked and impious, he responded, "In his poems Sophocles painted them as they should be, and I painted them in mine as they are."[52] For this reason, Planudes in the life of Aesop said that among all the harmful things it must be said that the worst is woman:

---

47. Isidore, *Etymologiae*, 11.2.23.

48. Ariosto, *Orlando furioso*, 33.121.5–6. Here Passi ignores the context of Ariosto's poem. The lines refer not to women, but to the monstrous harpies. The harpies descend upon a table set with food and defecate as the knight Astolfo attempts to dine with King Senapo in Ethiopia. Astolfo slays the harpies for his host.

49. Unable to be attributed.

50. Born in Narbonne, Rabbi David Kimchi (1160–1235), or Radak, as he was also known, wrote Hebrew grammars and Biblical commentaries.

51. Passi's text read "sòs," but this word does not exist in either Ancient or Christian Greek. I have assumed that this is a printing error for "*phos*," the Greek word for fire.

52. Philoxenus (ca. 436–ca. 380 BCE) was a Greek dythrambic poet.

The angry sea rages greatly,
also the headlong rivers, and the blasts of fire and air,
but there is nothing so bitter as a bad woman.[53]

Let us now see what this woman is for whom we find a definition in the thirty-second homily of Saint John Chrysostom. Explicating that passage in Matthew, he writes:

It is not advantageous to marry. Woman is a hostile friendship, an inescapable punishment, a necessary evil, a natural temptation, a desirable disaster, a domestic danger, a delightful [or, as others read, detestable] harm, the nature of evil, painted with the color of goodness.[54]

And another man says:

Woman is the devil's gateway, the pathway of iniquity, the scorpion's blow, and a harmful sort is a female.[55]

Simonides, asked in the end what a woman was, replied:

Woman is the bewilderment of humanity, an unstable beast, a perpetual care, an unending fight, a daily expense, an obstacle to solitude, the shipwreck of a moderate man, a vessel of adultery, a ruinous battle,

---

53. Maximus Planudes (ca. 1160–ca. 1220 CE) was a monk from Constantinople who wrote a *Life of Aesop* in Greek.

54. The passage is not found in Chrysostom's homilies on Matthew, although other Renaissance sources similarly credit the passage thus. An almost identical passage is found at Paschasius Radbertus's *Expositio in evangelium Matthaei* 9, 654A; because Paschasius was a great devotee of Chrysostom, Passi may well have lifted it from Paschasius. Note that the passage is a gloss on "It is not advantageous to marry" from Matthew 19:10, which clause has mistakenly been made part of Chrysostom's commentary.

55. A misquotation of (among many others) Amalarius of Metz, *Forma institutionis canonicorum et sanctimonialium*, 1.98 (889A): an unnecessary "woman is" has been added at the beginning of the passage.

the worst animal, the heaviest burden, a deadly asp, and human bondage.[56]

The female is a shipwreck for her husband, a storm for the family, an impediment to tranquility, a prison of life, a continuous punishment, a very costly war, a domestic beast, an ornate bitch, and finally, an excess. For this reason, when enumerating the evils that come from woman in the sermon on Saint John the Baptist's decapitation, Saint John Chrysostom says:

> Because of you wars start; because of you wise men ruin themselves; because of you saints are slain; because of you cities are burned; because of you the true path is lost; because of you death is found; because of you the rich become poor; because of you the strong become weak; because of you the honest become liars; because of you the chaste become dissolute; because of you the humble become arrogant; because of you the penitent become obstinate, and then loathsome to God.[57]

This means: because of you they wage war, because of you the wise are lost, because of you saints are killed, because of you cities burned, because of you life is lost, because of you death is found, because of you the rich are poor, because of you the beautiful are ugly, because of you the strong are weak, because of you the truthful are liars, because of you the chaste are lustful, because of you the humble are proud, because of you the penitent are stubborn and loathsome to God.

And another says that you must seal this with those two sententious verses:

56. Likely the elegiac poet Simonides is being paraphrased here. His fragment 7, a poem on the taxonomy of women, may have provided the inspiration, but nothing resembling the above passage is extant.

57. Not found in Chrysostom's extant works.

> Woman, strength, eyes, voice, goods, body, soul,
> Takes, bereaves, embitters, destroys, infects, kills.[58]

Bembo put it well that whoever said *"donna"* meant to say *"danno."*[59] Writing to Ruffino, Valerius said that woman was a Chimera because, like that triform monster, she had the face of a lion, the belly of a goat, and the tail of a viper, and woman is at first glance pleasant to behold, but her touch is foul, and an encounter with her brings death. Lastly, woman is called an "accidental male"[60] by the Philosopher, as Saint Thomas states in the first part of the *Summa*. Explaining this saying of Aristotle in the thirty-third chapter of the second part of Anthony of Melissa's work, Philonous said: "Scientists state that a woman is nothing other than an incomplete man."[61] This means "an error committed by nature," which, wishing to produce the man, the perfect animal, by some misfortune produced the woman, a most imperfect animal subject to a thousand passions, as Averroës says.[62] In recent times, woman is called a "necessary evil," and not only by Saint Chrysostom and Simonides, but also by Menander, as we read in Stobaeus:

> Marrying a woman, to tell the truth,
> is indeed an evil, but a necessary evil.[63]

And Philemo the Comic in the same author:

---

58. This popular Italian proverb was included in John Florio's collection of Italian proverbs, *Giardino di recreatione* (1591).

59. The popular proverb used here by Pietro Bembo plays upon the phonetic similarity in Italian of the words for "woman" (*donna*) and "harm" (*danno*).

60. The Scholastic translation into Latin of Aristotle's definition of woman. Aquinas gives the theory an extensive treatment in *Summa theologiae*, 1.92.1–3.

61. Aristotle says something roughly to this effect in *De generatione animalium*, 4.6 (775a15); Aristotle's precise meaning is, not surprisingly, much in dispute.

62. Born in Spain, Ibn Rushd (1126–1198), or Averroes, was a Muslim philosopher, theologian, and astronomer who commented on the works of Aristotle and Plato.

63. Menander, fragment 651. Rather than cite directly from Menander or Philemo, Passi refers to a fifth-century florilegium by the Greek anthologist Ioannis Stobaeus. Stobaeus's *Apophthegmata* circulated widely in early modern Italy in Latin translation and inspired a number of imitations in both Latin and Italian.

Undying is that necessary evil, the wife.[64]

The Emperor Severus referred to her in the same way, as Lampridius testifies. As Saint Augustine says in the questions on the New Testament, woman is necessary because man is not able to perform many tasks at which women are adept, both in the house and also "in order that through her there might be childbirth."[65] But happy and wholly fortunate would be men if life-giving nature had made it so man would be able to be born in the world without woman. Ariosto laments this fact through his character Rodomonte, saying:

> Why didn't life-giving Nature make it
> That without you man could be born;
> As one grafts with human care
> One onto the other, the pear, the sorb, and the apple
> trees?[66]

For this reason Metellus said in one of his orations cited by Gellius, "If we could live without a wife, my countrymen, we all would be free of this nuisance, but since nature has made it so that life is miserable with them and impossible without them, we have to look to our lasting well-being instead of temporary pleasure."[67] This is not very different from that which Aristophanes says in *Lysistrata*:

> That proverb was not at all bad; no, it was well said:
> "neither with those pests, nor without them."[68]

For this reason, when asked why he had given one of his daughters in marriage to an enemy of his, the philosopher Protagoras replied, "I could do nothing worse to that man."[69] This means: "I did not have anything worse to give him." And here I cannot leave out an elegant

64. Philemo, fragment 165.

65. Pseudo-Augustine, *Quaestiones ex veteri testamento*, 21.

66. Ariosto, *Orlando furioso*, 27.120.1–4.

67. Aulus Gellius, *Noctes atticae*, 1.6.2.

68. Aristophanes, *Lysistrata*, 1038–39.

69. The quote is not extant in the fragments of Protagoras.

Latin epigram written by a learned poet, in which he shows women to be always evil, saying:

> My friend, marriage is always bad; if you treat her
> badly
> she becomes worse, but worst of all if you treat her
> well.
> A good wife is a dead wife; better still, if she dies
> before you; best of all, if she dies quickly.[70]

But happy is he who stumbles upon a good wife, because a wicked wife is the ruin of the family! For this reason, wise philosophers believed marriage to be a very difficult and unhappy thing. Begged by his mother to take a wife when he was still young, Thales Milesius replied, "It isn't time yet." And when he had reached middle age and she begged him once again, he said, "There is no more time." Hippocrates used to say that the married man did not enjoy his life save for two days only: the one when he marries, and the one when he buries his wife. We see this well in the life of Emperor Claudius, who was fortunate to bury his wife Livia Medullina, who died the same day that they were to be married.[71] For this reason, the Latin comic used to say: "Oh, thrice unhappy the married man!"[72] And Metrodoros used to say that it rarely behooves a wise man to marry. Good Cato knew these damned animals very well, when he said in the Roman Senate: "If our generation could continue without women, we would be companions of and similar to the immortal Gods." But perhaps Arius had more experience with womanly wickedness, when his neighbor Pacuvius said to him, crying, "Alas, my dear friend, that I have a wretched tree in my garden, in which my first wife hanged herself, and then the second, and now the third!" To which Arius, knowing quite well how much ruin the married man brings upon himself, replied, "Is it possible, Pacuvius, that you have tears to shed for similar incidents? Oh God eternal, how many expenses this unfortunate tree has saved you! Kindly give me a twig to plant in my garden, and make sure not

70. Unable to be attributed.

71. This is Emperor Tiberius Claudius Caesar Augustus Germanicus, who ruled 41–54 CE.

72. Unable to be attributed.

to reveal the virtue of this tree to many others, because everyone will want a branch and there won't be any left in your garden."[73] About the very prudent King Phoroneus we read that turning to his brother Leontius on the day of his death, he said to him, "Nothing would prevent my happiness, if I had never married." Similarly, Eubulus used to say that the second man to take a wife deserved to die a terrible death. Theognis used to say that one cannot find anything sweeter and more dear than a good wife; but before him Hesiod said that one cannot find anything more unpleasant than a bad wife.[74] Therefore, whoever can live chastely without a wife lives far from grave dangers, and if someone cannot remain without a wife, let him pray to God that the one he is given is not the cause of his ruin, as Eve was for Adam. Now then, "Understand me if you can, I know what I am saying," and if anyone speaks badly of me, let God forgive him.[75] We will speak of their defects individually.

Discourse IV: On Lustful Women and *Their Intemperate Appetites in Lustful Acts*

There is no doubt that lust, the opposite of chastity and modesty, is but an unbridled appetite of dishonest, carnal thoughts that gives birth to intellectual blindness, thoughtlessness, rashness, love of oneself, and little love for God. Speaking of lust, Valerius Maximus said reasonably, "What could be fouler than luxury? What could be more ruinous? It wears down valor, weakens the intellect, puts glory to sleep and then disgraces it, and overwhelms the strength of body and mind."[76] One cannot hide lust; it spreads the stench of its infamy on every street

---

73. The earliest known source of the story of the hanging tree is Cicero, *De oratore*, 2.69.

74. Hesiod actually said that a man can find nothing better than a good wife, and nothing worse than a bad wife (*Opera et dies*, 703–4). There is nothing extant in Theognis that matches up with what Passi ascribes to him.

75. Petrarch, *Canzoniere*, 105. This verse has enjoyed great success, utilized by Ariosto (*Orlando furioso*, 43.5), Goldoni (*La serva amorosa*, 2.4), and Rossini (*L'equivoco stravagante*, act 2). In this sentence my translation assumes a reading of Passi's *alcuna* as short for "*alcuna persona*."

76. Valerius Maximus, *Facta et dicta memorabilia*, 9.1, ext. 1. Here Passi seems to have misunderstood the Roman author's diatribe against luxuries to be a denunciation of lust (*lussuria* in Italian).

corner. For this reason, Saint Jerome said: "You have polluted the land with your fornication."[77] It is that which, when used immoderately, harms the stomach, brain, and vision. "What has snatched away the light? Unrestrained lust,"[78] said the poet from Constantinople. It destroys one's strength and in the end shortens one's life. For this reason, Plautus called Venus Astarte, which means life and death, the well-being and ruin of the living:

> The goddess Astarte is the force, life, and salvation of men and gods;
> at other times this same goddess is their ruin, death, destruction.[79]

Cornelius Celsius was also of the opinion that the abuse of Venus cools and dries the blood and is the cause of dangerous illness. Epicurus always judged coitus—and in this woman is immoderate—to be unhealthy. For this reason, those in power, having experienced this womanly intemperance, assigned guardians to women by way of the law, *et Mulier. ff. de cur. furio.*, which did not apply to men, as Felinus says in the chapter "Pastoralis," *Il Barb.* in the law is *cui bonis. ff. de verb. oblig.*, and Saliceto in the first law *C. de cura. furio.*[80] And if

---

77. Jeremiah 3:2.

78. Isak Fehr ascribed this passage to an epigram to Cupid by Michael Tarchaniota Marullus, a fifteenth-century Greek poet born in Constantinople: "Fabeln om Kärleken och Dårskapen," *Samlaren* 4 (1883): 54.

79. The misattribution of this quote to Plautus did not begin with Passi, nor did it end with him; to this day it is wrongly attributed to Plautus's comedy *Mercator*.

80. Passi is citing three Italian jurists here and laws from the *Codex* (indicated by *C*) and the *Digestum* (indicated by *ff.*) of Justinian I's (483–565) *Corpus iuris civilis*, most likely via an intermediary source. The *Corpus iuris civilis* was a collection of Roman laws that were the foundational texts for the study of jurisprudence in medieval Italian universities. Felinus Sandeus (1444–1503) taught canon law in Ferrara and Pisa. Passi refers here to Sandeus's commentary on canon law (*Commentaria Felini Sandei ferr. in V librum decretalium commentaria*, 1571; "De pastoralis," 1110–26). Bartolomeo da Saliceto (1330–1412) taught law at the University of Bologna. Passi refers here to Saliceto's commentary on civil law regarding guardianship of the mad and disabled, "De curatore furiosi et prodigi" (*Barth. A. Salyceti in V et VI codicis libros commentaria*, 1586; ff. 54r–56r). The abbreviation "*Il Barb.*" refers perhaps to Gerolamo Barbarano or Barbaro from Vicenza, who lectured in Padua in 1473.

women, like men, do not display an unnaturally great appetite, this is not born from the cause (says Alberto Lavizola in his commentary on the *Orlando Furioso*) put forward by the old man introduced by Ariosto in canto XXVIII, but from fear of disgrace and the threat of death.[81] Because if these two were not heeded, the female would show this desire to be stronger and more impetuous in her. You hear Ovid say in the first book of *The Art of Love*:

> Love on the sly is as delightful for girls as for men.
> Men cannot keep a secret; girls hold their love under wraps.
> If we men decided not to be the first to proposition,
> women, overcome by love, would play that role.[82]

And he proves his opinion with the simile of the other animals, saying:

> In the tender meadow the heifer lows at the bull.
> The mare always whinnies at the horn-footed steed.
> For us, passion is stronger[83] and not so frenzied;
> Propriety sets a limit to the manly flame.[84]

But what fever do we believe that Arastinassa had, she who, according to Suidas, was the first inventor of the games of Venus, on which she wrote books? Just think, she need not have ever been otherwise occupied to have brought upon herself this deserved shame! I know that she must not have paid attention to the winter or the summer, for Woman tends to be inclined toward coitus much more during the summer than the winter, as Hesiod sings:

Our thanks to Maria Teresa Guerra Medici for her help in identifying the references to Sandeus and Saliceto.

81. Passi refers here to Alberto Lavezuola's *Osservationi sopra il furioso* (Observations on the *Furioso*, 1584).

82. Ovid, *Ars amatoria*, 1.275–78.

83. There are two variants for this passage from Ovid. Passi uses *fortior in nobis* (stronger in us), while most modern editions use *parcior in nobis* (more moderate in us).

84. Ovid, *Ars amatoria*, 1.279–82.

> In the summer's burning heat
> lust is more wanton in the female sex;
> it is milder in men, and if often called forth it wilts.[85]

What will we say about Cyrene, who was the inventor of twelve positions for putting Venus to work? For this reason, the Greeks called her "knowing twelve tricks,"[86] or Dodecamecane. What about Elephantis, who also described in verse the positions, kinds, types, and various forms with which one can variously exercise the same art? She wrote books on this subject, which Virgil mentions, saying:

> Taking smutty pictures from the booklet
> of Elephantis for the horny god.[87]

And Martial:

> You, Sabellus, cleverly (and excessively) read to me
> some lines concerning playboys,
> the sorts of things that Didymus's girls aren't versed
> in,
> nor the dainty books of Elephantis.
> Love there takes some new positions.[88]

What of Quartilla, who in the work of Petronius let it escape from her lips that she did not remember ever being a virgin?[89] What of the two Julias, the one the mother, the other the daughter? What of the two Faustinas in Julius Capitolinus? What of the two Giovannas, queens of

---

85. A loose paraphrase of Hesiod, *Works and Days*, 584–88.

86. Aristophanes, *The Frogs*, 1327. The correct spelling is δωδεκαμηχανη.

87. *Carmine priapea*, 4.1–2. The *Carmine priapea* is a collection of eighty Latin poems dedicated to the phallic god Priapus. Although Passi claims Virgil wrote these lines, Virgil's authorship had already been put in doubt during the sixteenth century. The question of authorship has not been resolved yet, and many scholars believe that a number of different authors contributed poems to the collection.

88. Martial, *Epigrams*, 12.43.1–5. The grammar is garbled; the accepted reading is "you, Sabellus, read to me some all-too-clever lines."

89. Petronius, *Satyricon*, 25.

Naples, who, when they saw a man who had a big nose, suffered great pain if they did not copulate with him, because as they say, "by the shape of his nose," with that which follows:

> Due to the vast size of your pendulous nose, Cato,
> you are thought to be dangling a huge member.[90]

What did Xiphilinus in the *Life of Claudius*, and Pliny in book X, not say about the unbridled libido of Messalina, who forced many women to engage in adultery in the presence of their husbands and had many of them killed because they did not want to satisfy her lust, and who, in order to find relief, wrapped herself in a cape, disguising herself as soon as she saw that her husband was asleep, and committed many adulterous acts?[91] She sang the praises of the prostitutes' brothels, and furthermore, having entered into competition with a dishonest woman and bested her in lust, and boasting about her abilities as a skillful whore, she claimed that between the day and the night she had been with more than twenty-five men and left the job more tired than satisfied. Juvenal speaks of her in the following way:

> She entered a cathouse reeking of an old quilt,
> entered a room cleaned out for her use. Then, naked
> and with her nipples gilded, she posed,
> displaying a placard bearing the pseudonym "She-Wolf"
> and paraded her belly that still carried you, noble Britannicus.
> Her winning ways welcomed visitors, and demanded cash up front.
> Later on, though the pimp had sent home his hookers,

90. Unable to be attributed.

91. The Byzantine monk John Xiphilinus lived during the second half of the eleventh century and was the epitomator of the work of the second-century Roman historian Dio Cassius. The incidents mentioned are in Dio Cassius, *Roman History*. The incidents attributed to Messalina are found in book 60. Passi refers here to Pliny's *Natural History*. Pliny mentions only her triumph over a prostitute with whom she competed in a twenty-four-hour sexual marathon, which she won with a score of 25 (10.83.171–72).

she was sad to go; the last to close up
shop, still burning in her clitoris, down in her swollen
sex.
Worn out by her johns—but unsatisfied—she departed.[92]

What did Plutarch not say about Myrrha, who was so lustful that she fell in love with her own father and never found peace until with the help of her nurse she copulated with him secretly? For this reason, Ovid says of her in the *Metamorphoses*:

Myrrha loved her father, but not as a daughter should.[93]

And Dante, placing her in his *Inferno*, says:

That is the ancient soul
of wicked Myrrha, who became
her father's lover beyond the bounds of just love.
So she came to sin with him
disguising herself in the form of another.[94]

Pelopea, Nitteme, Procris, Hippodamia, and Harpalyce did similar things, as one reads in the *Decreti canonici*.[95] But what Semiramis did was not inferior: she passed the unjust law that a mother could marry her son in order to be able to copulate with her Ninus, with whom she had fallen in love, as Justinian narrates, as does Saint Augustine in the second chapter of the eighteenth book of the *City of God*.[96] In canticle[97] V of the *Inferno*, Dante says, speaking of her:

She was the Empress of people of many tongues,
By the vice of lust she was so broken

92. Juvenal, *Satires*, 6.121–30.

93. The passage is not from the *Metamorphoses*, but from Ovid's *Ars amatoria*, 1.285.

94. Dante, *Inferno*, 30.37–41.

95. Here Passi refers to Gratian's *Decretum* by its Italian title.

96. Augustine, *City of God*, 18.2.

97. I have maintained Passi's imprecise terminology here by calling canto 5 of the *Inferno* "canticle V."

That she gave free reign to inclination in her law,
To remove the blame she had brought upon herself.[98]

[Diogenes] Laertius, in the life of Periander the philosopher, and Aristippus in the book *Antiquis delitiis*, write that Periander's mother Crateia was so ardently in love with him that she secretly copulated with him.[99] Agrippina did the same, according to Cornelius Tacitus in the first book of the *History of Augustus*,[100] as did Nerei and the mother of Ammianus, about whom Martial said:

O how pleasing you are, Ammianus, to your mother!
How pleasing is your mother to you, Ammianus![101]

Byblis, the daughter of Miletus, was so lustful that, enamored of her brother Canno, she forced him to use her carnally, a fact Ovid touches upon, saying:

Why should I bring up Byblis, and she burned with a forbidden love for her brother?[102]

Canace did the same thing with Macareus, for which Ovid says of her:

Canace is well-known from her love for her own brother.[103]

Canulia acted in the same way, according to Plutarch's *Parallel Lives*[104] and Chrysippus's *On Italian Things*. Statius sings of Cydon's sister in the ninth book of the *Thebiad*:

98. Dante, *Inferno*, 5.54–57.

99. Diogenes Laertius, *Lives of Eminent Philosophers*, "Periander," 1.7.

100. Cornelius Tacitus's story of Agrippina is actually found in *Annales*, 14.2.

101. Martial, *Epigrams*, 2.4.1–2.

102. Ovid, *Ars amatoria*, 1.283. The accepted reading is, "Why should I bring up *Byblis*, *who* burned with a forbidden love for her brother?" (emphasis added).

103. Ovid, *Tristia*, 2.384.

104. Although Canuleia is mentioned by Plutarch as a vestal virgin appointed by Numa, the legendary second king of Rome, he says nothing about her behavior in that office, though

And Cydon, wrongfully cherished by his miserable sister.[105]

Hippolytus, son of Theseus, is depicted by Seneca as so honest that, when beseeched by his stepmother Phaedra with many entreaties to consent to her depraved and dishonest desires, not only did he not cede to the mad request of the indecent woman, but from then on he developed such a great hatred of females that he could not in any way bear to hear tell of them. Whence Seneca says:

> Abhorring every name of woman he flees,
> and unrelentingly dedicates his remaining years to celibacy.[106]

In this way many other women loved their sons, stepsons, and sons-in law, for which Pausanias, Heliodorus, Dositheus, Plutarch, Philostratus, Apuleius, Suetonius, and Ammianus Marcellinus offer extensive proof.

Giovanna, Queen of Naples, the first daughter of Carlo the son of Robert, was so very lustful that she had her first husband Andrea hanged because his lovemaking did not satisfy her appetite. After this, she took Ludovico Terrentino as a husband, who, attempting to satisfy her lust, died within three years. Then she took her third husband, Othone Duke of Bransichi, and in the end, Carlo of Durazzo, who had seized Naples, had her decapitated in the very place where she had hanged Andrea her first husband. The poetess Sappho was so lustful that she copulated by turn with her maidservants Amythone, Telespina, Migara, Athis, and Cydno, whence in the Epistle to Phaedra in Ovid's *Heroides*, one reads:

> Amythone is beneath contempt to me, and also Cyd-
> no, glittering white;
> Athis is not delightful, as before, to my eyes.[107]

he describes the punishment for vestal virgins who violate their vows of chastity. See his *Life of Numa*, 10.

105. Statius, *Thebaid*, 9.759.

106. Seneca, *Phaedra*, 230–31.

107. Ovid, *Heroides*, 15.18.

We will not leave out the story of Barbara, the daughter of the Emperor Ghismondo, who, having been widowed, was told by a relative that she must imitate the turtledove, which remains chaste when its husband dies. To this the wicked woman replied, "If I must imitate the example of birds that lack reason, why not the doves or the swallows?"

The story of that woman from Burgos comes to mind that we read in the Spaniard Antonio Torquemada's *Giardino de' fiori*.[108] Torquemada relates that because she was a hermaphrodite, she was allowed to choose the sex she preferred and was prohibited from using the other under penalty of death. She chose the female sex. After this, it happened that she secretly used her male sex and through this deceit committed many evil acts for which she was burned publicly. I met someone similar, who, for as much as one could understand by her outward actions, gave great pleasure to as many young women as came into her hands. She was always flitting around one woman in particular, as if she were a sparrow. Wherefore, having left her city and gone to another one, when the Bishop there realized what she was doing, he made her depart immediately. For despite the great amount of favor she had gained, it was not enough to allow her to stay, for he was of a very religious mind. The women of Santa Cruz in the New World make a certain poisonous animal bite the men on certain parts of their bodies, which, swelling on account of the poison, give the woman greater delight. Quite often these men either die or lose those parts that were bitten.

Was not Pasiphaë's libido so great that, having fallen in love with a bull, she was not ashamed to copulate with him, and she gave birth to the Minotaur, who was half-man and half-bull? Virgil speaks of this in the sixth book of the *Aeneid*:

> He comforts Pasiphaë, blissful if only herds
> had never been, with her love for a snow-white bull.
> Unlucky maiden, what madness took you?

---

108. Originally published in Spanish in 1570, Antonio Torquemada's *Giardino de' fiori curiosi* (*The Garden of Curious Flowers*), trans. Celio Malaspina (Venice: Altobello Salicato alla Libreria della Fortezza, 1590), is a collection of marvels that includes chapters dedicated to extraordinary humans, wonders of nature, and supernatural beings, such as ghosts and elves.

> The daughters of Praetus[109] filled the fields with un-
> natural lowings,
> yet not a one went after such filthy couplings with
> beasts.[110]

And Propertius to Cynthia:

> Once the wife of mighty Minos, they say,
> was seduced by the gleaming beauty of a savage bull.[111]

Ovid was not silent on this point, saying in the first book of the *Art of Love*:

> Now down in the shady valleys of timbered Ida,
> there was a gleaming bull, the glory of the herd.[112]

And then:

> Pasiphaë was overjoyed at becoming the mistress of
> a bull;
> she had a jealous hatred of shapely cows.[113]

Was not the lust of Semiramis so great that she copulated with a horse? And that of Glauca the zither player, who took a dog for a husband, as Elianus narrates? Tatian in one of his orations against the heathen tells of a woman named Glaucippe who copulated with an elephant. Herodotus in the second book and Strabo in the seventh book based on the authority of Pindar relate that in Egypt there is an island

---

109. "Daughters of Praetus" should be "the daughters of Proteus" who, cursed by Dionysus, went insane and wandered the mountains of Arcadia, thinking themselves to be cows.

110. Although Passi attributes this passage to Virgil's *Aeneid*, the lines actually come from Virgil's *Eclogues* (6.45–50).

111. Propertius, *Elegies*, 2. 31–32.57–58.

112. Ovid, *Ars amatoria*, 1.289–91.

113. Ibid., 1.296–97.

called Mendes on which the women copulate with goats.[114] Volaterano in book 32 of the *Philology* recounts that a young woman in Italy copulated with a dog and gave birth to a half-dog, with the hands, feet, and ears of a dog and the rest human.[115] But it is very difficult to convince the masses of how this could be, of how these women sometimes give birth to perfectly formed, rational humans, since the fathers were brute beasts. To clear this up, one says that the seed of each of these women was the agent and shaper of the child on account of being more potent, so that it shaped the child with the characteristics of the human species. The seed of the brute beast, because it does not have the power, served as nourishment, and nothing else. It is not surprising that one reads of their insane and nefarious lust in Leviticus "nor shall any woman lie with a beast, nor give herself to it."[116] And in the twentieth chapter one reads these lines: "If a woman shall lie with a beast, she shall be killed along with it,"[117] which is also mentioned in the *Decreti canonici* in a chapter titled "Mulier."

Discourse XVI: How disgraceful it is that women paint their faces; what happens to them because of their overabundant use of cosmetics; with a discussion of their elaborate care of their hair, and of the ridiculous lunacy of their hairstyles

Some hold that the custom of women painting their faces derived from the Ancient Romans, who, during each festival, set themselves to painting the face of Jove. The Roman women of that time, seeing that Jove appeared very handsome and worthy of admiration, began to paint their own faces, and others followed in doing this. This custom has continued until our own day, because if one sees a poor woman who has six pennies to her name, four of them are on her face. It seems

---

114. In the second book of the *Histories*, Herodotus claims to have seen a goat copulate with a woman in the province of Mendes (2.46). There is nothing in Strabo, book 7, corresponding to what is said in the text here.

115. Passi is referring here to Raffaele Maffei (1455–1522), known as Volterrano, whose encyclopedic *Commentarium urbanorum* contained chapters on geography, philology, and anthropology, as well as a translation of Xenophon's *Economics*.

116. Leviticus 18:23.

117. Leviticus 20:16.

to me, however, that those who lend credence to this false opinion have made a serious mistake, because we know that a long time before the Romans, a type of cosmetic that contained the dung of crocodiles was in use. As Clement of Alexandria[118] tells us in the third book of his *Christ the Pedagogue*, the comic poet Antiphanes[119] recounts specifically the use of this ancient cosmetic, saying in the tragedy titled *Malthake*; "These women use the excrement of the crocodile, and they oil themselves with cuttlefish grease, dye their lashes with charcoal, and cover their cheeks with fire."[120] Therefore, the opinion of those who hold that the custom of women painting their faces originated with the Ancient Romans appears quite wrong on account of the authority of the Greek comic poet Antiphanes. And this is further proven inasmuch as it is confirmed by Galen, who says that the dung that was found in this cosmetic was not that of the aquatic crocodile, but that of the terrestrial crocodile. One can read his words in the tenth book of the herbal medicines, and they are cited here, translated into Latin: "The dung of land crocodiles (that is, those that are small and crawl on the ground) is highly valued by dainty, extravagant women who are not content with the innumerable existing cosmetics that make their faces firm and shiny; no, to these items they add the dung of crocodiles."[121] But don't you realize, women, that instead of making yourselves beautiful, instead of cleaning, smoothing, and coloring your skin, these poisoned mixtures corrode and wrinkle it? They upset your stomach and rot your teeth (which are a very admirable feature in women). Then you need to rub your teeth with coral powder, sage, and dragon's blood,[122] from which is born very bad breath, a pal-

---

118. Titus Flavius Clemens (150–215 CE), known as Clement of Alexandria, was an early Christian educator who included the study of pagan authors at his school in Alexandria. His *Christ the Pedagogue* is a sort of conduct book for Christians that instructs the reader on the proper ways of eating, drinking, sleeping, procreating, speaking, and grooming oneself.

119. The Greek poet Antiphanes (408–334 BCE) was a prolific writer best known for his comedies in verse.

120. Although the final part of this citation reads *cuoprono le guancie di fuoco* (they cover their cheeks with fire), the reference here is obviously to some sort of rouge.

121. Galen, *De simplicium medicamentorum tempermentis ac facultatibus*, 12.308.

122. Pulverized coral, sage, and dragon's blood (the reddish resin from the dragon tree indigenous to the Canary Islands) were all common items available at the apothecary employed for medicinal purposes or for personal grooming.

lid complexion, and a corruption of the humors that afflicts the entire body and destroys it. Regarding this matter, Clement of Alexandria said: "The wretches do not perceive that while they procure artificial beauty, they lose their innate beauty, because with all the washing, the rubbing, the scrubbing, and the applying of those creams they diminish and tone down that lively blush, and with those poisonous treatments they vex the flesh and lose the color and vigor of their own beauty." One must, nevertheless, praise that simple beauty that comes from nature, aided by cleanliness and proper grooming, not from the use of cosmetics, irons, or wires.[123] This belief was well-respected in the Twelve Tablets of Roman Law, which explicitly decreed that women should not shave or pluck either their foreheads or their cheeks.

Happy would be the women of our day—however much it would appear strange to them—if this law were observed, for they would not fall into a thousand disgraces and they would not give rise to a thousand malicious rumors, and what is worse [*sic*], they would not sin willingly, as they do. But one sees their every care and thought to be only for washing themselves, adorning themselves, prettying themselves, curling their hair, making ringlets of their tresses, crimping their hair, whitening their faces, and coloring their foreheads with various glosses and cosmetics. In doing so, they empty the apothecaries of white lead, mercury, alum cleanser, sugar alum, and saltpeter; they make themselves luminous with soft bread, distilled vinegar, broad bean water, and ox dung water; they soften their flesh with Persian almond water and lemon juice; and they keep themselves young with roses, wine, and native alum. They harden the horns in the front of their hairdos with tragacanth and quince seeds,[124] and they create a shortage of potassium carbonate, quicklime, and sulfur in order to make their hair perfectly straight or blond.[125] They always have set

---

123. As the next sentence reveals, irons and wires were used for depilation.

124. This hairstyle, which involved styling two small "horns" of hair that rose up from both sides of the top of the forehead, was popular at the end of the sixteenth century. The portrait of the Venetian writer Moderata Fonte found in an early edition of her dialogue *Il merito delle donne* depicts her wearing her hair in this style. The portrait is reproduced in Virginia Cox's translation, *The Worth of Women*, 42.

125. All the substances mentioned in this paragraph were utilized in the manufacture of early modern cosmetics. Sixteenth-century Italian women could obtain these substances

before themselves mirrors, combs, cloths, albarellos, ampullas, cases, small bottles, and little boxes full of a thousand vanities prepared only according to their specifications. Orange flower water, musk water, perfumes, and civet are always on their table.

Sophocles, wishing to present Venus to speak to the Cretans, presented her completely made up and perfumed. Homer, speaking once of Juno, describes her wearing perfumes and oils like lasciviousness enthroned, saying:

> First she washed the dirt from her sweet body with ambrosia,
> then thoroughly anointed her white skin and divine peplum.[126]

And we cannot forget Sappho the poet, who, as Atheneus recounts, used to make herself up and anoint herself with certain most expensive creams, and like a Nymph she wanted to lie nude among roses, lilies, amaranths, violets, and all sorts of precious and odoriferous flowers. We read about Susanna in the Book of Daniel, who, having washed her face, sent for the ointments, or for the *smerga*, which is a cosmetic that had the power to firm and cleanse the skin.[127] Notable is the case of Phryne who (as Galen recounts), finding herself once again at a banquet with many other women where each took turns playing the Queen and giving commands to the others, when it was her turn to rule ordered that a bowl of pure water be brought there in view of everyone and that each woman, as she did first, wash her face. While she remained beautiful, it happened that many made the dissolved cosmetics run down their cheeks, turning their faces pale, and uncovered their hidden blemishes. The words of Galen are written here below, translated into Latin:

at the apothecary and found recipes for cosmetics in books like *Gli ornamenti delle donne* (*Women's Ornaments*) by Giovanni Marinello, father of Lucrezia Marinella, one of Passi's most articulate critics.

126. The passage is a very loose translation of *Iliad*, 14.170–77.

127. Susanna 1:17 (chapter 13 of the Greek version of Daniel, belonging to the Apocrypha).

Once (speaking of Phryne), at a banquet where a game arose in which each woman took a turn telling the others what to do, she looked at the women painted with alkanet and white lead and rouge, and asked for water to be brought, and then told the women to plunge their hands in the water, then bring them to their faces, and finally wipe their faces clean with linen. She herself was the first to do it, and though the faces of all the other women were full of blemishes (you would have thought you were looking at busts designed to terrify), she herself seemed more lovely than before. For she alone was free from a cosmeticized beauty; she possessed a genuine loveliness, and had no need of dishonest arts to recommend her beauty.[128]

From these words one can clearly understand how disgraceful it is for a woman to paint herself with cosmetics, and with how much disgrace and shame the women banqueters were left on account of having left their colors in the water and revealed the blemishes on their faces, which before were hidden by the thickness of the cosmetics.

But what is this you're painting yourselves, ladies? Nothing other than a desire to cover and to adulterate the face that God has made for you, and to correct it, because it is not to your liking! Why is so much diligence applied to adulterate that which He has made with his own hands (says Saint John of Chrysostom)? Is not the form that he has given you, having made you in his own image, enough for you, woman? And you with colored corruptions make yourself like the Devil!

What is this endeavor of yours, which you presume to apply to the work perfected by God? Does not your divine formation suffice for you? Or, as if you were a more skilled craftsman than the Divine Craftsman, do you—with a woman's blasphemous daring—want to fix it, and as an affront to the Maker, decorate yourself so that you may entice herds of young men after you?

128. Galen, *Adhortatio ad artes addiscendas*, 10.43–52.

In fact, when I am restless, I can do the same, yet I do not wish to, but am compelled to do so for the man's sake—a woman who refuses will never be loved. God placed beauty in you so that he would be praised and his handiwork become a cause for admiration, not so that he would bear injury. God made you beautiful so that he could produce in you the rewards of virtue, that is, he did not make you a showpiece to be adored by many."[129]

He follows with those things that should be used to make women beautiful and says, "to hold on to virtue, and maintain chastity."[130]

If some idiot painter arrives at the unfinished image of some excellent painter and rashly put his hands on it and spoils it, although it seemed to him the most beautiful image that was ever seen, would not the excellent painter be required by his own honor to hold such a grudge that the clumsy painter would be rewarded for his rash behavior? So God will act against you women, and happy you would be if you had never seen cosmetics! "To hold on to virtue, and maintain chastity" says Saint John Chrysostom. Ladies, take care of your virtue and preserve your chastity; these are the white lead, the mercury, the sugar alum, and the saltpeter that make you beautiful. But what will we say about the brazen men who crimp their hair like women, and smear a thousand vanities on their faces, making the bumble bees of the swarm drown in honey, and are the shame of our century? For now I will be silent on the subject that I will address in *The Monstrous Smithy*.[131]

Returning to our subject, Xenarchus severely condemned women's use of cosmetics in the *Economics*. Xenophon, Clement of Alexandria in the tenth and twelfth books of *Christ the Pedagogue*, and Saint Bernard in the book *De Christiana religione* all did the same. Among the many things found in his verse opposing the vain cosmetics of women, Saint Gregory of Nazianzus wrote:

129. The passage is not found in Chrysostom's fourth homily on Matthew.

130. This passage is not found in Chrysostom's extant works.

131. Passi's treatise on the defects of men, *La mostruosa fucina*, would be published in 1603.

> Preserve your body as it has been made,
> and do not wish to appear as one thing instead of another.[132]

This means: "Preserve your body as it is made for you, do not wish to appear that which you are not." The poet Aurelius Prudentius composed the following verses opposing women who adorn themselves too much and paint their faces:

> For not content with her native grace,
> woman fabricates a foreign form.
> And as if the hand of the Lord, her Creator, had made
> an unsound face, so that there is yet need to adorn
> her lofty brow by wreathing it with strings of sapphires,
> or gird her chaste neck with fiery necklaces,
> or hang verdant pearls heavy on her ears.
> She even attaches to her gleaming tresses the seashell's
> white stone, and holds her hair with golden bands.
> It would be tiresome to review the blasphemous practices of women,
> who stain with rouge their lineaments, already enriched with dowries
> from God, so that their skin, smeared with paints, destroys
> its original look and lies unrecognizable beneath its
> false color.
> This is the conduct of the weaker sex.[133]

But little wretches, don't you consider the mistake that you make along with the sin that you commit in corrupting the work of God? Foolish women, in order to deceive people you cheat yourselves and deceive your souls! Listen to Saint Ambrose, who says to those of you who paint your faces:

---

132. Unable to locate this passage.

133. Prudentius, *Harmatigenia*, 264–77.

Woman, if you besmirch your countenance with material whiteness, or steep it in purchased redness, it is a painting of deformity, not of dignity; it is a painting of deceit, not of candor; it is a temporary painting, wiped away by rain or sweat; it is a painting that tricks and deceives: on the one hand you do not please the one you wish to, because he recognizes this supposed delight is not yours, but foreign, and on the other hand you displease your Maker, who sees his own work has been destroyed. Tell me, if you were to bring in an artist to superimpose new work over that just finished by another artist, might not the previous artist be outraged when he discovered his own work defiled? Do not destroy God's painting to gain a harlot's painting, for it is written: 'I shall take the members of Christ, and make them the members of a prostitute.'"[134]

This means: Woman, if you dirty your face with coarse whiteness, and acquire a blush by smearing it on, that is the painting of vice and not of reputation, that is a painting of fraud and not of candor, that is an earthly and fleeting painting that vanishes in the rain and with sweat. Nor are you even pleasing to the one you desire to please, but you very much displease your Maker who sees his work rubbed out. Tell me, if you persuade someone who is not his equal in that art to paint over the work of some excellent painter, and who in trying to make it graceful and beautiful, covers it, insulting him by so doing, knowing that his work has been corrupted.[135] Do not remove God's painting and take up that of the whore, because you deceive yourself and are raving mad if you believe that you paint better than the Supreme Maker.

But what will God say on the terrible day of judgment to those women who always had their cosmetics and who never attended to anything

---

134. Ambrose, *Hexaemeron*, 6.8.47. The opening sentence has no main verb because the apodosis has been omitted: "You destroy the painting." The concluding quotation (from 1 Corinthians 6:15) is also mistakenly turned from a question into a statement.

135. Passi's text here reads "mi *farà grandissima ingiuria*" (insulting *me*). This *mi* is most likely a typographical error for *gli* (him), which makes more sense in this context.

but rubbing them on their faces in order to seem that which they are not? Listen, woman, these aren't fairy tales, but the teachings of Saint Ambrose, and the very truth makes it clear: "I do not recognize my colors (he will say), nor do I perceive my image or the countenance which I myself shaped."[136] He will not recognize your colors because they will be artificial, and he will not recognize His own image because it will have been corrupted by you, wicked woman, and so he will say: "I reject that which is not mine. Seek out the one who painted you, and throw in your lot with him, and get deliverance from him to whom you have given payment. What will you reply?"[137] This means: "I reject that which is not mine. Seek out the one who painted you, and let your conversation be with him, and seek grace with him, to whom you have given payment and striven to please." What do you say to these words, vain and lascivious women, buried in the delights and vanities of this foul world? "How great is the madness (Augustine says) to alter the very image of nature in search of a painting? The crime would almost be more bearable were it adultery; for there chastity is defiled, but here it is nature."[138] In a certain way, adultery is tolerable, but you women with these cosmetics of yours adulterate both modesty and nature.

Similarly, when contemplating the eternal flames that you will face in the next life for these cosmetics of yours, the glorious Saint Cyprian left in writing the following words in *On the Dress of Virgins:* "This work is not mine (the eternal judge will say to you: woman, who has deformed your appearance) nor is this likeness mine. You have befouled your skin with deceitful rouge; you have altered your hair with a defiling tint; your face is overcome by falsehood; your form is corrupted; your appearance is not your own. You will not be able to see God; those eyes you have were not made by God, but stained by the Devil, whom you emulate. You have aped the serpent's painted red eyes. You are adorned like your enemy, and likewise you will burn with him."[139] This means: "This is not my work, nor the work of my hands, nor my image, since with false and artificial colors you have

---

136. Ambrose, *Hexaemeron*, 6.8.47.

137. Ibid.

138. Passi attributes the passage to Augustine (*De doctrina Christiana*, 4.21), who is actually quoting St. Ambrose (*De virginibus*, 1.6).

139. St. Cyprian, *De habitu virginum*, 0456B.

befouled the appearance we made, and with corrupting colors you have changed your hair, and this face is not your own, wherefore you cannot, nor do you deserve, to see God, and these eyes are not your own, nor those that he made for you, but they are the Devil's, who has clouded them because you have followed him. You have imitated the serpent's eyes who has deceived you, and with him you have adorned yourself, for which reason you will also go away with him to be burned always and never consumed." Similarly, Saint Jerome condemns the young women who, when adorning their heads, let their hair fall artfully from their foreheads, clean their foreheads, anoint themselves, and put too much study into dressing ornately. Saint John in Revelation likens women to locusts who adorn themselves and paint their faces to draw men into lascivious love.[140]

For the last word on this subject, we will end with the Doctors of the Church who say that painting one's face is always a mortal sin for women when it is done either out of lasciviousness or out of contempt for the Divine Majesty. If it is done lightheartedly, it is a venial sin; however, I do not find anything in this that lessens the guilt. Instead, I'll add further that women adorning themselves to flirt lightheartedly and in order to seem beautiful without having any other lascivious or depraved intent, easily fall into mortal sin, if one considers the circumstances of the people, place, time, and custom, as Saint Thomas asserts in the second part of the second part, at question 169 and on the third chapter of Isaiah.[141] Alessandro Alense affirms the same thing in the second part of his *Summa*, as does the Parisian Doctor in his book on temperance.

Let us speak now about hair care, and, to tell the truth, how many plasters our women use to make their hair blonde, how many types of distillations, and how many other mixtures to make their hair as they wish. They wash their hair with lye and put potassium carbonate, orange peels, ashes, eggshells, sulfur, and a thousand other vanities on their hair which I will not mention out of respect. It is a marvelous

140. In Revelation 9: 9–11, John writes of the fifth woe to plague the earth during the Apocalypse: locusts with hair like that of women. He does not mention their painted faces.

141. Here Passi is referring to the second part of the second part of Saint Thomas's *Summa* (also called *Secunda Secundae*) and the third chapter of his *Commentary on the Book of the Prophet Isaiah*.

thing to see the anxiety of these women as they pine for the sun and to see them pained and cursing the clouds that hide it when it does not appear. The little wretches give themselves over to sitting in the sun where it is strongest for four or six hours a day, and they endure each torture and pain and yet they got to great lengths for this imagined beauty of theirs. Certainly, for women the most important feature of their beauty is to have long, beautifully colored hair, like Paulina; because of which, although Nero was in and of himself very cruel, he was forced to become the kindly lover of that woman's hair, and he liked it so much that he enjoyed no greater delight than touching it. For this reason, Neptune became the lover of Medusa, Cunibert of Theodota, though their hair was natural, not aided by a thousand artificial plasters, like those our women apply all day long, believing that with them they lighten their hair to gold. Not content to enjoy their hair in the style that nature has given them, they want to counterfeit it with a thousand mixtures, even though they try any way and do not consider that many women have left this life for having cultivated their hair too much with malicious medicines. I know well that colored hair makes a woman beautiful to behold, and for this reason Petrarch, speaking of Laura's braids, likens them to pearls and gold, saying:

> One flower fell on the hem,
> One on her blond braids,
> That polished gold and pearls,
> They seemed to be that day.[142]

But leave aside these mixtures of yours, ladies, because you will cause harm to some other part of your body while you treat your hair! I am speaking to the young women, but even more so to the old women who experience such anxiety that they are bursting with the desire to dye their hair from white and black to blond and pale and dull to red, because of what they say about them:

---

142. Petrarch, *Canzoniere*, 126.46–49. These lines come from one of Petrarch's most famous poems, which begins "Chiare, fresche e dolci acque" (Clear, fresh, sweet waters).

> Nor can one speak of
> nor think of a thing more foul
> nor more vile than an old woman.

But black hair was still praised by the Ancients, as in Horace's *Art of Poetry*:

> Gazed at because of black eyes and black hair.[143]

And elsewhere:

> And Lycus, beautiful with his black eyes and black hair.[144]

Pindar also ascribed black hair to the Muses. But to return to these old women, I do not want to refrain from reciting the verses of Lucillus, with which he politely stings an old woman who used to paint her face and dye her hair:

> You dye your hair, but you will never dye your old age,
> nor will you ever smooth the wrinkles of your cheeks;
> and so don't daub all your face with white lead,
> I would see to have a mask and not a face.
> If it serves no purpose? Why so frantic? Rouge and lead
> will never turn Hecuba to Helen.[145]

And another sings these lines like this:

> Dye your white locks, and try
> To stretch the wrinkled skin, and use
> White lead to paint your face,
> Because you will not be able to dye old age.

143. Horace, *Ars poetica*, 37.

144. Horace, *Carmina*, 1.32.11–12.

145. Attributed to Lucian, *Greek Anthology*, 11.408.

Nor will the vermilion color have such power
That Hecuba, although dyed, seems to be Helen.[146]

And another poet used to say to these women:

And this hair you dye
Its first color, so that the color of the surface
Does not reveal that inner color.[147]

But what is worse, ladies, is what Saint Cyprian says when writing about you dyeing your hair:

With reckless impulse and sacrilegious contempt you
dye your tresses, with an evil portent of the future you
portend your fate with your now fiery-red hair, and—
oh, the horror!—you sin against your own head, the
better part of your body.[148]

This means: "With reckless effort and sacrilegious contempt you dye your hair, like an evil portent you already begin to have fiery-red hair, and you sin with your head, which is with the best part of you." But in order to stop these women from committing this sin, it would be necessary that the custom of the Arimphaeans, according to which the women went about shorn, as Solinus relates, were observed in our time, and in this way women would not sin.[149] If it were the custom only for women to feed on that bread made in Syria with blackberries, which has the property of causing all the hair on the head to fall out, our women would not have so much work to do, nor would they have to have their foreheads and eyebrows depilated, something about which I do not wish to speak because they sin and do penance

---

146. This citation is simply an Italian translation of the citation from Lucian that precedes it (see note 145). Perhaps this is Niccolò Leoniceno's (1428–1524) Italian translation of Lucian, which was published in Venice in the sixteenth century.

147. Unable to be attributed.

148. St. Cyprian, *De habitu virginum*, 0456A.

149. An encyclopedic description of many aspects of the ancient world, Gaius Julius Solinus's *Polyhistor* (250 CE) enjoyed a renewed popularity in early modern Italy.

simultaneously. The Satyr in the *Pastor fido* said this very thing when he said against Corisca:

> Often you stretch a thread across, and hold one end
> With your teeth, and with the left hand
> You hold the other end with the running knot;
> With the right hand you move it about, opening and
> closing it
> As if it were a shaving blade, and you fit it
> On your uneven and downy forehead
> Where you shave all the down and remove at the same
> time
> The ill-born and reckless hairs,
> With such pain, that the penance is the sin.[150]

Now let every woman be content with that which Nature has given her, if it seems to her that Nature was wanting and she thinks that nature has been more favorable to another, like the Roman Sulpitia, to whom were given such charming eyes that one couldn't gaze upon anything more charming; or Lavinia, to whom were given cheeks so blushing that she made fresh roses go pale; or Theodota of Athens, to whom was given such a beautiful bosom that Socrates stopped out of wonder to admire it; or Leda, to whom were given such beautiful breasts that the greatest painters of her age pursued her to portray her in their painting; or to Phryne, to whom was given shameful parts so beautiful that showing them to the judges counted more than all of eloquent Hyperides's learned oration.[151]

If we speak now of hairstyles, nests of pride and banners of lust, you see some woman who has wound up her hair on her head in so many shapes that one hundred sparrows could take up residence inside there, using the fake hair made from colored hemp as they do. For those women who are bald and have very little hair at their temples, Jewish women are not wanting who will assist them with this need, as they always have innumerable braids to sell and haggle over.

150. Battista Guarini, *Il pastor fido*, 1.5.

151. Hyperides (390–322 BCE) of Athens defended the courtesan Phryne in one of his orations.

And those who are bald, God knows how much skill and time they spend to cover up what seems to make them look bad! They do this with such diligence that whoever had not met them before would not be aware of their hidden defects. Every day one gazes upon braids arranged in new styles, and one always notes there a haberdashery of strings of gold, silver, and silk. Sheaths, rosettes, and hemp[152] are not wanting, nor are flowers in such abundance that they obstruct the vision of whoever looks at them, so that it seems as if they have fixed their eyes on the sun, so dazzled are they by the diversity of so many little tangles of silk and hair styled with bows or plumes that continually change—with garlands of pearls and gold, as with certain locks of hair styled in ringlets in which they stick so many real and artificial flowers that in a contest the most noble gardens of Italy would lose—demonstrating the inconstancy and instability of their minds. Therefore, one can rightly say that the only thing missing is this motto written above them: "An offense to God, the ruin of husbands, and the hope of lovers." They are an offense to God by deforming that which His Divine Majesty makes, made, and will always make well; the ruin of husbands because in one stroke they put him in the poorhouse with their ostentation, acquire a bad reputation, and show the world clear signs of immodesty and intemperance; the hope of lovers because women wearing so many ornamental accessories show signs of their corrupt mind. For this reason, the holy Fathers ordered that women cover their heads with veils, hiding their tresses, so that men cannot find in their beauty an opportunity for scandal. For this reason, Saint Paul ordered that women go into churches with their head covered and veiled. "Let women pray with a veiled head,"[153] he used to say to the Corinthians, a custom that is so far removed from Christianity that women go into Churches without anything on their heads, or if they perhaps put on a thin veil they arrange it in such a way that it does not cover their hair, but increases their charm and lasciviousness, like those Roman women about whom Symmachus says, "Their

---

152. Here I have interpreted Passi's word "*canache*," the meaning of which remains obscure, as "*canepa*."

153. A very loose translation of 1 Corinthians 11:4: "Any woman who prays or prophesies with her head unveiled dishonors her head—it is the same as if her head were shaven."

heads are graced by fillets."[154] This means: "The fillets add to their finery." It is against this disreputable practice that Saint Ambrose says, praising the virgins of his day: "Their heads are graced not by fillets, but by the common veil made noble through chastity; the pandering of beauty not sought out but parted with."[155] It is as if he said the Christian virgins do not deck themselves out with precious cloths on their heads to add to their personal finery, but they cover themselves with a rough veil to make their modesty shine. Nor do they seek to increase with lascivious artfulness their beauty, but instead flee from every vain adornment. Tertullian, also writing to Christian women, spoke to them like this:

> I beg you, whether you be mother or sister or unwedded daughter (so as to address each according to their age), cover your head! If you are a mother, do so for your sons; if a sister, for your brothers; if a daughter, for your father. Every stage of life is at risk because of you. Don the armor of decency, lay out a palisade of modesty, erect a wall for your sex that will neither let your eyes wander free, nor let another's enter in.[156]

All authorities oblige every woman to cover her head with veils, in order not to give cause for scandal. And I remember having heard tell by trustworthy people of the Illustrious Cardinal Borromeo that one morning a Milanese gentlewoman went to the Church of the Archbishop and wished to enter without having covered her hair. The Cardinal said to her: "Woman, either cover your head or do not enter the Church." And truly, the practice of women going about with their heads uncovered is quite worthy of correction in our country, because it is certainly an unworthy thing to see honest women openly display their flesh to everyone. The custom of women going about with their heads covered was praised by the ancient and modern poets, as Homer praised Penelope, who covered not only her head but also her face, as did Museus Hero, and Petrarch said of Laura:

154. Symmachus, *Tertia relatio*, 11.

155. Ambrose, *Epistle*, 18.12.

156. Tertullian, *De virginibus velandis*, 16.2.

Abandon the veil for sun or shade
Woman, I did not see you.[157]

We will discuss this more fully in *Porto delle perfettioni donnesche*, but for now this will suffice.

Discourse XX: *That one must not accept a woman's counsel, and that a woman's counsel is inconstant, invalid, fragile, and infirm*

I do not know where these women are coming from that they want to give counsel to men, because, as is widely known, Aristotle has written in the second book of *Politics*: "A woman's counsel is invalid." Emperors Honorius and Theodosius also said *in. si pater C. de spon.*: "the judgment of women working against their own advantage"; and Accursius in the first law of *C. de confir. tut.* says, "Fragile and changeable is the counsel of woman."[158] In the first § *de. fastid. tut* he calls it infirm. Another one said: "The judgment of women is weaker, so to speak."[159] And who is there who, meditating on it, would not consider Baldus and Decius to be fools when they said that the counsel of woman is immutable? Now one must say here in their defense that Decius and Baldus had surely been convinced by some woman to change their tune, and because of this they were quite right not to speak badly of them, not to speak badly but to speak the truth. Although it might seem that their thoughts were shared by Ariosto, who said in favor of women in canto 27:

Much of women's counsel comes out better
When spontaneous rather than thought out;
Because this is special and their own gift
Among many bestowed upon them by the Heavens.[160]

---

157. Petrarch, *Canzoniere*, 11.1–2.

158. Francesco Accursius (1225–1293) taught law at the University of Bologna.

159. Unable to be attributed.

160. Ariosto, *Orlando furioso*, 27.1.1–4.

He meant to say that women are quite prepared to offer counsel spontaneously, perhaps imitating that passage we read in Boccaccio's *Filocolo*: "Oh, Lelio, this is the part of my counsel that may be accepted by you, and don't mind that I am a female, because sometimes females offer better counsel than that offered by men immediately afterward."[161] But reflecting within himself and realizing the error he made, in the end of the same canto he says:

> Troublesome, proud, and disrespectful,
> Lacking love, faith, and counsel.[162]

What do you say against yourselves in Euripides:

> We women are unskilled in good planning,
> but are the wisest artisans of every evil.[163]

Cicero said the same in an oration for Lucius Murena.[164] But what counsel do the miserable little wretches want to offer if they have neither prudence nor wisdom? "The webs of women are ossicles, not plans,"[165] that wise Greek used to say. For this reason Plato doubted whether he should include women among the number of reasoning animals or among the brute beasts. Also for this reason some liken them for their imprudence to dogs. On account of this Martianus wrote that Minerva was born without a mother to make us understand that females lack prudence. One can read Martianus's verses in the Hymn to Pallas Athena, and they are written here below:

---

161. Boccaccio, *Filocolo*, 1.22.15. The modern Italian edition offers a slightly different reading: "Deh! Fa Lelio, che in questa parte sia il mio consiglio udito e servato da voi, e non guardare per che feminile sia, che tal volta le femine li porgono migliori che quelli che subitamento sono presi dall'uomo."

162. Ariosto, *Orlando furioso*, 27.121.5–6.

163. Unable to be attributed.

164. We were unable to find a similar line in Cicero's text; however, Cicero does write "because of their poor judgement, all women desire to be under the authority of guardians" (*Pro Murena*, 27).

165. Unable to be attributed.

> They say this man was born a woman from a father
> who had no union with a mother,
> because the Senate wisely does not recognize the
> opinions of women.[166]

But "with respect to bad judgment, women surpass men,"[167] says a moral maxim, because women do not have in them the ability to generate prudence and wisdom. So one reads in the histories of the Greeks that they gave tutors and administrators to the women on account of the weakness of their counsel, without the authority of whom they could not do anything nor negotiate. Concerning this, one reads the following words in that oration of Demosthenes *In neaeram*: "The law decrees that if a man should put away his wife, he must return the dowry or pay 1.5% of the dowry as a monthly tax to the guardian (by which is meant he who holds custody over the woman), and for the wife's property either in accordance with an agreement to sue for restitution of the dowry."[168] Cicero in his oration for Murena says: "Our forefathers decreed that on account of their poor judgment all women should be in the power of guardians."[169] This means: "They wanted all women on account of their poor judgment to be under the control of tutors." Cato the Censor is also not silent on this point, saying: "Our forefathers, in fact decreed that women could not conduct even a private transaction without a guardian."[170] Boethius on the second book of Cicero's *Topica* wrote: "Under an ancient law women were held by a perpetual guardianship."[171]

---

166. Martianus Capella, *De nuptiis philologiae et mercurii*, 6.573. A grammatical error garbles the sense and makes Pallas Athena a hermaphrodite; the passage should read, "They say she was born from a father who had no union with a mother for the following reason: because the Senate ... ."

167. Unable to be attributed.

168. Demosthenes, *In neaeram*, 52. The sense of the final clause is so garbled as to be untranslatable; the quote is a combination of Demosthenes's oration and the gloss of a commentator.

169. Cicero, *Pro Murena*, 13.27.

170. Livy, 34.2.11.

171. Boethius, *In topica Ciceronis*, 4.18, 1074C. The law pertained only to women with fewer than three children.

I do not want to pile high the sayings of the Doctors of the Church, which on this subject they would not be lacking, so that it not seem that I want to examine one by one all the defects and shortcomings of these miserable, infirm, and fragile females according to [the following laws]….[172]

Battista Mantovano wrote of them thusly:

Whoever you are (and I speak from experience), refuse to try,
while you can, the innumerable scorns this feeble sex has.[173]

And the beautiful Hero to Leander in Ovid:

I dare say men have the stronger nature.
As in the body, so in the mind of delicate women there is frailty.[174]

But to follow the order I began with, and to give some examples of this bad counsel of women who bear honey on their tongues and in their hands poison, according to the verse of that Poet:

---

172. Here Passi cites fifteen different laws from the *Codex* (indicated by *C*) and *Digestum* (indicated by *ff*) of Justinian I's *Corpus iuris civilis*, using Latin abbreviations: "Per la legge seconda al § verba. ff. ad Sen. Conf. Velleia. Per la legge regula ff. de iur. et fact. ignor. Per la legge cuius bonis ff. de iur. far. per la legge perferre ff. de iur. fisci. Per la legge prima § accusationem, ff. ad Sen. cons. Turpil. Per la legge prima C. quam mulie. tut. offi. fung. pot. per la legge quisquis C. ad legem Iul. maie. per la legge nullus C. deur. fisci. per la legge. nullus solius C. de decur. cond. lib. per la legge si mulier C ad Velleia. per la legge si pater al Cod. de sponsal. per la legge prima al paragrafo penultimo al C. de rei uxo. act. per la legge ultima al C. de don. ante nup. per la legge sicut al Cod. de praescript 30. vel 40. anno per la legge assiduis. C. qui poti. in pigno. habean." Most likely he copied this list from an intermediary source.

173. Battista Spagnoli (il Mantovano), *Adolescentia*, 4. A member of the Carmelite order, Spagnoli (1447–1516) was born at the Gonzaga court in Mantova, where he began his career as a Latin poet.

174. Ovid, *Heroides*, 19.6.

Impious poison lies hidden on the sweet head.[175]

We read that in order to carry out the counsel given to him by his stepmother, Crocus King of the Vandals ruined the greatest cities of France. That other enemy of virtue, Nero's mother, Agrippina, used to distract him from the study of philosophy, as if it were something contrary to the governing of the world and unworthy of an Emperor. Who made Gallus Augustus so perverse, if not the bad counsel of his wife? Because of the counsel of Isabella, daughter of Alphonse of Aragon the King of Naples and wife of Galeazzo Sforza, her husband died poisoned and her father was stripped of the Kingdom of Naples and of the Duchy of Milan. Because he followed the advice of his wife Lucilla and plotted against Commodus, Pompeianus was led to a miserable end. Advised by Thaide, Alexander the Great so ruined Persepolis, true dwelling of Emperors, that no trace remained of it where it had been built. Now having discussed sufficiently these fallacious counselors, we will discuss jealous women.

175. Ovid, *Amores*, 1.14.44.

7.
Love as Centaur: Rational Man, Animal Woman in Sperone Speroni's Dialogue on Love

JANET L. SMARR

Sperone Speroni (1500–1588) was the son of a medical doctor in Padua who encouraged young Sperone's education in both science and logic. After studying philosophy with Pomponazzi in Bologna, he returned at the age of twenty-five to teach that subject at the university in Padua. While living in Padua during the 1530s, he married, affectionately raised three daughters, and became an elected member of the Paduan governing council. His government work both in Padua and as an envoy for various negotiations won him a reputation for skillful rhetoric and oratory. He joined the Accademia degli Infiammati (Academy of the Burning Men), and, upon becoming its director in 1541, insisted that the group focus on vernacular literature, in contrast to the rival Studio's emphasis on Latin and Greek. Speroni's tragedy *Canace* (1542) was read to this academic audience; its performance, however, was canceled because of the death of the famous actor and playwright Ruzante. During these years of involvement with a vernacular intellectual society, Speroni began writing his dialogues, which he circulated without any apparent interest in their publication.[1]

Several of Speroni's dialogues deal with women's issues and include women's voices. "On the Dignity of Women" features a debate between two men on whether men or women are superior, capped by the indirectly quoted speech of their Paduan salon hostess, Beatrice Pia degli Obizzi, who argues that serving and obeying her husband is a woman's proper glory.[2] "On the Care of the Family," addressed to his goddaughter Cornelia for the occasion of her marriage, includes

---

1. The biographical information is based primarily on Mario Pozzi's much more detailed "Nota Introduttiva" to Speroni in his edited *Trattatisti del cinquecento* (Milan: Ricciardi, 1978), 1:471–509.

2. Beatrice Pia degli Obizzi appears again with a female friend, as well as Varchi, Alamanni, and other male intellectuals, in a dialogue praising the Obizzi villa at Cataio.

advice on how to live peaceably with one's husband by submitting one's will to his. Allegorical female speakers hold forth in the wittily paradoxical dialogues titled with the speakers' names, "On Usury" and "On Discord." Speroni's "Dialogue on Love" gives a speaking part to the famous courtesan Tullia d'Aragona, presumably an expert on love. It is the first dialogue to make a courtesan one of its speakers.[3] Dialogues on love often included a female speaker, but this dialogue is perhaps unique in that Tullia, herself a writer, responded to it with a dialogue of her own, "On the Infinity of Love" (1547). Although Speroni's acquaintances thought he had done her a great favor by immortalizing her in his text, Tullia's own dialogue radically refashions her representation.[4]

Other dialogues by Speroni, set among male intellectuals without female participation, discuss the uses of vernacular and classical languages and rhetorical styles. These were part of a broad intellectual discussion on how to create an Italian vernacular that could proudly hold its own against both the pedantic imitation of ancient languages and the political influence of the Spanish and French. Speroni's dialogues were considered a good example of this kind of Italian as well as a discussion about it. His strong advocacy of the vernacular was admired by Bernardo Tasso and Pietro Aretino, and Benedetto Varchi and Alessandro Piccolomini spread his ideas to men of letters in Tuscany. Speroni's influence was not limited to Italy; Joachim du Bellay translated and adapted passages from the "Dialogue on Languages" in his *Defense and Illustration of the French Language*.[5]

During the early 1560s Speroni spent a few years in Rome, hoping for employment by the pope, and joining in the meetings of

---

3. Rinaldina Russell, "Opinione e giuoco nel dialogo d'amore," in *Parola e testo: semestrale di filologia e letteratura italiana* 6, no. 1 (2002): 145.

4. See Janet Levarie Smarr, "A Dialogue of Dialogues: Tullia d'Aragona and Sperone Speroni," *MLN* 113, no. 1 (1998): 204–12; Campbell, *Literary Circles and Gender*, 22–29. Russell's introduction to the translation of Tullia's *Dialogue on the Infinity of Love*, especially 30–32 and 36–41, comments on relations between the two dialogues. Russell argues at the end of "Opinione e giuoco," 146, that Tullia was the only one who truly understood the philosophical point of Speroni's dialogue. However, that did not make her happy with his use of her as the defender of a purely physical passion.

5. H. Chamard's edition of the *Deffence et illustration de la langue françoyse* (Paris: Didier, 1961) points out these borrowings in the notes.

the Academy of Vatican Nights under the patronage of Carlo Borromeo. In 1573, when Ugo Buoncompagni, a former friend from the academy, became Pope Gregory XIII, Speroni once more returned to Rome to try for a post at the papal court. In 1574 someone brought a marked copy of Speroni's dialogues with a denunciation to the Roman Inquisition. Speroni's response, the *Apologia on Dialogues*, was written that same year; after circulating in manuscript, it was published in 1576. Despite his arguments that the speakers, like characters in a play, do not represent the author's own opinions, and that dialogue by its nature requires a variety of viewpoints—including tentative and even wrong ones—his dialogues were listed on the Index of Forbidden Books.[6] During 1575 Speroni revised some of his earlier works, including the "Dialogue on Love," in the vain hope of making them acceptable to the censors, and he composed a new "Oration against Courtesans." He continued writing until his death, but he never saw his dialogues in print.

From the start, his dialogues broke away from the courtly setting of Bembo's *Asolani* and Castiglione's *Book of the Courtier* to feature instead the society of urban men of letters. Valerio Vianello sees Speroni as an important figure in the general shift from the courts as centers of culture to the wider intellectual community, brought about by independent urban intellectuals and print technology.[7]

Three important editions exist of the dialogues. The first was published by Daniel Barbaro in 1542, during Speroni's lifetime but, as Barbaro notes, without his knowledge or consent, much less his supervision. Barbaro was concerned that copiers were introducing errors and even claiming authorship; his publication aimed to set the record straight. The second edition was published in 1596, after Speroni's death, as part of a complete works by Speroni's grandson Ingolfo de' Conti, based on manuscripts belonging to the family or sought from friends. This grandson, however, was not a scholar, and he faced the problem that Speroni had sometimes left several versions of a text,

6. Jon Snyder analyzes Speroni's defense of his dialogues in *Writing the Scene of Speaking. Theories of Dialogue in the Late Italian Renaissance* (Stanford: Stanford University Press, 1989), 87–133.

7. Valerio Vianello, *Il "giardino" delle parole: itinerari di scrittura e modelli letterari nel dialogo cinquecentesco*, Materiali e Ricerche N.S. 21 (Rome: Jouvence, 1993), 19–28, 111.

rewriting either to polish it further or to respond to criticisms of the Inquisition. Ingolfo's choice was generally to use the latest version. In the early eighteenth century a pair of scholars, Natale Dalle Laste and Marco Forcellini, highly critical of Ingolfo's work, undertook their own edition of Speroni's complete works based on a collation of existing manuscripts and editions. The "Dialogue on Love" was in their very first volume to appear, in 1740, using again the text that had been revised under pressure from the church. In 1978 Mario Pozzi reprinted the 1542 version in his *Trattatisti del Cinquecento*, while he chose the 1740 version for his reprinting of the entire *Opere* (1989).[8] Speroni himself, of course, supervised none of these editions. Which version, then, should a translator select? As Pozzi notes, Speroni himself seemed uninterested in producing finished texts for his dialogues, preferring to keep them close to the conversational mode and open to additions or modifications. Should we trust the judgment of Barbaro, a personal friend of Speroni's, or should we prefer the judgment of a pair of devoted scholars nearly two centuries later? Do we want the text as it first appeared, or the text as it was reworked to satisfy the Inquisition? Ideally, we want both.

My translation is based on Pozzi's edition of the earlier version, with endnotes indicating significant later revisions, though not every small change. In general, the revision tended to cut religious words, such as "God," "divine," or "miracle," and replace them with safer alternatives. Some portions of the conversation were dropped entirely, as I have noted. The revision, made long after Molza was dead, blames Molza for some of the controversial statements or suggests that Tullia, who quotes him, did not truly understand what he was saying. I have generally followed Speroni's long sentences, but occasionally the demands of clarity have required inserting a break. I have also altered punctuation to suit modern English usage and to clarify meaning. Speroni makes no paragraph divisions within each speech.

---

8. For the history of editions, see Pozzi's introduction to Sperone Speroni, *Opere* (Rome: Vecchiarelli, 1989).

Four people speak in this dialogue, situated in Venice around 1530.[9] Tullia d'Aragona (1510?–1556) was a well-known courtesan and poet who moved among a number of Italian cities, admired by men of the cultured elite. Her published volume of poetry, *Rime della Signora Tullia di Aragona e di diversi a lei* (1547), including many poems both to her and by her, reveals her connections to a wide circle of men of letters. Bernardo Tasso (1493–1569), father of the more famous Torquato Tasso, was a poet and admirer of Speroni. Born and raised in Venice, he was apparently amorously involved with Tullia there; after 1532 he served for many years at the court of the Prince of Salerno and married a woman of Naples.[10] Nicolò Grazia or Grassi (dates unknown) was part of the literary group around Speroni; Bernardo Tasso wrote several poems to him, one envying his ongoing residence near Speroni while Tasso was in Salerno.[11] Francesco Maria Molza (1489–1544) was born in Modena and spent much of his life in Rome, associated with the court of Cardinal Ippolito de' Medici, but he was obviously known to the others; he does not appear among the primary speakers but is quoted by Tullia in a previous dialogue with her, plausibly while they were both in Rome. Molza wrote burlesque poems, four *novelle* in imitation of Boccaccio, and a mock epic, *La ficheide* (1539). Russell observes that as the teacher who is cited only indirectly, he plays the Diotima to Tullia's Socrates.[12]

Speroni's dialogue combines the Christian distinction between two kinds of love, *amore* and *carità*, with many ideas borrowed from Plato's *Phaedrus*: that a jealous lover harms his beloved; that love comes in both rational and irrational kinds; that the lover becomes an image of the beloved, so that the beloved sees himself (for Plato both are male) in the lover as in a mirror. The image of the centaur may come

---

9. Julia Hairston suggests a date of 1528. Hairston, "Aragona, Tullia d'" Italian Women Writers, http://www.lib.uchicago.edu/efts/IWW/BIOS/A0004.html. The references to the imminent departure of Tasso for Salerno may imply a date closer to 1532.

10. Pozzi indicates that he may have been in Venice still or again in 1534 (Speroni, *Opere*, 1:518n.).

11. Bernardo Tasso, *Rime* Book II, 115, "Elegia sesta: A Messer Nicolò Grazia." This poem is available online at http://www.bibliotecaitaliana.it/xtf/view?docId=bibit001547/bib-it001547.xml&chunk.id=d6847e18200&toc.depth=1&toc.id=d6847e7144&brand=default.

12. Russell, "Opinione e giuoco," 136.

from the *Phaedrus's* image of the charioteer and his horses, which at the sight of the beloved sometimes pull forward violently and at other times pull back abashed just as violently, until eventually they become accustomed to the charioteer's rational control. Yet Aristotle is a source for the discussion about how sense impressions are taken up by the intellect. Rinaldina Russell argues that Speroni's dialogue takes an Aristotelian position counter to the Neoplatonic emphasis on spiritual love by underscoring, via the centaur image, the need for both reason and the senses. Thus he "opens a moral, non-religious dimension fundamentally diverse from that preached about love by the dialoguers of Asolo and Urbino."[13] Speroni's philosophical studies, in any case, show through despite the casual tone of the conversation. Tullia, in this dialogue, remains unconvinced that love can ever be rational.

The dialogue insists repeatedly on the distinction between male lover and female beloved. When Tullia speaks of herself as a lover on a par with Tasso, she is reprimanded for going too ambitiously beyond her proper boundaries and confusing the natural order of things. Women love for the glory and utility of having men praise them, declares Tasso, while men love for the pleasure caused by a woman's beauty. Thus, he implies, a woman looks for a man of intellect and eloquence like himself, whereas a man considers chiefly a woman's beauty, although her virtue helps her to maintain a kind of beauty as she ages. The fact that Tullia also wrote her own poetry is ignored here, or perhaps she had not yet written much at the time when the dialogue is set; however, with the ironic justice of history, she is now better known for her own writings than for Tasso's forgotten poems about her. Grazia offers Tullia the role of Diotima, i.e., an oral teacher of love who is written about rather than writing; furthermore, he suggests (counterfactually) that the ancient female poets were all courtesans. This would certainly have tended to discourage any respectable female reader of the dialogue from attempting to write. Tullia herself, however, was not discouraged. Besides her *Rime* and her *Dialogue on the Infinity of Love*, both published in 1547, she is believed to have

---

13. Russell, "Opinione e giuoco," 144: "Apre una dimensione morale areligiosa fondamentalmente diversa da quella predicata dell'amore dai dialoganti di Asolo e di Urbino." Her reference is, of course, to Bembo's *Asolani* and Castiglione's *Book of the Courtier*, both early sixteenth-century dialogues with an obvious Platonic discourse.

penned an epic, *Il meschino* or *Il guerrino*, published after her death in 1560, though this attribution is contested.[14]

14. See Virginia Cox, "Fiction 1560–1650," in *A History of Women's Writing in Italy*, ed. Letizia Panizza and Sharon Wood (Cambridge: Cambridge University Press, 2000), 58: "The work's authenticity may reasonably be doubted, given its posthumous publication and dissimilarity to Tullia's other writings." In addition, Russell asserts that "the attribution of *Il meschino* to Tullia d'Aragona (1510–1556) remains dubious, above all because there is no mention of it anywhere, before the Sessa brothers of Venice published it uner the name of the famous courtesan." Rinaldina Russell, "Margherita Sarrocchi and the Writing of the *Scanderbeide*," in *Scanderbeide: The Heroic Deeds of George Scanderbeg, King of Epirus* (Chicago: University of Chicago Press, 2006), 19n45.

Dialogue on Love

SPERONE SPERONI

Speakers: Tullia [d'Aragona], Bernardo Tasso, Nicolò Grazia, [Francesco Maria] Molza[15]

Tullia: Here, Signor Bernardo, comes just the person who will be able to give us the counsel we lack.

Tasso: O loving Signor Grazia, you have arrived at a good moment, for there is no one who can advise us better than you on how to resolve our disagreements.

Grazia: Any disagreements between you two must be sweet and fine, and blessed is that judge who can resolve them; but you who love and cherish each other so deeply, how can your heart permit you to quarrel with each other? Or how can anyone come between two of you so closely joined and united, so as to put an end to your disputes?

Tasso: The only cause of our discord is that my lady loves me too much, holding me in much higher esteem than I am worthy of.

Tullia: On the contrary, you hold me much higher than befits me; for although I am obliged to thank you for your labors,[16] through which I will live and die glorious, you not only refuse to let me thank you but, full of unaccustomed humility, you declare wrongly that you owe all your good qualities[17] to me.

---

15. See the introduction for the identities of these speakers.

16. I.e., his poems about her, as the revised version makes explicit.

17. *Vertù* here can mean both his moral virtue and his writing ability.

Grazia:	Does it possibly bother you, Signora Tullia, that your Tasso loves and appreciates you beyond measure?
Tullia:	Certainly, sir, yes, because I fear that, becoming aware of his error and avenging himself for his deception, he will cease to love me; and I would rather be loved by him forever and be held as dear as I ought to be, than to be loved too much for only a few days.
Grazia:	Let it satisfy you that he esteems you as he does and is content with his opinion.
Tasso:	Alas, Grazia, what are you saying? Are you supporting her view? Truly I am not deceiving myself in loving her, unless like someone who is too bold in undertaking a project beyond his capabilities. But in praising me beyond what is due, she seems almost to mistake me for some ideal, and to love perfectly that ideal to which she likens me.
Grazia:	This is nothing other than to deny your experience and, like a man desirous of jealousy, to betray her feeling with some strange reasoning; for if she loves you (which I don't believe you doubt), what's the point of talking emptily about ideals, seeking for what you don't want to find?
Tasso:	Whoever loves wholeheartedly, as I do, can't avoid being jealous; but my jealousy is much greater than another man's because the lady I love is so lovable and honorable in herself; and with inexpressible courtesy gladly welcoming whoever comes to see her, that she gives men the opportunity to express to her their desire.
Grazia:	Even though the place and her kindness give men an opportunity to speak, nonetheless her intellect and

virtue, which nothing base can hope to please, takes away their boldness.[i] But you, divine[ii] Signora Tullia, will you patiently permit Tasso to love you jealously?

Tullia: Jealousy is too evil a thing, as I know from feeling it myself; for I suffer its pangs because of Tasso's already extinguished loves, not to mention the new loves that might kindle him. And if this were not the case, I would gladly see him jealous, as jealousy is always a sign of love.

Grazia: O wretched sign of love! O vile pledge of a thing so precious! Truly you are both afflicted with a very serious error; and I will tell you how, if you will give me your attention.

Tullia: Reasons are in vain where experience holds sway. As for myself, I never love without dying of jealousy; nor have I ever been jealous without loving and burning. Therefore I believe that jealousy and love go together like rays and light, thunder and lightning, breath and life.

Grazia: Many things are united in such a manner that it is very difficult—but not impossible—to separate them; for just as one rarely finds pride and beauty apart from each other, nonetheless Tasso and I know a lady both so beautiful and so humble that it is hard to say which is greater.[18] So even if every jealous person loves and many lovers are jealous, nonetheless it is possible and must be the case that someone can love and not be jealous, and perhaps such a love is even more perfect than one accompanied by jealousy.

Tasso: We are going to hear something novel but, in my opinion, more ingenious than true.

---

18. Obviously a flattering reference to Tullia herself.

Tullia: I think so too; but Grazia must explain to us what sort of love he is calling "perfect." I know well, as for me, that while being extremely jealous, I love someone else as much as myself and my own life.

Grazia: That love is perfect whose knot binds and unites two lovers perfectly, in such a manner that, losing their own appearance, they become some—I don't know what—third thing, just as the fable describes Salmacis and Hermaphroditus.[19] Our poets have in various ways signified that mutual and miraculous union, one of them, for example, saying that Laura wore his heart in her face; and elsewhere that she had bestowed on him the greatest and best parts and had held back the lesser.[20] Thus similarly arise all those loving privileges, free and different (as they say) from every natural condition, and especially this one: to live in another and die in oneself. For just as in your harmony the sound of the lute is mingled with the voice, and in perfumes the amber, musk, and civet, their purity altered, render all together a fragrance sweeter than they do separately, so too love is perfect when both lovers are not what they once were but mingled together in such a manner that one can truly call them neither one nor two, or both one and two; and it would not be a grammatical error to say: "you loves."[21] Certainly, if love overcomes and forces nature by simultaneously burning and freezing, wounding and healing, killing and reviving, it should readily be able to make a rule

19. Ovid's *Metamorphoses*, 4.285–388, tells the story of how Salmacis clung so tightly to Hermaphroditus that they fused into one body.

20. Petrarch, *Conzoniere* 111:1, and *Trionfo di morte (Triumph of Death)* 2.151–53. Petrarch's *Triumph* verses say that he gave her the best of himself (his heart) and took something lesser (her glance), but Grazia's phrase seems to attribute the giving to the lady.

21. Italian, having both a singular and plural "you," allows Grazia to use here both the singular pronoun with the plural verb and the plural pronoun with the singular verb while maintaining the second person, so as to indicate that the two lovers are one and that each is both.

of grammar work as it wishes, without anyone repri-
manding it. Such then is the perfection of the love that
we are talking about, which cannot well hold place
in that heart where jealousy resides, that horrid and
fearful monster; for nothing else produces jealousy in
the lover's heart except finding in himself some defect
lacking in his rival and doubting at every moment the
faith and constancy of his lady.[22]

Tasso: To me it seems that, originating in such a way and
from such a root, jealousy is a good thing, because
the jealous man will continually seek to be so virtuous
that few or none can rival him; and with the fear of
seeing his lady change her favor, he will never change
his manner and behavior to her.

Grazia: In that same way sickness is a good thing, and an enemy is helpful: for a sick man avoids unhealthy food,
and often to guard himself against an adversary he is
more faithful to his friends. Therefore, just as a fever
that is causing us to die is still a sign of life in that a
dead man doesn't feel it, just so even if a jealous man
is in love, nonetheless jealousy is the route that leads
sooner to hating than to loving.

Tullia: It would be better to teach me how not to be jealous
rather than to leave me with my jealousy and blame
me for my error. But how can I ever cease being jealous, having continuously before my eyes the infinite
virtues of my Tasso, which make him worthy to have a
much greater lady than I love and adore him?

Tasso: I have reason to be jealous, because my worth is small
compared to your intellect; and the good in you that
led me to love you is known not only to me; and I see

22. Grazia consistently assumes that the active lover is male and that the female is the beloved, ignoring Tullia's assertions that she loves just as actively as Tasso.

that it is admired openly by everyone who recognizes it.

Grazia: Neither her goodness nor his virtues make each of you jealous, but the fear that those qualities may be found pleasing in another that ought to please only in you. And so that jealousy may become clearer to us, we need to know that amorous desire is truly, as we say, a flame and a burning, and as it is kindled in one moment, so in one moment it would be extinguished if hope did not prevent that; for in hope our appetite is maintained like fire in a candle. Therefore, since something beautiful is naturally seen and desired, the soul wishing to possess it compares himself to that object, and if it is such—or gives the appearance of being such—that its virtue or fortune or other kindness enables it to be enjoyed, hope is kindled and nurses his desire, which only then becomes worthy of the name of "love" when it has drunk such milk. Now it is the virtue of hope, this beautiful offspring of reason, this most holy and kindly goddess,[iii] mother and nurse of love, that she stirs up and extinguishes jealousy; and jealousy, depriving our wishes of the lively and sweet liquid of their hope and feeding it to our rival, is the cause that our wandering desire, which we named loved, becoming a madness and frenzy, burns and destroys charitable love[23] just as fire does the wick when the oil is gone. In this manner jealousy (which is a sign of love the way that vinegar is a sign of wine) lays the path to hatred with its fury.

Tullia: So then teach us the means to avoid such a furious thing.

---

23. *La carità.* Augustine, in his *De doctrina Christiana* 3.10, 16, defines the difference between a "concupiscent" and "charitable" love, and in 1.29, 30, he describes a "charitable" love that is happy rather than jealous when others share in admiring the beloved object. See also Augustine's *City of God* 14.7 on *caritas* versus *amor*.

Grazia: You will not easily learn not to be jealous unless you know how love makes of two lovers his miraculous[iv] composite. You must know, then, that as soon as we love each other and become aware of our mutual affection, a thousand amorous thoughts continually fly between the lover and the beloved, each of them dyed in the color of its object and as similar to it as impressed wax is to the seal. This does not calm but rather inflames our desires, which, eager for greater joy, leaving aside the shadows, run with all their senses to embrace each other in truth; this then transforms us entirely, when we recognize and treat the beloved object[24] just as well as she is fit for the man to enjoy and with her to satisfy his desires. Thus, not satisfied only to see and hear her, we make every effort to content the rest of our senses. From there, passing to our mind and with it subtly contemplating the virtues of the beloved (for we are not only eyes and hands but also intellect and reason), if those virtues are such that the lover in his contemplations is delighted with them, then the amorous hermaphrodite is already perfectly formed; nor can we generate this hermaphrodite and give it life in any other way, for the senses are the pathway to reason.[25] Therefore, anyone who is so foolish in love as not to heed his appetites but who, as if he were purely an intelligence, seeks only to content his mind is like someone who, swallowing his food without touching it with his teeth, gives himself more pain than nutrition. What remains to be explained (if I didn't already say it) is how jealousy inserts itself between the lover and beloved, prohibiting them from being transformed into each other.

24. Note that she is the object and he the subject of love, i.e., that the woman is the object, rather than the subject, of the action of loving.

25. Aristotle, *On the Soul*, 3.8.431b: Sense perception is necessary for the mind to form its images. Dante repeats this in *Paradiso*, 4.41–42. Speroni's revised text, "ladder and pathway," emphasizes a hierarchical progression.

Tullia:	Tell us first how reason and love can exist together; for I know already that no amorous joy can be perfect unless every sense is joined with its object. For we are necessarily driven back and forth without a moment's rest from sight to thought and from thought to the senses; but that love may pass from the senses to reason, I don't see, nor can I believe that it's true; rather, it seems to me that the greater and more fervent the love, the less it is tempered by reason. What's your view of this, Tasso?
Tasso:	In the past it may have been the case that I loved against reason, but with you, my dear lady, every reason persuades me to love you; and I get as much delight from contemplating your virtues as my senses do in enjoying your beauties.
Tullia:	So that's why you are permitting yourself to leave me and go to live in Salerno. But you may be sure that no matter how great and worthy an object your valor may be in itself and to every excellent mind, yet it is all nothing compared to your physical presence, without which I will never in truth be gladdened.
Tasso:	Please, let's not talk about my departure, for that cruel future greatly disturbs and darkens my present happiness.
Tullia:	Indeed your departure is a matter not for discussing but for weeping. Therefore it's better to be silent about it; but if I were its cause, as you are, I would consider the grief into which it threw me a just consequence.
Tasso:	The cause is my fate which, while obliging me to be elsewhere, caused me to see you, and, after I had been

taken up by the benevolence[26] of my Prince, put me into the hands of a love that bound and tightened with new snares in Venice my already given-away liberty. However, I do not reject sorrow but will gladly give way to it within myself. Would that I were causing grief to myself alone, for I would not feel half the pain! For seeing you grieve on my account will afflict me more than the pain that I myself will suffer in parting.

Tullia: O wretched me, o infinitely unhappy if I were alone in suffering this separation! Now how could I believe that you loved me and held me dear if it didn't cause you pain to leave me? Grieve, then, if you love me, for it is only by seeing you share that grief almost equally with me that I can console myself. But how can what you said before be true, o divine[v] Signor Grazia, that our love is perfect in such a way that Tasso and I are like a hermaphrodite, if the Prince's kindness and Tasso's service to him can take him away from me?

Tasso: For God's sake,[vi] Lady, don't question my love, and be content with your own opinion without trying to spy out someone else's; for no one knows my love better than yourself.

Tullia: Would that I were as much its master as I am sure of your love. Of that your amorous and lovely verses bear witness, by which you grant my name eternal fame;[27] for only the excessive love you bear me induced you to write them. But Grazia's talk of a loving composite that expels jealousy moved me to ask this question.

---

26. The prince's *carità* is contrasted with Tasso's *amore* for Tullia. See Grazia's further discussion of this below.

27. Tullia is actually more famous now for her own writings than for the largely forgotten verses of Bernardo Tasso.

Grazia: It's a good and subtle question, and not unworthy of your intellect. To answer it, I should say that some human operations are contrary to love, some are similar, and some are shared in common with it; we can approach this matter by loving and hating. So then, it is impossible that Tasso love you and not love you at the same time; nor can it ever be true that he love you and another woman equally and towards the same end; but that he love and serve in diverse manners, and that he act and fulfill both of these offices perfectly, is no more marvelous than that he can both love you and pursue poetry. This is because these kinds of love have different names and forms: yours is "love"; the Prince's is "benevolence";[28] one is affection between equals; the other is reverence and honor.[29] Who ever loved more and changed himself more into his beloved than Petrarch? Yet his same heart no less revered Colonna[30] than it burned for Laura. I'll tell you further, that the love of lovers is not only different from service to a Lord, but it can even coexist with the companionship of a husband and wife; and it's not true that every wife who falls in love [with another man] hates her husband, nor that a husband who deeply loves his wife can't fall in love with another woman; for love imposes itself with another aim and a higher[vii] law than those that ordered our marriages.

Tullia: This strange conclusion we grant you as the payment we owe to a judge, so that you, who are a married

---

28. On *amore* and *carità*, see above note 26 and sources cited. See also note 23 and related text.

29. The same question and a similarly argued response appear in Alessandro Piccolomini's *Institutione di tutta la vita de l'huomo nato nobile*, first printed in 1542, the same year that Speroni's dialogues were printed. The two men had met each other in 1540 when Piccolomini joined the Academy of the *Infiammati* in Padua. See Diana Robin, *Publishing Women*, 137, 145.

30. Petrarch's patron, a member of one of Rome's most powerful families.

man, may fall in love with your honor intact and so that your girlfriend may believe that you love her.[viii] Therefore, leaving that issue aside, resolve my doubt more thoroughly; for notwithstanding what you said, it seems to me that since Tasso's obligation of service to his Lord, taking place together with our love, parts him from me and makes him go to live in Salerno, our union is not perfect, and that his service to the Prince draws him more strongly than our love bound him to me. Nor can I understand how one can excuse such "benevolence" while accusing jealousy, which, even if it is the source of much bitterness in love, certainly never causes a lover to go far away. But it is above all strange to me to hear you equate in a lover the service to a Lord with the power of poetry, messenger of love, conserver of his joys, secretary of his thoughts, consoler of his desires, and witness to his heart. However it may be for others, for me certainly nothing can keep me alive without my Tasso except reading his poems, in which I will never read his praises of me and his affection for me without flying to Salerno and bringing him to me in Venice (despite the Prince) on the wings of my thoughts. And if I should die of love, it would seem to me small harm to lose ten or twenty years of my life to please one who makes my glory eternal with his verses.

Grazia: Now I want to tell you how a lover, seeing and hearing, can be happy with nothing further. Blessed are you, Signor Tasso, and fortunate are your muses, at whose praises a beautiful lady, eloquent and dearer to you than all else, burns with so great an affection and sparkles with words. It pains me only that such beautiful and ornate words come in defense of jealousy, and I fear that even though it is the cruelest venom that lovers drink—one that, when tasted by one of them, poisons and kills them both—nonetheless, being sea-

soned with the eloquence of such a tongue, it may
seem to be a sweet and good thing, especially when
compared to your departure, o Tasso, than which
nothing is more grievous to your lady. But I declare to
you, o kindest couple, that if jealousy is not a cause of
going far away, it is surely a source of being most miserable together. But since both of you are (as the proverb puts it) stained with that tar and giving as good as
you're getting, it shouldn't annoy either of you that I
tell you the truth. Whoever loves, then, should know
that jealousy is a sign of worse intention in the lover
toward the beloved than going away, for a jealous man
would rather that his lady be ugly and sick unto death
and begging for a living than that some other man
who likes her should make her immortal and queen
of the universe. Besides that, no behavior or virtue
in the beloved that moves others to praise her can be
pleasing to the jealous man; and although most often
he is such a person as to be worthless himself and unable to be of any benefit to her, nonetheless he would
be happiest if his lady, in constant need of his wisdom
and of his material goods, always in subjection, always
indebted, bowed down to him with every reverence
and remained obedient to him.[31] On the other hand,
whenever he hears his lady praised, he is accustomed
to blame her, rightly or wrongly, and maliciously to
darken and undermine the praises given her by another man. If she is described as witty, he says she is
shrewd and full of fraud; if she is described as kind, he
tries to depict her as foolish and sensual; if eloquent,
loquacious; if honest, crude and insensitive; if polite,
flattering and duplicitous.[32] In sum, her worst and
most deadly enemy would not do her as much harm

31. This argument about how the jealous lover is bad for the beloved derives from Plato's
Phaedrus, 232 and 239–40.

32. For the negative labeling of positive qualities, see Ovid's *Remedia amoris* (*Remedies for
Love*), ll. 322–30.

as a jealous lover, who, besides envying her well-being of mind and body, besides depriving her of the friendship of other people, which is the most appropriate thing for human beings, never lets her have any peace or rest by day or by night but continually molests her with his importunate company—much more than Tasso's departure will molest you, Signora Tullia. For if she is happy, he fears a rival; if she is pensive, he suspects her of being sorry to see him. Thus, regardless of what his lady does, his mouth is full of sighs; at one moment he silently gnaws himself; at another, losing his patience, he screams and curses aloud at her, himself, and his wretched lot, speaking even more ill of another person's good fortune, and calling ungrateful and disloyal a woman who perhaps has no idea why. Since this is how it is, who will ever say that a man sick with jealousy loves either himself or anyone else? Anyone who knows jealousy will affirm that it is an incurable disease, for the jealous man sees nothing that does not annoy him; rather, like someone with rabies who, seeing the water that can cure him, imagines in it the dog that bit him, he turns every good quality of the beloved, which should gladden a lover—that is to say her beauty, grace, wisdom and virtue and other such gifts—into something that pains and kills him, converting within himself into something suspect that which (if he were sane) would do him most good. Therefore Valerio[33] used to say, not without reason, that jealousy is like a plague proceeding from corrupted air, which is fatal because it harms us by the very breathing that ought to refresh and keep us alive.

Tullia: Either I am not jealous or there are various types of jealousy, some like the kind you describe and others

33. Mario Pozzi in his notes identifies this as Gian Francesco Valerio, illegitimate son of a Venetian gentleman, who befriended learned men, served the Marquis of Mantua, and later became a secretary to Bibbiena. Speroni, *Opere*, 1:11.

different, for it is not possible that I should envy Tasso for his good fortune, in that his departure pleases me—or to put it better, is not displeasing to me—only because he is doing it with the good favor of his Lord, from which he will gain both profit and fame. Yet for all that, I am no less fearful that some other woman, more lucky than I, may take him from me as I took him from another; and this fear is the jealousy that afflicts me.

Grazia: And you, Signor Tasso, in what manner are you jealous in your loves?

Tasso: Jealousy in me is made in the same fashion as that which my lady feels, but much greater in degree than hers; because, besides her divine[ix] qualities, besides the opportunity that everyone who loves her has of being with her, my departure against her will makes me fear that she, setting aside my true reasons and suspecting me of betraying her, may try to avenge herself. Then her valor, her courtesy, her great anger and little faith, and seeing her exalt and praise me unduly, loving me not as the Tasso I am but as the sort of person that many men are but I never was, fills me and overwhelms me with jealousy.

Grazia: I knew very well that such a vile passion could not exist among such noble intellects; that's why I did not hold back before from saying the evil that it does to lovers; and in thinking yourselves to be jealous, you are deceiving yourselves.[34] For it is not true that every fear is jealousy; indeed whoever loves perfectly fears and honors the beloved, and such fear does not extinguish but kindles hope, because a virtuous humility

---

34. Plato's *Phaedrus* 243C denies that two men "of noble and gentle nature" who love each other could be jealous in this harmful way. In *The Dialogues of Plato*, trans. Harold North Fowler, Loeb Classical Library (Cambridge, MA: Harvard University Press, 1977), 463.

most often makes the modest person worthy of favor. Therefore we read in one place:

That which teaches to love and to revere

and in another place:

that will make me always fear and hope.[35]

In such a manner and not otherwise, I would swear that both of you fear and frighten each other: you, Signora Tullia, admiring your good Tasso, and he adoring[x] your virtues. But whoever fears where and when he should hope, and distrusting himself gives away to another, like a prodigal, the hope that it is a virtue to hang onto greedily, is already a jealous lover, if one may call him a lover who lives "in desire without hope."[36] For just as one who is hungry but rejects the food that could nourish him is not starving but crazy, so when a man preserves in himself his desire for his lady while pouring out his hope onto his rival, it is not love but jealousy. It may well be, and you perhaps have experienced it, that an amorous heart lives for a while between these two, with hope finally overcoming fear. But he is much more to be praised who hopes without fear; for it is greater glory to a warrior to find no one who will stand against him than to vanquish someone who has wounded him.

Tullia: This war between fear and hope, which I have suffered for a long time and which still continues in my heart, do you not call it jealousy?

---

35. Both verses are from Petrarch's *Rime*: the first 5.9, the second 119.45.

36. Dante, *Inferno*, 4.42, describing the plight of virtuous pagans who died before the time of Jesus and thus before the hope of salvation. The phrase is echoed also by Petrarch, *Rime*, 73.78.

Grazia: My lady, no; jealousy is nothing other than the victory of fear together with the death of hope.

Tullia: Then we were wrong about the name, considering that to be jealousy which is not.

Grazia: You were wrong about both the word and the deed; for, if we granted that such a battle was jealousy itself, then being a mixture of two opposites, one a vice and the other a virtue, it could not be a sign of the good and perfect love of which we are speaking.

Tasso: To me it seems that the conflict you mention along with the victory of hope is a good and loving jealousy; which, even though it is a sign of truest love, still afflicts me no differently than civil unrest afflicts certain cities; for even if the better part wins, nonetheless the republic suffers so much that it is left tired and broken although safe.

Grazia: That was truly a fine comparison, but not appropriate to your conclusion: because just as it is much better for our city to have entirely good citizens or at least so few wicked ones that they do not dare to fight against the better ones, so he loves more who hopes without fear than he in whose divided heart two such adversaries combat each other; for regardless of which side wins, he will not be well-united with his beloved who is divided in himself, and ill can he find peace in another who wages war on himself.

Tasso: Truly jealousy is an evil thing, which saddens me not only to feel but even to hear about. At first there was a battle continually running through me between fear and hope; now another battle, no lesser, has begun between your speeches and my habit, because I see the true and right way, and yet habit with lively force car-

	ries me away in the opposite direction to my extreme displeasure.
Grazia:	Console yourself, Signor Tasso, for the pain of the sore is a good sign that the wound is beginning to heal.
Tasso:	The pain of the remedy is such that it would have been better to leave the illness without medication. So either abandon the cure or comfort it with a new and better plaster than this one that you have put on it. And since by blaming jealousy at length you made us both sad, now for our delight please talk a bit about that loving hermaphrodite of yours; for if you remember, you did not complete his creation.
Grazia:	The fault is yours, Signora Tullia, who took away from him that part which antiquity did not dare to take from the satyrs, sphinxes, and centaurs.
Tullia:	What part did I cut off, to leave it incomplete?
Grazia:	Reason, without which no human operation, especially love, can be considered either human or good.
Tullia:	Love and reason in one soul would be a greater monster than the Minotaur in Crete.[37] [xi] Truly I could neither see nor imagine a stranger and less pleasing shape than one composed of two such forms; because whether love may be nature or habit or destiny or fortune, surely no reason consents that I call it either reason or a rational thing.
Grazia:	Then what sort of thing is love, according to you?
Tullia:	What it is I don't know, but, according to what I once heard from Molza, if I called it either fortune or des-

37. The Minotaur was half bull, half man.

tiny, I believe I would be saying the right thing; it is always good in itself, coming as it does from heaven, although here among us it appears to cause some bad effects. But Molza used to say[xii] that when God (in his mercy) had given mortals the gift of intellect so that our nature, rising above itself, might find union with him, seeing on the contrary that the earth[xiii] that received it not only did not help it to rise but, wrapping it in the weight of earthly dust, weighed it down so much that its top joined its root, the gods lamented long and justly among themselves; then, taking counsel together, they uttered various judgments, and these drew one conclusion: that is, that taking back from mortals the ill-spent gift of a rational soul, they might heavily punish mortals' folly. But already the bodily senses and other material parts were so mixed and merged with the intellect that no sign could be discerned of its ancient divinity, so that it was impossible to separate it out from them and return it to its star in the pure and whole condition that it had once had. Mars and Saturn would gladly have let humans kill each other off. Mercury suggested binding them alive in perpetual exile at the bottom of the universe. Minerva was of the opinion that they should be turned into animals, and many of the other gods shared this view. Finally Jove and Apollo, having first with true reasoning demonstrated how necessary the human species was to the health and beauty of the world, advised that those first wicked men should die and others take their place, continuing their generations one after another as long as the heavens revolved. Next they decided to elect judges who would in various ways punish and afflict the wicked souls after death, at least until every base earthly stain, which they had acquired during life, was completely erased. The gathering was greatly pleased by this idea, and every god in the council was ready to consent to it with all their votes when Venus, who was sitting slightly apart from the other gods with Cupid in her lap, getting to her feet and looking once or twice reverently into the face of her father Jove, as if requesting his permission to speak, with a low and sweet voice began in this manner. Every god fell silent and attentively fixed both eyes and ears in her direction as if they all had no care to hear or see anything else. Only a few interrupted sighs sounded here and there, which not only did not interfere with her speech but, like the tenor to the soprano, sweetly harmonized with it. "Father," she said, "whose mercy is greater than any error and is not vanquished by justice, you know very well with what good will,[xiv] at just one of your nods and to the delight of the whole world, I produced this little son of mine. Now, seeing on earth the base experiences produced by the rational soul that, though born blessed, has deserved your wrath by its situation among mortals, frightened by its example I greatly fear that something similar might happen to me, and that my desire to gladden others by my giving birth may turn into woeful weeping. Therefore, as your prudence provided for the past, so let it provide for the future in such a way that every loving pleasure (a truly celestial thing)[xv] may remain among us; and should we wish to console others with it, let love be sent down below with a different law than that which sent down the intellect." Her request appeared just, and much more was said. In the end, after long discussion, all the gods decided in consensus that just as the sun, staying on high, grants to the earth a part of its splendor, so Love, not leaving their midst, with the rays of his grace should overcome the shadow and ice of our hearts, awakening in us the desire to follow our proper immortality.

"So then," said I, interrupting Molza's words, "now is it true that love is a celestial thing, born among us from the beauty and virtues of mortals?"[38]

Molza: No simile is more apt to give us some understanding of the marvel of love than that of the sun: both eternal, both of almost infinite power, readily observed in their effect on others but rendered invisible in themselves by the excess of light that hides them from our sight. Know, then, that just as the sun's ray, pure of any mortal quality, descends from heaven and, striking, heats and kindles everything, so love, descending from the appearance and actions of some beautiful and virtuous person, masters and compels our wills. Moreover, as the sun in a mirror not only burns and kindles but also represents in the most lively manner the face that looks into it, just so the more beautiful and more virtuous the object, the more gladly love appears there, letting the lover see that there lies his highest happiness, to which, loving and burning, he can rise. For just as the world's sun, illuminating the earth, raises from it some vapors that rise up to the moon, if the cold air around them does not transform them into snow or rain, so the sun of our hearts, love, with the sweet heat of its flames creates in us thoughts that, longing to rise, would make their way above the heavens if our simple humanity (which we call reason), envious of such good, distracting them from their flight, did not turn them back downwards, placing before them every error that entangles life, especially those two idols of the common herd: ambition and utility.

Tullia: It is difficult for me to believe that love, which you make a god, takes from a mortal face the power to

38. At this point Tullia reports a previous dialogue between herself and Molza, couched within the dialogue of Tullia, Tasso, and Grazia.

do its divine[xvi] operations among us. For I would say rather that love is born and lives among us and is mortal as we are.

Molza: All the world is in some sense full of God, especially we humans made in His image and likeness. From us, therefore, to us ourselves, inasmuch as we are divine,[xvii] love sends the darts and the flames of his torch; and a great indication of this is the eternity of being that (by his grace) our species acquires through the generation of one by another. Hence it comes about that neither place nor time limits love, but whoever loves perfectly wishes to have his beloved with him always and everywhere. What more? How many love, yet can't say what, being pleased by a grace in their lady that has no name? That grace, in order to make the world understand that it is something divine[xviii] and truly the companion of Venus, often deprives of its favor someone considered beautiful and makes us delight in those who are not beautiful, covering in them with his divine[xix] splendor every mortal accidental quality[xx] that might cause us displeasure.

Tullia: Ah, can it be that a god is the cause of so many errors and so many evils as we encounter in loving?

Molza: The errors and evils arise solely from us, for love in itself is the cause of nothing but good; therefore in heaven among the gods, as they are pure intellects, pure and optimal is their love.[xxi] But we mortals, whose lives are composed of little intellect and much dust, make room for love within us as the earth makes room for the sun; its material mass is illumined on the outside, but inside it is dark and horrid; moreover, what appeases the ears leaves the eyes full of desire, and what is food for one of the senses leaves the other four in hunger and thirst.

Tullia: Sometimes even the senses find peace among themselves, that is, when two lovers take their delight together, beyond which love can grant no greater.[xxii]

Molza: Ah, if love ever permitted you to feel his highest delight, tell me briefly, please, what do those long and frequent sighs mean that issue from lovers' mouths? What is the meaning of their biting each other? Of that beating of their hearts, as if, unable to remain in their breasts, the hearts wanted to jump out? And the interruption of kisses with words? And soon after, the interruption of those same desired and cherished words with other kisses? Drawing back a bit and relinquishing the touch of the beloved in order to fill the gaze? And once seen, immediately with greater fury than before hugging and drawing close again? And thus without pause, half drunk, halfway between being themselves and the other, neither living nor dead, enjoying that good than which (as you say) no greater can be granted them?

Tullia: Certainly I remained silent then, not knowing how to reply, until Molza began again.

Molza: The flesh and bone of which we are formed are the cause, by their imperfection, of our feeling those miraculous effects: for just as now it is not day all over the world, but our dusk is midnight for others, and the evening of this hemisphere is the dawn of the other, because the earth we tread and the heaven and the air around it are different bodies, this being opaque, those transparent; so too it is impossible that at the same moment love can make happy with its joys the eyes, touch, and ears of our body, things diverse and material. Nor should you be surprised by that, because, whenever a man touches his lady, he never completely fulfills his wish but, happy and content in his outer parts, he remains on the inside, where the pleasure doesn't reach, sad and full of desire. The lover, then, would like not just to embrace his beloved but alive and whole to penetrate her completely, as water enters a sponge; and not being able to do that, in the midst of all his joy he groans and sighs with desire. But reason, so highly praised by those who make little use of it, should arouse itself in mortal hearts at such a time of need, showing them who they are and of what mud they are composed, so that they may sooner thank Love, who does not scorn to visit them, than complain because he is not in them in the same manner that he is in heaven among the gods. For the fault belongs to these limbs, not more receptive to the grace of Love than the earth is to the rays of the sun; while the outer part of earth is illumined and kindled with its flames, the center remains cold and dark.[xxiii] Hence the sighs, hence the tears, hence the angers and outbursts, hence the jealousy of lovers, hence, finally, the tedium and displeasure that those same amorous delights bring them when continued too long. As the soil that last June produced grain, having lost its natural vigor that exhausted itself in the light of the sun, would not grow anything in the future, and therefore by plowing we cover the upper part and bring to the surface what lay below before we seed it; so mortal lovers, overcome in their pleasures by the divinity of Cupid, now gaze, now listen, and now embrace the beloved, making one sense a screen for the other, until the first sense, assailed and worn out, has regained its strength and courage to return to the war of its joys.

Tullia: Then are our limbs a bad thing, because they are the cause that this amorous felicity is converted into harm and displeasure?

Molza: Rather, they are good and very helpful to our imperfect nature, acting as a kind of shade between us and Love, reducing his overwhelming splendor so that we may be able to sustain it; otherwise, at the appearance of his presence our weak humanity, like Semele,[39] would turn into ash and flame.

Tullia: Is it possible, I responded, that someone enjoy such delight without being in love? And he, understanding my question, replied thus: "Who ever stopped eating…"And he, understanding my question, replied: "Who ever stopped eating in order not to tire his jaws? But what am I saying? Bring forward a philosopher who teaches us to love and unlove in my manner, just as one would learn to walk and sit, talk and be quiet and other such actions, which are caused not by destiny nor by fortune but only by our will. In how many forms, in how many ways, with what sort of arts and in how many places that we can't even imagine, can Love assail us and, despite our wishes, make himself lord of our minds?"

I certainly did not understand what he was saying then, but now I realize that the words spoken by that divine intellect two or three years ago were a prophecy of my Tasso,[xxiv] from whom every day Love sends me new flames. And no certainty that I may have of losing him can diminish my fire; nor am I any less his than I would be if he were to be mine perpetually. Nor does that surprise me, loving as I do. Indeed I would be very surprised (as if Love ever yielded to human foresight) if such a reason, diligently considered a thousand times and repeated to myself when I was not yet his, had preserved my liberty.[40] Verily, if what Molza

39. Semele, beloved by Jupiter, requested to see him in his full divine glory but was consumed and destroyed by that presence. Ovid recounts this story in *Metamorphoses*, 3.253–315.

40. I.e., even if she had known in advance that he would leave, no rational consideration of this fact could have prevented her from falling in love with him.

said, and what I feel at present, is true, then just as the eternity of the species is rather a gift of God than an action of mortals, so love, which is its cause, ought not to be subject to an individual's reason. It is a virtue to abstain from the baseness of gluttony; it is virtuous to be generous; very virtuous to be just: for with regard to food, gold, our prosperity, our adversity, rewards, punishments, things that are transient as we are and in some cases ordered for the well-being of a person or a city, it is worth providing oneself ahead of time with counsel. But amorous appetites lead us as they please, so that it is all our intellect can do to feed on the sight from afar, not daring to get on top and govern love with its laws. Who then will say that amorous appetites must be reined in and turned aside by reason, rejecting the path of love that leads those who follow it from earth to heaven, from time to eternity, and from death to life? Let the ignorant crowd come forward and praise wealth, as it is used to doing; let it place the tyrant and his lordship in their midst; let the philosophers admire their teachings and virtues; surely neither the former nor the latter will be so bold as to dare say that their professions can make another man as dear and similar to God as loving can. Those are the actions that adorn life, but this the one that renews life; those are proper to man, this alone we do not as humans but as immortals inspired by God; those benefit a few, this is ordered and arranged for the welfare of the entire species. So then, as much as it is a greater virtue to procure the public good than a private good, so much is it better to love one another than any other action that may bring either utility or glory.[xxv] But because the world has few people or none these days, or had ever in the past, who do not fight against and resist love, opposing reason to it (which ought to bow down to love), if it were permissible to me as it was to Molza to ascend into heaven and spy out the secrets of heaven's council and to reveal those secrets to mortals as did Tantalus,[41] I would say that when Venus, made pregnant by the will of her father, gave birth to Love, every god, on earth as in heaven, rejoiced with her wholeheartedly.[42] Only the rational soul, [xxvi] secretary and counselor of Jove in that time, as if guessing at her own harms, held that birth in contempt; and just as she had tried as hard as possible with every effort to interrupt that pregnancy, persuading the gentle goddess with vain reasoning to abort the intention of Jove, so too, after Love was born, Reason used every skill to seek his death, frequently bringing public allegations against Love: that his birth boded ill and that so strange a monster and one so different in appearance, born as he was blind and winged, should be exposed to wild beasts or drowned in the middle of the sea. But every argument was in vain; therefore, in deadly pain and blinded by envy, without thinking it over further, she plotted to poison him in such a manner that even if, being a god, he could not lose his life, yet at least he would become, like Scylla, so frightful that no god or goddess would fail to stay away from his rocks.[43] Mixing together a cruel and pestiferous brew of sighs, tears, fear, wrath, scorn, jealousy, and every other evil that a lover is used to feeling, and distilling this into a liquor, she planned to give this to Cupid to drink instead of nectar. But her treachery was discovered, and the gods, considering together how to punish her,

41. Tantalus revealed secrets of the gods to humans, or, in another version of the myth, stole nectar and ambrosia from the gods and gave it to humans, for which he was punished with eternal hunger and thirst. See Sir William Smith, *Smaller Classical Dictionary* (New York: Dutton & Co., 1958), 283.

42. This sentence may associate Venus with the Virgin Mary and Cupid with Christ, in which case the following sentence may indicate the mystery of faith at which rationality balks.

43. Scylla, once a beautiful girl, was turned by a jealous god into a hideous monster, living on a cliff by the sea; sailors tried to give that cliff a wide berth so as not to be snatched and devoured by her. She appears in the *Odyssey* 12.85–126 and in Ovid's *Metamorphoses* 14.8–74.

agreed that, as we read about Perillus and his ox,[44] the rational soul should be punished with those same means by which she wanted to afflict Love. Thus while Love remained pure and healthy above, Reason, the rebel, was condemned to taste the venom that she had brewed for him down among these limbs, where she still hates and persecutes every amorous delight and will hate them forever.

Grazia: Your own intelligence would have been enough to contradict me without having recourse to Molza and making use of the authority of such a man, who I cannot believe would have said and thought about love what you attribute to him. And even if he does think that way, we should not accept his view and give credence to fables that the poets are accustomed to tell and to make up by themselves about the doings of the gods. Surely if there were anyone who, narrating about matters of heaven, were worthy to be believed, you would be such a one; for as you are divine in every part, one must think that you were born in heaven and grew up there and, full of heavenly ideas, were sent by God to come among us to reveal to some of us the good that is up there. And someone who ought to know has already said such a thing in his poems.[45] Be careful, however, not to make things of this sort public to the common folk, and let that Tantalus whom you mentioned be a warning example to you.

Tullia: Your advice comes too late, for I have already been Tantalus for many days, expecting at every moment

44. Perillus invented for his tyrant a metal ox that, with a fire lit beneath it, would bellow with the cries of the person tormented inside it; the tyrant decided that a fitting reward for Perillus was to put him into his own ox to suffer the torment he had devised for others. See Pliny's *Natural History* 34.19.39. Ovid refers to him in *Ars amatoria (Art of Love)* 1.653–56.

45. A reference to Tasso's poetry about Tullia, but this poetic conceit has a long earlier history.

that the food with which my life is nourished will be taken away from me, leaving me starving.

Grazia: The person who will take him away from you will also give him back to you, and then you will eat all the more willingly, as your appetite will be bigger. But if you don't mind, we will talk about this a little later; now let's talk about reason and love, which you make out to be eternal enemies, and you are very much mistaken, for between them is that true and holy affection that exists between a mother and her son. Therefore, love willingly obeys reason and, blind as he is, is glad to let her approach and guide him. Otherwise one should expect from his flight only bad effects, for a ship without a rudder is more likely to sink the more strongly the winds blow it. Nor is it valid to say that, because love causes the perpetuity of the species, we ought, in following him, to abandon every other enterprise, both honest and useful; for eternity is a terrible pain when not accompanied by virtue. For that reason Ulysses, the wisest of all mortals,[xxvii] chose rather to die in Ithaca and be buried together with Penelope than to live forever in delights with Calypso. But by God, how happy will be the immortality of a love that is shared by both the virtuous and the vicious? By you, rare and divine Lady, and the vulgar herd?[xxviii] Let us go further. This same eternity, which love gives to our species, does he not give it as well to the beasts, to the plants, to the rocks and earth that we tread upon? Then after a thousand efforts and a thousand amorous trials, after burning and freezing, after the angers, the contempt, the jealousy, after sighs, after tears, after poverty, after public infamy, and finally after death, will man have acquired nothing but what makes him equal to a dog? God forbid that I should believe your thoughts to be so base that you love or deign to be loved to such an end.

Tullia: Not to make ourselves equal to such things but in or-
          der not to let them get ahead of us, we must by loving
          make ourselves immortal. But certainly the power of
          love must be very great when it makes the lowest crea-
          tures in the world act equal to the dearest.

Grazia: That lord would not please me at all who made no dis-
          tinction between me and some page boy of his, but
          rewarded our services equally.

Tullia: As long as you were rewarded fairly for your service,
          you shouldn't complain if he rewards someone else
          above that person's merits, for the lord is not miserly
          to you just because he's generous to someone else.

Tasso: Truly, Signora Tullia, you offer no small offense to the
          courtesy of Grazia when you interrupt his words after
          he listened so kindly to yours.[xxix] And you, Grazia, are
          no less in error against her, blaming her love instead
          of praising your own. For Venus did not get the apple
          from Paris by insulting the other two goddesses but by
          being more beautiful, or rather by giving him some-
          thing that Pallas and Juno could not offer. Therefore
          it would be better that, just as Signora Tullia showed
          us her sun, you bring forward this centaur composed
          of reason and love, whose strangeness may be no less
          beautiful to see than the light of the sun; especially as
          it supposedly carries lovers on its back to a better goal
          than the immortality of the species.

Grazia: I obey you promptly and am content if you wish the
          love that I am preparing to bring forth to be baptized
          by you as a centaur; on condition, however, that, in
          attaching this name to it, you don't conclude that Tul-
          lia's opinion is better and truer than mine, as much as
          the sun is a nobler and truer thing than any centaur
          ever depicted by poets or painters. For I warn you that

centaurs too have their place above, a place perhaps higher and closer to God than the sun in its chariot.[46] Therefore, leaving aside the disparity of the words and not caring which name might more beautifully signify the operations of love, but attending to the fact, I say that love is no other than the desire for something that is truly or appears to someone to be good. That desire comes in as many modes as there are natures in the universe, for each of the elements desires its proper place in a manner different from the way the plant desires water and animals desire their mates, and to those who understand, each is granted a different way of pursuing its own felicity: one way for us humans, another way for celestial creatures. And if it is permitted in talking about such a topic to mention the creator of all things, God loves the world that he created differently from the way that he is loved and desired by it. But talking about ourselves, it is true that we are born and die in the same manner as the beasts; yet our behaviors and manners of living are of quite another style than those of brutes. And that is because when we are taken from the arms of our mother nature, reason—without which there would be no humanity—raises and nourishes us with new and delicate foods; those foods (if I may make use of magnificent[xxx] words) I would call the nectar and ambrosia so much celebrated by antiquity. I would say similarly that the truth—which I told you was hidden by someone under a veil in that fable in which we read that Jove, at the death of his beloved Semele, drew Bacchus out from her womb and bound him to his thigh and carried him, so bound, until Bacchus had gone from his unfinished form to a perfected birth—is that he was

46. According to geocentric astronomy, the constellation of the centaur is in the eighth sphere with the fixed stars, whereas the sun is in the fourth sphere.

worthy to be born the son of such a father.[47] So then, when we see a fair lady (so that I may better explain what I mean), her beauties please a man no differently than the dove pleases its mate; and in the brute beasts love passes through the eyes and through the other senses of the body to the heart of whoever loves, to wound him, to kill him, and to dominate and compel him just as in man; except that in the beasts love, being something raw and material, does only those lowly actions that nature teaches them for the welfare of the species. But in us, as soon as we feel love in our breasts, reason, which dwells in a higher part, eager for this novelty, courteously welcomes it and considers with diligence on one side the mind and body of the lady, on the other side what noble and honorable effects a lofty spirit is likely to produce when enamored, hoping not only to enjoy the beloved object but through her also to raise itself so high that she may see perfectly her hoped-for happiness; finally reason forms an image with the sight of which she feeds the love that she governs not otherwise than the flowers of spring feed on the rays of the sun. That love, when it has grown as much as befits it, sitting in the highest place of the soul not far from its nurse, reason, in the same way that the sun moves the earth's liquid to create the fruits we gather, arouses every part of the body to its proper office so effectively that no one part envies another its good. It is true that as the earth, warmed and illumined by the light of heaven, often generates some nasty vapors that, converted into clouds, obscure the light of the sun; so sometimes this earthly body, too much afire with amorous desire, with its strange appetites, perturbs the clarity of reason, whereupon love is left blinded. For I forgot to

47. See Ovid's *Metamorphoses* 3.311–15: when Jupiter, appearing in his full glory, had caused the death of his lover Semele (see above, note 39), he took their unborn son Bacchus from her womb and carried him to term in his thigh.

mention that reason can do to love what the sun does to the moon, which without its light would be always cold and dark. But perhaps I am acting amiss in comparing love to the sun when I promised to compare it to a centaur. Therefore, to change similes, have you by chance ever heard how the bear is born as a shapeless piece of flesh and how after his birth the mother with her tongue licks him into the shape that we see? Just so reason does to that new love that the soul, full of the beauties it has seen, gives birth to in its heart; and because, in that part of itself that we share with the beasts, love is not capable of the shaping power of reason, its form turns out to be mixed: from the middle down being bestial and in the upper half, where reason shaped it, becoming human as we are. Here, then, in a few words is the centaur that you asked me to show you, like a Nessus or a Chiron, with both hands full of darts.[48] Although he is already swift and light on his own, in order to make him even speedier we can add to him two wings like those of the horse of Parnassus,[49] and now the picture is complete.

Tasso: If the actions of your love are anything like the figure you describe, little honor may a lover expect from it. For, without thinking further about it, I would rather err with my Lady by believing (as she believes) that love is entirely divine than, knowing the truth, be certain that he is half a horse; for whereas at present I am his and glory extremely that everyone knows that I write and sing about his arrows, in that other case being familiar with him, serving him, praising him,

---

48. Nessus and Chiron are famous classical centaurs. For Nessus, see Ovid, *Metamorphoses*, 9.98–171. For Chiron as the teacher of Achilles, see Ovid, *Ars amatoria (Art of Love)*, 1.11–18, and Statius, *Achilleid*, 1. Both centaurs are mentioned by Dante in *Inferno* 12.

49. Pegasus is the flying horse associated with the spring of Helicon and with Mount Parnassus as the sites of poetic inspiration.

and adoring him as lovers do would seem to be proper work for a stablehand and not for a poet.

Grazia: So then, not without cause did I make a deal with you, when politely accepting your name of centaur, that we should not argue about either names or images. But tell me, you who take so much delight in praising love, does such love as you experience not satisfy you?

Tasso: Yes, very well.

Grazia: Now what else is the life of man but a mixture of reason and sensation? So then, we are centaurs, our soul is a centaur.[xxxi] The centaur is love, who rules us; that love, mixed not only of man and beast but of infinite contraries united in him alone, mixing together two lovers and making of them a hermaphrodite, grants to both their due felicity.

Tullia: Tell me at least to which of them he gives more: to the lover or the beloved.

Tasso: As if anyone doubted the answer to that.

Tullia: Certainly I am very much in doubt about it; and if I were not hesitant to interrupt Grazia's speeches, I would insist on a reply.

Grazia: Rather in this manner you will finish and complete my words; for in resolving this question we will become sure of some things about love that are good and necessary to know. But let Tasso resolve the matter by serving us as an example; for to his most happy state no amorous felicity can be compared.

Tasso: A bit later we can talk about my supreme happiness, and I will show you how it happens that sometimes the lover by an excess of happiness becomes unhappy. Now, my Lady, responding to your question, to me it seems that the beloved, in whose judgment love places the lover's happiness, is by far the most happy and blessed, not so much with respect to the lover as with respect to love, which (as some say) continually resides and lodges in her face and from whose beauty it takes its power to work the miracles for which we always adore him as a god.[xxxii] Thus we read: "Blessed art thou who can bless another"; and elsewhere, the poet says of Love: "Your power fades at the closing of her fair eyes."[50]

Therefore, I would say that Love not only puts together two lovers to make a sort of hermaphrodite, but first of all unites himself to the beloved object and makes himself her, in such a way that I can truly call him "Tullia" and call you "Love," as Petrarch wrote in this verse among many others: "When Love bends earthward the fair eyes."[51]

But leaving aside miracles,[xxxiii] let us descend to experience. What do you think the lover is seeking? What does he value in his sighs? What end does his desire aim at? In what does he place his hope, his heart and his good, other than to be loved by the one he loves and adores? Ask the one in love with Laura, when he consoled himself by saying:

Perhaps over there
now you sigh at being far away.
And in this thought the soul breathes.

And shortly after:

Perhaps, worthless to yourself, you are dear to an other.[52]

---

50. The poet is, as usual, Petrarch: *Rime*, 341.9 and 270.105.

51. *Rime*, 167.1.

52. Petrarch, *Rime*, 129. 63–65 and 24. Thus "shortly after" should be "shortly before."

Now hear a great marvel concerning Tasso: that whereas this hope alone comforted and sustained Petrarch among the thousand travails that he felt in love, the sure knowledge that you love me as much as I know by experience you do, turns all my joy into wretchedness; for even though the sun with its light is the cause of all things becoming visible, nonetheless the eye in fixing itself too much on that splendor loses its sight, so your loving me more than befits my merits is a happiness beyond measure, dazzled by which my soul loses its sense of all joys, not otherwise than Semele in the presence of her lover Jove, surrounded by lightning flashes, lost her life. That is why I have often begged you, and I beg you anew, that you love me not as much as you are able to love but as much as I am worthy, tempering somewhat your inexpressible courtesy, so that I may not, in despair at ever compensating it, hate myself and my life.

Tullia: Yet for once the excessive love I bear you will do you good, for if I loved you a bit less, I would sooner believe you to be a flattering Spaniard than a man truly in love. Hear me then as to why it pains you so that I love and appreciate you too much, for if the effects are known to you, you may nonetheless be deceived about the cause; then let Grazia judge the truth. Whoever loves, as I love you, by loving moves the beloved to love;[53] and if he does it gladly, behold Grazia's hermaphrodite. But if he does otherwise and is forcibly compelled to love a lover for whom he naturally feels distaste, there arises between love and his heart a war that makes his life miserable. That war grows all the crueler the stronger the imprint left on his heart by the lover's love. For that reason, recognizing the cause of his pain, he complains about the one who loves him

---

53. An evocation of the verse in Dante's *Inferno* 5.103: "love that excuses no beloved from loving."

the way he would complain about someone who had wounded him. But it is true indeed that, in loving me as you say you do, I see that you deceive yourself, for I know who I am and who I would have to be to deserve such love. But either I will change my manner of life and be the master of my will, or I will die in the attempt.

Grazia: Be glad, Signora Tullia, for just a few days ago I saw an oration by Brocardo[54] in praise of courtesans, in which he exalts them in such a way that if Lucretia came back to life and heard it, she would live in no other way.[55] Among other things, after showing that it is proper to women to live the life of a courtesan and that those who live differently do violence to nature, which created them for that purpose, he shows in what way the manners of courtesans (if we rightly esteem those) are a path and ladder to the knowledge of God.[xxxiv] For just as the courtesan loves many men for diverse reasons—this man because he loves her entirely, that man because he is rich and noble, so-and-so because he is handsome, and another, finally, because he is full of every virtue—and with each of them at the appropriate time and place she shares (according to his rank) her favors, glances, laughter and words and all that nature formed in her to the delight of the crowd, yet giving her heart to one alone and in him only taking special pleasure and transforming herself into him; so God[xxxv] diversely bestows his favor and his being on diverse mortal objects, granting

54. Antonio Brocardo was a Venetian who wrote poetry and other texts, of which not much remains. Born like Speroni in 1500, he was dead by 1531. Tasso, a friend of Brocardo's, lamented his death in several sonnets in his first volume of *Rime*. The oration on courtesans was obviously witty and humorous, in the paradox genre of arguing a case opposed to common thought.

55. The ancient Roman Lucretia is a famously chaste wife who committed suicide to prove that the king Tarquin had raped her against her will.

to the more and less perfect according as their nature requires. And although all those things hold the elements in common and, whether fish, birds or other animals, equally enjoy them, yet among them all man alone was selected by the creator of all things to receive the imprint of an image of divinity so that man more than any other being might resemble him.

Tullia: This speech of yours is very similar to the paintings we commonly call "distant views," where there are landscapes in which one sees several small figures walking that appear to be humans but, examined up close, have not one part resembling human limbs. Therefore I would prefer that, setting aside poetry, you would consider the servitude, the lowliness, the baseness, and the inconstancy of this type of life,[xxxvi] blaming those who consider it good and excusing her (if there be any such) who, pushed into this error[xxxvii] when she was young and foolish, seeks to escape from it whenever she may be able, drawing close to those who, by admonishing and helping, are capable of raising her out of that misery. But Brocardo, because of the love he felt for some courtesan or in order to show off better the flower of his wit, and not in order to do justice, took to praising a cause so dishonest.

Grazia: He would not call a courtesan lowly or base, but servile and inconstant, yes; for she remains in one state for only a brief hour. For that reason more than for any other, he supremely praises and honors her life, comparing it to the sun, which, as a god,[xxxviii] never disdains to share with us its splendor, serving us (who adore[xxxix] it) like a handmaid. The sun never stands still, nor does it light always one same place, but moving continually and now arriving at the sign of Taurus and now Leo and now another sign, making distinct the hours and seasons, with invariable variety it maintains the state of the universe. Such was Sappho; such was she from whom Socrates, the wisest and best man, gloried to have learned what love is.[56] Accept, then, being the third in number among such worthies; and pray to Love that he may compose a little tale about our conversation wherein he writes your name just as the name of Diotima appears in the dialogues of Plato.[57] And so that it may be done to your glory, teach us in what manner the lover, loving the beloved object, moves her to love and how it can be possible that sometimes the beloved, while loving, hates and resents the lover; for these claims are quite divergent from each other and from the common opinion of men, and so they need your intelligence to explain to your listeners how they are, if not true, at least plausible.

Tullia: I don't think there is any woman born who loves more than I do and who understands less about the secrets of love. But everything I say about it is what I have read or heard said by someone else, and so that's how I will answer; except that occasionally, to show more clearly what I mean, I will make up things that God knows whether they are relevant at all.[xl] So then, what I was saying before, that is, that the lover draws the beloved to love, is a statement well known to everyone.[xli] And Dante already confirmed it, when he said:

Love that excuses no beloved from loving.[58]

---

56. Sappho was an ancient Greek poet but not, in fact, a courtesan. In Plato's *Symposium*, Socrates describes the priestess Diotima as teaching Socrates about love; she, too, was not a courtesan. The revision inserts as another example the Greek poet Corinna, thus numbering Tullia as the fourth.

57. In asking Tullia to glory in being written about like Diotima, Speroni is also comparing himself to Plato.

58. See above, note 53.

About that verse, very often contemplated and verified by me, hear the dream of someone awake. The lover (as it seems to me) is properly a portrait of what he loves; by considering his manners and the acts that the lover does for his love, one can better know what she is and how worthy she is than one could ever know through some accidental quality of her own. Therefore the poet said:

But as often as you turn back toward me
you see in another what you are.[59]

So then, the beloved loves the one who loves her in the way that a father loves his son who resembles him. For "to love" is not, as the word sounds, to do or act something, but rather to suffer something being done; and "being loved" is a verb not passive but active. I say this according to the rules of our teacher Love, a strange and marvelous grammarian, who writes not with syllables or words but with human hearts. And I dare say that, just as a painter with colors and skill portrays the likeness of a person, and the mirror lit by the sun's rays offers not only the likeness but even the movement of the person mirrored; so the beloved, with the stylus of love, makes in the face and in the heart of the lover an image of herself and all that is hers, both body and soul. So that just as in a mirror the same face simultaneously sees and is seen by itself, so the same love that enamors the lover, showing itself to the beloved, causes her forcibly to love and appreciate the one who loves her. Which, if she does willingly, delighting all the while to see in another's face that she is a person lovable and most honorable, no other thing can be more pleasing to anyone who has within any aspect of humanity. Thus, everyone likes to be loved and held dear by others, but we don't always yield to and love

59. Petrarch, *Rime*, 71.59–60.

the lover, for just as the love of the lover is destiny, that is a force and violence done by heaven, so the hatred we bear for another is fate and the disposition of the planets that govern us, which neither gods nor men are able to resist.[xlii] And certainly to love the one who loves us is no other than simply to love and wish well oneself and one's body; in the other we see as in a mirror in which our soul, more than usually desirous of its own beauty, enjoys and rejoices at contemplating itself. You, Signor Grazia, who along with many others think love is a mortal thing and subject to reason, would say otherwise: that is, even if the beloved naturally loves the lover for loving her, nonetheless it often happens that, looking him over and noting with diligence one by one the lover's conditions, which are perhaps not so divine[xliii] as would seem desirable, the beloved chooses in the end to dislike him; not otherwise than those great-spirited Romans used to do who, coming into the hands of their enemies, killed themselves, mortally hating nothing but the servitude in which the enemy wanted to keep them alive.[xliv] But another time I concluded with Molza[xlv] that Love is not a god of such little valor as to serve the wishes of mortals. Therefore, getting back to the similitude with which I began, I would say that the lover whom the beloved dislikes, due to his ill fortune or because of some defect he has, is in his love for her like those concave mirrors used to kindle fire, which, illumined by the sun, do not give back a proper image of the one who looks into it, but instead dazzle and strangely offend the eyes of the person mirrored.

Grazia: I'm not sure how correct it is in talking about the deeds of Love, a god (according to you) supreme and mighty,[xlvi] for us to take our arguments from portraits and images that, being only the dreams and shadows of our real being, cannot well make known to us the truth we seek.

Tullia: Now what else is the world other than a beautiful and large gathering of portraits made by nature? She, having in mind to paint the glory of God and not being able to collect it all into one spot, produced infinite species of things that, each in its own way, might resemble some part of him. The world as a whole, then, is a portrait of God made by the hand of nature.[xlvii] The lover is a portrait; the mirror and the artist portray; but the portrait by the painter (which is the only type commonly called "portrait") is less good than all the others, because of the life of a man it represents only the color of the skin and nothing further.

Tasso: You do wrong to Titian, whose images are of such a kind and so well made that it is better to be painted by him than to be generated by nature.[xlviii]

Tullia: Titian is not a painter nor is his power mere skill, but a miracle; and it is my opinion that his paints are mixed with that marvelous herb that, tasted by Glaucus, transformed him from a man into a god.[60] Truly his portraits possess a kind of divinity, for just as heaven is the paradise of souls, so it seems that in his paints God has placed the paradise of our bodies, not painted but made holy and glorified by his hands.

Grazia: Certainly Titian these days is a marvel of this age, but you praise him in such a manner that Aretino would be astonished.[61]

---

60. See Ovid, *Metamorphoses*, 13.898–968.

61. Aretino, living in Venice since 1527, wrote and published his praises and dispraises of many contemporaries. Note that the revision cut all reference to him.

Tullia: Aretino portrays things with words no less well than Titian does with paints. I have seen some of his sonnets written about portraits by Titian, and it's not easy to judge whether the sonnets derived from the portraits or the portraits from the sonnets; surely both together, the sonnet and the portrait, are perfect: the one gives voice to the painting, the other in return dresses the sonnet in flesh and bone. I think that being painted by Titian and praised by Aretino may be a new regeneration of men, who, no matter how little value they may have in themselves, in the paints and in the verses of these two become most noble and precious. But now no more of this; let's get back to what we were talking about when the mastery of both these men and my love for them made me digress. The lover, in sum, as a lover, is a portrait of the object he loves. That lover can be a person of such perverse intellect and behaviors that, like a poorly prepared cloth, he will not receive wholly the painting done by love or, having received it, will strangely transmute what was correct into something distorted. That must be no less displeasing to the beloved than it was to Alexander to be painted by a hand other than Apelles's.[62] Therefore, not without reason, I regret being incapable of bearing the portrait of Tasso in a manner that would show back to him exactly how he is, and I fear that, disdaining my fate, he may find some other woman in whom Love with greater mastery can paint and sculpt him the way he deserves. But let Love do as he will; to me it is enough to be loved by Tasso, even if it is only because I love him; and this little glory will console my loss in such a way that, if I do not live happy, at least I won't die of despair.

---

62. Apelles is the most famous Greek painter; Horace, *Epistles*, 2.1.237–41, and Pliny, *Naturalis historia*, 7.125, both mention Alexander not wanting his portrait painted by any other artist. The idea was repeated in Italian in Castiglione's widely read *Book of the Courtier*, 1.52.

Tasso: My lady, it is not your office to love but to be loved, and I ought sooner to be called your portrait than you mine. It is very true that you are so generous to me (not to say prodigal) with yourself that, not content to let me love you (going out beyond your boundaries) you come to meet my love so swiftly that your love seems to come first and not to respond to mine. But that is not the case, or else you would be perverting the condition of things.

Grazia: I know a number of women who love greatly; but these same women are loved in a way that they should be called rather beloveds than lovers; I don't yet know whether that is a sign of the perfection or imperfection of their sex. Therefore, watch out, Signora Tullia, that while believing to humble yourself, you don't exalt yourself.[63] And you, Tasso, consider a bit better whether the title of being beloved is a greater praise to your lady than the title of loving.

Tasso: Infinitely greater. For being loved means nothing other than possessing some good that the lover, lacking, desires and tries to gain. And to show that this is true, suppose that God[xlix] gave me all the gifts of my lady and that I enjoyed them in myself in the way that I currently enjoy them in her; surely loving her would be superfluous because, being sufficient to myself (like another Narcissus), I would not care about anyone else.[64] In truth, loving with respect to being loved is like serving with respect to being a lord, or receiving a favor with respect to granting one. Therefore, since God has foreseen that beauty and grace, the principal qualities of one who is loved and desired by another, would be much greater in women than in men, and

63. Tullia may think she is humbling herself by being the lover rather than beloved of Tasso, but by usurping the male role, she is rising above her proper status.

64. For the story of Narcissus, see Ovid, *Metamorphoses*, 3.339–510.

since he has, on the other hand, endowed the lover with a strong spirit fit to support the trials of love, as we men are,¹ who through every season, by day and by night, at the risk of our lives, swim the sea, scale the towers, and penetrate the depths of the earth in order to get near the beloved lady, we can be very certain how great and of what nature is the perfection of the lady and how deceived they are who hold the opinion that woman is born not as an ornament but as a defect of the male.⁶⁵

Grazia: If what you say is true, then the man loves the woman more fiercely than the woman loves him, and she consequently is rather ungrateful to him; but that, in the presence of Tullia, you will not dare to affirm. I surely not only would affirm it, and think it well said, but would boldly add that our love for women, being the greater and more ardent, is also the swifter to kindle; therefore they are deservedly called the beloveds and we the lovers. But that is because all that Love, residing in the heart of the lady, cannot achieve in her directly because of the coldness of her soul, he brings to effect by returning to her from the lover with redoubled effort, like a victorious leader, a matter that (to tell the truth), if we consider it carefully, is rather to be blamed than praised.⁶⁶

Tasso: When the woman loves the man as much as she ought to, even if her love is not equal to that of the man, I would not call her either stingy or ungrateful. Moreover, I tell you that if the man loves the woman principally with the aim that she love him, nonethe-

---

65. This Aristotelian view (see, e.g., *On the Generation of Animals*, 1.20.728a and 4.3.767b–768b) was widely repeated before and during the Renaissance debates about women.

66. Aristotelian science considered the female to be colder than the male. However, the greater ease with which men, being hotter, are kindled with love is not necessarily a good thing.

less the reward that the woman, grateful and generous according to the laws of love, is obliged to give him is not to love and caress him but only to be pleased that he loves her. In that way the lovers' wishes, and the lovers themselves, truly form a hermaphrodite. But for God's sake,[li] what good does the man do for the woman in loving her? And from what did you infer that the man's love is greater than the woman's? For as God, beloved and desired by the world, loves the world he created more than it loves him, so it may be that the woman, naturally loved and desired by us, loves us more than we love her; or is the comparison that you made rather empty and most inappropriate? For just as one ought not[67] to say that these walls are more or less white than whiteness itself, which is not white but makes the wall white, so the woman properly does not love but *is* the love of the man, for which he is called "lover." However, the ignorant crowd, incapable of the mysteries of love, believes and speaks the contrary, holding the opinion that to love a woman is a great favor to her, for which we make her out to be, alive and dead, obliged to us.

Grazia: I am extremely pleased with all your other claims, because with some you taught me many things that I now hold for very true, and with others you delighted me by fine wit. But in one alone you displease me: when you affirm that the lover, loving the beloved, does nothing other than desire to take part in the good that she possesses. Surely if that were the case, love would not be love but adulation, or rather a merchandising of the wills of men, who would enter into the sea of love with hope for some gain.

---

67. "Not" appears only in the revised text, but its omission seems to me an error in the editing of the earlier text.

Tasso: It is less bad that we make Love a merchant than so base and wretched a man as we see asking and begging from hour to hour for his life.

Tullia: Now is the world so bold as to dare to say that Love is an unfortunate beggar?

Tasso: Whoever thinks that weeping and sighing at every hour and appearing pale and lean of face is the way to make oneself loved by the beloved holds the opinion that love is nothing other than being wretched and begging bread for God's sake.

Tullia: I would have sworn that the sighs and tears were to the lover like water to the sea and light to the sun, or rather like a sword to a knight. For with such arms one sees hearts conquered that were as cold and hard as diamonds. I will say something about us, and it's something very true: I firmly believe every action of yours shows that you love me infinitely; but sometimes I have seen your love for me shining and sparkling in your tears just like a ray of sun in a pure and transparent crystal. And surely if when you leave, seeing my weeping, you do not weep with me, my heart will not feel sure of the love you bear me.

Grazia: Do me a favor, Tasso, and in the matters that pertain to you (such as what we're talking about) let me be your advocate; for it is not proper for you to praise yourself, nor can anyone respond to the lady without doing that. I say then, with your permission, that it is true that the sighs and tears of the innocent move another to have compassion; yet it is one thing to have pity for a mendicant and another to love and feel loving to a friend. Thus just as we gladly give, for God's sake, a coin or two[68] to a poor sick fellow without oth-

---

68. The reference here is to specific Venetian coins, a "*grosso*" or a "*marcello*."

erwise loving or caressing him, so a wise and kindly lady will be gracious enough to give to one of these lovesick men a glance, a laugh, and sometimes a word (without anything more). For if the lover's pain is a sign that he loves, it does not therefore cause anyone else to love him; so I don't believe that, even if Tasso were to weep for years and years at his departure, he would move your mind to love him and hold him dear unless his valor and virtue merited it. The damned person groans and sighs forever; and this same sorrowful and pained sinner never ceases being under the wrath of God because no goodness accompanies him that would make him worthy of God's grace.[lii] So then, tears by themselves are only a sign of desire, not a cause of mercy. Those tears streaming from the eyes of your Tasso have a special privilege of making him loved by others because he is a fine and lovable object, who, along with his intelligence and his admirable virtue, allows a large place to kindly behavior, treating as equal even the common folk; for if he (made proud by the talents of his mind) disdained to be born and live as a mortal, certainly his valor would make us feel more envious than charmed. But as to the manner in which he and you should lament his departure, and what good and what evil that departure may cause you, I will speak of that shortly. Now, my dear Signor Tasso, if I have made a satisfactory reply for you to the lady's argument, you must yourself satisfy both her and me; for it seems to me that you wronged any honest man and especially your own honor when you let slip from your mouth that love is flattery or a desire for gain.

Tasso: The end of every action of ours is something that we desire and aim at through our action, that is, glory, pleasure, or utility. These three ends, although sometimes they are found united so that the glory is pleasurable and useful, the pleasure useful and glorious, and the utility glorious and pleasurable, nonetheless they are naturally distinct; and they are divided in such a way that each of these ends has a corresponding beginning and middle that do not fit with the other two. But what do I mean by beginning and middle? By some of our human actions (if you please) we reach at glory, by others at what is useful, and others lead you toward delight so entirely that to turn them in another direction would be nothing other than to throw the world into confusion, depriving it of that order by which its creator distinguished its parts. A woman, then (joy and delight of the universe), loves not for pleasure that she might get from it, but so that by giving pleasure and joy to her lover, her courtesy, sweetness and generosity[liii] (not widely noticed on their own) may be celebrated and praised. This is the good, this is the reward, this is the aim[69] of her life and her love for us; surely it is no different from the divine, who, coming forth somewhat from himself, created heaven and earth for no other end than that there might be those who, coming into being and living, magnify his goodness.[liv] Now, my lady, if, on the contrary, I, being a man, love you, not for any utility nor for glory but only for that pleasure that your beauty and virtue bring to whoever admires them, and if, you being ugly and without virtue, I did not deign even to look at you, who would ever blame me? May you be still beautiful, and may you heal and refresh with your virtue the beauty that time or illness often consumes; then surely, young or old, you will be loved and held dear.

Grazia: Not only young and old but living and dead, from now until a thousand years hence.

---

69. I have used "aim" here to avoid the ambiguity of "end of her life."

Tullia:	How so?
Grazia:	In Tasso's poetry, in which, like a relic in its reliquary, your name, praises, and virtues will be devoutly adored by those faithful followers of Love.[lv]
Tullia:	They will be adoring not my relic but my reliquary.
Tasso:	May God grant that this reliquary of mine not turn out to be a cobweb. But let my verses be as they may, I am not without hope that however many people may blame their art, as many more will praise and admire my love, constant and firm as a jasper; my love is the way it is because you are the way you are, that is, beautiful of body and of mind, and in a manner so proportionate between them that to this body no other mind and to this mind no other body but yours could belong.
Grazia:	This same proportion can be found between the two of you, from which perhaps initially arose the love you feel; for to her no other lover and to you no other beloved could properly belong.
Tasso:	If this is true, I hope that my verses will bring her as much glory as she has brought me delight and virtue; and may that proportion be perfect. But let's return to my discussion of ends, which have a place not only in the love of lovers but also in the love between father and son, produced and nourished by the father with hope that the son may support the homeland, the family, and the father's own body when broken and weakened by age. Thus it happens that a father generally loves his sons much more than he is loved by them; and that among his children, he loves the male more than the female; and among the males, the oldest, as the one who can fulfill his desire sooner than the oth-

ers. Similarly friendship—I mean the kind that is an enemy of flattery (by which Theseus and Pirithous, Nisus and Euryalus, Laelius and Scipio were such loyal friends)[70]—is a pathway in our life into which man would not enter if it did not lead to one of the three aforementioned ends. At another time I will demonstrate this to you distinctly. For now it is time that you, Grazia, with your sweet comforts console us for my imminent departure, and then let us make place for Molino, Capello,[71] and so many other noble and rare intellects who (on the holiday, when they are through with their official advising) are in the habit of visiting my lady, poetizing and philosophizing with her.

Tullia: The consolation for Tasso's departure will be my death; for since he and I have the same relationship as my body and soul, when he leaves, my soul will depart that keeps me alive. Therefore your words will be to me as are those songs to the dead with which we accompany them to their burial.[lvi]

Grazia: Surely above all else I wanted to show you how great is the error of those[lvii] who believe that love is in us as a destiny and fatal violence; from that opinion (as from an evil root) spring up in you, Signora Tullia, some ideas that I would gladly (if I could) uproot from that divine intellect.[lviii] And to do that, I was starting to make a case about anger, which often quenches and occasionally inflames the love of lovers, depending on whether it blows more or less forcefully into their hearts—a very clear sign that love is a choice or

---

70. Famous classical pairs of friends. Nisus and Euryalus appear in Virgil's *Aeneid* 5.291–361 and 9.176–449. Cicero dedicated his treatise "On Friendship" to Laelius because of Laelius's friendship with Scipio.

71. Girolamo Molino was a Venetian patrician who corresponded with both Speroni and Tullia and attended the Venier salon, at which writers, musicians, and artists mingled with the upper class. Bernardo Cappello was another Venetian friend of Tasso and Molino.

a human affection, not a force of heaven; mortal is that from which love takes now food and now poison, which either kills or restores it. But you, full of passion whenever you talk or sigh about this departure, impress in my breast an image of you so worthy of compassion that the reasoning of which I ought to have told you (speaking of amorous angers and pacifications) has been converted into pity; spurred by that pity, I must run to the topic of Tasso's departure, which you compare to your death—wittily, as I don't deny, but certainly very wrongly. For it is not always the case that when our soul departs from our body, we cease to live; rather when we long to see God and his minister Nature by contemplation while in this flesh, it becomes necessary, while still living, to separate the intellect from the sense perceptions and to raise it so high above them that the smoke of their appetites does not interfere with our view of the desired bliss. So then, if I show you that Tasso's departure can achieve the same effect in you and your love, what will you have to complain about? And why will you not rather have to praise and thank him for that good that his going away will bring you? Of course, being in the presence of the beloved and completely enjoying her person is a good part of the happiness of a lover; but love can offer a much greater happiness, which, though it remains unknown to the common herd, love by a special grace concedes to his noble-minded elect[72] in such a manner that only then do they truly reach the summit of all their joy when others expect to see them downcast in wretchedness. Now I don't intend to repeat what you previously said you heard from Molza about the senses and love; but, confirm-

---

72. The contrast between the "*vulgari*" and the "*gentili*" is a class distinction; but since the thirteenth century, poets had argued that love creates or selects its own "nobility" among those men (especially poets) not of aristocratic birth. The religious imagery here was retained in the revision.

ing his claim, I now add two things: one, that since the lover, seeing, hearing, and touching, is still not happy, in order that we may not love each other in vain, it is necessary that we have recourse to reason, in which all our operations are refined like gold in the fire and become perfect.[lix] The second thing is that, as in amorous joys one sense impedes the other, so the soul, having wandered astray after sense perceptions, abandons reason so entirely that it forgets to behold the delight present before it, much less anything else. Therefore, even if the senses were capable of every amorous bliss, nonetheless only then would the lover be worthy of being called happy when reason, somewhat removed from the battle of the senses, showed him that the true felicity is that to which love, by means of the limbs and body, has brought him. For our consciousness of the state in which we find ourselves is not the function of the senses to give us but only of that noble power that above all others makes man human, that is, capable of understanding perfectly his own good and the good of others. The senses see, hear, and taste, but by themselves they don't know what they're doing; therefore not without cause they are compared to the streets we walk along, which directly (but not knowing it themselves) lead one to the desired inn. It is necessary, therefore, to leave aside the tumult and war of the senses, which, envious of each other, they usually engage in when the beloved object is present, and to approach the port of reason, where, like travelers arriving home rich after various adventures, we sort out part by part all the delight with which love, in a jumbled manner, loaded us: she laughed, she cried, she said this, she listened to that, she hugged me like this, she embraced me here. Who is more beautiful, who kinder, who wiser than she? Who is happier and more fortunate than I? And truly, just as we see things better when they are at a little distance, so that there is at least some room between the eye and the color for light to shine and make it visible to us, so the lover begins to notice his amorous felicity when, drawing apart from the senses, reason like a sun can illumine it, letting him focus one by one on joys that love put into his soul all mixed together with this material sand. I would not wish you to think, however, that reason (being a thing divine) completely scorns the delights of the world and only speaks of those that are heavenly. This would be the operation not of a man but of an angel, which is a pure intellect without body, and a pure light with no darkening veil. But reason, our own and special power, that is human as we are, which God gave[lx] the duty of moderating the appetites and calming their discord, turning now to one and now to another, with supreme prudence praises first the delights of our perceptions, making us see how this mortal life is greatly obliged to them; for deprived of such pleasures it would become not life but lead and wood.[lxi] A little while later, showing the senses that the envy that they bear each other, each wanting to be the first and only to enjoy the beloved, confounds the good of our joys, just as if a glutton at a delicate and sumptuous dinner were to stuff every food into his mouth at once, reason teaches them how, in proper time and place, one after another, each should engage in its own operations: you will see, you will speak, you will hear; meanwhile let the hand rest, and when it awakes, let the others wait aside until, called back again, they willingly serve the perception for which they are naturally ordained by her ministers. In acting this way, does reason not seem to you to be (as I said) the governess or rather the majordomo of the household of Love? Certainly, yes. Therefore, let no one in future dare to separate reason from love; for though its first roots grab hold in the earth of our senses, along the open and slender branches of reason it produces the fruit that nourishes the lover's heart. So far I think I have shown you quite well how the lover, if he wants to be happy, must distance himself from the beloved, at the sight of whom reason is dazzled and doesn't dare or is unable to function; the words and glances, hearing, touching, the anger, the peacemaking, the laughter, the repose, are imperfect and like those of a dreamer, and (what is marvelous to hear) the heart and soul of a lover, previously fire and sparks, suddenly become snow and ice.

Tullia: Truly to remain distant from the beloved just long enough, and not more, to let the loving memory ruminate the food that the senses devoured, not only gives the lover the opportunity to become aware of his good but also causes him to become day by day more lovable; for whereas at first, inexperienced in love, in the presence of the beloved the lover babbled, inappropriately speaking or remaining silent, now bold and now timorous (signs, to tell the truth, that the lover loves much but is worth little), soon afterwards that same lover, counseled by reason and returning to himself, displays his virtues one by one, doing with them what the senses, overwhelmed by new joy, had prevented him from doing. But this is a departure that has a return soon after, as is not the case with Tasso. Therefore the discourse by which you tried to console me is in vain; moreover, you did not talk about reason in the sense in which I was speaking of it earlier, namely, as a rebel against and murderer of the amorous life. That aspect of reason … But it's better that, postponing all other matters, we come back to the parting of lovers, where you promised us that we would linger for a while, speaking and replying.

Grazia: Tasso's departure is so fixed in your soul that to extract it I need the use of tongs. Therefore, if I leave blandishments aside and turn to force, don't take it amiss; for love, truth, and the situation compel me to do it, not any desire to displease you. Then it's true (as you say) that, after reason with her truthful arguments has demonstrated to the lover how to behave at the dinner table of Love and how to temper mortal sensations, a new desire, more fervent than the first, inflames his heart to return; he does return and, having left again, takes counsel anew with reason. And he does this so often that the senses, already used to confrontations with her, without waiting for a command, fulfill their duty in the way that reason herself, admonishing, habitually told them. Reason, naturally the enemy of idleness and desirous only (if she is up to it) of making us eternal, thinking that it is a lowly sort of dominion to rule continually, like a shepherd, a herd of sensations, distancing herself from this familiar care, begins to think over with herself how many and of what nature are the delights of sense perception, and how she has labored at length, and with much more zeal than was appropriate to her own nobility, to give them some order so that they might show themselves worthy of her. She sees and recognizes first of all that beauty of the body is a mutable and very frail good, which in the blink of an eye passes away like shadow and smoke or like flowers discolored by the midday sun, which at its rising in the east with rays cooled by the dew had displayed them lovely and fresh. Arraying and considering the carnal delights, she sees and recognizes that they are no more different from those of the beasts than wild horses are from bridled ones, or wild magpies from tame and speaking ones, which, although they obey man, remain no less beasts than the others. She sees and recognizes that no misery is equal to the life of the wretches who, without acquiring fame, consume their lives in sorry idleness, leaving such traces in the memory of others as wind leaves in the air or foam on the water. And she holds it as certain that all of what was fabled in ancient times about Circe and her potions becomes true in him who, having forgotten to be a human of speech and understanding, without even once lifting his eyes to the stars that continually signal to him, does nothing until his death but roll around in the dust and mud of this flesh; on his vile actions the adversaries of love once based their argument that one should slanderously vituperate love and his followers, publicly affirming that Love was the son of lust and idleness, two extreme miseries of mortal life.[73] For that reason such men are so far from calling and adoring him as a god[lxii] that they consider him less than human—a blasphemy truly worthy sooner of punishment than of reply. For wherever he is found, whether in the fields among the animals—where some think he was born and, while growing, practiced wounding and enamoring—or among laws and humans, where his temple and altar and statue stand, Love is always a thing divine and as such should be devoutly adored by persons of good will, yet not in such a way that, content with that first divinity of which Molza was talking, which is indeed common to us and to the beasts, we fail to aspire to another, higher divinity and one more suitable to man.[lxiii] Because, just as in the beauty of the body, a proper object for our eyes and beheld with pleasure not only by us alone but by all the other animals, love placed the sparks that set the lover on fire; so too it is right that such a fire finally rise and shine so high that no sight except the human has the grace to gaze at it.

---

73. Petrarch, *Trionfo d'amore* (*Triumph of Love*), 1.82: "Ei nacque d'ozio e di lascivia umana" (He was born of idleness and human lust). Boccaccio, *Genealogy of the Gods*, 9.4: "Seneca the tragedian in his *Ottavia*, with somewhat more ample license although with few words, describes his [Cupid's] origin saying: '… He was generated out of youth by lust, and nourished by idleness among the happy goods of fortune.'" Both are citing Seneca's *Ottavia* 562–63: "Iuventa gignitur, luxu otio / nutritur inter laeta Fortunae bona."

Considering all this within herself, and recognizing very well that her power was fit not only to distribute material food with fair order to the body's senses, but also to season them within herself in such a way as to turn them from bitter to sweet, from vile to precious, and from corruptible to incorruptible, and considering similarly that the beauties of the limbs, which correspond poorly to those of the mind, sooner cause us infamy than honor, our mother reason judges it well done that the lover, turned from the senses to the intellect and from the present to the future, live for months and years far from his beloved object. During that time, in a noble mind, every amorous action, both happy and sad, remembered and examined by reason, becomes such a thing that Apollo and Minerva would not scorn to behold.[lxiv] I hear that distillers of herbs do something similar, who, mixing together many flowers, white and red and of every color, of which the loveliness would not naturally last for long, distilling them with a slow and gentle fire, convert them into a liquid with which we adorn and conserve life.[lxv] Hence the "*Silvae*," hence the odes, hence the heroic poetry rhymed and unrhymed by your Tasso; those verses that he, not when playing or resting with you but when alone or withdrawn among the Muses, has sent forth to the perpetual glory of his rare powers.[lxvi] In those poems, besides sometimes tying your name and his together in indissoluble knots (a new kind of amorous union, and more marvelous than any other I have spoken of), the sighs, tears, hopes, desires, fire, ice, and all the passions that our weak humanity experiences in loving, like a nut or unripe olive that is coated in sugar, he transforms into sweet and health-giving food for mortals. This food, feeding our soul, marvelously induces us with his example to love better than we would.[lxvii] In this manner Orpheus, the most ancient and noble poet, tamed lions and pacified tigers and rested among the serpents of this life, safe from their venom. In this manner and in this way, raising his beloved Eurydice from the depth of the abyss (in spite of death), he was leading her back to a new and joyful life; and he would have done it had he not, overcome by disorderly appetite, turned too soon to the old familiar pleasures of seeing and embracing her, at which, as the murderer of his own lady, with shaming actions and words as if he were someone un-restrained, he was deservedly torn apart and wounded to death by other wise and prudent women.[74] The present age and the future, my dear Signora Tullia, with good reason would complain too much about Tasso and about you, and both he and you would lose too much, if, preferring your presence to his virtue, he so lightly exchanged an eternal and fixed glory, which his studies will bring forth for both of you, for a brief and fleeting pleasure, and if the flower of his intellect, from which now and a thousand years from now the world will gather fruit, were lost and wasted in a short time by you (by your foolishness or prodigality). I cer-tainly do not know these days any beautiful and kind-ly lady whose worth is so great that, if Tasso loved her as he loves you, he should, to gain her favor, stop writ-ing poetry even for one day; much less should he do it for your love, which (as you yourself judge) does not equal his merits. You are beautiful, you are virtuous; but these beauties either sickness or time will soon interrupt,[lxviii] and your virtues, without the light of his verses, would be buried in a dark night of oblivion. Therefore not only do not impede his departure but even, being full of prudence,[lxix] with as many prayers and with as many tears as you were prepared to shed for it, insistently urge and hasten it; and don't wish

---

74. Ovid tells the story of Orpheus in *Metamorphoses*, 10.1–85 and 11.1–66, but Grazia here has allegorized it, following a long tradition of such interpretation; see, e.g., Boethius's *Consolation of Philosophy* 3m12.

that his staying with you for a long time should cost him something for which you will in no way be able to compensate him. Let it suffice you that once every two years, pausing from his greater duties, he comes to see you and, remembering that he was born a centaur, gives some pleasure to that part of his life that makes him mortal, as we are. Meanwhile put your jealousy to rest and be sure that wherever you are, whether far or near, he is yours as you are his, both because you deserve it more than any other woman[lxx] and also because his senses, having appeased their every wish in you, lady, will disdain to make an effort elsewhere. Fear only, or rather hope, that his love, raising itself from the senses to the mind and carried upward from there to heaven like Ganymede,[75] may rise so high that the glory of the world, now reputed infinite, is shown to him to be small and low. This grace Tasso will not obtain from God[lxxi] without you, who are him and not just his. But no more of this; be content to let me fall silent, taking it as an excellent omen that Molino, who is arriving,[lxxii] puts an end to our talk of Tasso's departure.

75. Jupiter, in love with the young man Ganymede, took the form of an eagle and carried him up into the heavens to be his cupbearer among the gods: Ovid, *Metamorphoses*, 10.155–61.

Significant Textual Revisions

i. Adds: from the unworthy.

ii. judicious

iii. [This phrase is cut.]

iv. marvelous

v. my dear

vi. please

vii. another

viii. so that each of the two women may believe that you love them both.

ix. rare

x. bowing to [Because *adorare* derives literally from "praying to," it may have seemed too religious a term.]

xi. Inserts: (I speak according to one of our poets). [The rest of Tullia's speech here is cut.]

xii. Inserts: poetically as is his habit

xiii. flesh

xiv. how obedient and with good will

xv. [The parenthetical phrase is cut.]

xvi. marvelous

xvii. made thus

xviii. that it is one of the three nymphs [i.e., the Graces] that accompany Venus

xix. Cuts: divine

xx. every fleshly defect

xxi. The errors and evils arise solely from us, whose life is not pure intellect but a little spirit with much earth, wherefore we receive love in that manner in which the earth makes room for the sun ...

xxii. Tullia: Then is it impossible that at any time all the senses might be appeased at once? Molza: Just as now it is not day all over the world, ... [The speeches in between have been cut.]

xxiii. Cuts from "Nor should you be surprised by that" through "the center remains cold and dark."

xxiv. the words spoken by that great poet were a prophecy of my Tasso

xxv. Cuts from "Who then will say ..." through "... which may bring either utility or glory."

xxvi. [Here Grazia cuts Tullia off, saying:] Signora Tullia, God keep you from making public to the common crowd your lofty thoughts, and let that Tantalus, whom you recently mentioned, be an example to you.

Tullia: Don't think that I wanted to tell my own tale in order to compete with Molza; Molza is too great a man, but I wanted to see if I could imitate him.

Grazia: Molza is a true poet and has the privilege of telling lies and making fables as he wills in order to delight the listener, and it is no scandal to listen to him; therefore, while you were recounting his narrative, I did not interrupt the fable; but you are acting like the Sibyl, whom we are always supposed to believe is speaking in order to tell the truth and not in a playful or empty way. So then, since the discourse was trying to enter up into the heavens, it was good to cut off its path at the beginning.

Tullia: Well then, leaving out the beginning and middle of my speech, I will come to the end and stop. The end is this: that reason, enemy of loving, hates and persecutes love's every delight and always will.

Grazia: Your own intellect was enough to contradict me without turning to Molza, who I know for certain holds foolish what he said about those poetic gods of his and about love and the intellect. Let us talk, then, about the best wisdom we have, about reason and love, which you make enemies. [Here the speech reconnects with the original text.]

xxvii. the wisest of all the Greeks in his time [This avoids calling a pagan wiser than any Christian.]

xxviii. But please, how happy can that immortality be which is shared in common by a gentleman and a commoner, by the learned and the uneducated, by the good and the wicked?

xxix. Adds: except for that fable.

xxx. lofty and poetic

xxxi. So then, not only Love but we too are centaurs.

xxxii. to work marvels. [The rest of the sentence is cut.]

xxxiii. poetry

xxxiv. of nature and heaven.

xxxv. heaven

xxxvi. this unhappy life

xxxvii. Inserts: by bad advice

xxxviii. a heavenly object

xxxix. honor

xl. except that occasionally, to show more clearly what I mean or to delight my listener, I will make up things that God knows how true they are or whether they are relevant at all.

xli. Adds: either because Solomon once taught it to one of two men who went to him for advice, or because Dante confirmed it a couple of times. This divine poet in one place, distinguishing between man and woman in love and in this matter honoring the woman greatly, wrote: "Love that does not pardon any beloved from loving." In another place he said in three verses: "I saw one of them draw forward to embrace me with such great affection that it moved me to do the same." [The latter quotation is *Purgatory*, 2.76–78. The episode with Solomon appears in Boccaccio's *Decameron* 9.9.]

xlii. whose initial assault no man can resist.

xliii. excellent

xliv. Adds: as happened to Valerian with the King of Persia. [Valerian was a Roman emperor captured by the Persian King.]

xlv. But another time Molza concluded according to the authority of the poets and the common saying of the world, that ...

xlvi. that you and Molza, with the authority of the poets and the empty common crowd, call a god,

xlvii. The world as a whole, then, is a shadow or effigy or portrait of the omnipotence of God, made by the hand of nature.

xlviii. Tasso: You do wrong to Titian, whose images are of such a kind and so well made that great men hold them dearer than many of the things produced by nature. His paints seem to be mixed with that marvelous herb which, tasted by Glaucus, according to Ovid's verses, suddenly transformed him into an ocean god. Truly his portraits possess a kind of divinity, as we read about the figures made by Daedalus, which astonished those who beheld them.

Grazia: Certainly Titian these days is a marvel of his age. That's why, when one is speaking of painters, his name always comes up. But let's get back to where we left off. The lover then, as I was saying, insofar as he is a lover, may be called the portrait of what he loves; but this lover is sometimes of such different manners, that like a thick and badly prepared canvas, it does not receive very well the painting that Love makes in the soul … [This speech seems to have been erroneously attributed to Grazia rather than to Tullia. It is she who was speaking about this, and the end of the speech refers in the first person to her love for Tasso.]

xlix. love

l. Therefore, since beauty and grace, the two principal qualities of one who is loved and desired, are much greater in women than in men, and since on the other hand the lover is endowed with a stronger spirit and one more fit to support the travails of love, as we men are, …

li. please

lii. no goodness accompanies his weeping. [This cuts the reference to meriting God's grace.]

liii. her virtue and courtesy

liv. [This comparison is cut.]

lv. Grazia: In the poetry of your Tasso, in which your honor, name, and praises will be read and sung by whoever feels love.

Tullia: And perhaps envied.

Tasso: Let my verses be as they may, …

lvi. as medicines to the dead.

lvii. of Molza

lviii. from that opinion, as from an evil root, there spring up in the world diverse other thoughts, all false and wicked, and especially certain troublesome ideas which I would gladly uproot from your lovely mind.

lix. Cuts: and become perfect.

lx. was given

lxi. would be nothing but a plant. [In the hierarchy of living things and their faculties, plants take in food and reproduce but are without sensations, animals and humans have sensation, and humans alone have reason.]

lxii. Adds: as did Molza

lxiii. For Love, although he is not a god (which is the opposite extreme), wherever he is found, either in the fields among the animals—where some poets think he was born and, while growing up, practiced wounding and enamoring—or among laws and humans, where he reigns with reason; besides possessing that divinity common to men and beasts that Molza was talking about, he seems ordained by his nature for something greater and more specific to us humans.

lxiv. and appreciate.

lxv. adorn life and conserve the whole bodies of our friends after death.

lxvi. and with much honor for the friends whom he praises in his verses.

lxvii. better than the common crowd.

lxviii. but these beauties heaven itself, which gave them to you, will soon interrupt.

lxix. Adds: and made eager with good reason by your love of his honor and your own,

lxx. Adds: if I am not mistaken,

lxxi. from his worthiness

lxxii. that Cappello and Molino coming now to see you

8

Francesco Andreini: "On Taking a Wife"

JULIE D. CAMPBELL

As his character Teofilo recalls the "good memory of [his] most dear consort" in "Sopra del pigliar moglie," Francesco Andreini (ca. 1548–1624) mourns the loss of "Fillide," his *Anima cara e Consorte …carissima*," his soul and dearest consort, in his pastoral lament on the death of his wife, Isabella Andreini (1562–1604).[1] The marriage of these two actors who codirected the Gelosi, one of the most popular *commedia dell'arte* troupes of the period, was apparently a very successful one, as were their mutual careers. Their names appeared in theater records for the first time in 1578 in Florence upon their return from a tour in France,[2] and their fame increased throughout the rest of Isabella's life. Francesco is especially remembered for his role of Capitan Spavento da Vall'Inferna, the blustering, boastful soldier, while Isabella is renowned for her roles as Isabella and Fillide, beautiful *innamorate* who are highly educated and speak eloquent Tuscan, the language of lyrical poetry. Their names, along with that of their son Giovanni Battista Andreini, remain among the best known in the theater history of their time. Francesco retired from acting upon his wife's death, and the troupe dissolved shortly thereafter. During his retirement in Mantua, Francesco edited and published some of his wife's works, as well as his own, in effect memorializing their career.[3] As Robert Henke has observed, he also did so to "show 'future actors the true way of composing and performing comedies, tragicomedies, tragedies, pastorals,

---

1. Francesco Andreini's lament is found in *Le bravure del Capitano Spavento*, ed. Roberto Tessari (Pisa: Giardini, 1987), 450. Isabella Andreini died in Lyon, France, from a miscarriage of her eighth child.

2. Clubb, *Italian Drama*, 262.

3. See *Fragmenti di alcune scritture della signora Isabella Andreini, comica gelosa ed academica intenta*, ed. Francesco Andreini (Venice: Giovanni Battista Combi, 1620). Isabella's pastoral tragicomedy *La Mirtilla* (1588) had already been published during her lifetime, as had as her first book of *Rime* (1601) and her *Lettere* (1602). Her second book of *Rime* was published in 1605. For a bibliography of Francesco's and Isabella's works, see MacNeil, *Music and Women*, 325–26.

intermedi, and other theatrical inventions.'"[4] Clearly, he understood that the Gelosi's repertoire contained historically important material that resonated deeply in its cultural moment and that should be saved for posterity.

Regarding his own work, Francesco published his first collection of dialogues, called the *Bravure del Capitano Spavento*, in 1607; he published the second part of that work in 1615. Henke points out that these dialogues between Andreini's famous stage persona Capitano Spavento and Trappola, his servant, constitute his "magnum opus" and that he continued to work on editions of them up to his death in 1624.[5] In an indication of Andreini's widespread fame, the *Bravure* were translated and published in Paris as *Les bravachieries du Capitaine Spavente* in 1608.[6] In 1611, he wrote the introduction to Flaminio Scala's famous compendium of *commedia* scenarios, the *Teatro delle favole rappresentative*, and he published two plays, *L'ingannata Proserpina* and *L'alterezza di Narciso*.[7] The *Ragionamenti fantastici posti in forma di dialoghi rappresentativi* appeared in 1612. Between his retirement and the time of his death in 1614, Andreini had been writing, editing, and publishing his own works and those of Isabella, all the while remaining in close contact with Flaminio Scala, who would publish the *Fragmenti di alcune scritture*, a volume of Isabella's writings edited by Francesco, in 1620.[8] Andreini and Scala became literary lions of the *commedia* world during this period.

"Sopra del pigliar moglie" is from Andreini's *Ragionamenti fantastici posti in forma di dialoghi rappresentativi*, a collection of fantastical arguments in the form of dramatic dialogues. It is the sort of piece that could be used as a building block for a *commedia* performance. Louise George Clubb writes that such "full-length dialogues or *contrasti scenici*"[9] constitute "whole scenes" that could be "employed

---

4. Andreini quoted in Henke, *Performance and Literature in the Commedia dell'arte* (Cambridge: Cambridge University Press, 2002), 176.

5. Henke, *Performance and Literature*, 176.

6. MacNeil, *Music and Women*, 260.

7. See Henke, *Performance and Literature*, 176; MacNeil, *Music and Women*, 261–62.

8. See Henke, *Performance and Literature*, 176.

9. Richard Andrews examines the medieval roots of the *contrasti scenici* in *Scripts and Scenarios: The Performance of Comedy in Renaissance Italy* (Cambridge: Cambridge University

as movable blocks of theatrical material usable in any number of plays."[10] Regarding its subject matter (choosing a wife) and the sentiments expressed by Teofilo and Calistene—Counter-Reformation platitudes mixed with traditional *querelle des femmes* references—this dialogue resonates with other texts included in this volume. Clubb points out that the professional actors of the *commedia dell'arte* were quite vulnerable to "political and ecclesiastical power"; thus, the content of their work was at times designed to avoid giving offense in the "official culture."[11] Echoing Counter-Reformation ecclesiastical and Pauline pronouncements, Teofilo pontificates, "[M]arriage was contrived to preserve the human species, by having children to resemble ourselves, to restrain the disorderly carnal appetite, and to obtain glory and honor."[12] Calistene, however, warns Teofilo that his son should not marry for marriage's sake, especially with a beautiful woman. He argues that beautiful women are inevitably unchaste, not to mention greedy and spoiled, and he cites with apparent relish the example of the beautiful Fiammetta, from a tale in Ariosto's *Orlando furioso*, who was caught sleeping with two men at once.[13] These two characters thus perform a debate constructed of numerous intertexts belonging to the Counter-Reformation and *querelle* traditions, designed to please contemporary tastes.

When reading this particularly provocative *ragionamento*, "Sopra del pigliar moglie," in dialogue with the work of Isabella and that of her female Italian contemporaries, we must recall that although personal relationships between men and women may have often been cherished unions, the social pressures that fostered the *querelle des femmes* strongly encouraged the production of misogynistic literary works such as this one, which in large part denigrates marriage. Moreover, the two traditional sides of the *querelle*—those who would attack

---

Press, 1993). He connects them to the religious *laude*, the devotional poems performed by religious confraternities that may have developed into dramatized moral debates, and possibly the acts of the *giullari*, the professional medieval entertainers who featured *contrasti* in their acts; Andrews, *Scripts and Scenarios*, 22.

10. Clubb, *Italian Drama*, 267.

11. Ibid., 270.

12. See 1 Corinthians 7.

13. See footnote 32 below.

women and those who would defend them—were painfully similar in their oppression of women, as Calistene and Teofilo so nicely illustrate. Calistene[14] is a textbook case of an attacker of women; his approach echoes such classical predecessors as Hesiod and Juvenal, as well as more contemporaneous writers, such as Giovanni Boccaccio in his *Corbaccio* or Giuseppe Passi. From this perspective, women are evil, malignant beings whose only worth lies in their ability to bear children. Teofilo,[15] on the other hand, is a traditional defender of women who praises them through his references to the "good" *exempla* of classical antiquity and biblical history, in a manner reminiscent of Boccaccio in his recounting of good women in *De mulieribus claris*. Even so, Teofilo is staunch in his assertion that women should obey their husbands without question and that those who misbehave should receive "slaps, punches, kicks, and blows equal to twenty gauntlets!" Clearly, neither of these characters is particularly sympathetic to women. Teofilo adopts the oppressive stance of the traditional defender of women with his pronouncement that "women pass from paternal authority to marital authority through their wedding: males by law of nature hold command over females even as they do over beasts."

The same oppressive social impulses toward women that fueled the *querelle* and the misogynistic literature that propagated it also stigmatized women's efforts to have public artistic careers. The result was that a *virtuosa* seldom escaped the label, or at least the reputation, of a courtesan. Thus, Isabella's fame for her talent and virtue was, like her marriage, a rare phenomenon during this period. That marriage, a partnership between two famous artists, no doubt provided Isabella the protection and propriety that made her stellar career possible, and it was reputed to be a happy union. But the literary legacy that the Andreinis left for posterity provides an intriguing glimpse into the social complexities that a female artist and intellectual such as Isabella faced,

---

14. Calistene was a fairly common name in ancient Greek manuscripts. It was the name of Aristotle's nephew, who was a historian during the time of Alexander the Great. The name means "beauty and strength," particularly masculine strength. In the case of this dialogue, it may be a somewhat ironic choice, because here Calistene is an old man, deeply embittered toward women, who is ultimately impotent in his ability to change his friend's mind.

15. Teofilo's name means "God-loving." It is clearly a fitting name for one such as this character, who quotes scripture and refers frequently to Christian tradition.

as well as a two-sided commentary on men's and women's anxieties about the state of matrimony.

While Francesco develops his *ragionamento* thematically along traditional misogynistic *querelle* lines that denigrate women and support their virtue only as it is manifested in the persona of a "Signorina Tranquilla"—that is, a young woman who exhibits the stereotypical characteristics of a good woman: silence, chastity, and obedience—Isabella's writing problematizes and broadens the scope of virtuous behaviors for women. It does so ostensibly to publish her own protofeminist beliefs and to undergird her reputation for virtuous behavior in spite of the fact that she is indeed an actress. Although one could argue that Francesco's *ragionamento* is meant to be purely a work of comedy—and, in light of what is known about his marriage, it is probably not an accurate representation of his own notions about women—Francesco's inclusion of such a dialogue among others on such diverse topics as love ("Sopra amore"), the education of sons ("Sopra i figliuoli, che vanno alla scola"), and farmers and soldiers ("Sopra gli agricoltori, e soldati") illustrates not only how commonplace debates on the nature of women were but also the degree of complicity with which he willingly engaged in popular misogynistic literary traditions.

Isabella, however, took issue with such complicity. In *La Mirtilla*, she extensively explores questions about the nature of love and what constitutes a marriage between deserving partners. Her female characters, while virtuous with regard to issues of chastity, are most certainly not silent as they engage in witty dialogue, and they exhibit spunk and intelligence as they rescue themselves and their lovers from sticky situations.[16] Stereotypical Signorina Tranquillas they are not. Moreover, Isabella openly critiques sexist social injustices in her *lettere*, as her "Lettera del nascimento della donna" ("Letter on the Birth of Women") and "Dei pensieri honesti di giovanetta da marito" ("Of the Honest Thoughts of a Young Woman to be Married") illustrate. In the former, she chastises a gentleman who complains about the birth of a daughter, and in the latter she communicates the fears of a young woman about to be married, who laments both the strictness of her upbringing and her parents' right to marry her off to a man whom

16. See 2.2, 2.3, 3.3, 3.4, 4.3, 5.1, and 5.3 of *La Mirtilla: A Pastoral*.

she dislikes and fears.[17] The piece that most resonates with Francesco's "Sopra del pigliar moglie" is Isabella's dialogue "Sopra l'amor coniugale" ("On Conjugal Love"), an "*amoroso contrasto*" from *Fragmenti di alcune scritture*. In this dialogue the reluctant Hippodamia soundly interrogates her husband-to-be, Tarquinio, on their wedding day regarding the details of her future life in the home of his parents, and she expresses her fear of the "*tirannide*" (tyranny) that she knows a father can inflict upon his family.[18]

To begin, Hippodamia expresses her concern that fathers-in-law are typically not known for cherishing their daughters-in-law. Tarquinio immediately blames her doubts about marriage on her love of literature and the "*stravagante*"—extravagant, or, as John Florio puts it, "new-fangled"—material that she has been reading.[19] Tarquinio complains that young women read books too much these days, declaring that life was much easier when they stuck to the needle and the spindle, "*all'ago*" and "*al fuso.*"[20] Hippodamia, however, insists that her information comes from good authority and presses her case about fathers-in-law. She compares their rule to that of kings, explaining that the reign of a king can easily become tyrannous. She extends her metaphor to compare the state of a man's sons and their spouses to that of a tyrant's subjects. Tarquinio tries to ease her fears by countering that marriage can be a partnership between husbands and wives similar to that of magistrates and nobles who rule over a city-state or region, but Hippodamia argues that husbands usually prefer absolute rule. Tarquinio counters that he has heard of wives who do the same, but Hippodamia protests that one seldom encounters such situations, except perhaps when the wife in question is of higher birth or has greater wealth than her husband. She notes, however, that such would never be the case between Tarquinio and herself. Finally, she expresses her concerns that his mother and siblings will react badly to her being brought into the household, especially if they fear that she might cre-

---

17. See *Lettere della Signora Isabella Andreini, Padovana, comica gelosa, e academica intenta, nominata l'accesa* (Venice: Alla Minerva, 1647), 254–56.

18. "Sopra l'amor coniugale," in *Fragmenti di alcune scritture*, 79.

19. "Sopra l'amor coniugale," 78. For "*stravagante*," see "Florio's 1611 Italian/English Dictionary: Queen Anna's New World of Words," http://www.pbm.com/~lindahl/florio.

20. "Sopra l'amor coniugale," 78.

ate a financial burden. Ultimately, Tarquinio reassures Hippodamia on each of these accounts that all will be well in her new home after she is married and that he will be a willing partner in their union.[21]

Isabella expressed the woman's point of view on marriage in a number of contexts in her work, which suggests that she felt passionately about the subject, as did other women writers of the period. In *The Worth of Women* (1600), Moderata Fonte has her group of ladies debate the merits of marriage, and Lucrezia Marinella in *The Nobility and Excellence of Women and the Defects and Vices of Men* (1600) critiques misogynistic views of wives. Concern over the state of marriage was not limited to the literary confines of the *querelle*, however. Isabella's comparison of the rule of fathers to political rule strikes an intertextual note not only with Francesco's comic dialogue but also with political and legal situations related to patriarchy during the period. Stanley Chojnacki writes that "patriarchy was the principle that linked governmental and private spheres in securing elite hegemony. The ideology of Florence's increasingly aristocratic government after 1382 was modeled on the patriarchal family; in Venice the authority of fathers was enhanced by their inscription as channels of government authority to the family. Moreover, the new documentary initiatives reinforced patriarchy not just for the ruling class but for all fathers, whose status as family heads was enhanced by the official recognition it received from registration in fiscal censuses."[22]

For Francesco's characters, contracting a marriage is a business negotiation that is also encumbered with ramifications for a family's reputation and status. Their fear of choosing a daughter-in-law who is angry, proud, and diabolical ("*nuora arrabbiata, superba, e diabolica*") suggests their insecurities about taking into the family a woman who might bring shame to them, thus undermining their patriarchal power, status, and right to "promote social order among the populace," as Choijnacki puts it.[23] Isabella's dialogue, on the other hand, expresses the fears that beset women regarding their lack of agency and recourse in matrimony, as well as in the homes of their fathers or fathers-in-law. Considered together, Isabella's and Francesco's

---

21. Ibid., 77–81.

22. Chojnacki, *Women and Men in Renaissance Venice*, 31.

23. Ibid.

dialogues provide insight into the anxieties of both women and men regarding the institution of marriage and what it meant personally and politically for their lives.

On Taking a Wife

FRANCESCO ANDREINI

From *Ragionamenti fantastici*

Calistene, an old man, and Teofilo, the head of a household[24]

Calistene:	Good day, Signor Teofilo.
Teofilo:	Good day and a good year withal, Signor Calistene.
Calistene:	A good day would be encountering good fortune!
Teofilo:	Everyone has his fortune from the day he is born.
Calistene:	The important thing is in knowing how to recognize it.
Teofilo:	Crazy is he who does not recognize it!
Calistene:	And who is that sage who recognizes it?
Teofilo:	He who is wise and prudent.
Calistene:	Many things have the aspect of goodness that are not good.
Teofilo:	And what are those? Tell, that I may know them.
Calistene:	There are many, and particularly that of taking a wife, because sometimes a man thinks he's taking a lady and takes [instead] a hellish fury.
Teofilo:	You have completely confused me with your last words!

24. See footnotes 14 and 15 above.

Calistene: Why is that?

Teofilo: Because it was my intention to give a wife to my son, and now I am all confused. I don't know what I should do!

Calistene: As for me, I would say that you should proceed with more consideration, that you should think it over carefully, because once the thing is done, it is no longer possible to undo it, and so much more is it with marriage, which only death dissolves.

Teofilo: I went so far with promises that I wouldn't know how to retract my commitment to the marriage between the daughter of Signor Teodosio Tranquilli and my son, already nearly contracted and settled.[25]

Calistene: If Signorina Tranquilla has a mind consistent with her name, it will be a good thing for her and for your son, but otherwise, it will be bad for the one and worse for the other.

Teofilo: Oh, that I had never gotten into this! Even so, I am not entirely sorry, because I have always heard it said that marriage was contrived to preserve the human species, by having children to resemble ourselves, to restrain the disorderly carnal appetite, and to obtain glory and honor, as the Apostle[26] says.

Calistene: It is true that the marital state is much more necessary (for increasing the human lineage) than the state of continence and virginity; nevertheless, there are some

25. For discussions of the history of negotiating and contracting marriages in Renaissance Italy, see Klapisch-Zuber, *Women, Family and Ritual*, 181–96, 247–60, and Chojnacki, *Women and Men in Renaissance Venice*, 53–75, 132–52.

26. Teofilo refers to the Apostle Paul. See 1 Corinthians 7 regarding Paul's pronouncements on marriage.

who prefer to withdraw from the world rather than to live married.

Teofilo: It seems to me that everyone should marry, and the reason is this: it was God who instituted marriage to glorify man and to make him live by His law. God commands[27] marriage; thus, it is good, and one must observe His commandment. Another reason I find is that marriage was instituted in a most worthy place, since it had its beginning in His Paradise. Marriage is none other than a mystical body in which there are two bodies in the same flesh: God joins them together, and that which God joins together man cannot separate.[28]

Calistene: That is a most lofty speech; yet for all this, we have seen many repudiations and separations [in marriage].

Teofilo: These aren't valid objections. We hold that marriage was ordained when Adam and Eve, our first parents, had their consciences pure and clean, and after the Flood (sent by God to punish the wrongdoers) only married persons were saved in the Ark to signify and demonstrate the excellence of inseparable marriage.[29]

Calistene: I understand you. You mean that having a beautiful wife and beautiful children is the greatest happiness; but the business does not go this way; on the contrary, it goes quite another way.

---

27. The Italian text reads, "Dio comanda il manda il matrimonio." Here, "*il manda*" is an obvious printing error. It is omitted in the translation.

28. This description of marriage is paraphrased from words attributed to Jesus in Matthew 19:4–6.

29. The account of Noah and the flood is found in Genesis 6–9.

Teofilo:	And how does it go? I know very well that men who are not ignorant, who have sound intellect, should marry their children nobly, in order that they then be able to have the fruits so dear to God, the fruits of wedlock, which are legitimate children.
Calistene:	It is usually said that marriage makes a man wise, destroys his vices, and restrains him.
Teofilo:	I am not satisfied by these words alone; however, all the same, my determination to give a wife to my son increases.
Calistene:	You could repent of it, as others, too, have done. But, before you begin to repent without knowing why, I want to tell you what I understand about getting married. You know, sir, that it would be very much better to die quickly than to be married to an evil woman, who continually keeps you in suffering and torment: the husband dies all the time, and does not know why; he languishes and is not able to die; and finally he calls on death to relieve him of his suffering life. Where can one find a more harmful friend? A prison more dreadful than to have continually at home a foul-tempered wife, who always seeks to wear you down?
Teofilo:	Signor Calistene, you are too hard on the poor women!
Calistene:	Listen carefully, Signor Teofilo: if a man (as it happens) falls and is caught in some error against justice, and then he tells his wife about it, as he would a trustworthy friend, as soon as she is informed of such a misdeed, and as soon as she has received some offense or some small indignation, then she immediately runs off to accuse him, whence follows the ruin or unexpected death of the poor husband!

Teofilo: God save my son from so wicked an encounter!

Calistene: Observe, dear sir, how a man runs a great risk in tak-
                  ing a wife, the first risk being that he takes a person
                  whom he does not know, because if he knew her to
                  be a wretch and knew her customs, he would not take
                  her for all the gold in the world! But because he only
                  knows what he hears about her, and from her closest
                  relatives, he takes her blindly, and instead of finding
                  her nice, sweet, courteous, and amiable, he finds her
                  full of haughtiness, pride, [and] arrogance, scornful,
                  complaining, spiteful, envious, a gossip, a slanderer,
                  and finally, that she has all the evil traits!

Teofilo: Oh me, oh me! What do I hear? My most dear and
                  fondly remembered consort was never thus with me
                  as long as she lived; because living, she was a Giulia, a
                  Claudia, a Cassandra, a Nesterre, a Judith, and a Tam-
                  ar of goodness and honor![30]

Calistene: You had great luck in finding such a woman, since
                  it is good luck to be the first to find something good

30. Borrowing a strategy popular in the *querelle des femmes*, Teofilo argues for the goodness of his late wife by comparing her with virtuous classical and biblical *exempla*. Julia,
the daughter of Julius Caesar and Cordelia, was renowned for her goodness and virtue.
Claudia was a Roman vestal virgin to whom miraculous occurrences were attributed. Cassandra was the daughter of Priam and Hecuba, and she was famous for her powers of
divination. Nesterre remains unidentified, although it might be a version of Nestor, the
Homeric hero who, as king of Pylus and Messenia, was known for his prudence, eloquence, and wisdom. Interestingly, male figures are seldom included in lists of *exempla* for
women, but the virtues for which he was famous do fit Teofilo's theme. For these classical
references, see Lemprière, *Lemprière's Classical Dictionary*, 337, 170, 144, and 439. With
Judith and Tamar, Teofilo turns to apocryphal and biblical *exempla*. Judith, whose story
is in her eponymous book in the Apocrypha, was the beautiful and virtuous widow who
beheaded Holofernes, the leader of the Assyrian army besieging her city. The Tamar of
whom Teofilo is probably speaking was the daughter-in-law of Judah. Her story is found
in Genesis 38. She seduced Judah through trickery and gave birth to twin sons, Perez and
Zerah. Through Perez, she became an ancestor of Jesus in the line of King David; see Ruth
4:18–22 and Matthew 1:1–6.

before others. My Signor Teofilo, do not want (I pray you) to marry off your son so young, who, drawn by his senses, will not put up any resistance, but like a harebrained fellow will give his "yes" right away, not knowing that after it's done he'll regret it and for it he'll always live malcontent and full of displeasure. Remember that choosing a wife is not like buying a horse for goodness and beauty; if later one finds it full of defects, one may sell it, trade it, or give it away, but when the man is bound [in marriage], he is bound in that way until death.

Teofilo: I believe that the daughter of Signor Tranquilli must be, or, to put it better, is goodness itself, being a most beautiful young girl, since the beautiful and the good turn into each other.[31]

Calistene: You fool yourself, because beneath beautiful faces can also be hidden many vices. Everyone seeks to have a beautiful wife, permitting himself to be fooled by his own senses and desire, not realizing that sometimes these sorts of women are accustomed to wanting everything they can think of!

Teofilo: You hint at something—I don't know what, but I don't like it!

Calistene: I know that you understand me, and to a good listener a hint is enough: but again I offer that if a beautiful woman is not such [i.e., spoiled and all-desiring], you will never convince her jealous husband.

Teofilo: You are putting me to the test!

31. Here Teofilo echoes arguments about connections between goodness and beauty put forth by classical philosophers. In Plato's *Lysis*, for example, Socrates says, "I declare that the good is the beautiful"; *Plato III: Lysis Symposium Gorgias*, trans. W. R. M. Lamb. Loeb Classical Library (Cambridge, MA: Harvard University Press, 1967), 49.

Calistene: Think a minute about that *novella* by Ariosto, about the worthy Fiammetta, who knew so astutely how to please her lover, yet she was in bed with *two* other lovers![32]

Teofilo: Beauty doesn't last forever, since it is no other than a deceitful flower, which, if it lasts for a while, it is a short while. It is like a rhetorical pretense.[33] When old age or infirmity arrives, what a joke: soon that once beautiful body is changed and becomes ugly and droopy!

Calistene: You speak to me in *sdrucciolo*,[34] my Signor Teofilo, which seems to me to be appropriate among those Arcadian shepherds who sing *sdruccioli* lines to the sound of their pipes and make their wooly sheep run and leap.

Teofilo: Now you make me laugh with these fables of yours! I tell you, what you tell me about beautiful women is hard for me to believe.

32. In canto 28.1–74 of Ludovico Ariosto's *Orlando furioso* [trans. Guido Waldman (Oxford: Oxford University Press, 1974)], an innkeeper tells Rodomont a story about women's inability to be chaste. In the tale, Astolfo, king of the Lombards, and Jocondo, the brother of the king's Roman knight, Fausto, decide to leave their cheating wives and do unto other men as has been done unto them. Eventually, seducing other men's wives becomes too dangerous, so they take up with a young woman called Fiammetta, whom they magnanimously decide to share between them. She, however, manages to entertain yet another lover while Astolfo and Fausto lie sleeping on either side of her.

33. Andreini refers to the negative aspects of sophistry and rhetoric. Here he compares them to beauty's ability to lead men astray.

34. A *sdrucciolo* line contains an extra syllable vis-à-vis the *piano* line that prevails in Italian versification; the construction is thus rare in Italian and is considered artificial and belabored.

Calistene: Remember the one who says chaste are those women who have not been asked![35] And this is said with the leave of those women who know how to defend their honesty. A woman glories in her beauty, and when she hears that everybody desires her, she then becomes more proud, and very great in her grows the desire to have people see her.

Teofilo: The more you go on blaming women, the more my desire increases to give my son a wife!

Calistene: Make sure you don't repent [this action], because the sooner you marry him off, the sooner he will undergo pain and torments. For if a man doesn't have the luck to take a good wife, there is no greater burden or suffering in the world than being married for only one day! You think, my Signor Teofilo, that it is insignificant toil for a husband to suffer all that his wife says, suffer all that she does, to give her what she demands, to conceal what she doesn't want. I remind you that this is a labor so painful that I, myself, would not desire a greater revenge on my enemy than to see him married to a proud wife who loves everything her husband loathes and loathes everything he loves.

Teofilo: My Signor Calistene, for this, one finds the remedy with tolerance and patience, because there is no serpent in the world that has as much venom as an angry wife. And this [situation] will be easy to manage because my son is a fine tough boy and a good big cockerel, as they say.

---

35. In his *Amores*, 1.8.43–44, Ovid writes, "Chaste is she whom no one has asked—or, be she not too countrified, she herself asks first." *Heroides and Amores*, trans. Grant Showerman, rev. G. P. Goold, 2nd ed. (Cambridge, MA: Harvard University Press, 1977), 1:351.

Calistene: If your son is this way with his wife, he will do much harm, because it is necessary with wives to know how to divide up the good and the bad: sometimes show them a cheerful face and at other times an angry one—because women are of a nature that when their husbands show them a happy countenance they love them, and when husbands show an angry one they fear them.

Teofilo: If through misfortune my son took a bad-natured wife, she [would] receive slaps, punches, kicks, and blows equal to twenty gauntlets!

Calistene: This is medicine contrary to the nature of a bad wife, because the more you beat her, the worse she becomes. And [it does not matter] how proud and angry the husband is, since he knows that his wife will weaken and humiliate him; because one does not find a man so proud that a defiant, proud, and wicked woman does not put him under her feet.

Teofilo: Whether they are good or bad, they are our plants and we their fruit, and everyone should praise that plant which produced him!

Calistene: Yes, when he is able to do it.

Teofilo: What then will become of this son of mine? I would certainly like (as they say) at my death to regain my youth in my son and in my dear grandchildren.

Calistene: If I were you, I'd give it careful consideration, because once bound, if he fails to keep faith, he hurts himself and burdens his conscience.

Teofilo: What you say is true, but it still seems to me, as I understand it, that a young man may woo and love perfectly an honest young woman without taking her for a wife.

Calistene: This is another discussion: it is one thing to speak of giving him a wife and another to allow him to woo. Anyway, when you wish to give him permission to do so, don't give it, for then you will leave him in the power of Fortune, who is known to play some nasty tricks in love.

Teofilo: I don't believe it [would] put him in such danger!

Calistene: You will not find a status of being for this son of yours that satisfies you!

Teofilo: I will say to you: I have always heard said, lovers be careful not to get caught in the snares and the nets of those attractive ladies of yours, because many were those who, pricked and wounded by the arrow of love, in the end cried out and wept in sorrowful complaints and were reduced to a sad and miserable state.

Calistene: Before one comes to the act of love it first is necessary to know what virtues the lovers have in common. And if it happens that solely through the affection of loving they stay together, this is a love just and worthy of praise. But when one learns that under many enticements and charms are hidden vices and, upon discovery, they spring forth, then it is necessary to flee those caresses because they are similar to the fawning of a dog, feigned and dissembled, worth nothing!

Teofilo: And if by chance the young woman is of a nature seemly to her lover, that is, she is pleasing, agreeable, and in and of herself full of joy and delight, is it not meet that the man make every endeavor to love, serve, and honor her?

Calistene:	Yes, certainly, since in doing so, he is allowed to flee that most grave sin of ingratitude, and finding such qualities in her that he likes, he becomes calm in loving, coveting or desiring nothing more—in such love there is nothing shameful. But, when nature begins to grow dark, immediately it runs, and in this way deceives his mind so that he can think of no remedy: the poor lover doesn't sleep, doesn't rest, doesn't eat; always of his lady he speaks, of his heart; he leaps through the streets, runs, goes, comes, sweats, argues with himself, contradicts himself, and he leads and manages his miserable life among a thousand pains and a thousand torments. This is that love that transforms man into the most vile animal, without reason and without wit, and for which many fall into grave illnesses, dying miserably and [as] beggars, and others live the rest of their lives weakened in mind and unhappy.
Teofilo:	I can only say as the Poet says, evil oppresses me and worse frightens me![36] If I give him a wife, he runs the risk of being given a woman of little worth; if I give him a beautiful one, he runs the risk of being killed; if I allow him his freedom, he then becomes sick or loses his mind. My Signor Calistene, I resolve to think hard on this, for seeing before my eyes every hour a daughter-in-law angry, proud, and diabolical, and her children, almost like serpents, born of a Hydra and an infamous Chimera.[37]

36. The poet is Petrarch, and the line is from his *Rime*, sonnet 244: "Mal mi preme et mi spaventa il peggio."

37. In Greek mythology, the Hydra is a serpentlike monster with many heads, and the Chimera is a monster composed of parts of a goat, a lion, and a dragon. Lemprière, *Lemprière's Classical Dictionary*, 318, 161.

Calistene: You will do well! In any case, when he wants to take a wife, he will choose her in his own way, and like most young men he will not ask your permission.

Teofilo: Lucky you, Signor Calistene, that you never experienced the yoke of marriage, the torment of children, the pain of a daughter-in-law, and the trouble of grandchildren!

Calistene: A young man is like a new knife, which with time loses its sharpness in sentiments, becomes blunt in judgment, loses the strength of its steel, gets rusty in infirmity, twisted in adversity, and finally loses its edge in death.

Teofilo: If one were able to live without a wife, as Metellus Numidicus said, being Censor to the people of Rome, it is certain that men would be unburdened of a very troublesome load.[38] But because Nature has so ordained it that we can live neither in great comfort with women nor without them in any way (if not with difficulty), she wanted to have us in a perpetual state of good health rather than to provide [us] a brief pleasure, and therefore she established marriage between man and woman, since in human life one finds nothing so perfect and absolute nor friendship more stable nor more useful and full with natural affection than marriage.

Calistene: My Signor Teofilo, I don't know how to comprehend you! Sometimes you want one thing, and sometimes you want another! If you want to have a look at what has been said of marrying, I will tell you, citing the opinion of Aristotle, that for the present you don't have to arrange a marriage for your son, for he would

38. Quintus Caecilius Metellus Numidicus was elected censor of Rome in 102 BCE. For more on his life, see Plutarch, "The Life of Caius Marius," in *Lives*, trans. Bernadotte Perrin (Cambridge, MA: Harvard University Press, 1920, repr. 1968), 9:465–597.

have young women marry at eighteen years of age and young men at thirty-seven;[39] thus, you can wait a while to marry him off. Lycurgus (who gave laws to the Spartans)[40] required that those men of thirty-seven years [who] had not taken a wife be driven from the theaters in disgrace.[41] The Romans held married people in such esteem that they made them exempt from every public charge, and, on the contrary, they deemed those who had lived without a wife unworthy of having rank in the Republic. Think again about what you decide to do!

Teofilo: On the whole, I would like him to marry, and I would not like to go back on my word given to Signor Teodosio: God willing and he willing, Signora Tranquilla is a discreet young woman who will know how to love her husband as duty requires, and to hold him in reverence as judge and lord of her life, and she will call him such, because those wise and honest women of ancient times thus called their husbands, and did not stray from their commandments. Women pass from paternal authority to marital authority through their wedding: males by law of nature hold command over females even as they do over beasts, but the authority that the man holds over the woman is *politico*, and that which he holds over his children is *imperio*; thus, his

39. In book 7, chapter 16, lines 27–30 of *Politics*, Aristotle writes that women should be married at eighteen and men at thirty-seven because these are the ages at which they are in the prime of life regarding their ability to have children. *Politics*, trans. Benjamin Jowett (New York: Random House, 1943), 314.

40. Lycurgus, thought to have lived during the ninth century BCE, is credited with creating the laws that were enforced in Sparta for seven hundred years. See Plutarch, "Life of Lycurgus," *Lives*, 1:204–303.

41. In the "Life of Lycurgus," Plutarch writes, "Lycurgus also put a kind of public stigma upon confirmed bachelors. They were excluded from the sight of the young men and maidens at their exercises, and in winter the magistrates ordered them to march round the marketplace in their tunics only, and as they marched, they sang a certain song about themselves, and its burden was that they were justly punished for disobeying the laws" (*Lives*, 1:249).

marrying will entail all these privileges and all these prerogatives; what do you say, my Signor Calistene?[42]

Calistene: I will speak according to your humor: and briefly I will say that the virtue of matrimony is so great and powerful that it also reconciles and unites enemies, as happened between Pompey and Caesar.[43] Rome would have fallen from the beginning if the raped Sabine women, through the love that they bore their husbands, had not assuaged the enraged spirits of their fathers and brothers.[44] The man takes a wife not only for procreation but also for having company in the vicissitudes of his life, whence the couple sharing the same destiny call themselves consorts.[45] And since you do not want to go back on your word, it will be well done if as soon as possible you make the nuptials with good fortune, and remember to distinguish yourself, having no other son but this one, since you are rich and possess many goods.

Teofilo: The man who has good friends possesses many goods; where I lack, you will supply, Signor Calistene, since you are a friend to me, and you are richer than I am!

Calistene: If you were to need me, I would help, but I know that it is not necessary! Act quickly in this business, but not hastily, because being hasty or lazy in one's negoti-

42. Andreini utilizes *politico* in its etymological sense of "pertaining to equals ruling over a city," in opposition to *imperio*, or imperial, implying absolute power over subjects.

43. Pompey married Julia, the daughter of Caesar. *Lemprière, Lemprière's Classical Dictionary*, 337.

44. After the abduction and rape of the Sabine women, the majority of the Sabines eventually stopped making war against the Romans and became their allies. This occurrence, however, was more likely due to the Romans' crushing military might than to the virtuous acquiescence of the Sabine women. Nonetheless, Lemprière repeats the traditional view of the Sabines as a nation known for "chastity" and for "purity of morals." Ibid., 595.

45. Calistene comments on the etymology of "*consorti*" or "consorts" by referring to "*sorte*," translated here as "destiny."

ations are two dangerous extremes; however, of these two the worst is to be hasty, since if by deliberating too long one loses what he could have won, by deciding too soon, one loses what was already won. Farewell!

Teofilo: Farewell! Now I'll go conclude this blessed marriage!

9.
Dishonoring Courtesans in Early Modern Italy: The poesia puttanesca of Anton Francesco Grazzini, Nicolò Franco, and Maffio Venier

PATRIZIA BETTELLA

By the beginning of the sixteenth century on the Italian peninsula, a specific type of woman emerged in a particular social and cultural milieu, offering beauty, sexual delight, and cultivation to high-class men: the honored courtesans. Arturo Graf was the first scholar to note the peculiar and unique phenomenon of the rise of the "honored courtesan" in Italy during the first decades of the sixteenth century, prompting the distinction—unprecedented as late as the *quattrocento*—between the common prostitute (*meretrice* or *puttana*) and the honored or honest courtesan (*cortigiana onorata* or *onesta*). The *onorata*, modeled after the classic *hetaera*, paralleled court ladies with her mannerisms and social roles but also offered sexual pleasure, aesthetic allure, cultivation, refinement, and physical attraction. As Adriana Chemello points out, honest courtesans possessed all the qualities of the *donna di palazzo*,[1] as they were delineated in Castiglione's *Book of the Courtier*, except chastity. Fiora Bassanese notes that courtesans allied themselves with the ruling elite, becoming friends and mistresses of intellectuals, poets, painters, politicians, and other figures of authority, thereby achieving high social status. However, even for the most established courtesans such a high position was precarious at best, and their fortunes were often subject to changes and downturns. In fact, the courtesans' condition was highly ambiguous: in the general public's mind, the differentiation between *onesta* and *puttana* could often be blurred, and sentiments towards courtesans could easily range from the veneration of high-ranking admirers to the open hostility of moralists and other detractors. Because of their profession, courtesans were liable to exclusion, occupying a marginal zone on the

1. Adriana Chemello, "Donna di palazzo, moglie, cortigiana: ruoli e funzioni sociali della donna in alcuni trattati del cinquecento," in *La corte e il cortegiano*, ed. Carlo Ossola (Rome: Bulzoni, 1980), 128.

fringe of social and cultural conformity; thus, even at the peak of their success they were vulnerable to insult and abuse. Tullia d'Aragona, acclaimed in Rome, was later included in the infamous *Tariffa delle puttane di Venegia* (*Price List of the Whores of Venice*, 1535), a stain on her reputation that, according to critics, she went on to correct by fashioning her persona as a respectable *literata* in her collection of *Rime* (1547).[2]

In matters of legal and religious regulation, courtesans and *meretrice* were one and the same. Particularly after the Sack of Rome (1527) and the Council of Trent (1545–63)—which, to counteract the Protestant Reformation, imposed strict new moral and religious rules upon the Catholic Church—enforcement of existing laws became common and did not spare courtesans. Nevertheless, some high-ranking honest courtesans attained privileged status as writers and talented intellectuals, which granted them an elevated social position, financial wealth, and independence.

Tullia d'Aragona (ca. 1510–1556) and Veronica Franco (1546–1591), two of the most famous and revered courtesans and writers of the Italian Renaissance, experienced success and glory; but they were also the targets of attacks by *literati* such as Pietro Aretino, Giambattista Giraldi Cintio, and Agnolo Firenzuola.[3] Even venerated courtesans like Aragona and Franco did not elude the condemnation and danger inherent in their profession: such notorious incidents as Aragona's subjection to the yellow veil of prostitutes during her stay in Florence in 1547 and Franco's Inquisition trial for witchcraft in 1580 attest to that.[4] The immense popularity and prominence of courtesans in sixteenth-century Italy prompted opposing responses: curses, humili-

---

2. See Georgina Masson, *Courtesans of the Italian Renaissance* (London: Secker Warburg, 1975), chap. 4; and Francesco Bausi, "Le rime di e per Tullia d'Aragona," in *Les femmes écrivains en Italie au Moyen Âge et à la Renaissance*, ed. Georges Ulysses (Aix-en-Provence: Publications de l'Université de Provence, 1994), 277.

3. Firenzuola composed a sonnet against Tullia and her mother, and Giraldi Cintio describes Tullia in negative terms in *Ecatommiti*, his collection of novellas. For Aretino's opinion of Tullia D'Aragona, see below.

4. For d'Aragona's success in obtaining exemption from wearing the yellow veil of prostitutes—thanks to the help of her friend, the intellectual Benedetto Varchi—see Bongi, 183–87. For Franco's trial and acquittal for witchcraft, see Rosenthal, *The Honest Courtesan*, chap. 4.

ation, contempt for their immoral behavior, and yet respectability and veneration for their physical beauty and literary skills. Courtesans frequented and hosted renowned intellectual circles and were immortalized in figurative art and literary works.[5]

With the ever-growing numbers of prostitutes and courtesans in early *cinquecento* Italy, these women entered the debate of the *querelle des femmes* as subjects of praise or scorn. While literary pieces by prominent *literati* honoring and eulogizing famous courtesans were widely published, the vast array of satirical texts about prostitutes and courtesans—particularly those in verse, the *poesia puttanesca*—remain largely unknown today, possibly because of their obscene language and graphic details. In such works no distinction is made between *cortegiane* and *puttane / meretrici*. *Poesia puttanesca* flourished in the sixteenth century, often under anonymous authorship, and targeted common prostitutes as well as courtesans/writers like Tullia d'Aragona and Veronica Franco. Besides Pietro Aretino's prose "Sei giornate" (*Ragionamento e dialogo*, 1531 and 1536), a classic of the *letteratura puttanesca*,[6] many works appeared anonymously or with uncertain attribution; these included *Il catalogo di tutte le principali et più honorate cortigiane di Venetia* (*The Catalogue of the Most Honored Courtesans in Venice*, 1533), *La tariffa delle puttane di Venegia* (*Price List of the Whores of Venice*, 1535), *La puttana errante* and *Il trentuno della Zaffetta* by Lorenzo Venier (*The Wandering Whore* and *The Rape of Zaffetta*, 1531), and *Ragionamento dello Zoppino*, attributed to Aretino (*The Dialogue of Friar Zoppino*, 1539), as well as numerous poems in both Italian and the vernacular.[7]

5. *Cortigiane oneste* such as Tullia d'Aragona and Veronica Franco were exalted by famous literati and artists. Benedetto Varchi, Girolamo Muzio, and Sperone Speroni honored Tullia d'Aragona in their verses. Marco and Domenico Venier praised Veronica Franco. Franco was also the sitter for a famous portrait by Jacopo Tintoretto, about which she writes in a letter to the artist.

6. Although Aretino admired and frequented many courtesans, he was a detractor of Tullia d'Aragona, of whose literary aspirations he disapproved. In book 2 of the *Ragionamenti*, in the "Art of Being a Whore," he accuses Tullia (without mentioning her by name) of being too old and affected in a Petrarchan manner. In his comedy *Il filosofo* (1546), Aretino chose to call one of the characters Tullia *meretrice*.

7. This is a vast area that deserves a separate study. Some examples are the anonymous *Trionfo della lussuria* (*Triumph of Lust*, 1537) said to be composed by the Roman statue Pa-

Here I present *poesia puttanesca* texts composed by Anton Francesco Grazzini, Nicolò Franco, and Maffio Venier, three poets of the Italian Renaissance known as irregulars and rebels. These men occupied a peripheral literary space, but their satirical work, mainly in the genre of burlesque anti-Petrarchan poetry, gives a sense of the pervasive attacks launched against prostitutes and courtesans during this period. These writers' marginality derived from their failure to settle for and conform to the models and rules of decorum of the court *literati*. This exclusion and instability fostered their interest in anti-classicist, realistic, and even obscene subject matter, often targeting prostitutes and famous courtesans. While Grazzini writes in moralistic tones about the dangers that common prostitutes pose for respected young men, Nicolò Franco and Maffio Venier attack famous courtesans, namely Tullia d'Aragona and Veronica Franco, respectively. Given such writers' marginal literary status, attacking courtesans or prostitutes may have been a strategy for them to boost their literary careers by writing in an established genre of satirical poetry. As Margaret Rosenthal says, for a satirist like Maffio Venier—i.e., a writer not fully in control of his literary persona—poetry becomes a weapon in the attempt of exorcising a woman and "rhyming her to death."[8] While in Grazzini's poetry we find a distinct separation between courtesan and *meretrice*, with corresponding dichotomous attitudes of praise and blame, the work of Nicolò Franco and Maffio Venier debases two famous courtesans and writers to the level of harlots. Rather than boosting their careers, however, such slandering proved unfruitful. Nicolò Franco paid with his life (he was executed for the obscenity of his poetry), while Maffio Venier, who achieved no literary fame during his lifetime, spent his entire existence in search of recognition and died prematurely of syphilis, in poverty and anonymity.

---

squino, to which satirical verses were affixed. *Pronostico alla villotta sopra le puttane* (*Forecast in Verses about the Whores*, 1558) was written in verse in the rustic dialect of Padua. In Tuscany there appeared *I germini sopra le quaranta meritrice della città di Fiorenza* (*The Origins of the Forty Whores of the City of Florence*, 1553), a long list of Florentine prostitutes living at the time of Duke Cosimo de' Medici. *Il vanto e il lamento della cortigiana Ferrarese* (*The Bragging and the Lament of a Ferrarese Courtesan*, 1532) was published anonymously but was attributed to Giambattista Verini. In it we hear the voice of the courtesan herself, mainly repenting for her dissolute life.

8. Rosenthal, *The Honest Courtesan*, 39.

Anton Francesco Grazzini (Il Lasca) (1503–1584)

Grazzini was an editor, dramatist, and poet of the Florentine middle class, and one of the founders of the Accademia degli umidi (Academy of the damp men). Although Grazzini is acknowledged today as the author of some of the best Renaissance novellas and comedies, during his lifetime he was known primarily as a burlesque poet and the composer of humorous verse. The academy, a short-lived literary gathering of like-minded Florentine friends and free spirits, promoted informal discussions and lectures on Tuscan literature. The Accademia degli umidi lasted only a few months (November 1540 to February 1541) and had a mainly burlesque and comic agenda, fed by the strong tradition of popular poetry and *canti carnascialeschi* (carnival song) prevalent in Florence and throughout Tuscany. The academy included young men of modest culture, mostly middle-class artisans and merchants who organized literary discussions and gave themselves bizarre names of plants and animals. Grazzini himself was nicknamed "Il Lasca," a word that designated a variety of carp but that also had phallic connotations in the equivocal language of early modern comic literature.

The academy attracted the interest of Duke Cosimo I de' Medici, who, under the pretext of offering his patronage and support, was seeking to establish cultural dominance in Florence for his newly formed dukedom. This resulted in a quasi-hostile takeover of the academy, which was promptly renamed Accademia Fiorentina in 1541 and was transformed from an informal circle of lighthearted *dilettanti* into the cultural organ of the Medici regime.[9] Grazzini, as founding member of the academy and an independent spirit, did not fare well under the new regime, and on various occasions he made known his disapproval and strong disdain for some policies introduced in the academy. His refusal to comply with the rules led to his expulsion in 1547, a ban that lasted for nearly twenty years. Grazzini's removal from the now prestigious Florentine Academy resulted in his exclusion from the official cultural scene for a long period. From the periphery, however, Grazzini continued his activity of preserving the

---

9. Domenico Zanrè, *Cultural Non-Conformity in Early Modern Florence* (Burlington, VT: Ashgate, 2004).

Tuscan burlesque poetic tradition while attacking and mocking the cultural establishment.[10]

Grazzini opposed the empty eloquence of the Petrarchists and advocated instead the simplicity of the Tuscan language, promoting the strong Tuscan tradition of burlesque poetry and authors such as Burchiello and Francesco Berni, whom he considered his principal inspiration. In 1548 Grazzini wrote a preface for and edited an important anthology of burlesque poetry by Francesco Berni and others for the publisher Bernardo Giunti, titled *Il primo libro dell'opere burlesche di M. Francesco Berni* (*The first book of burlesque poetry by M. Francesco Berni*), successfully followed by a second, expanded edition of *Opere burlesche* in 1555. Another important literary enterprise was Grazzini's edition of *Tutti i trionfi, carri, mascherate o canti carnascialeschi* (*All the Triumphs, Floats, Masquerades and Carnival Songs*, Florence: Torrentino, 1559), a collection of Florentine festival and carnival songs dating from the time of Lorenzo the Magnificent to his day.

Remarkably, in 1566 Grazzini was reinstated in the Accademia Fiorentina, despite the fact that his main literary production—anti-Petrarchan burlesque poetry—was sharply different from the classicist taste of the academy. According to Zanré this was due, paradoxically, to his production of homoerotic poetry addressed to younger members of the Florentine Academy, whom he praised in conventional Petrarchan tones. Whether he was on good or bad terms with them, Grazzini was acquainted with famous *literati* of his time such as Agnolo Firenzuola, Pietro Aretino, Benedetto Varchi, and Tullia d'Aragona, for whom he composed a laudatory sonnet that she included in her collection of *Rime* (1547). Critics have stressed Grazzini's ambivalent position on the boundary of conformity; such duality is visible in his literary production, in which he cites classical Petrarchan lines, a style he often rejected but which he used to praise famous literary figures of his time. One such example is his adulatory homage to the famous courtesan Tullia d'Aragona in the sonnet "Se 'l vostro alto valor donna gentile," a reverent homage in canonical language and conventional tone, which Aragona herself deemed appropriate to her image as tal-

10. He made a famous vitriolic attack on Pierfrancesco Giambullari, a prominent member of the Accademia Fiorentina, regarding the origin of the Tuscan language.

ented *literata*.[11] This poetry is in stark contrast with his comic verses, where he uses crude language and equivocal references with sexual undertones.

Although the distinction between courtesan and common prostitute was not clear in early modern Italy, there were substantial differences between the lives and working conditions of high-class courtesans like Tullia d'Aragona and those of prostitutes. Grazzini's poetic work reflects this distinction and reveals his ambiguous position, ranging from his appreciation for Tullia the poet to moralistic disapproval for prostitutes. Grazzini, most likely inspired by Berni (who himself attacked prostitutes in his verse), composed various poems for or about prostitutes and courtesans.[12] Grazzini's *ottave* "Alle puttane" are remarkable; they address prostitutes at a time when Florentine law prohibited them from traveling by coach and from wearing jewelry and fine clothing.[13] The *ottave* open with a tone of moderate support for prostitutes, but the conclusion reveals Grazzini's moral stand: the *puttane* are advised to repent and adopt a pious life or otherwise run the risk of becoming beggars, contracting syphilis, or being robbed and injured. All these clichés are ubiquitous in the *poesia puttanesca*. Grazzini's disapproval of prostitutes is also found in a sonnet about Milla Capraia, a woman of the *bordello* (brothel) whom he accuses of deceit and insincerity. In these poems Grazzini uses moralistic, disparaging terms for misogynistic verses about the *puttane*. Despite this, Grazzini was very much involved with both *cor-*

11. This sonnet to Tullia is in the most traditional classicist Petrarchan style. Tullia herself included it in her collection of *Rime*. "Se 'l vostro alto valor Donna gentile / esser lodato pur dovesse in parte, / uopo sarebbe al fin vergar le carte / col vostro altero, & glorioso stile. / Dunque voi sola e voi stessa simile, /a cui s'inchina la natura, & l'arte, / fate di voi cantando in ogni parte / TULLIA; TULLIA, suonar da Gange a Thile. / Si vedrem poi di gioia & maraviglia, / et di gloria, e d'honore il mondo pieno / drizzare al vosto nome altare, & tempi. / Cosa che mai con l'ardenti sue ciglia non vide il Sol rotando il Ciel sereno, / o ne gli antichi, o ne moderni tempi."

12. Berni rails against prostitutes in a "Sonetto delle puttane" and in a "Capitolo a Messer Antonio da Bibbiena," both dated 1518.

13. This poem probably dates to the time when Aragona was subjected to the yellow veil. Grazzini advises the "puttane" to wear simpler clothing and no jewelry and to save and accumulate as much money and wealth as possible for their old age, because many prostitutes—even famous courtesans—spent their last years in poverty.

tigiane and *puttane*; he wrote in positive terms about Nannina Zinzera and Giulia Napoletana, two famous Florentine courtesans, and he frequented the salon of Maria da Prato, another prominent courtesan in Florence, whose house provided an ideal setting for a performance of his farce *Il frate* in 1541. Courtesans' salons welcomed many members of the Accademia Fiorentina and original members of the *umidi*, who found there an alternative space for informal gathering and free expression that was not limited to men only. Grazzini frequented the Florentine salon of Tullia d'Aragona, who had shown her favor for the *umidi* even before she settled in Florence.[14] Grazzini, then, had every reason to praise a woman writer like Aragona; in fact, his sonnet to her is his first to appear in print, in Aragona's collection of *Rime* published in 1547. This sonnet shows that Grazzini's attitude toward honored courtesans was very different from his attitude toward prostitutes. While he praised Aragona's "*alto valor*" (high value) and her poetic talent, which he defined as "*altero e glorioso stile*" (haughty and glorious style), he deprecated the *meretrici*.

"Canto di giovani impoveriti per le meretrici" is a *canto carnascialesco*, a carnival song, in which young men of good families blame whores for their financial ruin, misery, and illness. *Canti carnascialeschi* were songs of dance and carnival, a distinctive literary form indigenous to Florence. During carnival and spring celebrations, the city hosted elaborate processions with masquerades, chants, and dancing; these processions included recitations of poetic compositions, the often anonymous *canti carnascialeschi*. Under the rule of Lorenzo the Magnificent, *canti carnascialeschi* became a learned genre of popular poetry. Grazzini collected and published such *canti* in an effort to preserve a popular literary genre that exhibited the witty, joyous spirit of the Florentine people. Often couched in sexual double meanings, carnival songs celebrated young loves and the spring season while often expressing social satire. Lorenzo the Magnificent and Politian were celebrated authors of such songs. Grazzini was noted not only as editor of the 1559 collection of *canti carnascialeschi* but also for adopting this genre in his own literary corpus. His equivocal *canti* "De' magnani" ("Of Key Makers"), "Dell'uova" ("Of the Eggs"), and "De' giocatori di palla a

14. D'Aragona addressed three pastoral sonnets to the *umidi* when she was living in Rome. See Zanré, *Cultural Non-Conformity*, 146.

maglio" ("Of Mallet Players"), with their clear sexual double entendres, are especially notable. In most carnival songs the poetic voice addresses the gentlewomen or speaks in a collective "we" to express the voice of a group. "Canto di giovani impoveriti per le meretrici" was probably composed around the middle of the sixteenth century, as it appears in some codices of that time, most of them exclusively dedicated to *canti carnascialeschi*. With a moralistic tone—and witty and equivocal undertones—the poetic persona warns respectable young men about the consequences of associating with the *meretrici*: exile, poverty, and syphilis and its disfiguring effects. The discourse of misogyny in this canto touches upon such classical topoi as prostitutes' false beauty and their greed for money and jewelry.

Carnival song (*canto carnascialesco*) by Anton Francesco Grazzini (Il Lasca)

| Di giovani impoveriti | Of Young Men Made Poor |
| per le meretrici[15] | by Prostitutes |

Pover huomini siamo hoggi condotti	We are miserable men who live
In vile e basso stato,	Today in base and low state,
Che le Puttane ci hanno rovinato.	Because the whores have ruined us.

Gia ricchi fummo e nella giovinezza	We were rich once and in our youth
Di lor molto honorati	Many of us were honored by them;
E dalla finta, et non vera bellezza	Enticed by the fake and untrue beauty[16]
Di quelle innamorati	Of those women,
Fummo ognhora sforzati,	We were constantly forced,
Per contentar lor voglie disoneste,	To satisfy their dishonest desires,
Anella comperar, catene e veste.	To buy them rings, chains and dresses.
Ancor ci bisognava alla giornata	We still needed every day

15. According to Carlo Verzone, this *canto carnascialesco* appears in the following manuscripts: Magliabechiano 1178, a miscellaneous codex of *canti carnascialeschi* by Lasca and anonymous authors; Codex Riccardiano 2731, from the mid-sixteenth century; Panciatichi Codex 123 of Biblioteca Palatina in Florence; and Codex 9, 310 of Biblioteca Marciana in Venice. It was also included in the *Rime di Anton Francesco Grazzini detto il Lasca* (Florence: Francesco Moücke, 1742), the main ancient edition of Grazzini's poetry.

16. Female beauty being regarded as false and deceitful is a misogynous *topos* ubiquitous in religious precepts and literary works, and it is a cornerstone in the *querelle de femmes*.

La casa provvedere,	To provide for their houses,
E saziar la lor gola sfondalata	And to satisfy their insatiable throats
Di ben mangiare, e bere	With good food and drink;
Che le malvagie fere	Since those evil beasts
Han padre e madre e sorelle, e parenti	Have fathers and mothers and sisters and relatives,
Che menon tutti ben le mane, e i denti.	Who all use their hands and teeth well.

Così per mantenere, e nutricare	So in order to support and feed
Loro, e la lor brigata	Them and their company
Fummo costretti a vendere, e impegnare,	We were forced to sell and pawn,
Non bastando l'entrata;	As our income did not suffice;
Tanto che consumata	So we have exhausted
La Robba habbiamo, e noi siam diventati Sudici, scussi, brulli ed affannati.	All our wealth, and we have become Dirty, deprived, bare, and worn out.

Questi fur già prelati	These men once were prelates,[17]
Ricchi di conto, hor son lordi e infelici,	Rich and esteemed, now they are dirty and wretched
Colpa delle ribalde meretrici.	Because of the dishonest whores.

Quest'altri sono in grado assai peggiore,	These other men are in much worse state,
Perche dopo alle spese	Because after expenses
Hanno la robba perduta e l'honore,	They have lost their possessions and honor,
Han tanto malfranzese,	They are so sick with the French disease.[18]

Che è coperto, e palese,	Which is both hidden and not,
Anzi, doglie, e gomme e piaghe enfetti,	Indeed they are so infected with wounds, and sores and pain,
Non trovano spedal che gli raccetti.	That they find no hospital that will take them in.

17. During the sixteenth century the Church had become so corrupt that many men of the cloth—even at the highest ranks, such as cardinals, prelates, and popes—were regular frequenters of courtesans and prostitutes.

18. In Italy syphilis was also known as "the French disease" because it was commonly believed that this sickness had been spread by French soldiers during their military campaigns in Italy in the sixteenth century.

Pigliate esempio ò voi giovani amanti,	And so, look, now, you young lovers,
Quel che si trae da loro,	At what you will see from them,
Esilio, povertà, tormenti e pianti	Exile, misery, torment and tears
Ed angoscia e martoro.	And anguish, and suffering.
O felice coloro	Oh happy, indeed blessed,
Anzi beati, chi le fuggiranno,	Are those, who flee them,[19]
Che sarà loro esempio in nostro	And our ruin shall be an example to
danno!	them!

Nicolò Franco (1515–1570)

Nicolò Franco was a polemist, polymath, and author of satirical verses, letters, and poetry in both Italian and Latin. Critics often mention him as an adventurer of the pen who, like Grazzini and Venier, struggled at the margins of the cultural and literary scene and strove but failed to find a stable position in a court setting. His desire for affirmation in the literary arena brought him from his native town— Benevento, in the Campania region—to the region's capital, Naples (1535–36), and then to Venice (1536–40), where he was introduced to the world of publishing. Franco probably worked as a copy editor for Giolito and Marcolini and then as a secretary for Pietro Aretino, who hired him to help with Latin and with the editing of his collection of *Lettere*. During Franco's stay in Venice, Giolito published his *Dialoghi piacevoli* and *Il Petrarchista* (both in 1539). During his Venetian years Franco also published *Pistole vulgari* (1539), an epistolary collection put together after the great success of Aretino's letters. These three works of Franco's present a polemical stand against contemporary culture and society and against Petrarchism, a recurring theme in his entire literary production. Franco's relation with Aretino was crucial in shaping his literary persona and in helping him forge important contacts in the Venetian cultural scene of his time. Franco began as Aretino's young protégé, but because of his ambition and rebellious temperament, Franco soon became Aretino's rival and antagonist in his desire to surpass his mentor. Aretino's deep jealousy was supposed to have been the cause of a physical attack on Franco, committed by an

---

19. It is remarkable to note that the *meretrici* of the poem's title are referred to here simply through the pronoun "them" and are not actually mentioned directly.

emissary of Aretino. Franco was wounded and was forced to flee Venice forever in 1541.[20] En route to France in search of patronage at the court of Francis I, Franco stopped in Casale Monferrato, which became for him a safe haven from Aretino's thugs for the next five years. There, in 1541, Franco prepared for publication a collection of *Rime contro l'Aretino* and *Priapea* (Torino: Guidone, 1541), two works that vilify Aretino. In constant search for a stable position, Franco spent three years in Mantua and the last years of his life in Rome, where he was prosecuted for the blasphemy of his literary work. The Inquisition sentenced him to death by hanging in 1570.

Franco's stay in Venice at Aretino's palace allowed him to establish contact with the *literati*, artists, and courtesans who frequented the house. It may have been during this time that Franco became acquainted with Aragona, the famous courtesan whom he addressed in negative terms in one of the 198 sonnets of his *Priapea*. Although Franco may have personally met Aragona in Venice, where she and her mother moved in 1535, there is no evidence to support this idea. By 1535 Tullia was already quite famous both in Rome and elsewhere, so Franco may have simply composed verses against her based on her fame rather than on personal knowledge of her. Because Aretino was a habitual frequenter of prostitutes and courtesans and had gone to great lengths to praise some courtesans such as Angela Zaffetta, it is remarkable to note his negative opinion of Aragona, which is attested both in the *Ragionamenti* and elsewhere. In fact, Franco and Aretino, despite their strained and ultimately hostile relationship, shared a negative opinion of her.

The sonnet against Tullia d'Aragona appears in Franco's *Priapea*, a collection of satirical and lewd verses, dedicated to "Aretino

---

20. The reasons for and exact timing of the break between Aretino and Franco are not clear. Most scholars hold that jealousy would not explain such strong and persistent hate. During his first month in Venice, in August 1537, Franco was a guest of the Mantuan ambassador, Bendetto Agnello, and was already acquainted with Aretino. Apparently he moved to Aretino's house later that year, because he was helping Aretino with the edition of the first book of *Lettere* that was published in January 1538. According to Bruni, Franco had already left Aretino's house in May 1538. Roberto L. Bruni, "Le tre edizioni cinquecentesche delle rime contro l'Aretino e la Priapea di Nicolò Franco," in *Libri, tipografi, biblioteche: ricerche storiche dedicate a Luigi Balsamo*, ed. Università degli Studi Parma Istituto di Biblioteconomia e Paleografia (Florence: Olschki, 1997), 1:125.

il flagello dei cazzi" (Aretino, the scourge of dicks). *Priapea* and the *Rime contro Pietro Aretino* (*Rhymes against Pietro Aretino*) not only contain crude and obscene verses; they also denounce Aretino's moral depravity, as well as that of princes, popes, prelates, and nuns. Such impudence made these works a primary target of the Inquisition, which confiscated and destroyed them. The first editions of *Rime contro Pietro Aretino* and *Priapea* have not been preserved; to this day, even subsequent editions are extremely rare and hard to find. These collections were listed in the Index of Forbidden Books, a fact that helped lead to Franco's trial and death sentence. Franco's *Priapea* was inspired by Aldus Manutius's 1534 publication of the *Diversorum veterum poetarum in Priapum lusus* (*Jocular Verses of Various Poets about Priapus*), a collection of eighty Latin epigrams accompanied by an appendix of similar texts by Virgil. Franco claimed to have worked on commentaries to this collection, as stated in the dedicatory letter to Giovan Antonio Guidone that opens his *Priapea*. Franco kept working on this commentary for the next two decades without ever publishing it, until the manuscript was confiscated and destroyed after his incarceration in Rome in 1558–59. Franco's open attack on powerful people in the *Priapea* gained him the reputation of an immoral and slanderous *literato*.

Priapus is the mythological god of harvests and orchards that Franco invokes as inspiration for his poetry; after the first six sonnets, the god becomes the main addressee of the verses. Priapus was also synonymous with the phallus; the god was represented as a phallic-shaped wooden statue. During the Renaissance, Latin verses devoted to Priapus were popular and widely imitated.[21] In the *Priapea* Franco denounces the corruption and obscene customs of his archenemy Aretino, of women (who are mentioned as insatiable fans of the phallus), and of Pope Paul III, Emperor Charles V, courtesans such as Flaminia and Tullia d'Aragona, and even Vittoria Colonna, although her name is not explicitly mentioned.[22]

---

21. One Latin collection of verse to Priapus (*Carmina Priapea*) was composed by the classicist Pietro Bembo. Burlesque poet Giovanni Mauro composed a *Capitolo in lode di Priapo*.

22. Roman courtesan Flaminia was the dedicatee of comic poet Giovanni Mauro's series of two *Capitoli della fava* and of a *Capitolo in lode di Priapo*.

Franco had satirized prostitutes in some of his other literary works: he spoke in satirical terms about the *puttane* in one letter of the *Pistole vulgari* and in his *Dialoghi piacevoli*.[23] Unlike Grazzini—who makes a clear distinction between the talented poet d'Aragona and the *meretrici*—Franco, following his rival Aretino, dishonors Tullia and dismisses her literary skills. In the sonnet "Priapo, l'alma Tullia Rangona," Franco contradicts Sperone Speroni's promotion of Aragona as a celebrated writer and debases her to the level of a common prostitute, famous only as a connoisseur of male members and sexual pleasure. Franco's sonnet ridicules Aragona for her Petrarchist pretentions, Petrarchism being for Franco (as it was for Grazzini) the pedantic result of empty imitation of Petrarch's poetic style.

Sonnet to Tullia d'Aragona by Nicolò Franco

A Priapo[24]   To Priapus

Priapo, l'alma Tullia Rangona   Priapus, the great Tullia Rangona
Sendo dal favor tuo tanto esaltata,   Was, due to your favor, so extolled,
Ond'è dal gran Sperone immortalata,   That great Sperone immortalized her, [25]
Che se ne fan moresche in Elicona.[26]   And in Helicon they dance for that.
Oggi, che il giorno tuo questa corona   Since today is your day, all bejeweled

23. In *dialogo* 4, the prostitute Giulia talks about her financial ruin and her venereal disease in old age. In the letter to the "*puttane*" of the *Pistole vulgari*, Franco effects a paradoxical praise of prostitutes.

24. This sonnet is part of the first edition of the *Priapea*, published in 1541 (now lost). It was published in subsequent editions in 1546 and 1548 and in *Il vendemmiatore, poemetto in ottava rima di Luigi Tansillo; e la Priapea, sonetti lussuriosi-satirici di Niccolò Franco* (Peking [Paris?]: Regnante Kien-Long [J. C. Molini?], n.d. [1790?]), from which I quote, 114.

25. Sperone Speroni was a famous Paduan *literato* who loved and admired Tullia, whom he selected as a female interlocutor in his treatise *Dialogo d'amore* (composed around 1535, published in 1541), translated here in chapter 7.

26. *Moresche* or Moorish dances were wild dances with music and warlike instruments. Mount Helicon in Greece is known in mythology as the site of residence of the Muses and is celebrated as a symbol of poetry and place of poetic inspiration. In the *Tariffa delle puttane di Vinegia* (1535), an infamous catalog listing the names of all Venetian prostitutes, Tullia is ranked eighth in importance and is referred to in offensive terms with a similar mention of Mount Helicon, whose springs are filled with urine produced by her poetic skills.

Di fine perle, e tutta inorpellata	She places this crown of fine pearls
Ti pone al capo, tal che poco grata	On your head, so that she won't be
Non sia tenuta e perfida persona.	considered an unwelcome or perfidious person.
E vuol che il don di così ricca spoglia	And she wishes that the gift of such rich spoils
Sappia non solamente il popolazzo,	Be known, not just by common people,
Ma qualunqu'erba ha 'l tuo giardino, o foglia.	But by any plant or leaf in your garden.
Perché né in Carampana, né in palazzo[27]	Because neither in a brothel nor in a palace
Donna fu mai, che con più grata voglia	Was ever a woman who, with greater lust
Riconosca i piacer che fa il cazzo.	Could recognize the pleasures that the dick dispenses.

Maffio Venier (1550–1586)

Maffio was the son of Lorenzo Venier and belonged to one of the most illustrious noble families in Venice. The Venier clan included some of the most influential personalities of the Venetian republic, such as his uncle, Domenico Venier, as well as three doges and several senators and ambassadors. Maffio himself became the archbishop of the Greek island of Corfu in 1583, three years before his death. Both Maffio's father, Lorenzo, and his uncle Domenico were well-known in the Venetian cultural scene. Lorenzo, a pupil of Pietro Aretino, wrote anticlassicist, obscene *poesia puttanesca*. Maffio's Uncle Domenico was for decades the host of Venice's most important literary salon, later to become the Accademia Veneziana or Accademia della fama (Academy of Fame). A follower of Pietro Bembo and promoter of the Petrarchan tradition, Domenico welcomed the most illustrious intellectuals and thinkers of his time to discuss and debate literature and enjoy music in his palace in Santa Maria Formosa.

While his uncle gained the coveted title of arbiter of poetic taste, patriarchal heir, and mentor for the Venetian *literati*, Venier led a libertine and dissolute life among prostitutes and brothels that eventually

27. The word "Carampana" refers to a neighborhood in Venice where many common prostitutes resided.

caused his death from syphilis at the age of thirty-six. In a biographical note to Venier's collection of *Rime e sonetti*, Attilio Carminati emphasizes the contradictions in his life.[28] Venier's religious appointment as archbishop of Corfu contrasts deeply with his hedonism; although the post was meant to provide economical stability for the chronically penniless Maffio, it actually turned out to yield next to no monetary benefit. Venier's constant financial strain sent him on various trips around the Italian peninsula in search of a position at some court, which he never obtained. He visited Rome, Florence, Pisa, Bologna, and Ferrara, where he was Alfonso II d'Este's guest. It is believed that Venier contracted syphilis during a business trip to Constantinople in 1580. He is celebrated as the best poet in the Venetian dialect of the *cinquecento*; his literary fame is attached to his *canzone* "La strazzosa," a Venetian-dialect poem that uses anti-Petrarchan yet gracious tones to praise the beauty of a poor young woman in rags. Despite being recognized as the best vernacular poet of the Venetian Renaissance, Venier remains largely unknown, perhaps because of the obscene content of some of his poetry. His works include the tragedy *Idalba* (1585), which was well-received in Florentine literary circles, and an ample collection of sonnets, *canzoni*, *terze rime*, and madrigals in dialect, which follow the anti-Petrarchan Renaissance tradition in burlesque style for entertainment in mid- to late-*cinquecento* Venice.

Venier is largely known for his poetry defaming Veronica Franco. He appears to have penned at least three poems against Franco: two *capitoli in terza rima*—"Franca, credéme, che, per San Maffio" ("Franca, believe me, by Saint Maffio") and "An fia comuodo? A che muodo zioghemo" ("Well, my dear, what sort of game is this?")—and the tailed sonnet "Veronica, ver unica puttana," which paints an obscene, physically repulsive, grotesque portrait of Franco. In this 128-line poem, Franco is debased to the level of the common whore and accused of being a syphilitic, depraved, disfigured old procuress, a true antithesis of Petrarchan beauty. Venier's sonnet fully conforms to anti-Petrarchism in the *stile bernesco*, the burlesque form inaugurated in the early decades of the sixteenth century by the founder of the

---

28. Attilio Carminati, "Presentazione," in *Canzoni e sonetti* by Maffio Venier (Venice: Corbo e Fiore, 1993), 29.

genre, Francesco Berni, himself a harsh chastiser of prostitutes and a most successful user of *terze rime* and tailed sonnets.

Venier's familiarity with the *poesia puttanesca* tradition of defamatory attacks on prostitutes derived from direct exposure. His father, Lorenzo, had dishonored famous courtesans both in *La puttana errante* (1531) and in *Il trentuno della Zaffetta* (1531). Venier, following his father's cue, penned pornographic verses and poems against prostitutes in Venetian dialect. Exemplary is his *capitolo* "Daspuò che son entrá in pensier sì vario / de cantar de puttane la nequizia" ("Ever since I found a peculiar way / to rhyme about the wickedness of whores"), featuring his own *catalogo* of Venetian prostitutes, each one mentioned in one *terzina* (tercet) for what made her most (in)famous; Franco was noted for her ability to squeeze money out of foreign clients. Venier focused principally on Franco's physical deformity and aged body, most likely drawing such themes from the tradition of *poesia puttanesca* as well as from misogynist anti-Petrarchan texts about woman's ugliness. In Venier's region, Veneto, and in Tuscany, there flourished comic authors such as Francesco Berni, Niccolò Campani, Anton Francesco Doni, and Anton Francesco Grazzini, all of whom produced either invectives against female ugliness or paradoxical verbal portraits of female grotesques.[29] Stefano Bianchi speculates that Venier's venom against Franco may be derived from personal envy and literary rivalry, because Franco was more successful as a poet than Venier ever was.[30] Through denigration and verbal abuse of Franco's body, Venier creates a rhetorical stance that protects him against the woman's charms.

In her *capitolo* 16, Franco counters Venier's fierce attacks, engaging him in a poetic competition (*tenzone*) in which, without triviality or invective, she courageously and elegantly responds to Maffio's defamatory verses in 209 lines in *terza rima*, far exceeding the length of her opponent's poem. Invoking the power of her rhetorical skills, Franco intends to challenge Venier's crude insults. Franco's counterattack consists of swerving from his boorish tones and base language

29. For the genre of anti-Petrarchan poetry about female ugliness, see my book *The Ugly Woman: Transgressive Aesthetic Models in Italian Poetry from the Middle Ages to the Baroque* (Toronto: University of Toronto Press, 2005).

30. Stefano Bianchi, "Introduzione," in *Rime* by Veronica Franco (Milan: Mursia, 1995), 15.

and inviting him to a dramatic confrontation in order to expose his lack of refinement and honor and to demonstrate her ability to defeat him on any poetic turf. Franco's tactics proved successful; her strategy to vanquish Venier's dishonoring verse produced vigorous, combative, elegant poetry, a far cry from Venier's obscene verse.

Venier's virulent dialect poems against Franco expressed deeply rooted feelings against the woman poet, but they do not represent the Venetian poet's only position with respect to women. To appreciate and fully understand Venier's stance toward women, it would be necessary to evaluate his complete oeuvre, which, in fact, shows a fluctuation between admiration and celebratory tones, interspersed with denigration and mockery. With regard to Veronica Franco, however, it is clear that Venier spared no effort to attack her on numerous occasions, and this has contributed to his infamous reputation as a wretched *poète maudit*.

Tailed sonnet to Veronica Franco[31] by Maffio Venier

Veronica, ver Unica Puttana,[32]	Veronica, verily unique whore,
Franca, *idest* furba, fina, fiappa e frola,	Franca, i.e., foxy, flimsy, faded, flabby,
E muffa, e magra, e marza, e pi mariola,	And musty, meager, moldering, and the worst thief
Che sia tra Castel, Ghetto e la Doana,[33]	That there is between Castello, Ghetto and the Customs,
Donna reduta mostro in carne humana,	Woman reduced to a monster in human flesh,
Stucco, zesso, carton, curame, e tola,	Plaster, chalk, pasteboard, leather, and plank,
Fantasma lodesana, orca varuola,	Scary ghost, a poxy ogre,

31. The sonnet is quoted from the Codex Marc. It. 9, 217 cc. 56r–59r.

32. In Veronica Franco's *Rime* there are some puns on her name, which became a satirical target for these verses of Venier. In Venier's *capitolo* 1 Franco is praised as *"donna di vera ed unica beltade,"* and in *capitolo* 7 by an unknown author she is called *"vera, unica al mondo eccelsa dea."*

33. These names refer to neighborhoods in Venice. The Ghetto was the Jewish quarter, which in 1516 the senate of the Venetian Republic decreed as a restricted area where all Jews were to be confined. This confinement lasted until 1797.

Cocodrilo, Hippogriffo, Struzzo, Alfana.	Crocodile, hippogriff, ostrich, wild mare.
Ghe vorrìa centenara de concetti, E miara de penne, e caramali, E un numero infinito de poeti,	It would take hundreds of concepts,[34] And thousands of quills and inkwells, And an endless number of poets,
Chi volesse cantar tutti i to mali, Tutte le to caie, tutti i diffetti, Spettativa de ponti, e de hospedali.	To sing all your evil, All your baseness, all your flaws, For you will end up by bridges and in the hospital.[35]
Fronte verde, occhi zalli, Naso rovan, masselle crespe e guanze, Recchie d'ogni hora carghe de buganze,	Green forehead, yellow eyes, Rusty nose, wrinkly jaws and cheeks, Your ears are always laden with chilblain,
Bocca piena de zanze, Fia spuzzolente, denti bianchi, e bei,	Your mouth is full of nonsense, Your breath is foul, and your beautiful teeth
A par delle cegie e dei cavei,	Are as white as your eyelashes and hair,
Oh vendi cavei,	And now you have become a seller of hair,[36]
Petti pieni de piaghe e pi magnai	Your breasts are covered with sores and more worn out
Che nò xe su la schena quei cavai	Than the backs of horses
Che se tien nolizai, Tette, che par la terra ghe xe aviso, Che siando in letto un di co un a Treviso	That are kept for hire, Rumor has it everywhere that, While you were in bed one day with one fellow in Treviso,

34. The word "concetti" can also be referred to conceits, that is, special rhetorical skills used in poetry making.

35. Many prostitutes spent their last years in the hospital, sick with syphilis. Bridges were used in Venice to display bodies of convicts after capital execution. In the *Lamento della cortigiana Ferrarese*, the courtesan refers to bridges and hospitals as two possible places where fallen courtesans might end their days. Ponte Sisto in Rome was a bridge where impoverished courtesans could end up begging and soliciting clients. As Lawner points out, "the bridge and the hospital" becomes a formula in satirical literature about Roman courtesans (13), a cliché that was well-known to Venier.

36. According to Dazzi, this refers to a despicable job: *Il libro chiuso di Maffio Venier (la tenzone con Veronica Franco)* (Venice: Neri Pozza, 1956), 37.

Ghe ne cazze sul viso	One of your tits fell onto his face
Una d'esse e 'l meschin puoco accorto	And the poor ill-advised man suffocated,
Se soffeghette, e ti, vedendol morto,	And you, thinking he was dead,
No 'l fu sì presto acorto	Before he was even aware of it
Che ti te 'l sepelissi in te la potta,	You buried him in your cunt,
Azzo no se sapesse della botta.	So that nobody would know of this incident.
El lo disse la zotta,	This is what the lame woman said
Che giera quella volta to massera,	Who was then your servant,
E si zuré per Dio che la xe vera.	And she swore by God that this was true.
No estu po fratiera	Aren't you also a fan of friars?
No xe de Don Donato quel bastardo,	Doesn't that bastard belong to Friar Donato,
Che ti dissi del Tron, e del Bernardo?	Whom you claim is of Tron and of Bernardo?[37]
Respondi, lion Pardo.	Answer, you leopard.[38]
Potta pi largha che no xe un battello,	Your cunt is wider than a boat,
Bus de culo pi largo d'un mastello,	Your asshole is wider than a tub,
Rezina del bordello,	Queen of the brothels,
No fostu a son de trombe, e da campane	Weren't you to the sounds of bells and trumpets
Un zorno incoronà da le puttane	One day crowned by the whores
In mezzo Carampane?	In the middle of Carampane?[39]
E per questo ogni primo dì del mese	And for this reason every first day of the month
Ancora per salario e per le spese	For your expenses and needs, still
Ti ha un cocon de marchese,	You use a menstrual pad,

---

37. Andrea Tron was a prominent member of the Venetian gentry. It is believed that he may have been the father of Enea, one of Franco's six children. Gian Battista Bernardo was a military commander and ducal counselor of the Venetian Republic, to whom Franco entrusted the future of her children. See Rosenthal, *The Honest Courtesan*, 79.

38. "Leopard" is to be read here as insult based on the animal's predatory, avid nature. Many prostitutes were decried for their greediness.

39. "Carampane" refers to an area of Venice not far from the Rialto bridge, where the government confined Venetian prostitutes in the sixteenth century, locking them up at night.

Un bùssolo d'onguento e una ampoletta	A jar of ointment, and a little cruet
De belletto, e de pi, d'ogni carretta,	With make-up, and moreover, from each copulation
Te tiri una gazzetta,	You receive some money as commission[40]
E te manda, da Pasqua e da Nadal,	And at Easter and Christmas,
Un sturuol de regallia ogni Hospedal.	Every hospital sends you a mat as present.[41]
No estù del gran mal	Aren't you the dear adoptive daughter
Francese la diletta fia adottiva,	Of the French disease,
Relita della *quondam* pellativa,	Orphan of what was called skin disease,
Causa che tanti scriva	About which so many are writing?
Herede universal del Lazzaretto,	Universal heir of the Lazaret,[42]
Quella Vacca, che satia tutto Ghetto,	You are the slut who satisfies the whole Ghetto,[43]
Quel stupendo soggetto	That fantastic subject
Che ti nassevi al tempo del Petrarca,	Who, whether you were born in Petrarch's time,
Anca lù de certezza andava in barca,	For sure he too, would not have known,
Quella, e ha fatto un arca	You are the one who built a tomb[44]
Per seppellir colu in la bottega,	To bury him in your shop,
Quella, che non ha nessuna parte integra,	The one who carries no intact part in her body,
Quella ciera de Gregha,	The one with a Greek face,[45]
Quella solene strega, quella herbera,	That solemn witch and herbalist,
L'insegna della infamia, e' la bandiera,	You are banner and sign of infamy,

40. Venier is accusing Franco of procurement.

41. Franco would have made so many ill that hospitals would be grateful to her and would send her presents packaged with the straw mats used to accommodate sick people.

42. "Lazaret" was the hospital for the contagiously ill.

43. This refers again to the Jewish quarter of Venice.

44. The reference here is to Franco's falsification of her age and her literary preference for Petrarchan poetry.

45. "Greek face" may refer to Franco being untrustworthy, as were the Greeks in the literary tradition.

Quella che mantien guerra	The one who feeds the war
Contro la sanità, mare del morbo,	Against good health, the mother of infection,
Quella che venne al mondo con el corbo,	The one who came into this world with the crow,
Quella che rende orbo	The one who blinds
Sto seculo presente, e che l'infetta,	And corrupts the present age,
Quella contra de chi no val recetta,	The one against whom there is neither remedy,
Ne medesina eletta,	Nor appropriate medicine,
Quella, che sti vuol dir la verità,	The one, to tell the truth,
Nianca la puoca carne, che ti ha',	Where not even the scanty flesh that covers you
Xe de natività,	Is natural,
Ma a' forza de cerotti, impiastri e onguenti,	And by using bandages, plaster and ointments,
Ti xe' un corpo formao senza elementi,	You are a body shaped without elements,
Quella, che dai frangenti	The one who, from the grated crusts
De broze, che ti vendi ai scovazzieri,	That you sell to the garbage men,
Che i le tuo da inmarcir, i leameri,	Who buy them to manure dunghills,
Da ingrassar i vignieri,	And to fertilize the vineyards,
El se sa che ti cavi un tanto al mese,	It is known, you make a monthly profit,
Che ti te vesti e ti te fa le spese,	Enough money for clothing and expenses,
Quella per chi zà presse	You are the one because of whom
Un mar de zentilhomini la gotta,	Before you became so repulsive,
Innanzi che ti fossi sì zavatta,	Many gentlemen fell ill with gout,[46]
Quella magra desfatta,	You are so skinny and wasted,
Anzi, secca, incandìa, arsa destrutta,	So very scrawny, so parched,
Quella, che nome in ossi sta redutta	One who is now reduced to skin and bone,

46. Allusion to Domenico Venier, poet and Franco's admirer and mentor, who suffered from gout.

Che cazze dalla brutta,
Quella, che spesso, i putti per la via

Tio in fallo per la morte stravestia,

E corre, e scampa, e cria,
Cosi estù tremenda, e spaventosa,
Cosi paristù al veder dolorosa

Quella che e' tosegosa
Che se non me vegnia a manco el di,
La matteria m'abbonda sempre pi,

Che chi te vede ti,
Vede el summario d'ogni malatia,
E l'alfabetto della furbaria,

Quel ragno, quell'Arpia,
Quella che del continuo ha in casa a' nolo
Do de quei fratti da san Zanne e Polo.

Quella che con el collo
Per sagramenti falsi in più mattine
Ha sverzena forsi cento berline,

Quella che non ha visine,
Che con el putrefar l'aer d'intorno,

Ti ha desabità mezzo quel contorno

Che se no' fosse el forno
El vesin, che ti ha' a' lai, quel squararuol
Con la fazza sul campo onde da el sol,

Who fell in ruin,
The one whom the children in the streets often
Mistake for death in disguise,

And so they flee, and run away screaming.
You are so terrible and frightful,
You are you so painful to see

You are so poisonous
That, if I did not lack the time,
I could largely expand on this subject,

Since those who see you,
See the sum of all illness,
An alphabet of wiliness,

A spider, a harpy,
One who constantly hires in her house

Two friars from Saint John and Paul.[47]

You are one who, with her own neck
Under false oath, on several mornings
Has inaugurated hundreds of pillories,

You are one who has no neighbors,
For with the stench that fouls the air all around you
You have chased away half the neighborhood

And if it weren't for the tar kiln
That one of your neighbors owns, the boat builder
Whose shop faces the sunny side of the square,

47. Here Venier refers to the Dominican church of Saint John and Paul, known in Venetian dialect as Zanni and Polo.

Che tien, altro ti puol	You could poison anything
Corromper con el fiao', ne' 'l sol,	With your breath, except the sun and
ne"l fuogo,	fire,
No sassemo seguri in nessun luogo.	We would not be safe anywhere.
E qua finisso el zuogo,	And here I finish my game,[48]
E, se no me tignisse per honor,	Since, if I didn't hold back for decency,
E per farte a ti mazzor favor	And in order not to do you a greater favor
Con el darte stridor,	By spreading news about you,
Fa' conto, che sarave sul invero	Be sure that I would be singing about you
Per cantar fino al zorno del Giudicio.	Until the day of the final judgment.
Perché ti è un precipitio,	Because you are an abyss,
Un profondo, un abisso, un caos di quanto	A precipice, a deep chasm, a chaos
Me reservo de dirte in l'altro canto.	About which I will tell you in another poem.

---

48. Venier is alluding here to the ludic aspect of his poem, which is indeed a harsh attack on Franco but also a poetic game, an exercise meant to demonstrate his rhetorical skills in composing satirical verses.

10.
Giulia Bigolina and Pietro Aretino's Letters

CHRISTOPHER NISSEN

Giulia Bigolina, one of the earliest Italian women to gain fame as an author of works of prose fiction, was born into an aristocratic family in Padua in or shortly after 1516. Very little biographical information concerning her has survived, but archival evidence indicates she was married, although she was widowed by the 1550s, and that she had three children.[1] By the early 1550s she had attained considerable local renown, and it would seem that her only known surviving works, the prose romance *Urania* and the novella "Giulia Camposanpiero and Thesibaldo Vitaliani," also date from this period.[2] None of her works was published during her lifetime, which is known to have ended by 1569, and it appears that her career as a writer did not attract a great deal of attention outside her native Padua.

While she lived, her name was undoubtedly most widely seen when it appeared in the fifth book of Pietro Aretino's *Lettere*, published in 1550.[3] Aretino (1492–1556), one of the most controversial literary figures of the age, was well known in Italy and beyond the Alps as a writer and a correspondent with famous artists and rulers. He had single-handedly created a new literary trend, as well as a cultural

---

1. For studies of the documents relating to Bigolina's life, see Valeria Finucci's introduction to *Urania*, by Giulia Bigolina (Rome: Bulzoni, 2002), 13–22; Nissen's introduction to *Urania: The Story of a Young Woman's Love*, 4–8; and Finucci's introduction to *Urania: A Romance*, 5n.; and Nissen, *Kissing the Wild Woman: Concepts of Art, Beauty, and the Italian Prose Romance* (Toronto: University of Toronto Press, forthcoming).

2. On the dates of composition of Bigolina's works, see Nissen's introduction to *Urania: The Story of a Young Woman's Love*, 20, 29, 33, 42–44, and Finucci's introduction to *Urania*, 49–50. Finucci places the composition of *Urania* between 1554 and 1558, whereas I would place it in or shortly after 1552.

3. For Aretino's letters to Bigolina, see Nissen's introduction to *Urania: The Story of a Young Woman's Love*, 9–14, Nissen, "Giulia Bigolina, la prima romanziera italiana: una donna dell'alta padovana tra i letterati del '500," *Alta Padovana* 4 (2005): 57–59, and Nissen, *Kissing the Wild Woman*, forthcoming. See also Finucci's introduction to *Urania*, 22–23 and 22–23n.

sensation, with the publication of more than three thousand of his vernacular letters in six volumes over a period of nearly twenty years. Many of these letters, addressed to famous writers and artists, reveal the author's deep fascination with the arts and with the lives and acts of creative individuals.[4]

Aretino's letters reflect a curious commingling of the magnificent and the mundane: letters of praise or admonition to kings, popes, and emperors are interspersed with such trivialities as thanks to minor figures for gifts of food or complaints about the doings of his household servants. Among these myriad correspondences there is no shortage of letters addressed to women of both high and low degree; however, letters acknowledging the creative talents of women are much scarcer. Although Aretino addressed several letters to the poet Vittoria Colonna in the first two volumes of the *Lettere*, in only one of them (1.217) does he acknowledge "*l'opre che avete prodotto con l'ingegno*" (the works that you have created with your mind); otherwise he is more inclined to praise Colonna for her piety and devotion to virtue (2.13, 2.16, 2.87).[5] Aretino also wrote several letters to the renowned poet Veronica Gambara, such as one of the best-known letters in the volume (1.222), which includes a sonnet describing Titian's portrait of the Duke of Urbino. In this letter Aretino discusses the aesthetics of portraiture with someone whom he seems to regard as an intellectual equal.[6] In other letters he thanks her for the sonnets of praise she has sent to him (1.128, 1.179).

---

4. On the significance and popularity of Aretino's *Lettere*, see Christopher Cairns, *Pietro Aretino and the Republic of Venice: Researches on Aretino and his Circle in Venice, 1527–1556* (Florence: Olschki, 1985), 125–26; Raymond B. Waddington, *Aretino's Satyr: Sexuality, Satire, and Self-Projection in Sixteenth-Century Literature and Art* (Toronto: University of Toronto Press, 2004), 47–58; and Luba Freedman, *Titian's Portraits through Aretino's Lens* (University Park: Pennsylvania State University Press, 1995), 29–33.

5. Pietro Aretino, *Lettere*, ed. Paolo Procaccioli, 6 vols. (Rome: Salerno, 1997–2002). Aretino also refers to the poetry of Colonna and Gambara in his "Dream of Parnassus" letter (1.280, 386). In citing Aretino's *Lettere*, modern scholars refer to them by the number designations that Procaccioli has established for them. Letters sent to him by others are not so numbered and will be cited by volume and page number.

6. For a study of this letter, see Freedman, *Titian's Portraits*, 69–90. However, Aretino's feelings for Gambara were ambivalent at best: in an earlier document, dated 1534, he had called her "*meretrice laureata*" (whore laureate), despite her effusive praise for him; see Pietro

Aside from these two poets of the highest aristocracy, whose literary talents were highly esteemed by their contemporaries and whose good will provided Aretino with bragging rights, Aretino mentions very few creative women in all of his thousands of letters. The poet and dialogist Tullia d'Aragona, of whom he was not fond, is referred to but once, in a letter to Sperone Speroni (1.139). Here Aretino heaps adulation upon Speroni for his *Dialoghi d'amore*, in which Aragona appears as an interlocutor; however, he only mentions Aragona briefly, saying that her immodesty ought to attract the envy of modest women, because it has gained her so exalted a place in Speroni's work. This, a typical example of one of Aretino's backhanded compliments to women, shows that Tullia's profession as a courtesan was of more interest to him than her skills as a writer, which he mentions not at all.[7] On a few occasions Aretino does praise certain courtesans for their musical abilities, recognizing this as a traditional and entirely appropriate art for a unique social group (2.316, 4.573, 5.50, 5.103, 5.463).[8] He never mentions the contemporary poet and musician Gaspara Stampa, who was also active in Venice.

Aretino provides words of praise for only two other women writers, apart from Colonna and Gambara. However, it must be noted that the letters in which they appear are not addressed to the women directly, nor can these encomia be regarded as entirely separate from the compliments that Aretino pays to the distinguished men for whom the letters are actually intended. In his letter of 1540 to Paolo Interiano, Aretino is primarily intent on expressing his feelings of friendship for the addressee. When he mentions that the Genoese poet Maria Spinola is as deserving of praise for her pastoral style as Sappho was in her own day, he does so in order to express his appre-

---

Aretino, *Un pronostico satirico di Pietro Aretino*, ed. Alessandro Luzio (Bergamo: Istituto Italiano d'Arti Grafiche, 1900), 9, 68–69n.

7. Aretino's scorn for d'Aragona has been documented by Rita Casagrande di Villaviera, *Le cortigiane veneziane del cinquecento* (Milan: Longanesi, 1968), 221, 225, and by Robert Buranello, "*Figura meretricis*: Tullia d'Aragona in Sperone Speroni's *Dialogo d'amore*," *Spunti e ricerche* 15 (2000), 55. See also chapter 7 in this volume.

8. For the noteworthy association between Venetian courtesans and music, see Casagrande, *Le cortigiane veneziane del cinquecento*, 187–90, and Lynne Lawner, *Lives of the Courtesans: Portraits of the Renaissance* (New York: Rizzoli, 1987), 53. Lawner describes Aretino's often ambivalent attitude toward the numerous courtesans he knew (65–72).

ciation for the gift of three of Spinola's sonnets that Interiano has sent to him, and also as a means of urging Interiano to become a better writer himself (2.165). Aretino's tone is more equivocal in the case of Franceschina (Checca) Baffa, a Venetian courtesan who was the lover of the dialogist Giuseppe Betussi.[9] Aretino mentions her in a letter of 1542 addressed to Betussi (2.445), in which he attributes Betussi's own skill as a writer to his association with Baffa. However, it is significant that Aretino seems less interested in the things that Baffa herself wrote than in what she might inspire Betussi to write. This attitude is borne out by Betussi's own efforts, as can be seen in his dialogue on love, "Il Raverta," where he portrays Baffa as a naive interlocutor in need of erudite lectures that men deliver for her benefit.

No creative woman received more heartfelt admiration from Aretino than Marietta Talatina, who apparently was renowned throughout Venice for her skill at the typically domestic art of embroidery (4.583). In another letter (3.606), Aretino also praises a certain Nicolosa for her sewing skills. It is evident that Aretino liked his artistic women to fit into convenient categories: ruling-class nobility, courtesans known for their musical talent, lower-class artisans who were distinguished for their domestic abilities, and poets who might serve as an inspiration to his distinguished male friends. At best, Bigolina made a rather awkward fit in this scheme.

Aretino wrote to Bigolina late in his career, long after the heyday of his correspondences with Colonna and Gambara. His three letters are dated September and October 1549. Bigolina was probably just beginning to make a name for herself in Padua at this time, because only one of her datable references predates Aretino's.[10] By all evidence, Bigolina initiated the correspondence by introducing herself in a letter of her own, perhaps in an effort to publicize her budding career, as

---

9. For Baffa's poetry, see Giuseppe Bianchini, *Franceschina Baffo, rimatrice veneziana del secolo XVI* (Verona: Drucker, 1896), and Casagrande, *Le cortigiane veneziane del cinquecento*, 178–80.

10. For the single reference to Bigolina that predates Aretino's letters, that of the poet Giovanni Maria Masenetti, see Nissen's introduction to *Urania: The Story of a Young Woman's Love*, 8–9; Finucci's introduction to *Urania*, 19 and 19n; and Finucci's introduction to *Urania: A Romance*, 5n.

other correspondents of Aretino's had often done.[11] Bigolina's letter to Aretino has not survived, so we can only speculate about its contents on the basis of the response that Aretino provides.

As his letters continually attest (one of those to Gambara mentioned above, 1.128, may stand as a case in point), Aretino was greatly pleased to receive recognition from others throughout his life. This characteristic is quite evident in this first letter to Bigolina, which expresses his gratitude for the praise that she has apparently lavished upon him in her own letter. Aretino seems genuinely grateful for her compliments, attributing them to an excess of kindness on her part. It would also seem that he is mindful of preserving her good name, since he is careful to call the affection she has shown him "filial," so that no one might suspect his motives in publishing his correspondence with her.[12]

Of course, such a reference to a father-daughter relationship might also serve to convey a tone of paternalism, to provide a subtle reminder that a neophyte woman writer from Padua must perforce recognize the literary authority of the world-famous Aretino. Moreover, he takes pains to mention that he was in the company of another most distinguished personage, the painter Titian, while he read her letter. Aretino's response strongly hints that he felt Bigolina would like to become better known through her association with so famous a writer, whose pen might make her name "a trumpet peal, resounding in its own glory, in the temples of the ages." Aretino's formulaic humility does not entirely disguise a sort of smugness, as if he wants Bigolina to know that he considers her gesture to be yet another attempt by an admirer to use him as a means of gaining publicity, even as he "rewards" her by publishing his response. Unfortunately we cannot know how Bigolina introduced herself to him; if she mentioned her accomplishments as a writer in her own letter, Aretino provides no clue. Aretino does not speak of her works or her "*ingegno*," as he

---

11. For evidence of such publicity seeking, see the letters sent to Aretino by Alessandro Piccolomini, Sperone Speroni, Lodovico Dolce, and Bernardino Daniello, *Lettere*, 1:486, 490, 503–5, and Aretino's letter to Giovanni Agostino Cazza (2.107). On this topic, see also Nissen, *Kissing the Wild Woman*, forthcoming.

12. On the topic of Bigolina's distinguished male acquaintances taking pains to preserve her good name in their writings, see Nissen's introduction to *Urania: The Story of a Young Woman's Love*, 3–4, 11.

occasionally did in his earlier letters to Colonna and Gambara, and he says nothing about what she might have done to deserve the thing he imagines she wants, that is, a name to resound through the ages. Instead, his conclusion stresses very different characteristics: she does indeed deserve his praise, but certainly not as an erudite writer of prose fiction. In his view, she stands as a paragon of all the traditional womanly virtues: moderation, chastity, piety, and the like. Only for these things will he celebrate her.

Aretino's second letter is also dated September 1549, and it immediately follows the first in the volume. Once more we find that Bigolina has sent something to Aretino, but this time she has chosen a very different gesture: having noted his advertisement for a servant to look after his daughters, she has taken it upon herself to sponsor a country girl and send her to Aretino's house in Venice for an interview. Aretino often wrote in his letters of his perennial need for reliable servants, as Bigolina might well have been aware. However, this act was bound to elicit a very different response from Aretino, for whom serving girls were a special concern and a special obsession.[13] In his second letter he reveals his true colors, the nastier side of his attitudes toward women, which is certainly not limited to this place in his writings.[14] The undisguised lechery of Aretino's comments is made even more derisive by his sarcastic misappropriation of neo-Platonic notions concerning the relationship between beauty and the good: after he has said that he prefers more mature and more attractive serving girls than the one Bigolina has sent, he proceeds to cite the most mundane examples of how the term *bello* is used in everyday urban life. In lewdly equivocal terms, he compares the words of shoppers who loudly proclaim the "beauty" of the fruits, vegetables, or fish that they buy in market squares to the admiring cries of men who

---

13. For Aretino's interest in hiring maidservants see Nissen's introduction to *Urania: The Story of a Young Woman's Love*, 11–12. Evidence of his habit of seducing them can be seen especially in letters 4.275, 4.295, 4.434, and 4.447.

14. For Aretino's creation of an often misogynistic "counterculture of the illicit" in his pornographic writings, see Guido Ruggiero, "Marriage, Love, Sex and Renaissance Civic Morality," in *Sexuality and Gender in Early Modern Europe: Institutions, Texts, Images*, ed. J. Grantham Turner (Cambridge: Cambridge University Press, 1993), 11–16.

see attractive women passing by on the street.[15] There is no gratitude for Bigolina's kind acts here; only scarcely veiled insults and words of reproach, culminating in a blast for her insufficient efforts to find the sort of girl he preferred ("I will send her back to you, providing you with more words of thanks than the words you yourself employed in seeking the girl out").

This is hardly a letter expressing one writer's admiration for another, much less a letter of friendship.[16] Bigolina was a married woman of a distinguished noble family, whose surviving literary works describe the deeds of female protagonists such as Urania and Giulia Camposanpiero, women devoted to traditional notions of virtue who make great sacrifices in the name of love. Her other writings, such as her one surviving letter and her will, reveal a fondness for charity, decorum, and polite comportment.[17] She was not likely to have appreciated the mocking tone of Aretino's second letter.

Nonetheless, by all appearances she sent yet another item to Aretino, to which he refers in his third letter to her, dated a month later. This time she has sent just the sort of thing he could always ap-

15. The link between beauty and the good was a commonplace in early modern neo-Platonic treatises; for example, see Marsilio Ficino, *Commentary on Plato's Symposium on Love*, trans. Sears Reynolds Jayne (Dallas: Spring Publications, 1985), 5.1 (84). On Bigolina's rejection of the Renaissance cult of female beauty in an art-historical context, see Christopher Nissen, "*Paragone* as Fiction: The Judgment of Paris in Giulia Bigolina's *Urania*," *Italian Quarterly* 42, no. 165–66 (2005): 5–17, and Nissen, *Kissing the Wild Woman*, forthcoming. For a study of the pervasive link between food and sex in the more ribald schools of Italian Renaissance poetry, see Jean Toscan, *Le carnaval du langage: le lexique érotique des poètes de l'équivoque de Burchiello à Marino (XV–XVII siècles)*, 4 vols. (Lille: Presses Universitaires de Lille, 1981), especially 3:1436–51 (for fruit, including Aretino's peaches, melons and figs), 3:1460–65 (salad), and 3:1595–1621 (fish). Alimentary metaphors for sex may be found in Aretino's own *Strambotti a la villanesca* (1544), especially *strambotti* 78 and 94 in Pietro Aretino, *Edizione nazionale delle opere di Pietro Aretino*, vol. 1, *Poesie varie*, ed. Giovanni Aquilecchia and Angelo Romano (Rome: Salerno, 1992), 199, 204.

16. For the notion that these letters indicate that Bigolina was a friend of both Aretino and Titian, see Finucci's introduction to *Urania*, 23–24, 36.

17. For Bigolina's letter to Francesco Barozzi, see Finucci's introduction to *Urania*, 20–21 and 20–21n., and Nissen's introduction to *Urania: The Story of a Young Woman's Love*, 14–16. For Bigolina's will, see Nissen's introduction to *Urania: The Story of a Young Woman's Love*, 5–8, and Nissen, *Kissing the Wild Woman*, forthcoming, which includes the full text and translation of this document.

preciate: a sonnet of praise for him (now lost). Aretino's assertion in this letter that Bigolina only knows him through his fame is a sign that the two writers had never met face to face. It also corroborates the impression given in the first two letters that Bigolina sought Aretino out and initiated the series of correspondences on her own. Here we find the clearest indication of Aretino's opinion of Bigolina's efforts to make herself known to him: he believes she is motivated by an almost obsessive desire to meet him in person. He pretends he does not deserve her attentions, but a more careful reading of his words reveals that he almost certainly did not think her attentions worth very much of his time. Surely the comparison between Bigolina's words of greeting and those of "any little chambermaid," a clear reference to his lecherous comments in the second letter, is not intended to express any great respect for her.

What conclusion could Bigolina have drawn from this brief, equivocal flurry of communication with one of the most famous men in Italy? The publication of those letters, while surely a memorable moment in her life, must have also been something of a mixed blessing. On the one hand, her name was now spread far and wide in print just as she was starting to make her mark as a writer, for now she was a correspondent of the great Aretino; on the other, everyone could now see his subtle backhanded compliments to her, as well as his snide comments about chambermaids and the true nature of beauty. The presence of the renowned painter Titian as an onlooker to this very public humiliation could only serve to make things worse. In any case, Aretino published no further letters to Bigolina, and it is unlikely she saw any sense in approaching him further, once she realized how he regarded her. Instead, after 1550 Bigolina turned her attention to composing the prose works that have come down to us, works that clearly communicate not only her faith in the powers and abilities of clever women but also her notion, central to *Urania*, that the true beauty of a woman lies not in her physical appearance but in her artistic accomplishments and her steadfast devotion to virtue.

Letters by Pietro Aretino

TO LADY GIULIA BIGOLINA

If ever letters were dear to me, most dear was the one that your kind chambermaid delivered to me with her own hand. When she appeared before me, Titian was with me; I mean that painter who is as famous as fame itself.[18] His most excellent soul was one with mine as he listened to me reading the things which you write to me through simple courtesy. He took as much pleasure from it as he would have if the kindness you show me had been meant for him. Indeed, we were uncertain for a time how to regard the great praise you bestowed upon me; eventually we decided to attribute it more to your kindness than to any merit of mine, and I wish my powers were capable of expressing in some way the feelings I hold in my heart for you. Even though nothing is lacking where good intentions come to the fore, affection of this sort triumphs over any mere action; for this reason, a spirit which is grateful and brimming with fervor gives itself in place of that which it cannot give. Therefore, take me in the place of those things which I am not, and let your name be satisfied with the honor with which my pen will find ways to memorialize it, even though my pen's inkwell is sufficient in itself to make your name a trumpet peal, resounding in its own glory, in the temples of the ages. It might be necessary that I consider serving you rather than celebrating you, but since I am not good at such things, I am forced to employ my tongue rather than my feet. I confess that I feel obliged to you, on account of the filial love which you, Lady Giulia, have shown me; for you feel nothing but love in your heart and soul. On this account, the human kindness which we see you are made of rejoices with Nature; for Nature has fashioned you in just the way that she, in her benevolence, would wish to create every woman born. For if it were so, then virtue instead of vice, moderation instead of haughtiness, and chastity instead of lasciviousness would predominate in that sex which you honor with kindness, adorn with manners and illuminate with reverence. In order to appreciate heaven

---

18. Tiziano Vecellio (ca. 1488–1576), one of the most influential Renaissance artists, was a close friend of Aretino's throughout his years in Venice, as well as a constant presence in the *Lettere.*

all the more instead of worldly things, you are married to continence, and religion is your teacher. Because of this, I am proud to be in your good graces. In Venice, September 1549.

Pietro Aretino

TO THE SAME

The country girl whom, in your kindness, you have sent to me has more need of being looked after herself than she is capable of looking after others. Certainly her appearance would do great wrong to the herding of lambs, were she to begin spending time with little girls.[19] Her mother made me laugh when she said that the girl is twelve years old, but she has not yet turned eleven. Perhaps *Messer* Titian will take her into his house to join the servants of his daughter and sister; if so, she will be very well lodged and situated. In addition to the three I have already, I need a servant who can train them, instead of one who requires training from them. I told His Reverence Brother Giulio[20] that I desired girls from fourteen to sixteen years of age, or up to eighteen; and not too unattractive, inasmuch as where beauty resides, good may almost always be found as well. And then, what man, wishing to buy something, fails to require his purchaser to see to it that he buys, for example, a beautiful head of lettuce, a beautiful squash, or a beautiful watermelon? "O what beautiful peaches, what beautiful melons, what beautiful figs!" one calls to another in the market square. "What beautiful fruit, what a beautiful sturgeon, and what beautiful *menole*[21] they have in the fish market!" says this serving boy to that. After all, if upon seeing different kinds of women, one shouts out, "What a beautiful maid, what a beautiful bride!" or "What a beautiful widow!" or "What a beautiful nun!" or "What a beautiful housewife!" it is all quite appropriate. Therefore, in the event that the great painter will not keep her, I will send her back to you, providing you with more words of

19. Aretino's point here, delivered with some sarcasm, seems to be that the girl looks more like a shepherdess than a governess.

20. This friar, otherwise unidentified by Procaccioli, apparently served as Aretino's agent for recruiting serving girls in Padua. He is not mentioned elsewhere in the *Lettere*.

21. A term applied to various species of small Mediterranean fish.

thanks than the words you yourself employed in seeking the girl out. And she may stop by at my house on her way home, for I have compassion for a maid who is born without means, wretched and poor. In Venice, September 1549.

Pietro Aretino

TO LADY GIULIA

Most gracious Bigolina, it is certainly true that those who have not yet made a name for themselves must send forth fame in the place of the reputation they wish to gain. I say this because it seems I must still be rather famous myself, for you only know me on account of my fame, and yet you have taken it upon yourself to write so lively, original, and brilliant a sonnet in praise of me. Kindness has moved you in this, rather than good judgment; nonetheless, you have done it in order that you might take as much delight in good words as you have in good deeds. Whatever the case, if I presume to be what you are, I presume to be more than I am, that is certain. And if this letter does not show as much happiness as the occasion merits, it is because joyful feelings expand the vital spirits in just the same way as the act of displeasure restrains them; therefore we know better how to make ourselves sad than how to make ourselves happy. That is how matters stand, so it is necessary that you accept my words as if they were deeds, especially since from its depths my heart bears witness to them with profound emotion.

Meanwhile, I am wondering in just what way I might show you my gratitude, not only for the honor I have gained through your verses, but also for your desire to meet me in person, a desire which so burns your soul that it yearns for nothing else quite as much. I hear of this desire, yet I do not glory in it excessively, and for this I blame my modest nature; and in the same fashion I have praised my own nature for not being overly proud. Virtue of this sort permits me to indulge only a little in the visceral pleasures I would feel if I were an arrogant man. But if any little chambermaid can make me hers through an insignificant word of greeting, how am I to regard the fact that I have been made yours by the affection that you, a woman of distinction,

have shown me? Well then, I will employ my wit, the only thing I have, to pay tribute to your lovely name. In this way your noble generosity will never have cause to regret the benevolent gesture whereby you make me so very fit to recognize it. In Venice, October 1549.
Pietro Aretino

11.
Centrality and Liminality in Bernardino Ochino's "Sermon Preached ... on the Feast Day of St. Mary Magdalen"

MARIA GALLI STAMPINO

The "Sermon Preached in Venice by the Reverend Father Friar Bernardino Ochino from Siena, a Capuchin Monk, on the Feast Day of St. Mary Magdalene 1539" is an excellent example of how a focus on gender reveals the tensions pervading early modern lives and culture. Paradoxes inform this text, as they do Ochino's own life and his relationship to powerful women, on whom he came to rely occasionally.

To begin at the textual level, Ochino's sermon on Mary Magdalene shows the ambiguous attitude toward women prevalent in early modern times among the Catholic hierarchy and those following its dictates. Women played a significant role in both Old and New Testaments; however, there is no woman-authored book in the New Testament, and the process of forming the Christian canon excluded some that were. Even the Gospel according to Luke—traditionally believed to be the book in which the presence and activities of women among the earliest disciples are constantly underscored—offers numerous episodes in which women characters (especially, but not solely, the Magdalene) are marginalized and male ones (especially Peter) made central to the narrative.[1]

Church teachings went hand in hand with views of women in the culture at large (including so-called high culture). As the sermon's second paragraph makes clear, women were considered to be genetically inferior to men, an attitude derived from Aristotle's *Generation of Animals*. Studies such as Laqueur's[2] and Maclean's[3] have amply shown

---

1. See Ann Graham Brock, *Mary Magdalene, the First Apostle: The Struggle for Authority* (Cambridge, MA: Harvard Theological Studies, 2003), 32–38, 55–60, 164.

2. Thomas Laqueur, *Making Sex: Body and Gender from the Greeks to Freud* (Cambridge, MA: Harvard University Press, 1990).

3. Ian Maclean, *The Renaissance Notion of Woman: A Study in the Fortune of Scholasticism and Medical Science in European Intellectual Life* (Cambridge: Cambridge University Press, 1980).

that, according to the scientific view prevailing at the time (i.e., that of Galenic medicine), women were imperfect men, lacking the necessary heat and dryness that make a human being whole (and hence male).[4] Women wanted rationality and were subject to the tyranny of their senses and emotions. Paradoxically, then, Mary Magdalene is only partially responsible for her sins, while the Pharisee who appears in the episode in the Gospel according to Luke[5] is fully responsible for his and is therefore far guiltier than the Magdalene. Such paradoxes would not have raised eyebrows, as they are part of a long rhetorical tradition in the Catholic Church.[6]

Mary Magdalene provides an even more puzzling example to be held up to worshipers: she was not only a woman but a reformed sinner—indeed, in the common view of the time, a reformed prostitute.[7] Following a homiletic tradition that goes back at least to St. Augustine, Ochino singles Mary Magdalene out as a worthy example for human repentance and the radical change of one's behavior.

In this sense Ochino's sermon provides one of many examples of male mediation, interpretation, and authorization of female religious experience—a circumstance given greater weight by the fact that when he delivered this sermon he was vicar general of the Capuchin order (a position he held from 1538 to 1542).[8] However, we should resist reading this sermon solely in a Foucauldian vein, placing it on the modern side of the divide between, to quote Marina Caffiero, "a medieval, mysticism-based model of sanctity and the proposal

4. On this issue, see note 5 in chapter 5 above.

5. Lk 7:36–50.

6. See, for other examples, the excerpts from Antoniano's treatise *Three Books on the Christian Education of Children* in chapter 2 of this volume.

7. Brock opines that "this association results from the identification of Mary Magdalene as the unnamed female sinner (later interpreted as a prostitute) of Luke 7:36–50, the passage immediately preceding Mary Magdalene's introduction into the Gospel of Luke." Brock, *Mary Magdalene*, 1n2. In her opinion, this identification is purely based on textual proximity, and "it provides another essential factor in the diminishment of Mary Magdalene's apostolic authority." Brock, *Mary Magdalene*, 168–69.

8. As Diana Robin explains, "The Capuchins preached the rejection of worldly goods; and they distanced themselves from the preoccupation of the ecclesiastical hierarchy with the acquisition of capital and lands, calling instead for a return to the simple values and faith of the early Church fathers." Robin, *Publishing Women*, 15.

in its stead of a model centered on heroic virtues, on religious commitment, both held up as worthy of being imitated by Christians."[9] Both mysticism and religiously motivated practical action are present in Ochino's sermon, evidence of a period of transition and thus of a rich, vibrant text. Indeed, Ochino himself, as we shall see below, was a liminal figure.

Beyond exemplifying an attitude toward women that was widespread in the early modern period, this sermon merits our attention because of the large following Ochino had among the learned. Extant letters by noble men and women indicate that they had witnessed his preaching in various Italian cities.[10] In addition, he frequented the gatherings in Giulia Gonzaga's home in Naples, which attracted many noblewomen, including Vittoria Colonna, as well as "poets, literary patrons, editors, translators, and the proprietors of presses."[11] In this sermon, the citation from Virgil is an unmistakable indication that Ochino assumed that at least some of his listeners would be familiar with it. Ochino's biographer, Roland Bainton, has pointed out that the Capuchins were opposed to scholastic subtlety as well as classical references, because they perceived such rhetorical devices as betrayals of a simple and direct expression of God's teaching;[12] hence, the Virgil citation is all the more notable. In particular, Vittoria Colonna heard Ochino preach in Rome in 1535, in Ferrara and Florence in 1537,[13] and in Verona, Bologna, and Pisa in 1538.[14] Tullia d'Aragona also

9. "Il modello mistico medievale [della santità] e la proposta, in sua vece, del modulo centrato sulle virtù eroiche e sull'impegno religioso, additati all'imitazione del popolo cristiano." Marina Caffiero, "Tra modelli di disciplinamento e autonomia soggettiva," in *Modelli di santità e modelli di comportamento: contrasti, intersezioni, complementarità*, ed. Giulia Barone, Marina Caffiero, and Francesco Scorza Barcellona (Turin: Rosenberg & Sellier, 1994), 265.

10. In 1535, for example, "during Lent [Juan de] Valdés and [the noblewoman Giulia] Gonzaga visited the church of San Giovanni Maggiore in Naples where the Capuchin friar Bernardino Ochino was preaching. Costanza d'Avalos and Giovanna d'Avalos also attended Ochino's sermons." Robin, *Publishing Women*, 17.

11. Ibid., 18.

12. Roland H. Bainton, *Bernardino Ochino: esule e riformatore senese del cinquecento* (Florence: Sansoni, 1940), 30.

13. Ibid., 33, 37–38.

14. Robin, *Publishing Women*, 27.

heard him preach in Ferrara in 1537,[15] and she addressed a sonnet to him criticizing his rejection of socially accepted pastimes of the age.[16]

Ochino invoked Colonna's political protection that same year,[17] at a time when the very existence of the Capuchin order was threatened. Interestingly, Colonna was not the only noblewoman whom Ochino addressed; his first printed work, *Dialoghi sette*, consists of conversations between "*padre* Bernardino" and the Duchess of Camerino, who in real life was a woman to be reckoned with[18] and was willing to help a group of Franciscans determined to return to the original rule of the order. In addition to the monk's connection with Colonna, Diana Robin has recently pointed out similarities between Ochino's *Dialoghi sette* and Tullia d'Aragona's own dialogue on the levels of style[19] and content.[20]

This sermon in particular had an indirect (though no less meaningful) impact on Vittoria Colonna. She devoted a sonnet to Mary Magdalene,[21] and as Giovanni Bardazzi has recently shown,[22] linguistic similarities with Ochino's homily are evident in it and in

15. Ibid., 171.

16. She wrote specifically of "le finte apparenze, e'l ballo, e'l suono," that is, "theatre, dance, music." See *Shining Eyes, Cruel Fortune: The Lives and Loves of Italian Renaissance Women Poets*, trans. Irma B. Jaffe with Gernando Colombardo (New York: Fordham University Press, 2002), 77, 95.

17. Bainton, *Bernardino Ochino*, 24.

18. "devota, potente come nipote del Papa, e decisa," that is, "devout, powerful as the Pope's niece, and resolute." Bainton, *Bernardino Ochino*, 6, 16. The pope was Clement VII (Giulio de' Medici).

19. "In the dialogues of Ochino, Valdés, and d'Aragona, the effectivemess of the drama depends on the stripped-down quality of the exchange: a man and a woman engage in an intellectually and emotionally intense discussion, and there are no other characters to buffer the space between them." Robin, *Publishing Women*, 163–64.

20. "These [Ochino's, Valdés's, and d'Aragona's] are conversations about ideas; yet all three, because of the female-male casting, are to some degree sexually suggestive—though the traces of it are faintest in Ochino's works" (ibid., 164); also, "All three dialogues come out the milieu of the salon" of noble Italian women (ibid., 176).

21. This is *rima spirituale* 155, reprinted in Vittoria Colonna, *Rime*, ed. Alan Bullock (Bari, Italy: Laterza, 1982), 162, and also translated by Abigail Brundin in *Sonnets for Michelangelo: A Bilingual Edition* (Chicago: University of Chicago Press, 2005), 76–77.

22. Giovanni Bardazzi, "Le rime spirituali di Vittoria Colonna e Bernardino Ochino," *Italique: poésie italienne de la Renaissance* 4 (2001): 61–91.

other poems of Colonna's.[23] Bardazzi rightly concedes that while Ochino's sermons cannot be considered direct sources for Colonna's poems, Colonna absorbed their thematic and linguistic elements, such that both sets of texts offer similar semantic qualities. Emidio Campi has convincingly argued that the important relationship between Colonna and Michelangelo was influenced by Ochino, as the latter exposed both to the spiritual teachings of the reformer Juan de Valdés.[24] In sum, the web of personal, intellectual, and religious relations around Ochino makes him highly worthy of consideration in the context of the complex network of personal and intellectual relationships that we refer to as "dialogue" in this volume.

Yet there are no modern editions of Ochino's sermons, presumably due to the fact that in 1542 he fled Italy, took refuge (and a wife) in Geneva, and converted to Protestantism. His published sermons are exceedingly rare even in Italian libraries, which is no surprise, given that his "books had been banned as heresies in every *catalogo* sponsored by the Roman Holy Office since 1549," that is, every *Index librorum prohibitorum* promulgated by the Inquisition.[25] The liminal nature of this sermon and of its author, linking a religious man and learned lay women, vernacular and Latin languages, and Catholicism and protestant leanings, make this text exceedingly rich if we consider that preaching and translation were, in Katherine Gill's words, "complementary enterprises"[26] that allowed for the spreading of religious texts in Latin (such as the Bible) among nonlearned audiences. Further, aside from the sermon's potential influence on Vittoria Colonna's *Rime spirituali*, its gender dimensions cannot be ignored, as they are central in Ochino's choice of topic, examples, implied au-

23. Bainton and Bardazzi also point out that the Magdalene is present in a letter of Colonna's, again described in terms similar to those of Ochino's sermon. Roland H. Bainton, "Vittoria Colonna and Michelangelo," *Forum* 9, no. 1 (1971), 37; Bardazzi, "Le rime spirituali," 80.

24. Emidio Campi, "'Non vi si pensa quanto sangue costa!' Michelangelo, Vittoria Colonna e Bernardino Ochino," *Michelangelo e Vittoria Colonna: un dialogo artistico-teologico ispirato da Bernardino Ochino e altri saggi di storia della Riforma* (Turin: Claudiana, 1994), 9–126.

25. Robin, *Publishing Women*, 102–3.

26. Katherine Gill, "Women and the Production of Religious Literature in the Vernacular, 1300–1550," in *Creative Women in Medieval and Early Modern Italy: A Religious and Artistic Renaissance*, ed. E. Ann Matter and John Coakley (Philadelphia: University of Pennsylvania Press, 1994), 64.

dience, and reception. Lastly, as historians of literature, culture, and society become even more interested in nontraditional aspects of the past—namely, the positions, roles, and activities of women, lower strata of the population, and eccentric groups (such as heretics, witches, and homosexuals)—Ochino will certainly find his place among those writers who left a mark on the thinking and writing of their contemporaries.

Sermon Preached in Venice by the Reverend Father Friar Bernardino Ochino from Siena, a Capuchin Monk, on the Day of St. Mary Magdalene[27] 1539

When I read the Gospel, I see that Christ highly commended St. John the Baptist for his gift of prophecy: "Verily I say unto you, Among them that are born of women there hath not risen a greater than John the Baptist."[28] Nathanael was highly praised by Christ for his simplicity: "Behold an Israelite indeed, in whom there is no guile!"[29] I hear the Roman centurion praised for his faith: "I have not found so great a faith, not in Israel."[30] The tax collector was praised for his humility: "This day is salvation come to this house."[31] The woman from Canaan was praised for her loyalty: "O woman, great is thy faith."[32] But I do not find anybody more praised or extolled for her true and perfect love and her great virtue than the sinful woman that today the Church presents to us. Christ told her: "Her sins, which are many, are forgiven; for she loved much."[33] Christ asserts that Magdalene, a sinner, gave him great joy.

Be advised: this is a difficult passage from the Gospel, indeed its meaning is very difficult.[34] A little silence, I pray you![35] I would like to know, so let me ask you now: whom do you think had more

27. In the Catholic calendar, the feast day of St. Mary Magdalene is celebrated on 22 July. This allows us to date the delivery of Ochino's sermon precisely.

28. Mt 11:11. All Biblical citations in English are from the King James Version, which occasionally capitalizes words that would not be capitalized in contemporary English.

29. Jn 1:47. Note that in the Johannine episode Nathanael is praised for his faith rather than his simplicity.

30. Mt 8:10.

31. Lk 19:9. Zaccheus was, according to Lk 19:2, "the chief among the publicans [tax collectors], and he was rich."

32. Mt 15:28.

33. Lk 7:47.

34. Here Ochino addresses his audience directly and individually, using the familiar "*tu*." He thus establishes a strong contact with audience members and simultaneously (and implicitly) exhorts them to pay close attention to the sermon as it concerns difficult theological concepts.

35. This interjection makes the oral nature of the sermon vividly clear; it reinforces the need for Ochino to request the appropriate behavior on the audience's part.

sins, the sinful, lascivious, sin- and iniquity-filled Magdalene, or the religious, law-abiding, Scripture-learned Pharisee?[36] I believe without a doubt that you would answer: "The sinful woman!" But perhaps that was not the case. Her sins were due to her sensuality; his were intrinsic.[37] The Pharisee's sins were greater: he was a man, she a mere woman. She sinned out of ignorance; he sinned out of wickedness. He is imbued with religion; she is secular. He is superb; she is humble. This is why you see her lying at Christ's feet as he is eating at the Pharisee's house, crying for her sins. With her tears of concern she washed Christ's holy feet and dried them with her hair and kissed them. The Pharisee, observing this, thought to himself: "This man, if he were a prophet, would have known who and what manner of woman this is that toucheth him: for she is a sinner."[38] So he was scandalized and did not believe that Christ was the Son of God and that he knew that she was a sinful woman. But Christ, to whom all our heart's secrets are open and visible, replied: "I want your opinion. There was a gentleman who had two debtors. One owed him fifty dinars (let's say fifty *scudi*), the other five hundred. Neither one could pay him back, so he forgave both their debts. Whom do you think loved the gentleman more?" The Pharisee answered: "I suppose he to whom he forgave most." Christ replied: "Thou hast rightly judged. Consequently, all the more she loved me more. This is why: I entered into your house, and you gave me not even a kiss on the forehead; she hath not ceased to kiss my feet. You did not anoint my head with oil, while this sinful woman has comforted me with her precious ointment. This converted sinner knows me as the Son of God. You, on the contrary, not only do not believe that I am the Son of God, but you think that I am no prophet and that I do not know this woman's sins. Wherefore I say unto thee, Her sins, which are many, are forgiven; for she loved much."[39] Pay attention

36. Pharisees belonged to a Jewish religious party that flourished from the sixth century BCE to 70 CE. In the New Testament, and hence in the Catholic tradition, Pharisees become shorthand for those who follow the interpretation of the Bible slavishly, to the letter, without understanding it or paying attention to its spirit.

37. That is, his sins proceeded from his soul, not his senses.

38. Lk 7:38–39.

39. While the Pharisee's answer, Christ's reply to it, and his final statement are taken verbatim from the Gospel (in Latin in the original) (Lk 7:43, 47), Ochino adapts the rest of the

that Christ did not simply call her, but he becomes her defender.[40] The Pharisee should love Christ much more, as this sinful woman has but fifty sins, and you, Pharisee, have five hundred.[41] Why is that? Because this sinful woman's sins are rooted in her sensuality, in her wish for delights, and in her bent toward voluptuousness; she sinned out of fragility and ignorance, out of scarce knowledge of the Scriptures, and on the basis of extrinsic qualities. Yours, instead, are far more serious before God, because they are rooted in the very heart of your heart, in your haughtiness, in your ambition, in your vainglory, in your very own complacency, in your hypocrisy and curiosity. Hence you should love me more than she did because I forgave you more sins.

Let us move to another explanation that covers another meaning. Someone might say: "Magdalene's sins were more serious." All the more: if the Pharisee did not have any sins, then he had to love God who had preserved him from sinning. As St. Augustine says, it is not simply that the crucified Christ forgave us our sins, but he also forgave us all those sins that we might have committed if we had not come into God's grace—sins that would have been numberless. Still we sin, but God keeps us from many out of his pure and absolute generosity. Indeed, if it depended on us we would do nothing but wrong and we would deserve a thousand hells. So we should love him more because he keeps us from sinning.

There is another, purer and more genuine meaning. Following Christ's word in the gospel, I gather that this Pharisee was not one of the nasty and evil ones; in other words, he was a religious, catholic man.[42] When he said: "This man, if he were a prophet" etcetera. he said so out of zeal for Christ's honor, because he did not want anyone to be scandalized to see that Christ would let himself be touched by a

---

passage (Lk 7:41–46), making it easier for his audience to understand and relate to; see the reference to contemporary currency.

40. Because this sermon was delivered orally, it would not have always been easy to determine whether "you" referred to Ochino's audience or to Christ's. This distinction was also lost in the original written text, as it does not contain quotation marks.

41. This is the most evident example yet of Ochino's rhetorical strategy of blurring the identities of his addressees and Jesus's, i.e., the Pharisees.

42. That is, a good member of the Church.

sinful woman.[43] This I say because I see that he invited Christ into his home, fed him, and shared what he had with him. I also see that in the parable of the two debtors Christ said that he forgave them both, so the Pharisee was already saved and had had his sins already forgiven.

Let us go back to Magdalene. He said: "Her sins, which are many, are forgiven; for she loved much"; all her sins were forgiven, for she loved much.[44] In her sins she has fallen more than other sinners. Some say that during her conversion seven devils were driven out of her;[45] but there is great discrepancy among Luke, Mark, and Matthew. One says that there was but one Mary Magdalene;[46] another, that she was Martha's sister; and a third one, that there were three different Marys.[47] St. Gregory believes that there was but one, and I follow him.[48] So we will take her from the Gospel: after she got to

43. Honor was one of the most important possessions of early modern men and women, in Venice and elsewhere in Italy. For an interesting and concise overview, see Sharon Strocchia, "Gender and Rules of Honour in Italian Renaissance Cities," in *Gender and Society in Renaissance Italy*, ed. Judith C. Brown and Robert C. Davis (London: Longman, 1998), 39–60.

44. This repetition is necessitated by the fact that the original cites the Gospel in Latin. To ensure that everybody in his audience understands, Ochino says the verse in Latin first and then translates it into Italian. This allows him to insist on scriptural citations by dwelling on them longer.

45. This is the Mary Magdalene whose story is told in Lk 8:2.

46. This is the version found in Jn 11 (for the identification of Lazarus's and Martha's sister with Mary Magdalene, see Jn 11:2).

47. That is: the nameless prostitute in Lk 7; the Magdalene freed from the devils in Lk 8:2; and Lazarus's and Martha's sister in Jn 11. Ravasi mentions that the town of Magdala was (in)famous in Jewish tradition for the corruptness of its sexual mores; Gianfranco Ravasi, "Maria di Magdala, santa calunniata e glorificata," in *Maddalena*, ed. Giovanni Testori (Milan: Franco Maria Ricci, 1989), 18. He suggests that this might be a reason behind the superimposition of the two women from Lk 7 and Lk 8. Another Mary from Magdala (that is, Mary Magdalene) is a close disciple of Christ who is present at the crucifixion, as Ochino will point out: see Mt 27:56, Mk 15:40, and Jn 19:25. Matthew and Mark also place her at Christ's burial; see Mt 25:61 and Mk 15:47.

48. Pope Gregory I (Gregory the Great) delivered a sermon in September 591 in the church of San Clemente in Rome in which he identified the unnamed sinner of Lk. 7 with John's Mary (Lazarus's and Martha's sister) and with Luke's sinner whom Jesus freed from seven devils. This identification gained ample currency during the Middle Ages and the early modern period. Katherine Ludwig Jansen, *The Making of the Magdalen: Preaching and Popular Devotion in the Later Middle Ages* (Princeton, NJ: Princeton University Press, 2000), 32–35.

know God and got to come back to Christ because of her love, you will not see anybody more inflamed, more in love than her, to such a degree that she deserved to be Christ's sister, as you'll hear; therefore, pay attention.

There once was a noble, wealthy, great, learned lord, surrounded by a nice court, a pleasure-rich group of virtuous companions.[49] One day, while strolling with his courtiers, he felt such joy, contentment, and happiness in his soul and mind that he told his companions: "I would like to understand what reason makes man happy in this life. I'm not talking about his fatherland,[50] because there he enjoys a divine, clear, open view of God; let us not talk about that one; let us limit ourselves to our current life. Where do our happiness and contentment come from?"

One of his learned courtiers answered thus: "I will tell you, my Lord, what the reason for this is. You should know that our contentment and peacefulness consist of feeding and nourishing our senses, each according to its objective. This is: eyes must be shown beauty and colors; ears must hear sounds, songs, and harmonies; taste must be fed delicate and sweet tastes to its liking; and so on for the other senses. In this manner our potentialities reach their objective, and then are at rest and content and at peace, not to mention happy and joyful. My Lord, for the past few days you have exerted yourself to satisfy each appetite of yours; from this follows that you are happy and contented."

Another one answered: "I believe that the reason is pure knowledge of God and of heavenly things. In that well of truth one sees all other truths shine. That is because we inhabit the jail of our body; further, due to our sins this jail is dark and gloomy, and we only see the light of truth a little bit, as it enters through the window of our senses. Indeed man lives imprisoned in his body, but this jail was open above us. We knew and loved God and through him we knew all other truths. Our souls have been put to the test by sin and cannot be at rest or happy until they come to the knowledge that makes man

---

49. Here Ochino follows the pattern of Luke's passage closely: just as Christ explained to the Pharisee why he had forgiven the Magdalene through a parable, Ochino resorts to a tale to make his meaning clear.

50. That is, heaven, where the saved will dwell after Christ's second coming and the final judgment.

happy. This is what the prophet meant when he said: 'My soul failed.'[51] My Lord, for the past few days you have tried to understand this truth; I am sure that this is the reason for your happiness."

A third one replied: "This is not why. Instead I believe that if an evangelic preacher came who had Christ in his heart and who made flames of love start in human hearts (as a white-hot piece of iron does) and who detached us from worldly things, we would then desire nothing but to hear the word of the living God and to nourish ourselves of it. This is what we did. Indeed people run to Christ's sermons without paying attention to what they will eat or drink. Christ himself said it: 'Man shall not live by bread alone, but by every word that proceedeth out of the mouth of God.'[52] God's word is what nourishes and feeds us, as it is said: 'The word of God is quick and sharper than any two-edged sword, piercing even to the dividing asunder of soul and spirit.'[53] The word of God is living, more efficacious than all knives, and it enters the human heart so deeply that it separates the soul from the spirit.[54] My Lord, since you attended the sermon of that true, inflamed evangelic preacher, you have found peace in God's word. This is why you feel so contented and happy."

Yet another one answered: "This is not the reason; I will tell you why. I hold the following to be certain: a pious action performed on behalf of one's neighbor out of love gains more merit and thanks from God than any other action we might perform. Therefore when one performs such an action, he feels much happiness, as he considers what Christ said: 'Inasmuch as ye have done it unto one of the least of my brethren, ye have done it unto me.'[55] Imagine: would you be happy if you knew that you had fed and clothed Christ, and shared your wealth with him? He accepts pious actions performed unto a poor person as if you had performed them unto him. Christ added: 'I

---

51. Song of Sol. 5:6. The Vulgate uses the verb "*liquefacere*," literally "to melt," which, as Jansen points out, was particularly suited to Mary Magdalene's tears. *The Making of the Magdalen*, 209. Ochino will address this later in his sermon.

52. Mt 4:4.

53. A modified citation from Heb 4:12.

54. See above, note 45.

55. Mt 25:40.

was an hungred, and you gave me meat,' etcetera.[56] Therefore he who frequently performs such pious actions, seeing how welcome they are to God, finds himself in a state of beatitude, happiness, and joy. Given that you, my Lord, these past few days have devoted yourself to these loving actions more than usual, you feel steeped in jubilation and joyousness."

Another one answered: "I am of another mind. Nothing makes man more contented than converting to God and feeling a real pain and contrition for his sins. This is what stops the worms of fear from gnawing at one's conscience. While man is in a state of sin, these worms never allow him to rest and be contented, as he is under constant stimulation, fear, and dread of God's judgment. He is also eaten away by animosity and hatred, so overall he never feels good. Once he has converted and repented of his sins he feels light, he feels no longer bound to Lucifer's kingdom;[57] he feels emancipated from the chains of hell. Indeed he would like to have a thousand gold chains to bind himself to Christ's yoke. My Lord, since you have converted to Christ and repented and felt contrition for your sins, now you feel such beatitude, happiness, and joy."

The last one answered: "This is not the reason. It consists of gazing upon Christ crucified for us. This gaze comes out of your living eyes but emerges from your faith-filled heart. Thanks to it, you will see how burning Christ's charity was when, out of love for us, he became man and our brother, sharing our flesh, our passions; he suffered many hardships, pains, and persecutions for thirty-three years and finally ascended to the wood of the cross to pay the debt of our sins, to extinguish it, to purge it with his very blood. If a human being carefully considers all this, then he/she will clearly know God's profound charity;[58] He was not satisfied with having given us life, thus went beyond that, and fashioned us in His image. Then He was dissatisfied even with steering and keeping us, preserving us from sinning,

56. Mt 25:35.

57. That is, hell. Lucifer is one of the many names for the devil.

58. Because Italian verb conjugation includes a clear reference to the subject in the endings, Ochino does not specify if the subject here is male or female. I have therefore opted for the admittedly anachronistic "he/she" to indicate that he addressed all audience members, presumably both men and women.

and benefitting us in many ways every day. So finally He gave Himself to pay back and extinguish our debts on the wood of the cross—he could not have done anything more! Therefore a soul feels inflamed by love and true charity when gazing upon Christ if it chooses to love but Christ on the cross, from whom we receive such sweetness. You, my Lord, have devoted yourself to the contemplation of Christ more than your wont during these past few days; this is why you feel contented, happy, joyful."

Let us now pause a little; then we will see what the reason for this contentment is.[59]

Strolling along, that gentleman chanced upon a rock along the Baume, near Marseilles;[60] a woman was there, alone, naked, but covered by her hair.[61] I have been to the same spot myself.[62] She asked him: "What are you looking for in this austere place? What do you discuss?"[63] The gentleman replied: "I wanted to know what it is that makes man happy and joyful in this life." This woman, a converted and repenting sinner, replied: "Well, what did your learned friends offer by way of answer?" The Lord answered: "One says it is sensuality, a second says it is knowledge of God, another one says it is hearing the word of God, yet another says it is pious actions done unto others, another says it is converting to God and repenting of one's sins, and the last one says it is gazing upon Christ on the cross, dead for love of us."

59. This pause, too, reflects the oral nature of Ochino's sermon.

60. The Baume is a river in the Vivarais region of southern France, northwest of Marseilles. The thirteenth-century *Golden Legend* by Jacobus de Voragine tells that Mary Magdalene followed her brother Lazarus to Provence, where she announced the Gospel before becoming a hermit.

61. This depiction of the Magdalene occurs frequently in the visual arts, especially after the Council of Trent (1545–63), when it afforded painters and patrons a suitable and dignified topic that included female nakedness. Earlier examples are also extant, such as a wooden statue by Donatello now at the Museo dell'opera del Duomo in Florence.

62. Ochino attests to the existence of the place, and hence to the verisimilitude of the story, by his own experience.

63. Ochino's audience would have immediately understood that the naked woman's behavior was uncommon at best; as a woman, and a naked one at that, she would have normally waited to talk to a gentleman until she had been spoken to. Her behavior, however, is consistent with the image of the Magdalene that emerges from the Bible: uncommon and forward, yet deserving of Christ's affection and forgiveness.

The contrite Magdalene answered: "You should know that not one of those things can make a creature perfectly contented and happy. I can attest to this, as I experienced it all myself.[64] First, let me say that sensuality does not sate. I do not think that the world ever saw or will see a more sensual woman than I was, in every imaginable way. God is no longer the point of reference of a sensuous person, after she has turned her back on Him and converted to the world. All vain things are in front of her, and she enjoys them; she becomes impudent and shows no respect or concern for anything. If a woman did not know God but had a father and a mother, then out of shame and respect for them she would refrain from doing bad deeds. But this is not what happened to me: not only did I not see God, but I did not have a father or a mother. And if a woman had no father nor mother and were not rich, then necessity would restrain her; she would not pay attention to her vanity. Well, I was rich, noble, young, and beautiful. You know that it is dangerous to merely look at a beautiful woman, let alone talk to her. I was not happy with my beauty, so I made myself up time and time again, I cleaned myself time and time again, I dolled myself up time and time again, I pampered my body time and time again. I used many ribbons, ornaments, fashions; I utilized various dyes, chemicals, perfumes, little bottles and containers, ambergris, musky smells, many ornaments and idle things (woman: you know what I am talking about: these are not Scotus's rules.[65] Do not be surprised if I know them all!)." Magdalene continued: "I eschewed no pain to look

64. Another element of exceptionality in Mary Magdalene is her ability to explain to men what they do not understand. This aspect is explored in Jane Schaberg, "The Woman Who Understood (Too) Completely: Legends, Apocrypha, and the Christian Testament," in *The Resurrection of Mary Magdalene* (New York: Continuum, 2002), 121–203.

65. Scotus was known as "the subtle doctor" for his ability to draw out distinctions. Ochino alludes to the fact that, although these are not liturgical or clerical rules, he is familiar with them, so as to impress on his female listeners that he is well-acquainted with their behavior and their tricks. Further, Ochino addresses each woman in his audience individually.

beautiful or plump.[66] I will tell you, I even partook of God's food.[67] I would go to church to be seen and to push and capture souls and give them over to Lucifer's hands. I tried every sensuous pleasure and everything that can be imagined, like Solomon.[68] But in the end, I was not happy, because the more I followed my senses, the more I craved sensuous experiences. On top of that, I never felt contented, because I felt continually gnawed by shame, by my respect for other human beings, by fear of hell, by the thought of dying, by the apprehension that I might be ill; so overall I never felt happy.

"I also know what it means to know God; I even tried to understand God's truth, but our intellect cannot get there because it is not capable of such height and goodness. After my conversion, I felt incredible emotions and sentiments; still, you ought to know that undoubtedly our happiness does not consist of this.

"Nor is a human being happy when he/she hears the word of God. I was not taught by an evangelic preacher or by a saint; I heard the word of God from the mouth of the living Christ, the true Son of God. I nourished and sated myself with his word for a long time. He taught me, but still I was not happy.

"Pious actions likewise were not enough to fill me with contentment: I performed those, too, and not unto the poor, but unto Christ himself. I took him into my home, I hosted him and his disciples, too, as well as the Blessed Virgin. This did not happen only once, but many times. Then, at the end of his life, at the Pharisee's house I anointed him with precious oils.[69] Still, I did not feel contentment through these actions.

---

66. Though "plump" might refer to her body's voluptuousness, this (to us, surprising) adjective fits well within the context of its time. In early modern times, being fat was a mark of wealth and of social superiority, as it implied that the person was not engaged in manual labor. It therefore constituted a highly desirable physical trait.

67. That is, Mass, where Christians share God's nourishment in the form of the scriptures and Communion.

68. In 1 Kings 11:1ff, Solomon—the son of King David, and himself a king in the tenth century BCE—turns away from God because of the influence of his seven hundred wives and three hundred concubines.

69. Here Ochino merges two Magdalenian episodes: the one in Lk 7:36–50 (set in the Pharisee's home) and another one that Matthew, Mark, and John place in Bethany, in Lazarus's home, a few days before Christ's passion. See Mt 26:6–13, Mk 14:3–9, and Jn 12:1–8.

"Nor did I feel that way through my conversion and my repentance and contrition for my sins. I did go through that, when Jesus said: 'I forgive you your sins.' His forgiving my countless sins was a great gift, and thus I felt great happiness for it. But know for sure that one has to go beyond that.

"To the one who maintains that contemplating Christ on the cross makes a human being happy, I say that I saw him lifted to the cross with my very eyes. I was with his mother where he was crucified between two thieves. Nevertheless, I was not happy."

Let us stop for a while; we will continue later. I call upon you, take good care of the *convertite* from Padua;[70] they will be at the door to their house. I recommend them to you as strongly as I can.

Holy sinner,[71] woman so far fallen, come from such lasciviousness to such perfection, tell us:[72] "Our happiness does not consist in any of these reasons. True happiness is found in shedding some tears. Be advised that there are many kinds of tears: some come from fear, some from contrition. I am not talking about either of these, but about tears of delight. These tears are sweet and delicate and they bring happiness. When I saw the love that God had for me, when I saw that he had sent his only Son to save me and make me his bride, I strove to burn with a living, ardent love. I was in the darkness of sin, in Lucifer's hands; I went to hear him preach, in the middle of the crowd, so that I could be easily seen and everybody could say: 'Here's the pretty woman'; so I went to Christ's feet."

---

70. *Convertita* is a term designating prostitutes who had repented and converted. Such women had an asylum in Padua, though this was initially a Venetian institution that, as Ochino's remarks indicate, had also taken root in Venice-controlled mainland cities. For more on the way in which early modern Italian city-states dealt with unmarried women, women abandoned by their husbands, or reformed prostitutes, see Sherrill Cohen, "Convertite e malmaritate: donne 'irregolari' e ordini religiosi nella Firenze rinascimentale," *Memoria: rivista di storia delle donne* 5 (1982): 23–65, and Sherrill Cohen, "Asylums for Women in Counter-Reformation Italy," *Women's Studies* 19 (1991): 201–8.

71. Paradoxical phrases such as this one are common to Christian prayers and poems. See the many examples in Catholic litanies and in John Donne's "Holy Sonnets."

72. Again Ochino conflates the two audiences: the gentleman and his courtiers, and his own in Venice. Far from being a slip, this is an effective rhetorical device that captures the preacher's listeners more fully as they identify with the characters involved in the sermon.

And here I remain: you women are always the closest to the preacher, while men stand a little behind. Now I see that there are men in front of me who take your place; so claim your spot, make the men move back, so that they do not take over your privileges.

"His words were so effective that I converted on the spot, just as Peter converted with one look from Christ, after he had denied knowing him.[73] My city,[74] notice that a converted sinner is similar to a bow. If you put your hand close to the front of the bow, its arrow would not hit with great strength. But if you put your hand farther [back], the arrow builds a circle with the air around it, and it hits with greater strength from a longer distance. Something similar occurs to the sinner: when he is very far from God and feels that he has been hit by the arrow of love, he becomes aware of his misery, considers how abundant his wickedness is, and humbles himself before God, because he does not feel worthy of such light and grace. This is not the reaction of someone who has lived according to the precepts and the law; he has no reason to humble himself as much as the sinner above. Therefore he does not recognize God's assistance to him as deeply."

When this sinful woman went to hear Christ preach, he looked at her with his gaze, and it encountered Magdalene; so she started to burn and became inflamed with love for him. She no longer enjoyed worldly delights, pleasures, vanity, or lascivious behavior; she could only be sorry for her sins. We must believe that when she went home she took all her makeup, hair products, perfumes, and other vain things; she lined them up in front of herself before burning them, and said: "My vanity, you were weapons to send me to the deepest chasm of hell; you were the reason why I could attract so many poor souls with my negative example; you caused many nasty actions. Now I do not love you nor do I want to enjoy you any longer, because I only want to love my Christ and bless him: 'Thou hast ravished my heart with one of thine eyes.'[75] Therefore for the rest of my life I want

---

73. The detail of Christ looking at Peter after the latter's denial and of Peter realizing what he had done because of that look is only in Lk 22:61; it is missing from the other three gospels (Mt 27:69–75; Mk 14:66–72; Jn 18:15–18).

74. Mary Magdalene now belongs fully to the city of her listeners, in Ochino's words; this increases their proximity to the saint on whose story the sermon centers.

75. Song of Sol. 4:9.

to cry, but not just out of contrition, also out of delight. Seeing how much Christ loves me, I want to love him alone; I do not want to love anything else."

This is why she goes into the Pharisee's home and cries for her sins at Christ's feet. This is also why you only see the Magdalene at Christ's feet: at Christ's feet at Christ's preaching; at Christ's feet in the Pharisee's home;[76] at Christ's feet in her own home; at Christ's feet at the crucifixion;[77] at Christ's feet at his burial.[78] Finally, everywhere she was she always cried: she cried at Christ's preaching when she converted; she cried in the Pharisee's home;[79] she cried when her brother Lazarus died;[80] she cried when Christ bade farewell to his mother; she cried when Christ entrusted her to his mother's care, asking that she would accept her as his sister;[81] she cried when she saw Christ being scourged and scorned; she cried when she heard that Christ had been smitten in the face;[82] she cried when Christ arrived where the Virgin had fainted because of the pain she felt; she cried at the feet of the cross;[83] she cried when Christ's body was taken from the cross; she cried in his tomb; she cried in the garden; she cried when she saw him ascend into heaven;[84] she cried along the Baume for thirty-two years,

---

76. Lk 7:38.

77. See Mt 27:56, Mk 15:40, and Jn 19:25. Luke writes that "the women that followed him from Galilee" were in attendance (Lk 23:49).

78. See Mt 27:61 and Mk 15:47. Here, too, Luke does not mention any woman by name (Lk 23:55).

79. Lk 7:38.

80. This detail is missing from John's episode (Jn 11:1–44).

81. This apocryphal detail is modeled after the episode of Christ on the cross entrusting John to his mother, and vice versa (Jn 19:26–27).

82. Mary Magdalene is not a witness to Christ's ascent to Calvary, according to the gospels. However, the details that Ochino lists here underscore her exceptional status among early followers of Jesus and make her into an even more exemplary model.

83. In Matthew, Mary Magdalene is one of two women to find Christ's tomb open (Mt 28:1). In Mark, she is one of the three women to whom the resurrected Christ first appears (Mk 16:1–8); he then appears to her alone (Mk 16:9). In John, it is Mary Magdalene who first finds Christ's tomb open and empty, and it is to her that the resurrected Christ appears (Jn 20:1–18). Specifically, she "stood without at the sepulcher weeping" (Jn 20:11).

84. Neither Mark nor Luke (the only two gospels to include the ascension episode) mentions who was present by name: Mk 16:19–20; Lk 24:51–52.

when she was doing penance; now that she is in heaven she cries for the sins of the poor sinners (though in heaven there can be no sorrow: "I have learned to bring healing to the wretched, since I know evil").[85]

So this is the sinful woman that the militant church offers to your attention today. She used to be the most lascivious, sinful, sensuous woman in the world. Now the church holds her up as a mirror and a model for every penitent sinner. She spent thirty-two years on a rock along the Baume, where I went with a companion and celebrated Mass. There is a small church in which there is a wooden statue of Magdalene with a placard around her neck that says: "Do not despair, you who are accustomed to sinning; through my example you can prepare for God."[86] Magdalene consoles the sinners by saying: "Do not despair for the number or weight of your sins, for I was a great sinner and an enemy of God. Seven devils were driven out of me. Nevertheless I received so much grace and so many gifts from my spouse Christ crucified on the cross! Do this, you sinners: as you followed me in sin, now, following my example, make true penance for your sins." That is as much a place of worship as any I have seen. My companion received a great gift there, so he said: "Happy sins of the Magdalene!"

In that area there is a hill from which water still flows.[87] There Magdalene was doing her penance and did not care about any sustenance other than crying and contemplating God. She was lifted in her spirit by angels seven times a day.[88] At Matins she would contemplate Christ taken prisoner, bound, sold, and insulted by the Jews; she would pass out, so angels would come and lift and comfort her. At

85. Virgil, *Aeneid*, 1.630.

86. Ochino's citation differs from the one found in thirteenth-century paintings, where Mary Magdalene's scroll typically reads: "Ne desperetis vos qui peccare soletis exemploque meo vos reparate Deo," that is, "Do not despair, you who are accustomed to sinning, and in keeping with my example, return yourself to God."

87. Ochino's personal experience of the place where the Magdalene did her penance allows him to point out another aspect that would be appealing to his audience: such a place is not only closer than Palestine, but it still existed unchanged at the time of the sermon.

88. As the rest of this passage makes clear, at that time daily public worship in the Catholic church was articulated in seven services that took place at specific times of day. Matins would be said before dawn; Prime was recited at dawn; Terce, Sext, and None took place at midmorning, noon, and midafternoon, respectively; Vespers was the service of sunset, and Compline was to be recited before going to bed.

Prime she would be back on the ground; she would see Christ in Pilate's house when he was falsely accused, smitten, bound up, and spit at. She would faint, so angels would come and lift her and console her with heavenly sweetness. At Terce on her way down she would see Christ purple-clad, crowned with thorns, saddled with the cross. Imagine: she was annihilated by the pain felt by her spouse; but the angels would come back and nourish her with divine love. At Sext she would see Christ crucified between two thieves, in pain, distressed, fed gall and vinegar; so she would feel like she was failing,[89] but God would will that the angels come and help her in her sadness. At None she would turn her thoughts to the moment when Christ died and his side was torn open[90] (at which point the militant church was born); she would feel like she was melting out of sweetness, but the angels would support her. At Vespers she would ponder when Christ was taken down from the cross. Lastly at Compline she would medidate on the burial of Christ in the sepulcher, and again she would feel like she was melting, but the angels would comfort her.[91]

Women, this sermon is all yours. I would like that, just as you followed the Magdalene in her pomp and vanity, you imitate her in her conversion. So much of the word of God has been spread in vain, without any fruit or repentance! I will tell you the truth. You are all gentle and noble women, I would say: do not pay attention to so much nonsense, because people expect generosity from noble hearts such as yours. Do not follow the example of base and low women. I am happy that you go about well dressed, refined, according to your rank; but avoid tall clogs![92] Do not follow the example of a bread maker or other similar woman, do not put on makeup, do not paint yourselves, for the love of God! I am ashamed for you. I entreat you, be happy with the beauty that God bestowed on you; He made you in His image! I assure you that you will look more beautiful, because an honest and

---

89. See also above, note 51.

90. Jn 19:34 (the only gospel to mention this detail).

91. Mary Magdalene's devotion to the passion is clearly an example that Ochino offers his listeners for their daily meditations.

92. Tall clogs were a clothing item reserved for courtesans; thus, they indicate immodest behavior and self-display. Visual examples and descriptions of women wearing tall clogs are given in Lawner, *Lives of the Courtesans*, 18, 20, 21.

modest woman possesses a loveliness that everyone has to revere. You will reply: "I do all this to please my husband." Well, if that is the case, then use makeup at night, and I would be fine with that.

Gentlemen, if your women are beautiful and well behaved, why are you not happy with them? Why do you have to go with prostitutes? If you were in the army, where there are no women, I would understand. But each one of you is married and has a companion; so, be satisfied with her!

Women, you should abandon all pomp. In each neighborhood three or four or five or six of you should get together and form a society in the name of Christ, founded on love.[93] Even those who are poor can practice charitable deeds to those who are poorer, searching the neighborhood house by house to distribute them. You should follow the example of a poor older woman from Florence, where I preached last year. There I saw this little old woman, not rich and not very tall. God had allowed her to marry off two noble girls. So she started performing the following charitable action: each year, she marries off twenty or twenty-five girls. I just received a letter from her. She writes that she has found a noble family with many daughters; those who want to serve God will go to a convent, the others she will marry off. If this old woman sees a girl whose father and mother have died and who is in danger of falling into sin, she takes her and puts her in a monastery for maybe fifteen days. Then she goes around the city: when she finds a girl without clothes, she goes to a noblewoman and says: "I would like for you to give me one of your old dresses," and she gives it to her. Then she goes to a gentleman, and tells him: "I need to marry a girl so that she does not fall into the wrong kind of life; so I need some money," and he gives her some. This is what you should do as a penance for your past sins.[94]

If you cannot follow the Magdalene's example in purity and innocence, then make an effort to imitate her as a mirror of penance.

---

93. Toward the end of his sermon, Ochino offers his audience a concrete example of charitable work that would visibly express their penance and help women who are in danger of falling into prostitution.

94. This is in direct contradiction to Magdalene's stated belief that poor women have no time or money for vanity. For Ochino and his audience, the fear that indigent orphan women would fall into prostitution was well-established.

Her conversion was so strong that she immediately deserved to be Christ's sister, Mary's daughter, Christ's spouse, Christ's secretary: he revealed to her the wondrous secrets of his passion and death because he saw that she was inflamed and lit up by divine love for him.[95] She was on earth, but lived in heaven. Therefore I urge and exhort you: amend your ways, make violent penance, deeply repent of your sins with good, saintly intentions, so that you may be happy on earth and later gain heaven.

95. Divine love for Christ was the model for nuns, often referred to as "Christ's brides." That terminology is present in this sermon as well, but with a different connotation: it suggests emotional proximity and identification between Ochino's contemporary married women and his subject matter (Magdalene), who knew both carnal and divine love.

Bibliography

A Select List of Male-Authored Texts in Translation

Alberti, Leon Battista. *An Autograph Letter from Leon Battista Alberti to Matteo de' Pasti, November 18, 1454.* Translated by Cecil Grayson. New York: Pierpont Morgan Library, 1957.

_____. *Dinner Pieces.* Translated by David Marsh. Binghamton, NY: Medieval and Renaissance Texts and Studies / Renaissance Society of America, 1987.

_____. *The Family in Renaissance Florence.* Edited and translated by Renée Neu Watkins. Columbia: University of South Carolina Press, 1969.

_____. *Ippolito e Lionora.* Edited by M. Faigel. Verona: Officina Bodoni, 1970.

_____. *Leon Battista Alberti's Delineation of the City of Rome (descriptio vrbis Romæ).* Edited by Mario Carpo and Francesco Furlan, translated by by Peter Hicks. Tempe: Arizona Center for Medieval and Renaissance Studies, 2007.

_____. *Momus.* Edited by Sarah Knight and Virginia Brown. Translated by by Sarah Knight. I Tatti Renaissance Library 8. Cambridge, MA: Harvard University Press, 2003.

_____. *On Painting and On Sculpture: The Latin Texts of* De pictura *and* De statua. Edited and translated by Cecil Grayson. London: Phaidon, 1972.

_____. *On the Art of Building in Ten Books.* Translated by Joseph Rykwert, Neil Leach, and Robert Tavernor. Cambridge, MA: MIT Press, 1988.

_____. *Renaissance Fables.* Translated by David Marsh. Tempe: Arizona Center for Medieval and Renaissance Studies, 2004.

_____. *The Use and Abuse of Books: De commodis litterarum atque incommodis.* Translated by Renée Neu Watkins. Prospect Heights, IL: Waveland Press, 1999.

Aretino, Pietro. *Dialogues.* Translated by Raymond Rosenthal. Toronto: University of Toronto Press, 2005.

_____. *Horatia*. Translated by Gillian Sharman. In *Trissino's Sophonisba and Aretino's Horatia: Two Italian Renaissance Tragedies*, edited by Michael Lettieri, 111–262. Lewiston, NY: Edwin Mellen, 1997.

_____. *The Letters of Pietro Aretino*. Translated by Thomas Caldecot Chubb. Hamden, CT: Archon Books, 1967.

_____. *The Marescalco*. Edited and translated by Leonard G. Sbrocchi and J. Douglas Campbell. Ottawa: Dovehouse, 1986.

_____. *The Marescalco*. In *Five Comedies of the Italian Renaissance*, edited and translated by Guido Ruggiero and Laura Giannetti, 117–204. Baltimore: Johns Hopkins University Press, 2003.

_____. *The ragionamenti: The Lives of Nuns, the Lives of Married Women, the Lives of Courtesans*. London: Odyssey, 1970.

_____. *Selected Letters of Aretino*. Edited and translated by George Bull. Harmondsworth, UK: Penguin, 1976.

_____. *Talanta*. In *Three Renaissance Comedies*, edited and translated by Christopher Cairns, 218–350. Lewiston, NY: Edwin Mellen Press, 1991.

Ariosto, Ludovico. *Cinque canti: Five Cantos*. Translated by Alexander Sheers and David Quint. Berkeley: University of California Press, 1996.

_____. *The Comedies of Ariosto*. Edited and translated by Edmond M. Beame and Leonard G. Sbrocchi. Chicago: University of Chicago Press, 1975.

_____. *Lena*. In *Three Renaissance Comedies*, edited by Christopher Cairns, translated by C. P. Brand, 25–78. Lewiston, NY: Edwin Mellen Press, 1991.

_____. Orlando furioso: *A Romantic Epic*. Edited and translated by Barbara Reynolds. Harmondsworth, UK: Penguin, 1975.

_____. *Orlando furioso*. Translated by Guido Waldman. Oxford: Oxford University Press, 1974.

_____. *The Satires of Ludovico Ariosto: A Renaissance Autobiography*. Translated by Peter DeSa Wiggins. Athens: Ohio University Press, 1976.

_____. *The Supposes*. In *Ariosto's The Supposes, Machiavelli's The Mandrake, Intronati's The Deceived: Three Italian Renaissance Comedies*, edited by Christopher Cairns, translated by Jennifer Lorch, 57–129. Lewiston, NY: Edwin Mellen Press, 1996.

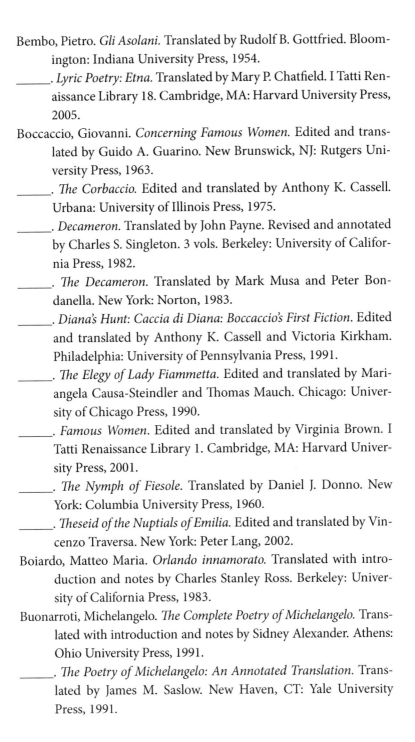

Bembo, Pietro. *Gli Asolani*. Translated by Rudolf B. Gottfried. Bloomington: Indiana University Press, 1954.

_____. *Lyric Poetry: Etna*. Translated by Mary P. Chatfield. I Tatti Renaissance Library 18. Cambridge, MA: Harvard University Press, 2005.

Boccaccio, Giovanni. *Concerning Famous Women*. Edited and translated by Guido A. Guarino. New Brunswick, NJ: Rutgers University Press, 1963.

_____. *The Corbaccio*. Edited and translated by Anthony K. Cassell. Urbana: University of Illinois Press, 1975.

_____. *Decameron*. Translated by John Payne. Revised and annotated by Charles S. Singleton. 3 vols. Berkeley: University of California Press, 1982.

_____. *The Decameron*. Translated by Mark Musa and Peter Bondanella. New York: Norton, 1983.

_____. *Diana's Hunt: Caccia di Diana: Boccaccio's First Fiction*. Edited and translated by Anthony K. Cassell and Victoria Kirkham. Philadelphia: University of Pennsylvania Press, 1991.

_____. *The Elegy of Lady Fiammetta*. Edited and translated by Mariangela Causa-Steindler and Thomas Mauch. Chicago: University of Chicago Press, 1990.

_____. *Famous Women*. Edited and translated by Virginia Brown. I Tatti Renaissance Library 1. Cambridge, MA: Harvard University Press, 2001.

_____. *The Nymph of Fiesole*. Translated by Daniel J. Donno. New York: Columbia University Press, 1960.

_____. *Theseid of the Nuptials of Emilia*. Edited and translated by Vincenzo Traversa. New York: Peter Lang, 2002.

Boiardo, Matteo Maria. *Orlando innamorato*. Translated with introduction and notes by Charles Stanley Ross. Berkeley: University of California Press, 1983.

Buonarroti, Michelangelo. *The Complete Poetry of Michelangelo*. Translated with introduction and notes by Sidney Alexander. Athens: Ohio University Press, 1991.

_____. *The Poetry of Michelangelo: An Annotated Translation*. Translated by James M. Saslow. New Haven, CT: Yale University Press, 1991.

Castiglione, Baldassarre. *The Book of the Courtier: The Singleton Translation: An Authoritative Text Criticism.* Edited by Daniel Javitch. New York: W. W. Norton, 2002.

———. *The Book of the Courtier.* Edited and translated by George Bull. London: Penguin, 1976.

Cellini, Benvenuto. *The Autobiography of Benvenuto Cellini.* Translated by John Addington Symonds. New York: Modern Library, 1927.

———. *Memoirs.* Translated by Anne Macdonell. London: Dent, 1907.

———. *The Treatises of Benvenuto Cellini on Goldsmithing and Sculpture.* Translated by C. R. Ashbee. New York: Dover Publications, 1967.

Da Vinci, Leonardo. *The Art of Painting.* New York: Philosophical Library, 1957.

———. *Fables of Leonardo da Vinci.* Translated by Bruno Nardini. Northbrook, IL: Hubbard Press, 1973.

———. *Leonardo da Vinci on the Human Body: The Anatomical, Physiological, and Embryological Drawings of Leonardo da Vinci.* Translated by Charles Donald O'Malley and J. B. de C. M. Saunders. New York: H. Schuman, 1952.

———. *Leonardo on Painting: An Anthology of Writings.* Edited by Martin Kemp. Translated by Martin Kemp and Margaret Walker. New Haven, CT: Yale University Press, 1989.

———. *Paragone; a Comparison of the Arts.* Translated by Irma A. Richter. Oxford: Oxford University Press, 1949.

———. *Philosophical Diary.* Translated by Wade Baskin. New York: Philosophical Library, 1959.

———. *Treatise on Painting (Codex Urbinas Latinus 1270).* Translated by A. Philip McMahon. Princeton, NJ: Princeton University Press, 1956.

Dovizi da Bibbiena, Bernardo. *La Calandra (The Comedy of Calandro).* In *Five Comedies of the Italian Renaissance*, edited and translated by Guido Ruggiero and Laura Giannetti, 1–70. Baltimore: Johns Hopkins University Press, 2003.

Ficino, Marsilio. *The Book of Life.* Translated by Charles Boer. Irving, TX: Spring Publications, 1980.

_____. *Commentary on Plato's Symposium on Love.* Translated by Sears Reynolds Jayne. Dallas, TX: Spring Publications, 1985.

_____. *Gardens of Philosophy: Ficino on Plato.* Translated by Arthur Farndell. London: Shepheard-Walwyn, 2006.

_____. *The Letters of Marsilio Ficino.* Translated by members of the Language Department of the School of Economic Science. London: Shepheard-Walwyn, 1975.

_____. *Meditations on the Soul: Selected Letters of Marsilio Ficino.* Translated by members of the Language Department of the School of Economic Science. Rochester, VT: Inner Traditions International, 1996.

_____. *The Philebus Commentary.* Edited and translated by Michael J. B. Allen. Berkeley: University of California Press, 1975.

_____. *Platonic Theology.* Edited by James Hankins and William Roy Bowen. Translated by Michael J. B. Allen and John Warden. 6 vols. I Tatti Renaissance Library 2. Cambridge, MA: Harvard University Press, 2001–6.

_____. *Three Books on Life.* Edited and translated by Carol V. Kaske and John R. Clark. Binghamton, NY: Medieval and Renaissance Texts and Studies / Renaissance Society of America, 1989.

Guarini, Giovanni Battista. *Pastor fido.* In *Three Renaissance Pastorals: Tasso, Guarini, Daniel,* edited and translated by Elizabeth Story Donno, 55–182. Binghamton, NY: Medieval and Renaissance Texts and Studies, 1993.

Guicciardini, Francesco. *Dialogue on the Government of Florence.* Edited and translated by Alison Brown. Cambridge: Cambridge University Press, 1994.

_____. *The History of Florence.* Edited and translated by Mario Domandi. New York: Harper & Row, 1970.

_____. *The History of Italy.* Edited and translated by Sidney Alexander. New York: Macmillan 1968.

_____. *Maxims and Reflections of a Renaissance Statesman (Ricordi).* Translated by Mario Domandi. New York: Harper & Row, 1965.

Machiavelli, Niccolò. *Art of War.* Edited and translated by Christopher Lynch. Chicago: University of Chicago Press, 2003.

_____. *The Discourses of Niccolò Machiavelli.* Edited and translated by Leslie J. Walker. London: Routledge and Paul, 1975.

_____. *Discourses on Livy.* Translated by Harvey C. Mansfield and Nathan Tarcov. Chicago: University of Chicago Press, 1996.

_____. *Florentine Histories.* Translated by Laura F. Banfield and Harvey C. Mansfield Jr. Princeton, NJ: Princeton University Press, 1988.

_____. *La mandragola.* In *Five Comedies of the Italian Renaissance,* edited and translated by Guido Ruggiero and Laura Giannetti, 71–116. Baltimore: Johns Hopkins University Press, 2003.

_____. *The Literary Works of Machiavelli: Mandragola, Clizia, Dialogue on Language, Belfagor; with Selections from the Private Correspondence.* Edited and translated by J. R. Hale. Westport, CT: Greenwood Press, 1979.

_____. *The Mandrake.* In *Ariosto's The Supposes, Machiavelli's The Mandrake, Intronati's The Deceived: Three Italian Renaissance Comedies,* edited by Christopher Cairns, translated by Kenneth and Laura Richards, 179–247. Lewiston, NY: Edwin Mellen Press, 1996.

_____. *The Prince.* Edited and translated by Peter Bondanella. Oxford: Oxford University Press, 1984.

_____. *The Prince.* Translated by George Bull. London: Penguin, 2003.

_____. *The Prince.* Translated by Harvey C. Mansfield. Chicago: University of Chicago Press, 1998.

Petrarca, Francesco. *Africa.* Edited and translated by Thomas G. Bergin and Alice S. Wilson. New Haven, CT: Yale University Press, 1977.

_____. *The Canzoniere, or, Rerum vulgarium fragmenta.* Translated by Mark Musa. Bloomington: Indiana University Press, 1996. Reprint, 1999.

_____. *Invectives.* Edited and translated by David Marsh. I Tatti Renaissance Library 11. Cambridge, MA: Harvard University Press, 2003.

_____. *Letters of Old Age: rerum senilium libri.* Translated by Aldo S. Bernardo, Saul Levin, and Reta A. Bernardo. Baltimore: Johns Hopkins University Press, 1992.

_____. *Petrarch's Bucolicum Carmen.* Edited and translated by Thomas G. Bergin. New Haven, CT: Yale University Press, 1974.

_____. *Petrarch's Lyric Poems: The Rime Sparse and Other Lyrics.* Edited and translated by Robert M. Durling. Cambridge, MA: Harvard University Press, 1976.

_____. *Petrarch's Songbook: rerum vulgarium fragmenta.* Translated by James Wyatt Cook. Binghamton, NY: Medieval and Renaissance Texts and Studies, 1995.

_____. *Remedies for Fortune Fair and Foul: A Modern English Translation of* De remediis utriusque fortunae. 5 vols. Translated by Conrad H. Rawski. Bloomington: Indiana University Press, 1991.

_____. *Rerum familiarium libri.* 3 vols. Translated by Aldo S. Bernardo. Albany: State University of New York Press, 1975.

_____. *The Secret.* Edited and translated by Carol E. Quillen. Boston: Bedford/St. Martin's, 2003.

Piccolomini, Alessandro. *Alessandro.* Translated by Rita Belladonna. Ottawa: Dovehouse, 1984.

_____. *Raffaella of Master Alexander Piccolomini, or Rather, A Dialogue of the Fair Perfectioning of Ladies.* Translated by John Nevinson. Glasgow: University of Glasgow Press, 1968.

Pico della Mirandola, Giovanni. *Commentary on a Poem of Platonic Love.* Translated by Douglas Carmichael. Lanham, MD: University Press of America, 1986.

_____. *Heptaplus: or, Discourse on the Seven Days of Creation.* Translated by Jessie Brewer McGaw. New York: Philosophical Library, 1977.

_____. *Of Being and Unity (De ente et uno).* Translated by Victor Michael Hamm. Mediaeval Philosophical Texts in Translation 3. Milwaukee: Marquette University Press, 1943.

_____. *On the Dignity of Man.* Translated by Charles Glenn Wallis, Paul J. W. Miller, and Douglas Carmichael. Indianapolis: Bobbs-Merrill, 1965.

_____. *On the Imagination.* Translated by Harry Caplan. New Haven, CT: Yale University Press, published for Cornell University, 1930.

Poliziano, Angelo. *Letters.* Edited and translated by Shane Butler. I Tatti Renaissance Library 21. Cambridge, MA: Harvard University Press, 2006.

_____. *Silvae.* Edited and translated by Charles Fantazzi. I Tatti Renaissance Library 14. Cambridge, MA: Harvard University Press, 2004.

———. *The Stanze of Angelo Poliziano*. Translated by David Quint. Amherst: University of Massachusetts Press, 1979.

Tasso, Torquato. *Aminta, a Pastoral Play*. Edited and translated by Charles Jernigan and Irene Marchegiani Jones. New York: Italica, 2000.

———. *Aminta*. In *Three Renaissance Pastorals: Tasso, Guarini, Daniel*, edited and translated by Elizabeth Story Donno, 1–54. Binghamton, NY: Medieval and Renaissance Texts and Studies, 1993.

———. *Creation of the World*. Translated by Joseph Tusiani. Edited by Gaetano Cipolla. Binghamton, NY: Center for Medieval & Early Renaissance Studies, 1982.

———. *Jerusalem Delivered: An English Prose Version*. Edited and translated by Ralph Nash. Detroit: Wayne State University Press, 1987.

———. *Jerusalem Delivered*. Edited and translated by Anthony M. Esolen. Baltimore: Johns Hopkins University Press, 2000.

———. *King Torrismondo*. Edited and translated by Maria C. Pastore Passaro. New York: Fordham University Press, 1997.

———. *Tasso's Dialogues: A Selection with the "Discourse on the Art of the Dialogue."* Edited and translated by Carnes Lord and Dain A. Trafton. Berkeley: University of California Press, 1982.

Vasari, Giorgio. *Life of Michelangelo*. Translated by George Bull. London: Folio Society, 1971.

———. *Lives of the Most Eminent Painters*. Edited by Marilyn Aronberg Lavin. Translated by Mrs. Jonathan Foster. New York: Heritage Press, 1967.

———. *The Lives of the Painters, Sculptors, and Architects*. Translated by A. B. Hinds. 4 vols. London: Dent, 1927.

———. *Vasari on Technique; Being the Introduction to the Three Arts of Design, Architecture, Sculpture, and Painting, Prefixed to the Lives of the Most Excellent Painters, Sculptors, and Architects*. Translated by Louisa S. Maclehose. New York: Dover Publications, 1960.

Primary Sources

Alighieri, Dante. *The Divine Comedy.* Edited and translated by Allen Mandelbaum. 3 vols. Berkeley: University of California Press, 1982.

_____. *Purgatory.* Edited and translated by Mark Musa. New York: Penguin, 1985.

Andreini, Francesco. *Le bravure del Capitano Spavento.* Edited by Roberto Tessari. Pisa: Giardini, 1987.

_____. "Sopra del pigliar moglie." In *Ragionamenti fantastici*, 35–42. Venice: Giacom'Antonio Somasco, 1612.

Andreini, Isabella. *Fragmenti di alcune scritture della signora Isabella Andreini, comica gelosa ed academica intenta.* Edited by Francesco Andreini. Venice: Giovanni Battista Combi, 1620.

_____. *La Mirtilla: A Pastoral.* Edited and translated by Julie D. Campbell. Medieval and Renaissance Texts and Studies 242. Tempe: Arizona Center for Medieval and Renaissance Studies, 2002.

_____. *Lettere della Signora Isabella Andreini, padovana, comica gelosa, e academica intenta, nominata l'accesa.* Venice: Alla Minerva, 1647.

_____. *Selected Poems of Isabella Andreini.* Translated by James Wyatt Cook, edited by Anne MacNeil. Lanham, MD: Scarecrow Press, 2005.

Antoniani, Silvio. *Tre libri dell'educatione Christiana de i figliuoli ad instanza di Monsig. Illustriss. Cardinale di S. Prassede, Arcivescovo di Milano.* Verona: Sebastiano dalle Donne and Girolamo Stringari, 1584.

Aragona, Tullia d'. "Dialogo della infinità di amore." In *Trattati d'amore del cinquecento*, edited by Giuseppe Zonta, 187–243. Bari: Laterza, 1912.

_____. *Dialogue on the Infinity of Love.* Edited and translated by Rinaldina Russell and Bruce Merry. The Other Voice in Early Modern Europe. Chicago: University of Chicago Press, 1997.

_____. *Le rime di Tullia d'Aragona cortigiana del secolo XVI.* Edited by Enrico Celani. Bologna: Forni, 1968.

Aretino, Pietro, *I ragionamenti.* Edited by Antonino Foschini. Milan: Dall'Oglio, 1960.

_____. *Lettere.* Edited by Paolo Procaccioli. 6 vols. Rome: Salerno, 1997–2002.

_____. *Edizione nazionale delle opere di Pietro Aretino.* Edited by Giovanni Aquilecchia and Angelo Romano. Vol. 1, *Poesie varie.* Rome: Salerno, 1992.

_____. "Ragionamento della Nanna e dell'Antonia." IntraText. http://www.intratext.com/IXT/ITA1035/_P4.HTM.

_____. *Un pronostico satirico di Pietro Aretino.* Edited by Alessandro Luzio. Bergamo: Istituto Italiano d'Arti Grafiche, 1900.

Ariosto, Ludovico. *Orlando furioso.* Translated by Guido Waldman. Oxford: Oxford University Press, 1983.

Aristotle. *The Complete Works.* Edited by Jonathan Barnes. 2 vols. Princeton, NJ: Princeton University Press, 1984.

_____. *On the Generation of Animals.* Translated by A. L. Peck. Loeb Classical Library. Cambridge, MA: Harvard University Press, 1979.

_____. *On the Soul.* Translated by W. S. Hett. Loeb Classical Library. Cambridge, MA: Harvard University Press, 1975.

_____. *Politics.* Translated by Benjamin Jowett. New York: Random House, 1943.

Augustine. *The City of God.* Translated by Henry Bettenson. New York: Penguin, 1977.

_____. *De doctrina Christiana. On Christian Doctrine.* Edited and translated by R. P. H. Green. Oxford: Clarendon Press, 1995.

Battiferra degli Ammannati, Laura. *Laura Battiferra and Her Literary Circle.* Edited and translated by Victoria Kirkham. The Other Voice in Early Modern Europe. Chicago: University of Chicago Press, 2006.

Bembo, Pietro. *Gli asolani.* Edited by Giorgio Dilemmi. Florence: Presso l'Accademia della Crusca, 1991.

_____. *Gli asolani.* Translated by Rudolf B. Gottfried. Freeport, NY: Books for Libraries Press, 1954. Reprint, 1971.

_____. *Prose della volgar lingua.* Edited by Claudio Vela. Bologna: Cooperativa Libraria Universitaria Editrice, 2001.

Betussi, Giuseppe. "Il Raverta." In *Trattati d'amore del cinquecento,* edited by Giuseppe Zonta, 3–150. Bari: Laterza, 1912.

Bigolina, Giulia. *Urania: A Romance.* Edited and translated by Valeria Finucci. The Other Voice in Early Modern Europe. Chicago: University of Chicago Press, 2005.

_____. *Urania: The Story of a Young Woman's Love & The Novella of Giulia Camposanpiero and Thesibaldo Vitaliani.* Edited and translated by Christopher Nissen. Medieval and Renaissance Texts and Studies 262. Tempe: Arizona Center for Medieval and Renaissance Studies, 2004.

Boccaccio, Giovanni. *Concerning Famous Women.* Translated by Guido A. Guarino. London: Allen and Unwin, 1964.

_____. *The Corbaccio.* Translated by Anthony K. Cassell. Rev. ed. Binghamton, NY: Medieval and Renaissance Texts and Studies, 1993.

_____. *Famous Women.* Edited and translated by Virginia Brown. Cambridge, MA: Harvard University Press, 2001.

_____. *Il corbaccio.* Edited by Giulia Natali. Milan: Mursia, 1992.

Boethius. *Consolation of Philosophy.* Translated by S. J. Tester. Loeb Classical Library. Cambridge, MA: Harvard University Press, 1973.

Bondanella, Julia Conway, and Mark Musa, eds. *The Italian Renaissance Reader.* New York: Meridian / Penguin, 1987.

Bongi, Salvatore. "Rime della Signora Tullia d'Aragona." In *Annali di Gabriel Giolito de' Ferrari I,* 150–98. Rome: Presso i Principali Librai, 1890.

Burgess-Van Aken, Barbara. "Barbara Torelli's *Partenia*: A Bilingual Critical Edition." PhD diss., Case Western Reserve University, 2007.

Campiglia, Maddalena. *Flori: A Pastoral Drama.* Edited and translated by Virginia Cox and Lisa Sampson. The Other Voice in Early Modern Europe. Chicago: University of Chicago Press, 2004.

Capella, Galeazzo Flavio. *Della eccellenza e dignità delle donne.* Edited by Maria Luisa Doglio. Rome: Bulzoni, 1988.

Castiglione, Baldassarre. *The Book of the Courtier.* Translated by George Bull. London: Penguin, 1967. Reprint, 1976.

Cereta, Laura. *Collected Letters of a Renaissance Feminist.* Edited and translated by Diana Robin. The Other Voice in Early Modern Europe. Chicago: University of Chicago Press, 1997.

Chrysostom, John. "An Address on Vainglory and the Right Way for Parents to Bring Up Their Children." In *Christianity and Pagan Culture in the Later Roman Empire*, edited by M. L. W. Laistner, 85–122. Ithaca, NY: Cornell University Press, 1951.

Colonna, Vittoria. "Rime amorose." In *Rime di tre gentildonne del secolo XVI*, edited by Olindo Guerrini, 19–79. Milan: Sonzogno, 1882.

_____. *Rime*. Edited by Alan Bullock. Bari, Italy: Laterza, 1982.

_____. "Rime sacre e morali." In *Rime di tre gentildonne del secolo XVI*, edited by Olindo Guerrini, 81–166. Milan: Sonzogno, 1882.

_____. *Sonnets for Michelangelo*. Edited and translated by Abigail Brundin. The Other Voice in Early Modern Europe. Chicago: University of Chicago Press, 2005.

Dolce, Lodovico. *Dialogo de i colori*. Venice: Gio. Battista et Marchio Sessa, 1565.

Du Bellay, Joachim. *Deffence et illustration de la langue françoyse*. Edited by Henri Chamard. Paris: Didier, 1961.

Fedele, Cassandra. *Letters and Orations*. Edited and translated by Diana Robin. The Other Voice in Early Modern Europe. Chicago: University of Chicago Press, 2000.

Ficino, Marsilio. *Commentary on Plato's Symposium on Love*. Edited and translated by Sears Reynolds Jayne. Dallas: Spring, 1985.

Florio, John. "Florio's 1611 Italian/English Dictionary: Queen Anna's New World of Words." http://www.pbm.com/~lindahl/florio.

Fonte, Moderata (Modesta Pozzo). *Floridoro. A Chivalric Romance*. Translated by Julia Kisacky. Edited by Valeria Finucci. The Other Voice in Early Modern Europe. Chicago: University of Chicago Press, 2006.

_____. *The Worth of Women: Wherein Is Clearly Revealed Their Nobility and Their Superiority to Men*. Edited and translated by Virginia Cox. The Other Voice in Early Modern Europe. Chicago: University of Chicago Press, 1997.

Franco, Nicolò. *La Priapea*. Edited by Enrico Sicardi. Lanciano: Carabba, 1916.

_____. *Il vendemmiatore, poemetto in ottava rima di Luigi Tansillo; e la Priapea, sonetti lussuriosi-satirici di Niccolò Franco*. Pe-king [Paris?]: Regnante Kien-Long [J. C. Molini?], n.d. [1790?].

Franco, Veronica. *Poems and Selected Letters.* Edited and translated by Ann Rosalind Jones and Margaret F. Rosenthal. The Other Voice in Early Modern Europe. Chicago: University of Chicago Press, 1998.

_____. *Rime.* Edited by Stefano Bianchi. Milan: Mursia, 1995.

Garzoni, Tommaso. *La piazza universale di tutte le professioni del mondo, nuovamente ristampata et posta in luce, da Thomaso Garzoni da Bagnacavallo.* Venice: L'herede di Gio. Battista Somasco, 1592.

_____. *Opere di Tommaso Garzoni da Bagnacavallo cioè il theatro de' varii et diversi cervelli mondani, la sinagoga de gli ignoranti, l'hospitale de' pazzi incurabili.* Venice: Seravalle ad Istanza di Roberto Meglietti, 1605.

Grazzini, Anton Francesco (il Lasca). "Canto di giovani impoveriti per le meretrici." In *Codice Marc. It. IX 310.* Venice: Biblioteca Marciana.

_____. *Le rime del Lasca.* Edited by Carlo Verzone. Florence: Le Monnier, 1882.

_____. *Rime di Anton Francesco Grazzini detto il Lasca.* 2 vols. Florence: Stamperia Francesco Moücke, 1742.

Guazzo, Stefano. *The Civil Conversation.* Translated by George Pettie. London: Richard Watkins, 1581.

_____. *La civil conversatione.* Venice: Presso Altobello Salicato, 1584.

_____. *La civil conversazione.* Edited by Amedeo Quondam. 2 vols. Ferrara: Istituto di Studi Rinascimentali, 1993.

Horace. *The Essential Horace: Odes, Epodes, Satires, and Epistles.* Translated by Burton Raffel. San Francisco: North Point Press, 1983.

Lavezuola, Alberto. *Osservationi sopra il furioso.* Venice: Francesco de' Franceschi, 1584.

Machiavelli, Niccolò. "Letter to Francesco Vettori." In *Norton Anthology of World Masterpieces*, edited by Maynard Mack, Bernard M. W. Knox, John C. McGalliard, P. M. Pasinetti, Howard E. Hugo, Patricia Meyer Spacks, René Wellek, Kenneth Douglas, and Sarah Lawall, 1708–9. New York: W. W. Norton, 1999.

_____. "Niccolò Machiavelli a Francesco Vettori." In *Lettere a Francesco Vettori e a Francesco Guicciardini*, edited by Giorgio Inglese, 192-201. Milan: Rizzoli, 1996.

Marinella, Lucrezia. *The Nobility and Excellence of Women and the Defects and Vices of Men.* Edited and translated by Anne Dunhill. Introduction by Letizia Panizza. The Other Voice in Early Modern Europe. Chicago: University of Chicago Press, 1999.

Marinello, Giovanni. *Gli ornamenti delle donne.* Venice: Francesco de' Franceschi, 1562.

Morata, Olympia. *The Complete Writings of an Italian Heretic.* Edited and translated by Holt Parker. The Other Voice in Early Modern Europe. Chicago: University of Chicago Press, 2003.

Nogarola, Isotta. *The Complete Writings of Isotta Nogarola (1418–1466).* Edited by and Translated by Margaret King and Diana Robin, The Other Voice in Early Modern Europe. Chicago: University of Chicago Press, 2003.

Ochino, Bernardino. "Predica predicata in Vinegia dal Reverendo Padre Frate Bernardino da Siena dell'ordine di frati capuzzini il giorno della festa di S. Maria Maddalena, MDXXXIX." In *PREDICHE NOVE PREDICATE DAL REVERENDO Padre Frate Bernardino Occhino Senese, generale dell'ordine di Frati Capuzzini nella inclita citta di Vinegia: del MDXXXIX,* 63v–73v. Venice: Nicolò d'Aristotile da Ferrara, detto il Zoppino, 1541.

Ovid. *The Art of Love and Other Poems.* Translated by J. H. Mozley. Loeb Classical Library. Cambridge, MA: Harvard University Press, 1979.

———. *Heroides and Amores.* Translated by Grant Showerman, revised by G. P. Goold. 2nd ed. Loeb Classical Library. Cambridge, MA: Harvard University Press, 1977.

———. *Metamorphoses.* Translated by Frank Justus Miller. 2 vols. Loeb Classical Library. Cambridge, MA: Harvard University Press, 1977.

Passi, Giuseppe. *Dello stato maritale.* Venice: Giacomo Antonio Somascho, 1602.

———. *Discorso del ben parlar per non offendere persona alcuna.* Venice: Giacomo Antonio Somascho, 1600.

———. *I donneschi difetti.* Venice: Giacomo Antonio Somascho, 1599.

Passi, Pietro [Giuseppe]. *Della magic'arte overo della magia naturale.* Venice: Giacomo Violati All'Insegna della Nave, 1614.

Petrarca, Francesco. *Petrarch: The Canzoniere, or, Rerum vulgarium fragmenta*. Edited and translated by Mark Musa. Bloomington: Indiana University Press, 1996. Reprint, 1999.

_____. *Petrarch's Lyric Poems*. Edited and translated by Robert M. Durling. Cambridge, MA: Harvard University Press, 1976.

_____. *Rime, trionfi e poesie latine*. Edited by Ferdinando Neri. Milan: Ricciardi, 1951.

_____. *Selections from the Canzoniere and Other Works*. Edited and translated by Mark Musa. World's Classics. Oxford: Oxford University Press, 1985.

_____. *Triumphs*. Translated by E. H. Wilkins. Chicago: University of Chicago Press, 1962.

Piccolomini, Alessandro. *La Raffaella ovvero dialogo della bella creanza delle donne*. Edited by Giancarlo Alfano. Rome: Salerno, 2001.

Plato. *Great Dialogues of Plato*. Translated by W. H. D. Rouse. Edited by Eric H. Warmington and Philip G. Rouse. New York: New American Library, 1956.

_____. *Lysis*. In *Plato III: Lysis Symposium Gorgias*, translated by W. R. M. Lamb, 6–71. Loeb Classical Library. Cambridge, MA: Harvard University Press, 1983.

_____. *Phaedrus*. In *The Dialogues of Plato*, translated by Harold North Fowler, 405-579. Loeb Classical Library. Cambridge, MA: Harvard University Press, 1977.

_____. *Republic*. Edited and translated by I. A. Richards. Cambridge: Cambridge University Press, 1966.

_____. *Symposium*. In *The Collected Dialogues*, edited by Edith Hamilton and Huntington Cairns, 553–63. New York: Bollingen Foundation / Pantheon Books, 1961.

Pliny. *Natural History*. Translated by H. Rackam, W. H. S. Jones, and D. E. Eichholz. 10 vols. Loeb Classical Library. Cambridge, MA: Harvard University Press, 1967–80.

Plutarch. *Lives*. Translated by Bernadotte Perrin. 11 vols. Loeb Classical Library Cambridge, MA: Harvard University Press, 1914–26. Reprint, 1968.

Ruscelli, Girolamo. *Lettura de Girolamo Ruscelli, sopra un sonetto dell'illustriss. Signor Marchese della Terza alla diuina Signora Marchesa del Vasto*. Venice: Giovan Griffio, 1552.

Seneca. "Octavia." In *Tragedies*, edited and translated by Frank Justus Miller, 2: 401–89. Loeb Classical Library. Cambridge, MA: Harvard University Press, 1968.

Speroni, Sperone. "Apologia dei dialoghi." In *Trattatisti del cinquecento*, edited by Mario Pozzi, 1:683–724. Milan: Ricciardi, 1978.

———. "Dialogo d'amore." In *Trattatisti del cinquecento*, edited by Mario Pozzi, 1:511–63. Milan: Ricciardi, 1978.

———. "Dialogo di amore." In *Opere*, edited by Natale dalle Laste and Marco Forcellini, 1:1–45. Venice: D. Occhi, 1740. Reprint, Rome: Vecchiarelli, 1989.

———. *Opere*. Edited by Mario Pozzi. Rome: Vecchiarelli, 1989.

Stampa, Gaspara. *Selected Poems*. Edited and translated by Laura Anna Stortoni and Mary Prentice Lillie. New York: Italica Press, 1994.

———, and Veronica Franco. *Rime*. Edited by Abdelkader Salza. Scrittori d'Italia. Bari: Laterza, 1913.

Statius. *Achilleid*. Translated by J. H. Mozley. Loeb Classical Library. Cambridge, MA: Harvard University Press, 1989.

Stevenson, Jane. *Women Latin Poets*. Oxford: Oxford University Press, 2005.

Stortoni, Laura Anna and Mary Prentice Lillie, eds. *Women Poets of the Italian Renaissance*. New York: Italica Press, 1997.

Tarabotti, Arcangela. *Paternal Tyranny*. Edited and translated by Letizia Panizza. The Other Voice in Early Modern Italy. Chicago: University of Chicago, 2004.

Tasso, Bernardo. *Rime*. Rome: Biblioteca italiana, 2003. http://www.bibliotecaitaliana.it/xtf/view?docId=bibit001547/bibit001547.xml&chunk.id=d6847e18200&toc.depth=1&toc.id=d6847e7144&brand=default

Tasso, Torquato. *Aminta*. Edited and translated by Charles Jernigan and Irene Marchegiani Jones. New York: Italica Press, 2000.

———. *Discorso della virtù feminile e donnesca*. Venice: Giunti, 1582.

———. *Discorso della virtù femminile e donnesca*. Edited by Maria Luisa Doglio. Palermo: Sellerio, 1997.

Tertullian. *Gli ornamenti delle donne*. Edited and translated by Maria Tasinato. Parma: Pratiche, 1987.

———. *La toilette des femmes*. Edited by and translated by Marie Turcan. Paris: Éditions du Cerf, 1971.

Titian. *Amor sacro e amor profano*. Galleria Borghese Web site. http://www.galleriaborghese.it/borghese/it/amor.htm.

Torquemada, Antonio. *Giardino de' fiori curiosi*. Translated by Celio Malaspina. Venice: Altobello Salicato alla Libreria della Fortezza, 1590.

Venier, Maffio. *Canzoni e sonetti*. Edited by Attilio Carminati. Venice: Corbo e Fiore, 1993.

_____. "Veronica, ver unica puttana." In *Codice Marc. It. IX, 217*, 56r–59r. Venice: Biblioteca Marciana.

Virgil. *Aeneid*. Translated by H. R. Fairclough. 2 vols. Loeb Classical Library. Cambridge, MA: Harvard University Press, 1986.

_____. *Eclogues, Georgics, Aeneid I–VI*. Translated by H. Rushton Fairclough. Loeb Classical Library. Cambridge, MA: Harvard University Press, 1978.

Secondary Sources

Altieri Biagi, Maria Luisa, Clementina Mazzotta, Angela Chiantera, Paola Altieri, eds. *Medicina per le donne del cinquecento*. Turin: UTET, 1992.

Andrews, Richard. *Scripts and Scenarios: The Performance of Comedy in Renaissance Italy*. Cambridge: Cambridge University Press, 1993.

Audi, Robert, ed. *The Cambridge Dictionary of Philosophy*. Cambridge: Cambridge University Press, 1995.

Avery, Catherine B., ed. *The New Century Classical Handbook*. New York: Appleton-Century-Crofts, 1962.

_____. *The New Century Italian Renaissance Encyclopedia*. New York: Appleton-Century-Crofts, 1972.

Bainton, Roland H. *Bernardino Ochino: esule e riformatore senese del cinquecento*. Florence: Sansoni, 1940.

_____. "Vittoria Colonna and Michelangelo." *Forum* 9, no. 1 (1971): 34–41.

Baldi, Andrea. *Tradizione e parodia in Alessandro Piccolomini*. Lucca: Maria Pacini Fazzi, 2001.

Bardazzi, Giovanni. "Le rime spirituali di Vittoria Colonna e Bernardino Ochino." *Italique: poésie italienne de la Renaissance* 4 (2001): 61–91.

Bassanese, Fiora A. *Gaspara Stampa*. Twayne's World Authors 658. Boston: Twayne, 1982.

———. "Mythological Representations of the Renaissance Cortegiana." *RLA: Romance Languages Annual* 1 (1989): 81–86.

Bausi, Francesco. "Le rime di e per Tullia d'Aragona." In *Les femmes écrivains en Italie au Moyen Âge et à la Renaissance*, edited by Georges Ulysses, 275–92. Aix-en-Provence: Publications de l'Université de Provence, 1994.

Benson, Pamela Joseph. *The Invention of the Renaissance Woman*. University Park, PA: Pennsylvania State University Press, 1992.

———, and Victoria Kirkham. "Introduction." In *Strong Voices, Weak History*, edited by Pamela Joseph Benson and Victoria Kirkham, 1–13. Ann Arbor: University of Michigan Press, 2005.

Bettella, Patrizia. *The Ugly Woman: Transgressive Aesthetic Models in Italian Poetry from the Middle Ages to the Baroque*. Toronto: University of Toronto Press, 2005.

Bianchi, Stefano. "Introduzione." In *Rime*, by Veronica Franco, 5–34. Milan: Mursia, 1995.

Bianchini, Giuseppe. *Franceschina Baffo, rimatrice veneziana del secolo XVI*. Verona: Drucker, 1896.

Bloch, R. Howard. *Medieval Misogyny and the Invention of Western Romantic Love*. Chicago: University of Chicago Press, 1991.

Boccia, Carmine. "Il quarto libro delle lettere di Nicolò Franco: l'epistolario inedito nel ms. Vaticano latino 5642. Nuovi contributi ai casi di un peregrino ingegno." *Critica letteraria* 32, no. 1 (2005): 3–46.

Brock, Ann Graham. *Mary Magdalene, the First Apostle: The Struggle for Authority*. Cambridge, MA: Harvard Theological Studies, 2003.

Broomhall, Susan. *Women and the Book Trade in Sixteenth-Century France*. Surrey, UK: Ashgate, 2002.

Bruni, Roberto L. "Le tre edizioni cinquecentesche delle rime contro l'Aretino e la Priapea di Nicolò Franco." In *Libri, tipografi, biblioteche: ricerche storiche dedicate a Luigi Balsamo*, edited by Università degli Studi Parma Istituto di Biblioteconomia e Paleografia, 1:123–43. Florence: Olschki, 1997.

Buranello, Roberto. "*Figura meretricis*: Tullia d'Aragona in Sperone Speroni's *Dialogo d'amore*." *Spunti e ricerche* 15 (2000): 53–68.

Burckhardt, Jacob. *The Civilization of the Renaissance in Italy*. Translated by S. C. G. Middlemore. 2 vols. New York: Harper and Row, 1958.

Caffiero, Marina. "Tra modelli di disciplinamento e autonomia soggettiva." In *Modelli di santità e modelli di comportamento: contrasti, intersezioni, complementarità*, edited by Giulia Barone, Marina Caffiero, and Francesco Scorza Barcellona, 265–93. Turin: Rosenberg & Sellier, 1994.

Cairns, Christopher. *Pietro Aretino and the Republic of Venice: Researches on Aretino and His Circle in Venice, 1527–1556*. Florence: Olschki, 1985.

Campbell, Julie D. *Literary Circles and Gender in Early Modern Europe: A Cross-Cultural Approach*. Surrey, UK: Ashgate, 2006.

Campi, Emidio. "'Non vi si pensa quanto sangue costa!' Michelangelo, Vittoria Colonna e Bernardino Ochino." In *Michelangelo e Vittoria Colonna: un dialogo artistico-teologico ispirato da Bernardino Ochino e altri saggi di storia della Riforma*, 9–126. Turin: Claudiana, 1994.

Carminati, Attilio. "Presentazione." In *Canzoni e sonetti* by Maffio Venier, 23–71. Venice: Corbo e Fiore, 1993.

Casagrande de Villaviera, Rita. *Le cortigiane veneziane del cinquecento*. Milan: Longanesi, 1968.

Cerreta, Florindo. *Alessandro Piccolomini: letterato e filosofo senese del cinquecento*. Siena: Accademia Senese degli Intronati, 1960.

Chemello, Adriana. "Donna di palazzo, moglie, cortigiana: ruoli e funzioni sociali della donna in alcuni trattati del cinquecento." In *La corte e il cortegiano*, edited by Carlo Ossola, 2:113–32. Rome: Bulzoni, 1980.

Cherchi, Paolo. "Juan Luis Vives: A Source for Pedro Mexìa's *Silva de varia lecciónes*." In *Sondaggi sulla riscrittura del cinquecento*, 149–57. Ravenna: Longo, 1998.

––––––, ed. *Sondaggi sulla riscrittura del cinquecento*. Ravenna: Longo, 1998.

––––––, ed. *Ricerche sulle selve rinascimentali*. Ravenna: Longo, 1999.

Chojnacki, Stanley. *Women and Men in Renaissance Venice.* Baltimore: Johns Hopkins University Press, 2000.

Clubb, Louise George. *Italian Drama in Shakespeare's Time.* New Haven, CT: Yale University Press, 1989.

Cochrane, Kirsty. "A Civil Conversation of 1582: Gabriel Harvey's Reading of Guazzo." *A.U.M.L.A.: Journal of the Australasian Universities Modern Language Association* 78 (1992): 1–28.

Cohen, Sherrill. "Asylums for Women in Counter-Reformation Italy." *Women's Studies* 19 (1991): 201–08.

———. "Convertite e malmaritate: donne 'irregolari' e ordini religiosi nella Firenze rinascimentale." *Memoria: rivista di storia delle donne* 5 (1985): 23–65.

Cox, Virginia. "Fiction 1560–1650." In *A History of Women's Writing in Italy*, edited by Letizia Panizza and Sharon Wood, 52–64. Cambridge: Cambridge University Press, 2000.

———. "Moderata Fonte and *The Worth of Women*." In *The Worth of Women: Wherein Is Clearly Revealed Their Nobility and Their Superiority to Men*, by Moderata Fonte, edited and translated by Virginia Cox, 1–23. The Other Voice in Early Modern Europe. Chicago: University of Chicago Press, 1997.

———. "Seen but Not Heard: The Role of Women Speakers in Cinquecento Literary Dialogue." In *Women in Italian Renaissance Culture and Society*, edited by Letizia Panizza, 385–400. Oxford: European Humanities Research Centre, University of Oxford, 2000.

———. *Women's Writing in Italy 1400–1650.* Baltimore: Johns Hopkins University Press, 2008.

———, and Lisa Sampson. "Volume Editors' Introduction." In Maddalena Campiglia, *Flori, a Pastoral Drama*, edited and translated by Virginia Cox and Lisa Sampson, 1–35. The Other Voice in Early Modern Europe. Chicago: University of Chicago Press, 2004.

Dazzi, Manlio. *Il libro chiuso di Maffio Venier (la tenzone con Veronica Franco).* Venice: Neri Pozza, 1956.

DeJean, Joan. *Tender Geographies: Women and the Origin of the Novel in France.* New York: Columbia University Press, 1991.

Derrida, Jacques. "Différance." In *A Derrida Reader: Between the Blinds*, edited by Peggy Kamuf, 61–79. New York: Columbia University Press, 1991.

Feldman, Martha, and Bonnie Gordon, eds. *Courtesan's Arts: A Cross-Cultural Perspective.* Oxford: Oxford University Press, 2006.

Fehr, Isak. "Fabeln om Kärleken och Dårskapen." *Samlaren* 4 (1883): 44–54.

Fenlon, Dermot. "The Movement 'ad fontes' and the Outbreak of Reformation." In *Heresy and Obedience in Tridentine Italy: Cardinal Pole and the Counter Reformation*, 1–23. Cambridge: Cambridge University Press, 1972.

Finucci, Valeria. "Introduction." In *Urania: A Romance*, by Giulia Bigolina, edited and translated by Valeria Finucci, 1–35. The Other Voice in Early Modern Europe. Chicago: University of Chicago Press, 2005.

_____. "Introduzione." In *Urania*, by Giulia Bigolina, edited by Valeria Finucci, 13–66. Rome: Bulzoni, 2002.

Frajese, Vittorio. *Il popolo fanciullo: Silvio Antoniano e il sistema disciplinare della Controriforma.* Milan: Franco Angeli, 1987.

Freedman, Luba. *Titian's Portraits through Aretino's Lens.* University Park: Pennsylvania State University Press, 1995.

Giannetti, Laura. *Lelia's Kiss: Imagining Gender, Sex, and Marriage in Italian Renaissance Comedy.* Toronto: University of Toronto Press, 2009.

Gill, Katherine. "Women and the Production of Religious Literature in the Vernacular, 1300–1550." In *Creative Women in Medieval and Early Modern Italy: A Religious and Artistic Renaissance*, edited by E. Ann Matter and John Coakley, 64–104. Philadelphia: University of Pennsylvania Press, 1994.

Graf, Arturo. "Una cortigiana fra mille: Veronica Franco." In *Attraverso il cinquecento*, 215-351. Turin: Chiantore, 1888.

Grendler, Paul. *Critics of the Italian World, 1530–1560: Anton Francesco Doni, Nicolò Franco & Ortensio Lando.* Madison: University of Wisconsin Press, 1969.

Hairston, Julia. "Aragona, Tullia d'." Italian Women Writers Web site. http://www.lib.uchicago.edu/efts/IWW/BIOS/A0004.html.

_____. "Out of the Archive: Four Newly Identified Figures in Tullia d'Aragona *Rime della Signora Tullia di Aragona et di diversi a lei* (1547)." *MLN* 118 (2003): 257–63.

Haskins, Susan. *Mary Magdalen: Myth and Metaphor.* New York: Harcourt Brace, 1993.

Henke, Robert. *Performance and Literature in the Commedia dell'arte.* Cambridge: Cambridge University Press, 2002.

Honderich, Ted, ed. *The Oxford Companion to Philosophy.* Oxford: Oxford University Press, 1995.

Jaffe, Irma B., with Gernando Colombardo. *Shining Eyes, Cruel Fortune: The Lives and Loves of Italian Renaissance Women Poets.* New York: Fordham University Press, 2002.

Jansen, Katherine Ludwig. *The Making of the Magdalen: Preaching and Popular Devotion in the Later Middle Ages.* Princeton, NJ: Princeton University Press, 2000.

Javitch, Daniel. "Rival Arts of Conduct in Elizabethan England: Guazzo's Civile conversatione and Castiglione's *Courtier.*" *Yearbook of Italian Studies* 1 (1971): 178–98.

Jones, Ann Rosalind. *The Currency of Eros: Women's Love Lyric in Europe, 1540–1620.* Bloomington: Indiana University Press, 1990.

———. "Surprising Fame." In *Feminism and Renaissance Studies,* edited by Lorna Hutson, 317–36. Oxford: Oxford University Press, 1999.

Kelly, Joan. "Did Women Have a Renaissance?" In *Women, History, and Theory,* 19–49. Chicago: University of Chicago Press, 1984.

Kennedy, William J. *Authorizing Petrarch.* Ithaca, NY: Cornell University Press, 1994.

King, Margaret L., and Albert Rabil, Jr. "The Other Voice in Early Modern Europe Introduction to the Series." In Moderata Fonte, *The Worth of Women: Wherein Is Clearly Revealed Their Nobility and Their Superiority to Men,* vii–xxvi. Edited and translated by Virginia Cox. The Other Voice in Early Modern Europe. Chicago: University of Chicago Press, 1997.

Kirkham, Victoria. "Introduction." In *Laura Battiferra and Her Literary Circle,* edited and translated by Victoria Kirkham, 1–54. The Other Voice in Early Modern Europe. Chicago: University of Chicago Press, 2006.

———. "Laura Battiferra degli Ammannati's *First Book* of Poetry: A Renaissance Holograph Comes Out of Hiding." *Rinascimento* 36 (1996): 351–91.

Klapisch-Zuber, Christine. *Women, Family, and Ritual in Renaissance Italy*. Translated by Lydia G. Cochrane. Chicago: University of Chicago Press, 1987.

Kolsky, Stephen. "Moderata Fonte, Lucrezia Marinella, Giuseppe Passi: An Early Seventeenth-Century Feminist Controversy." *Modern Language Review* 94. no. 1 (2001): 973–89.

Laqueur, Thomas. *Making Sex: Body and Gender from the Greeks to Freud*. Cambridge, MA: Harvard University Press, 1990.

Lawner, Lynne. *Lives of the Courtesans: Portraits of the Renaissance*. New York: Rizzoli, 1987.

Lemprière, John. *Lemprière's Classical Dictionary*. London: Bracken Books, 1994.

Lievsay, John Leon. "Notes on *The Art of Conversation* (1738)." *Italica* 17, no. 2 (1940): 58–63.

Luzio, Alessandro. "L'Aretino e il Franco." *Giornale storico della letteratura italiana* 29 (1897): 228–83.

Maclean, Ian. *The Renaissance Notion of Woman: A Study in the Fortune of Scholasticism and Medical Science in European Intellectual Life*. Cambridge: Cambridge University Press, 1980.

MacNeil, Anne. *Music and Women of the Commedia dell'Arte*. Oxford: Oxford University Press, 2003.

Magnanini, Suzanne. "*Una selva luminosa*: The Second Day of Moderata Fonte's *Il merito delle donne*." *Modern Philology* 101, no. 2 (2003): 278–96.

Marotti, Arthur F. *John Donne, Coterie Poet*. Madison: University of Wisconsin Press, 1986.

Masson, Georgina. *Courtesans of the Italian Renaissance*. London: Secker Warburg, 1975.

Migiel, Marilyn, and Juliana Schiesari, eds. *Refiguring Woman: Perspective on Gender and the Italian Renaissance*. Ithaca, NY: Cornell University Press, 1991.

Milligan, Gerry. "The Politics of Effeminacy in *Il cortegiano*." *Italica* 83, no. 3–4 (2006): 345–66.

Musa, Mark. "Introduction." In *Petrarch: The Canzoniere, or, Rerum vulgarium fragmenta*, by Francesco Petrarca, xi–xxxvi. Bloomington: Indiana University Press, 1996. Reprint, 1999.

Nissen, Christopher. "Giulia Bigolina, la prima romanziera italiana: una donna dell'alta Padovana tra i letterati del '500." *Alta padovana* 4 (2005): 50–64.

_____. "Introduction." In *Urania, The Story of a Young Woman's Love & The Novella of Giulia Camposanpiero and Thesibaldo Vitaliani*, by Giulia Bigolina, edited by Christopher Nissen, 1–54. Tempe: Arizona Center for Medieval and Renaissance Studies, 2004.

_____. "The Motif of the Woman in Male Disguise from Boccaccio to Bigolina." In *The Italian Novella*, edited by Gloria Allaire, 201–17. New York: Routledge, 2003.

_____. "*Paragone* as Fiction: The Judgment of Paris in Giulia Bigolina's *Urania*." *Italian Quarterly* 42, no. 165–66 (2005): 5–17.

_____. "Subjects, Objects, Authors: The Portraiture of Women in Giulia Bigolina's *Urania*." *Italian Culture* 18 (2000): 15–31.

Ormsby, Eric. "Petrarch: A Splendid Excess." *New Criterion*, 23 September 2004, 18–23.

Panizza, Letizia. "Introduction to the Translation." In *The Nobility and Excellence of Women and the Defects and Vices of Men*, by Lucrezia Marinella, edited and translated by Anne Dunhill, 1–34. The Other Voice in Early Modern Europe. Chicago: University of Chicago Press, 1999.

_____, and Sharon Wood, eds. *A History of Women's Writing in Italy*. Cambridge: Cambridge University Press, 2000.

Peck, Harry Thurston, ed. *Harper's Dictionary of Classical Literature and Antiquities*. New York: American Book Company, 1896.

Piéjus, Marie Françoise. "Venus bifrons: le double idéal féminin dans *La Raffaella* d'Alessandro Piccolomini." In *Images de la femme dans la littérature italienne de la Renaissance: préjugés misogynes et aspirations nouvelles*, edited by José Guidi, Marie Françoise Piéjus, and Adelin-Charles Fiorato, 80–167. Paris: Université de la Sorbonne Nouvelle, 1980.

Pozzi, Mario. "Nota introduttiva [to Sperone Speroni]." In *Trattatisti del cinquecento*, edited by Mario Pozzi, 1:471–509. Milan: Ricciardi, 1978.

Ravasi, Gianfranco. "Maria di Magdala, santa calunniata e glorificata." In *Maddalena*, edited by Giovanni Testori, 15–28. Milan: Franco Maria Ricci, 1989.

Rebonato, Alessandro. "Di alcuni imitatori di Tommaso Garzoni." *Studi secenteschi* 45 (2004): 195–215.

Richter, Bodo L. O. "Petrarchism and Anti-Petrarchism among the Veniers." *Forum Italicum* 3 (1969): 20–42.

Robin, Diana. *Publishing Women: Salons, the Presses, and the Counter-Reformation in Sixteenth-Century Italy.* Chicago: University of Chicago Press, 2007.

Rodini, Robert J. *Antonfrancesco Grazzini: Poet, Dramatist and Novelliere, 1503–1584.* Madison: University of Wisconsin Press, 1970.

Rosenthal, Margaret F. *The Honest Courtesan: Veronica Franco, Citizen and Writer in Sixteenth-Century Venice.* Chicago: University of Chicago Press, 1992.

Ross, Sarah Gwyneth. *The Birth of Feminism: Woman as Intellect in Renaissance Italy and England.* Cambridge, MA: Harvard University Press, 2009

Ruggiero, Guido. "Marriage, Love, Sex and Renaissance Civic Morality." In *Sexuality and Gender in Early Modern Europe: Institutions, Texts, Images,* edited by James Grantham Turner, 10–30. Cambridge: Cambridge University Press, 1993.

Russell, Rinaldina. "Introduction." In *Dialogue on the Infinity of Love,* by Tullia d'Aragona, edited and translated by Rinaldina Russell, 21–42. The Other Voice in Early Modern Europe. Chicago: University of Chicago Press, 1997.

———. "Margherita Sarrocchi and the Writing of the *Scanderbeide.*" In *Scanderbeide: The Heroic Deeds of George Scanderbeg, King of Epirus,* by Margherita Sarrocchi, edited and translated by Rinaldina Russell, 1–61. The Other Voice in Early Modern Europe. Chicago: University of Chicago Press, 2006.

———. "Opinione e giuoco del dialogo d'amore." *Parola e testo: semestrale di filologia e letteratura italiana* 6, no. 1 (2002): 133–46.

Sampson, Lisa. *Pastoral Drama in Early Modern Italy: The Making of a New Genre.* London: Modern Humanities Research Association / Maney, 2006.

Schaberg, Jane. "The Woman Who Understood (Too) Completely: Legends, Apocrypha, and the Christian Testament." In *The Resurrection of Mary Magdalene,* 121–203. New York: Continuum, 2002.

Simiani, Carlo. *Nicolò Franco: la vita e le opere.* Turin and Rome: Roux, 1894.

Slim, H. Colin. "Music and Dancing with Mary Magdalen in a Laura Vestalis." In *The Crannied Wall: Women, Religion, and the Arts in Early Modern Europe,* edited by Craig Monson, 139–60. Ann Arbor: University of Michigan Press, 1992.

Smarr, Janet Levarie. "A Dialogue of Dialogues: Tullia d'Aragona and Sperone Speroni." *MLN* 113, no. 1 (1998): 204–12.

———. *Joining the Conversation: Dialogues by Renaissance Women.* Ann Arbor: University of Michigan Press, 2005.

Smith, Sir William. *Smaller Classical Dictionary.* New York: Dutton & Co., 1958.

Snyder, Jon. *Writing the Scene of Speaking: Theories of Dialogue in the Late Italian Renaissance.* Stanford: Stanford University Press, 1989.

Stampino, Maria Galli. *Staging the Pastoral: Tasso's Aminta and the Emergence of Modern Western Theater.* Medieval and Renaissance Texts and Studies 280. Tempe: Arizona Center for Medieval and Renaissance Studies, 2005.

Strocchia, Sharon. "Gender and Rules of Honour in Italian Renaissance Cities." In *Gender and Society in Renaissance Italy,* edited by Judith C. Brown and Robert C. Davis, 39–60. London: Longman, 1998.

Sullivan, Edward. "Introduction." In *The Civile Conversation of M. Steeven Guazzo,* translated by George Pettie and Bartholomew Young. 1:v–xcii. New York: AMS Press, 1967.

Toscan, Jean. *Le carnaval du langage: le lexique érotique des poètes de l'équivoque de Burchiello à Marino (XVe–XVIIe siècles).* 4 vols. Lille: Presses Universitaires de Lille, 1981.

Ultsch, Lori J. "Epithalamium Interruptum: Maddalena Campiglia's New Arcadia," *MLN* 120, no. 1 (2005): 70–92,

Vianello, Valerio. *Il "giardino" delle parole: itinerari di scrittura e modelli letterari nel dialogo cinquecentesco.* Materiali e ricerche N.S. 21. Rome: Jouvence, 1993.

Vickers, Nancy. "Lyric in the Video Decade." *Discourse* 16, no. 1 (1993): 6–27.

_____. "Vital Signs: Petrarch and Popular Culture." *Romanic Review* 79, no. 1 (1988): 184–95.

Waddington, Raymond B. *Aretino's Satyr: Sexuality, Satire, and Self-Projection in Sixteenth-Century Literature and Art.* Toronto: University of Toronto Press, 2004.

Weaver, Elissa, ed. *Arcangela Tarabotti: A Literary Nun in Baroque Venice.* Ravenna: Longo, 2006.

Wiesner, Merry E. *Women and Gender in Early Modern Europe.* Cambridge: Cambridge University Press, 1993.

Zanfagna, Sr. Mary Lauretana. *Educational Theories and Principles of Cardinal Silvio Antoniano.* Washington, DC: Catholic University of America Press, 1940.

Zanré, Domenico. *Cultural Non-Conformity in Early Modern Florence.* Burlington, VT: Ashgate, 2004.

Zarri, Gabriella. "Living Saints: A Typology of Female Sanctity in the Early Sixteenth Century." In *Women and Religion in Medieval and Renaissance Italy,* edited by Daniel Bornstein and Roberto Rusconi, 219–303. Chicago: University of Chicago Press, 1996.

_____. *Recinti: Donne, clausura e matrimonio nella prima età moderna.* Bologna: il Mulino, 2000.

Zorzi, Alvise. *Cortigiana veneziana: Veronica Franco e i suoi poeti 1546–1591.* Milan: Camunia, 1986.

Notes on Contributors

PATRIZIA BETTELLA teaches in the Department of Modern Languages and Cultural Studies at the University of Alberta in Canada, where she is the coordinator of the Italian Language Program. She has published articles on Renaissance treatises on female beauty and on the anti-Petrarchan poetry of Berni, Doni, and Firenzuola. She is the author of *The Ugly Woman: Transgressive Aesthetic Models in Italian Poetry from the Middle Ages to the Baroque* (University of Toronto Press, 2005). She has just completed the chapter "Marked Body as Otherness in Renaissance Italian Culture" for the volume *A Cultural History of the Human Body in the Renaissance* (Oxford: Berg Publishers, 2010).

JULIE D. CAMPBELL is professor of English at Eastern Illinois University. Her areas of study are Renaissance and seventeenth-century literature, with a specialization in the works of Continental and English women writers. She is the editor and translator of Isabella Andreini's pastoral tragicomedy *La Mirtilla* (MRTS, 2002) and the author of *Literary Circles and Gender in Early Modern Europe* (Ashgate, 2006). She has contributed work to *Women Players in England, 1500–1660* (Ashgate, 2005), *Reading Early Women* (Routledge, 2004), and the *Encyclopedia of Women in the Renaissance* (ABC-CLIO, 2007). With Anne R. Larsen, she edited *Early Modern Women and Transnational Communities of Letters* (Ashgate, 2009). Her current research examines cross-cultural connections between Italian actresses and French noblewomen at the Valois court.

DAVID LAMARI is a lecturer in classical studies at the University of Western Ontario, Canada. His interests include imperial Latin historiography and Roman Stoic philosophy.

SUZANNE MAGNANINI is associate professor in the Department of French and Italian at the University of Colorado, Boulder. She is the author of *Fairy-Tale Science: Monstrous Generation in the Tales of Straparola and Basile* (University of Toronto Press, 2008). She is currently translating Giovanfrancesco Straparola's *Le piacevoli notti*, a sixteenth-century collection of novellas and fairy tales.

CHRISTOPHER NISSEN is associate professor of Italian at Northern Illinois University. He has published numerous studies of medieval and early modern Italian prose fiction, including several articles on Giulia Bigolina. His critical edition with translation of Bigolina's surviving works was published in 2004 by the Arizona Center for Medieval and Renaissance Studies. His monograph *Kissing the Wild Woman: Concepts of Art, Beauty, and the Italian Prose Romance in Giulia Bigolina's Urania*, is forthcoming with the University of Toronto Press.

JANET LEVARIE SMARR is professor of theatre and of Italian studies at the University of California, San Diego. She is the author of several articles on women writers of the sixteenth century, including "A Dialogue of Dialogues: Tullia d'Aragona and Sperone Speroni," *MLN* 113, no. 1 (1998), and of *Joining the Conversation: Dialogues by Renaissance Women* (University of Michigan Press, 2005). Her study and translations of Louise-Geneviève Gillot de Sainctonge's *Dramatizing Dido, Circe and Griselda* appeared in The Other Voice series in 2010. She has also published translations of *Italian Renaissance Tales* and *Boccaccio's Eclogues*.

MARIA GALLI STAMPINO is associate professor of Italian and French at the University of Miami. Her research concentrates on Italian literature of the late sixteenth and early seventeenth centuries, especially performed theater and lyrical and epic poetry. She is the author of *Staging the Pastoral: Tasso's* Aminta *and the Emergence of Modern Western Theater* (MRTS, 2005). Her edition and translation of Lucrezia Marinella's *Enrico, or Byzantium Conquered* appeared in 2009 in The Other Voice in Early Modern Europe series for the University of Chicago Press. The critical edition of the same poem is forthcoming from Mucchi in Modena. Currently, she is at work on a monograph exploring the decline of *commedia dell'arte* from *seicento* sources in Italy.

LORI J. ULTSCH is associate professor of Italian at Hofstra University. Her research and publication interests range from the early modern period to contemporary women's literature in Italy and focus on the interplay between gender and genre as the mirror of changing social realities. In the context of the early modern period in Venice, she has published articles on Maddalena Campiglia and Sara Copio Sullam that examine the institution of women's semireligious communities, emerging trends in secular celibacy, gender transgression and the pastoral genre, the history of the Venetian ghetto, and the forms and functions of literary exchange between Jews and Christians in the early-seventeenth-century ghetto.

Index

Academy of Vatican Nights 197
Accademia degli infiammati 89–90, 195, 211n.29
Accademia degli informi 143
Accademia degli intronati 89, 89n.3, 108n.30
Accademia degli umidi 31, 31n.54, 293, 296
Accademia Fiorentina 31n.54, 293–94, 296
Accademia olimpica 52
Accademia Veneziana (a.k.a. *della fama*) 303
Accursius, Francesco 190
Alcuin 156n.36
Aldine Press 10, 20, 32, 47
Alfano, Giancarlo 90n.7, 93n.13, 93n.14, 95n.24
Alighieri, Dante 20–21, 117–118, 134, 134n.53, 146, 169, 169n.84, 170n.98, 208n.25, 216n.36, 233n.48, 236n.53, 239, 262n.xli
Amalarius of Metz 159n.55
Ambrose, Saint 180, 181–82, 189
Andreini, Francesco 10, 19, 265–87
Andreini, Giovanni Battista 265
Andreini, Isabella 5, 10, 28, 48–67, 76–78, 265–72
Andrews, Richard 266n.9
Anna of Aragon 140n.76
Antiphanes 175
Antoniano, Silvio 8, 59–67, 68–71, 326n.6
Aquinas, Saint Thomas 154n.27, 161n.60

Aragona, Tullia d' 1–5, 10, 12, 19, 27–29, 30–31, 42–46, 196–200, 201n.14, 202–64, 290–92, 294–96, 300–302, 315n.7, 317, 327–28
Aretino, Pietro 11–12, 20, 66, 196, 242, 243, 290, 291n.3, 292, 293–302, 313–24
Ariosto, Ludovico 80, 146, 156, 158n.48, 162, 191n.162, 267, 279
Aristophanes 162, 167n.86
Aristotle 9, 115–17, 122n.16, 122n.17, 126–32, 134, 138, 146, 154n.27, 156, 161, 190, 200, 208n.25, 268n.14, 284, 285n.39, 325
Artemisia 136
Aspasia 140
Augustine, Saint 146, 156, 162, 169, 182, 207n.23, 326, 333
Averroes (a.k.a. Ibn Rushd) 161

Bainton, Roland 327, 328n.17, 328n.18, 329n.23
Baldi, Andrea 89–95
Barbara of Austria 141
Bardazzi, Giovanni 328–29
Bartolomeo de Saliceto 165, 165–66n.80
Bassanese, Fiora 25–27, 289
Battiferra degli Ammannati, Laura 5, 20, 25, 29n.47, 30, 31, 59n.1
Bembo, Pietro 18–19, 34n.65, 36–40, 44, 84, 140n.74, 140n.77, 161, 197, 200n.13, 301n.21, 303

Benson, Pamela Joseph 6, 7n.29
Berni, Francesco 294, 295, 305
Bianchi, Stefano 305
Bigolina, Giulia 5, 12, 65–67, 77, 78, 313–324
Boccaccio, Giovanni 2, 3n.4, 19, 80, 86, 115, 121n.12, 135n.55, 136n.57, 137n.59, 146, 153n.25, 155, 156n.35, 191, 199, 257n.73, 262n.xli, 268
Boethius 192, 193, 259n.74
Bologna 156n.37, 165n.80, 190n.58, 195, 304, 327
Borgia, Lucrezia 140
Borromeo, Carlo 59, 189, 197
Bronzino, Agnolo 20, 30
Buonarroti, Michelangelo 3n.4, 328n.21, 329
Burgess–Van Aken, Barbara 50
Burchiello (Domenico di Giovanni) 294
Burckhardt, Jacob 3–7

Caffiero, Marina 326–27
Campbell, Julie D., 5n.21, 10n.39, 29n.45, 33n.61, 42n.93, 43n.95, 43n.96, 196n.4
Campi, Emidio 329
Campiglia, Maddalena 5, 31n.54, 48–54, 57
Capella, Martianus 192n.166
Capra, Flavio Galeazzo 121
Castiglione, Baldassare 3, 8, 17, 19, 32–47, 57, 73–75, 93–95, 118, 121, 122n.14, 140n.75, 140n.77, 197, 200n.13, 243n.62, 289
Catullus (Gaius Valerius Catullus) 85n.31
Cereta, Laura 4
Chemello, Adriana 289

Cherchi, Paolo 146n.14, 147n.15
Chojnacki, Stanley 7, 60, 271, 274n.25
Chrysostom, Saint John 60, 61, 62, 64, 68, 70, 156, 159, 160, 161, 178, 179
Cicero 80, 154, 164n.73, 191, 192, 251n.70
Clement of Alexandria (a.k.a. Titus Flavius Clemens) 175, 176, 179
Cleopatra 119, 135, 136, 139
Clubb, Louise George 66n.17, 265n.2, 267
Cochrane, Kirsty 74
Cohen, Sherrill 341n.70
Colonna, Vittoria 5, 12, 24–28, 90, 212n.11, 140, 211, 301, 314–18, 327–29
Cook, James Wyatt 5n.22
Corinna 140, 239n.56
Corinthians 131n.134, 188, 267n.12, 274n.26
Cornelia 141n.73
Counter–Reformation 2n.3, 7n.31, 49–60, 65–67, 74–80, 122, 267, 341n.70
courtesan 1, 3, 4, 7, 10, 11, 12, 28, 35, 42, 43, 46, 60–62, 82n.23, 140n.72, 187n.151, 196, 197, 199, 200, 201, 237, 238, 239n.56, 268, 289–312, 315, 316, 345n.92
Cox, Virginia 4n.11, 5n.23, 8, 12, 13n.41, 17n.2, 31n.54, 43, 45, 50, 51n.120, 52, 59n.1, 79, 84n.27, 90, 94n.22, 176n.124, 201n.14
Cyprian, Saint 146, 182, 186

Daniello, Bernardino 317n.11

Demosthenes 154, 192
Dido 119, 137, 138n.61
Diogenes Laertius 170
Diotima 10, 35, 40, 140, 199, 200, 239
Dolce, Lodovico 149, 317n.11
donna 84n.27, 84n.28, 118–19, 128n.39, 133–34n.52, 154, 155, 161
du Bellay, Joachim 196

Elizabeth I 139n.64
Este, Alfonso I d' 125, 140n.74,
Este, Alfonso II d' 47, 116, 139n.68, 141n.78, 304
Este, Anna d' 139n.68
Este, Eleonora d' 117, 125n.25, 139n.68
Este, Isabella d' (Gonzaga) 140
Este, Lucrezia d' 139n.68

Farnese, Vittoria 141
Fedele, Cassandra 4
femina (foemina) 118, 154–58
Ferrara 12, 47, 59n.1, 115–16n.4, 125, 139, 140n.74, 141n.78, 165n.80, 304, 327, 328
Finucci, Valeria 313n.1, n.2, n.3, 316n.10, 319n.16, n.17
Firenzuola, Agnolo 290, 294
Florence 6, 31n.54, 265, 271, 290, 291–92n.7, 293, 296, 297n.15, 304, 327, 338n.61, 346
Fonte, Moderata (Modesta Pozzo) 4, 5, 10, 17, 43–47, 50–55, 62–67, 79, 80, 84n.27, 94n.22, 95, 143, 144, 150, 153n.25, 176n.124, 271
Forteguerri, Laudomia 90, 95n.24
Franco, Nicolò 11, 289, 292, 299– 303

Franco, Veronica 4, 7, 26n.32, 62, 290–92, 304–12

Galen 157, 175, 177, 178n.128, 326
Gambara, Veronica 90, 314–18
Garzoni, Tommaso 147–49, 153n.25
Gellius, Aullus 162
Gelosi 10, 265–66
Genesis 275n.29, 277n.30
Gill, Katherine 329
Giolito Press 22, 29, 299
Giraldi Cintio, Giambattista 290
Gonzaga, Cesare 10n.5, 45
Gonzaga, Eleonora 9, 116, 117
Gonzaga, Elisabetta 33–37, 41
Gonzaga, Francesco II 140n.75
Gonzaga, Francesco III 124n.20
Gonzaga, Giulia 327
Gonzaga, Guglielmo 124n.20
Gonzaga, Margherita 34n.65, 35n.67, 125n.24
Gonzaga, Vincenzo 115–16n.4, 124n.21
Graf, Arturo 289
Gratian 156–57
Grazia (Grassi), Nicolò 199–201, 202–60
Grazzini, Anton Francesco 11, 31n.54, 289, 292–99
Guarini, Giovan Battista 49, 52, 187n.150
Guazzo, Stefano 8, 19, 73–88, 121n.13

Hairston, Julia 29, 199n.9
Henke, Robert 265–66
hermaphrodite 151, 172, 192n.166, 208, 210, 218, 234–36, 246
Hesiod 156n.39, 164, 165, 167n.85, 268

Homer 148, 156n.38, 229, 227n.43
Horace 85n.31, 124, 185, 243n.62
Hyperides 187

Iliad 156, 177n.126
Index of Forbidden Books 93n.14,
    197, 301, 329
Isidorus 156n.36

Jansen, Katherine 334n.48, 336n.51
Javitch, Daniel 74
Jerome, Saint 146, 158, 165, 183
John, Saint 160, 183, 311, 331,
    334n.48, 340n.69, 343n.80,
    343n.81, 343n.83
Jones, Ann Rosalind 21, 25n.27,
    25n.29, 26n.34, 27, 65
Justinian I 165n.79, 169, 193n.172
Juvenal 157, 168, 169n.92, 268

Kelly, Joan 3, 6, 36n.72
Kennedy, William J. 21
King, Margaret L. 4n.8, 152n.25
Kirkham, Victoria 5n.19, 6, 7n.29,
    20n.10, 29, 30n.49, 30n.50
Kisacky, Julie 5n.25
Klapisch–Zuber, Christine 6, 274n.5
Kolsky, Stephen 144n.6, 144n.8

Lactantius 156, 157
Laqueur, Thomas 325–26
Lawner, Lynne 307n.35, 315n.8
Leviticus 174
Livy 192n.170
Love, types of 199–200, 205–06,
    208, 211–12, 221–22, 223–24,
    231–34, 240–41, 244–48, 282–
    83, 337, 341
Luke, Saint 325, 326, 334, 335n.49,
    343n.76, 343n.77

Lycurgus 129n.43, 285

Machiavelli, Niccolò 3n.4, 20
Maclean, Ian 325–26
MacNeil, Anne 5n.22, 265n.3,
    266n.6, 266n.7
Margherita of Austria 116
Margherita of Savoy 139
Maria of Hapsburg 138n.62
Marinella, Lucrezia 4, 9, 10, 12, 63,
    65, 67, 80, 93n.14, 95, 115, 118,
    119, 122, 143, 144, 145n.12,
    150, 151, 177n.125, 272
Mark, Saint 334, 340n.69, 342n.73,
    343n.77, 343n.78, 343n.83,
    343n.84
Martial 167, 170
Marullus, Michael Tarchaniota
    165n.78
Matthew, Saint 99n.27, 156, 159,
    179n.129, 275n.28, 277n.30,
    331n.28, 336n.30, 336n.32, 334,
    336n.52, 336n.55, 337n.56,
    340n.69, 342n.74, 343n.77,
    343n.78, 343n.83
Medici, Caterina de' 139
Menander 161
Metellus 162, 284
Migiel, Marilyn and Juliana
    Schiesari 6
Milligan, Gerry 36–37
Molza, Francesco Maria 198–199,
    202–60, 261n.xxii, 261n.xxvi,
    262n.xlv, 262n. xlvi, 263n.lvii,
    263n.lxii, 263n.lxiii
Morata, Olympia 4, 47n.106
Musa, Mark 3n.4, 18n.3, 19n.6, 20,
    21n.12, 86n.35, 134n.53
Muzio, Girolamo 291n.5

Nardi, Bianca 10, 143–144

Neoplatonism 1, 8, 21, 26, 27, 32, 34, 36, 37, 38, 40, 42, 52, 200, 318, 319n.15

Neoptolemus 126

Nogarola, Isotta 4

Ochino, Bernardino 12, 325–47

Ovid 80, 146, 151, 166, 169, 171, 173, 193, 194n.175, 205n.19, 213n.32, 225n.39, 227n.43, 228n.44, 232n.47, 233n.48, 242n.60, 244n.64, 259n.74, 260n.75, 263n.xlviii, 280n.35

Panizza, Letizia 4n.12, 4n.13, 7, 8, 9n.38, 43n.97, 80, 93n.14, 145, 201n.14

Passi, Giuseppe 9, 10, 80, 143–94, 268

Paul, Saint 40, 60, 65, 70, 188, 257, 274n.26, 311

Peter, Saint 60, 64, 70, 323, 342

Petrarca, Francesco (Petrarch, Petrarchism) 1, 2, 8, 17, 18, 32, 47, 56, 57, 80, 115, 117, 128, 129, 146, 148, 154n.28, 155, 164n.75, 184, 189, 190n.157, 205n.20, 211, 216n.35, 216n.36, 235, 236, 240n.59, 257n.73, 284n.36, 291n.6, 292, 294, 295n.11, 299, 302, 303, 304, 305, 309

Petronius 167

Pettie, George and Bartholomew Young 73, 85n.32

Philemo 161, 162n.64

Philoxenus 158

Piccolomini, Alessandro 8, 89–111, 196, 211n.29, 317n.11

Piéjus, Marie Françoise 91n.89, 92n.12, 95n.23

Pisa 165n.80, 304, 327

Planudes, Maximus 158, 159n.53

Plato 27, 33, 54, 57, 75n.8, 76, 80, 87n.36, 117, 120, 126, 127, 128, 131n.46, 133, 135, 140n.71, 161n.62, 191, 199, 213n.31, 215n.34, 239, 240n.56, 240n.57, 278n.31

Plautus 165

Pliny the Elder 168, 228n.44, 243n.62

Plutarch 80, 120, 126, 131, 169, 170, 171, 284n.38, 285n.40, 285n.41

Poesia puttanesca 11, 289–312

Pozzi, Mario 198, 199n.10, 214n.33

Propertius 151, 173

Prudentius, Aurelius 180

Puteanus, Erycius 66, 67

Pythagoras 127n.34

Querelle des femmes 8–13, 33, 36, 40, 43, 44, 46, 73–80, 115, 120, 121, 135n.55, 145, 151, 267–71, 277n.30, 291, 297n.16

Rabil, Albert, Jr. 153n.25

Radak (a.k.a. Rabbi David Kimchi) 158n.50

Ravasi, Gianfranco 334n.47

Reason (rationality) 39, 43, 55, 56, 86, 128n.38, 133, 172, 200, 207, 208, 209, 218, 221, 224, 226–34, 241, 253–56, 258, 262n.xxvi, 263n.lxi, 263n.lxiii, 283

Renata of Ferrara 139

Robin, Diana 2n.3, 4n.8, 4n.9, 4n.10, 7, 22, 29n.46, 31, 32n.57, 211n.29, 326n.8, 327n.9, 327n.14, 328, 329n.25

Rome 20, 76, 124n.20, 135–36n. 55, 136–37n.58, 170n.104, 196, 197, 199, 211n.30, 284, 286, 290, 296n.14, 300, 301, 304, 307n.35, 327, 334n.38

Rosenthal, Margaret 7, 290n.4, 292, 308n.37

Ross, Sarah Gwyneth 7

Ruscelli, Girolamo 155

Russell, Rinaldina 196n.3, 196n.4, 199, 200, 201n.14

Sampson, Lisa 5n.23, 31n.54, 48, 50, 51n.120, 52

Sandeus, Filenus 165–66n.80

Sappho 139, 171, 177, 239, 315

Sarto, Andrea del 20

Scala, Flaminio 266

Schaberg, Jane 339n.64

Scipio the Younger 136, 251

Scotus 339

Semiramis 135, 136, 139, 169, 173

Seneca (Lucius Anneus Seneca the younger) 171, 257n.73

Smarr, Janet Levarie 7, 10, 11, 17n.1, 23, 32, 34, 35, 39, 40n.85, 40n.86, 40n.87, 41, 42, 44, 47n.106, 196n.4

Snyder, Jon 197n.6

Socrates 40, 42, 117n.6, 126n.27, 126n.32, 128n.38, 140n.71, 187, 199, 239, 278n.31

Solinus, Gaius Julius 186

Solomon 82, 137, 262n.xli, 340

Spagnoli, Battista 193n.173

Spinola, Maria 315–16

Speroni, Sperone 1, 10, 11, 17, 42–43, 80, 89, 115, 195–264, 291n.5, 302, 315, 317n.11

Stampa, Gaspara 5, 24–28, 315

Stampino, Maria Galli 12, 48n.110, 49n.113, 68n.23

Statius 134n.53, 170, 171n.105, 233n.48

Stobaeus, Ioannis 161

Strocchia, Sharon 334n.43

Sullivan, Edward 73

Susanna 177

Symmachus 188, 189n.154

Tacitus, Cornelius 170

Tarabotti, Arcangela 4, 144

Tasso, Bernardo 140n.77, 196, 199, 200, 202–64

Tasso, Ercole 80, 95, 115

Tasso, Torquato 8, 9, 17, 47–57, 80, 115–41, 199

Tertullian 189

Thucydides 177, 126, 131

Timothy, Saint 60, 70

Tintoretto, Jacopo 291n.5

Titian (Tiziano Vecellio) 76n.8, 242–43, 263n.xlviii, 314, 317, 319n.16, 320, 321, 322

Torelli, Barbara 48–52, 57

Torquemada, Antonio 172

Ultsch, Lori 9, 11, 53–55

Valdés, Juan de 327n.10, 328n.19, 328n.20, 329

Valla, Lorenzo 157

Varchi, Benedetto 30, 42, 45, 59n.1, 89, 195n.2, 196, 290n.4, 291n.5, 294

Venice 10, 22, 29, 47, 60, 62, 63, 143, 144n.7, 145, 186n.46, 199, 201n.14, 210, 212, 271, 290, 291, 297n.15, 299, 300, 303, 304, 306n.33, 307n.35, 308n.39,

309n.43, 314n.4, 315, 316, 318, 321n.18, 322–24, 325, 331, 334n.43, 341n.70, 341n.72

Venier, Maffio 289, 292, 299, 303–312

Venus/Aphrodite, earthly and heavenly 75–78, 81, 86, 91n.89, 92n.12, 96n.23, 156, 165–67, 177, 220, 222, 227, 230, 261n. xviii

Vianello, Valerio 197

Virgil 47, 125n.23, 151, 167, 172, 173n.110, 251n.70, 301, 327, 344n.85

Volterrano (a.k.a. Raffaele Maffei) 174n.115

Weaver, Elissa 144n.7

Wood, Sharon 8, 9n.38, 201n.14

Xenarchus 179

Xenophon 117, 120, 126, 174n.115, 179

Xiphilinus, John 168

Zenobia 136